AF564645

Hotel Asset Management: Principles and Practices

Hotel Asset Management: Principles and Practices

Surinder Kumar Rai

RANDOM PUBLICATIONS
NEW DELHI (INDIA)

Hotel Asset Management: Principles and Practices

ISBN 978-93-5111-336-2

Published in 2014 in India by

RANDOM PUBLICATIONS

4376-A/4B, Gali Murari Lal, Ansari Road
New Delhi-110 002
Phone : +91-11-43580356, +91-11-23289044
e-mail: randomexports@gmail.com, sales@randompublications.com,
info@randompublications.com

Type Setting by : Keystoneprintads, Delhi-110051
Printed at : Thomson Press (India) Ltd

Preface

Hotel asset management is the fiduciary responsibility of managing the lodging investment to meet the specific objectives of ownership. Hotel Asset Management is a specialised hotel consulting business. We are recognised as hotel industry leaders in maximising returns from hotel assets in the accommodation sector. Whether you are a hotel owner, investor, operator, financier or receiver we will work with you to attain maximum value according to your needs.

The role and mandate of any property engineering department is the protection of the building's/owner's assets; the structure from the façade or building envelope, to the integrity of the floors, walls, ceilings and all of the furniture, fixtures, and equipment (FF&E) contained therein. This includes the electrical transformers and the distribution throughout, the domestic water distribution and sewage, the heating-ventilation-air conditioning system, (HVAC), the fire alarm system and fire safety components, the vertical transportation system (elevators), the property surroundings like parking and landscaping and pest control.

Utility management such as electrical, gas, steam, water. Kitchen and laundry equipment. Lighting and sound systems and on and on.

The hotel industry has undergone fundamental structural changes over the last two decades. Hotels are now owned by a diverse range of investors, while operators much prefer to focus on management only. Hotels are specialist assets and require active management in order to generate optimal returns. This, along with the differing objectives of asset owners and the hotel operating/brand companies, has led to the need for owners to obtain specialist hotel asset management advice to help them maximise cash flows and asset value.

This book is an asset for scholars, students and general readers alike.

I would like to thank my team for standing beside me throughout my career and writing this book. My special thanks go to "Random Publications" who have published the book.

— ***Surinder Kumar Rai***

Contents

1

Engineering Management in Hotel Assets

The role and mandate of any property engineering department is the protection of the building's/owner's assets; the structure from the façade or building envelope, to the integrity of the floors, walls, ceilings and all of the furniture, fixtures, and equipment (FF&E) contained therein. This includes the electrical transformers and the distribution throughout, the domestic water distribution and sewage, the heating-ventilation-air conditioning system, (HVAC), the fire alarm system and fire safety components, the vertical transportation system (elevators), the property surroundings like parking and landscaping and pest control. Utility management such as electrical, gas, steam, water. Kitchen and laundry equipment. Lighting and sound systems and on and on.

Aside from the base building, office buildings are quite easier to maintain. Generally, offices and shops within commercial buildings are subject to various lease arrangements, with the tenant often being responsible for all maintenance and repairs within their space and proportionate costs of the utilities and taxes.

The property operators are usually only responsible for the base building and common areas. The same concept being applied to apartments and condominiums. The important element here is what is contained within the lease or rental agreement. Office building hours are usually fixed, say, from 7:00am to 6:00pm; electronically controlled locks securing every outside door and alarm systems readied by time clocks. Security guards sweeping all areas at random and responding to any alarm calls. Weekends are generally in lock-down mode 24hrs a day. The after hours involvement of building staff are the building cleaners, normally contracted, however, engineering is rarely called for after hour situations. Tenants that would use their offices during off base building hours may contract for HVAC services and pay for the cost.

Hotels are much more extensive and demanding. The engineering department has the responsibility for everything in the building as well. Depending on the organizational structure of the hotel, some elements are assigned to other departments. The Security or Loss Prevention department may take on the task of fire systems but ultimately this is the responsibility of the engineering department as the building operators to monitor for regulatory compliance. Hotels have often been given the analogy of a cruise ship or a hospital in that the operation is 24 – 7. Twenty-four hours a day and seven days a week. When the guests are sound asleep the systems of the building continue to operate. The heating and ventilation units are running, the domestic hot water is being heated, the laundry may be operating, the night cleaners making their rounds, desk clerks and night auditors all doing what they have to do. Behind the scenes, there is a flurry of activity, and everything has to work so that everyone can do their jobs and the guests are safe and comfortable.

Without minimizing the contribution of other departments, of which there may be as many as ten or more, the bottom line is if there is no engineering department there is no hotel. Take away those services like hot water or elevators, heating or cooling, electricity, kitchen equipment, laundry equipment etc., you simply would have no customers.

When everything is working the next most significant department of course is housekeeping whose efforts keep the property clean and attractive, tending to the guests comfort in their rooms. Removing a restaurant from the system will not close the hotel, or closing the bar or lounge will not cause the hotel to cease operations. Again, all departments should contribute to a seamless operation where the guest comfort and safety and satisfaction are paramount. The pages following will attempt to shed some light on the various segments of hotel engineering although some aspects are interrelated and not really separable. Hopefully, by narrowing the focus the reader will gain a rudimentary or cursory understanding of the role of the engineering department.

FIXED ASSETS MANAGEMENT

Fixed assets management is an accounting process that seeks to track fixed assets for the purposes of financial accounting, preventive maintenance, and theft deterrence. Many organizations face a significant challenge to track the location, quantity, condition, maintenance and depreciation status of their fixed assets.

A popular approach to tracking fixed assets utilizes serial numbered Asset Tags, often with bar codes for easy and accurate reading. Periodically, the owner of the assets can take inventory with a mobile barcode reader and then produce a report. Off-the-shelf software packages for fixed asset management are marketed to businesses small and large. Some Enterprise Resource Planning systems are available with fixed assets modules.

Free cash Flow

Free cash flow measures a firm's net increase in:

- Cash from operations (this includes the reduction for interest),

- Less the dividends paid to preferred shareholders, and
- Less expenditures necessary to maintain assets.

Increases in non-cash current assets may, or may not be deducted, depending on whether they are considered to be maintaining the status quo, or to be investments for growth.

Problems with CapX

1. The expenditures for maintenance of assets is only part of the capx reported on the Statement of Cash Flows. It must be separated from the expenditures for growth purposes. This split is not a requirement under GAAP, and is not audited. Management is free to disclose maintenance capx or not. Therefore this input to the calculation of free cash flow is easy to manipulate. Since it is a very large number, maintenance capx's questionable validity is the basis for some people's dismissal of 'free cash flow'.
2. A second problem with the maintenance capx measurement is its intrinsic 'lumpyness'. By their nature, expenditures for capital assets that will last decades are infrequent, but costly when they occur. 'Free cash flow', in turn, will be very different from year to year. No particular year will be a 'norm' that can be expected to be repeated.

Uses of the Metric

1. Free cash flow measures the ease with which businesses can grow and pay dividends to shareholders. Even profitable businesses may have negative cash flows. Their requirement for increased financing will result in increased financing costs reducing future income. It is easier to grow with organic cash flows than with additional financing.
2. According to the discounted cash flow valuation model, the intrinsic value of a company is the present value of all future free cash flows, plus the cash proceeds from its eventual sale. The presumption is that the cash flows are used to pay dividends to the shareholders. Bear in mind the lumpyness discussed.
3. Some investors prefer using free cash flow instead of net income to measure a company's financial performance, because free cash flow is more difficult to manipulate than net income. The problems with this presumption are itemized at cash flow and return of capital.
4. The payout ratio is a metric used to evaluate the sustainability of distributions from REITs, Oil & Gas Royalty Trusts, and Income Trust. The distributions are divided by the free cash flow. Distributions may include any of income, flowed-through capital gains or return of capital.

This metric is used only by shareholders. Debt holders are not concerned with maintaining the operating capital assets, or with growing the business. Nor are they concerned with taxes paid since their payments come first. The appropriate metric for debt holders is EBITDA.

Change Management

There are several phrases regarding organizational change and development that look and sound a lot alike, but have different meanings. As a result of the prominence of the topic, there seems to be increasingly different interpretations of some of these phrases, while others are used interchangeably. Without at least some sense of the differences between these phrases, communications about organizational change and development can be increasingly vague, confusing and frustrating.

There are different overall types of organizational change, including planned versus unplanned, organization-wide versus change primarily to one part of the organization, incremental (slow, gradual change) versus transformational (radical, fundamental), etc.. Knowing which types of change you are doing helps all participants to retain scope and perspective during the many complexities and frequent frustrations during change.

Successful change efforts often include several key roles, including the initiator, champion, change agent, sponsor and leaders. Organization-wide change in corporations should involve the Board of Directors. Whether their members are closely involved in the change or not, they should at least be aware of the change project and monitor if the results are being achieved or not. As the change agent, you might be performing different roles during the project.

Appreciative Inquiry is a recent and powerful breakthrough in organizational change and development. It's based on the philosophy that "problems" are often caused as much by our perception of them as problems as by other influencing factors. The philosophy has spawned a strong movement that, in turn, has generated an increasing number of models, tools and tips, most of which seem to build from the positive perceptions (visions, fantasies, wishes and stories) of those involved in the change effort.

There are numerous well-organized approaches (or models) from which to manage a change effort. Some of the approaches have been around for many years — we just haven't thought of them as such. For example, many organizations undertake strategic planning. The implementation of strategic planning, when done in a systematic, cyclical and explicit approach, is strategic management. Strategic management is also one model for ensuring the success of a change effort. There are numerous, major methods and movements to regularly increase the performance of organizations. Each includes regular recurring activities to establish organizational goals, monitor progress toward the goals, and make adjustments to achieve those goals more effectively and efficiently. Any or all of the following approaches will improve organizational performance depending on if they are implemented comprehensively and remain focused on organizational results.

Some of the following, e.g., organizational learning and knowledge management, might be interpreted more as movements than organization performance strategies because there are wide interpretations of the concepts, not all of which include focusing on achieving top-level organizational results. However, if these two concepts are instilled across the organization and focus on organizational results, they contribute strongly to organizational performance. On the other hand, the Balanced Scorecard, which is deliberately designed to be comprehensive and focused on organizational results, will not improve performance if not implemented from a strong design.

STAFFING

Staffing levels are going to be dictated by quite a number of variables. The variable that seems to pre-empt all others is the financial performance of the property, although manipulating the contribution or size of the engineering department will only defer more costs to further down the road. Factors other than financial can be building specific; the amount of rooms, meeting space, grounds, age of building, available talent pool, plant size (boiler room etc.) swimming pools and peripheral equipment. The class of hotel also influences the caliber of maintenance. You can repair everything with sticky tape and glue, or you can do it right and replace the part. Scheduling plays a role depending on how busy it can be on any given shift. Hotels can be very busy in the evenings after dinner when guests return to their rooms and start using all equipment. More engineering staff may be required on the afternoon shift. Does the hotel require a midnight or graveyard shift?

The general rule/formula for the staffing level or department size is expounded by Frank D. Borsenik, a professor of engineering at an American University who gives a relatively accurate basis around which to set parameters. Reviewing my notes from the School of Hotel Administration at Cornell University compliment his opinion. When all the operating equipment, systems, building surfaces, are taken into consideration it is determined by following manufacturer's recommendations and current best methods, that in the areas of preventive maintenance and frequencies of maintenance required, the formula is 3.1 engineering full time equivalents per 100 available rooms.

That means that a hotel of 500 rooms would have 15.5 FTE's to properly maintain a hotel building in a state of good repair. Some hotels have other "appendages" such as retail and commercial, residential, or convention or marinas, which will add to the maintenance requirements. Mistakes are made in dismissing these areas as "self maintained" because of triple-net leases, where the tenants handle their own maintenance. This is not to be confused with a building of unitary function as previously mentioned, such as, office buildings, apartment buildings, factory or retail malls. Forgotten behind the scenes is that the plumbing, ventilation and virtually all systems are sized larger and are generally more extensive in providing services to these locations. The tenants themselves have requests of maintenance and their own work has to be approved and monitored. The common areas still have to be maintained. Adjustments to the recommended number of FTE's are feasible if the work is contracted out. Unionized properties may or may not have issues with contracting out.

The formula of 3.1/100 available rooms is arbitrary as the physical property will dictate the staff required to maintain a building in a state of good repair. The cyclical "financial pressure" that has plagued most building operators and the slash and burn mentality that prevails will have a negative impact on the quantity and quality of maintenance. The hotel is a business, and the prudent operator should operate it as such, however, should be cognizant, that saving a dollar on maintenance today will cost him two dollars tomorrow. During the course of my thirty-seven years in the business of hotels, commercial, and residential I've seen all too often where managers have cut costs irregardless of financial performance but based on their own political ambitions. The other greatest folly is rewarding by way of bonus or other accolades the engineering manager for budget performance.

We have seen where engineering managers have received hefty bonuses at the end of the year and behind the scenes have left devastation. Fan damper motors tied together with coat hangars, leaking pipes with little wooden wedges hammered into the holes, fire dampers wedged open because the fusible links had failed. Had these things been repaired and money spent the bonus would have been less. Temporarily increasing profits may lead to a manager's promotion or transfer, and in a year or two they are gone leaving the successor holding the bag as the "deferred maintenance" comes back to haunt. These temporary measures are sometimes necessary and a recent survey of several hotels has shown that the common level for engineering during a "crisis" period is 2.3/100 available rooms after cutbacks. This is crisis management. These levels of cut-backs should only be sustained for a number of weeks as guaranteed deterioration will make it difficult to catch up or recover.

Never, should it be expected that requests for projects or creating what never existed should be handled by in-house staff when a department is staffed at the lower level; a misconception is that it is business as usual and other departments wonder why it may take so long to honour their wish list. Generally, without getting into specific trades, a smaller operation can do well with generalists. A person who is proficient in electrical, in plumbing, in mechanical, in carpentry, painting; suffice a person with the necessary mechanical aptitude and skill. Caution should be exercised in the level of repair that is undertaken by any one trade person so as not to exceed his or her expertise or to do work when a permit or license is required.

Local regulations and authorities having jurisdiction should be consulted to determine if there are any code violations. Depending on the staffing level you could hire a kitchen and or laundry mechanic, at minimum staffing levels – these could be contracted out. Generalists by nature can be quite proficient in a variety of trades and excel at either one or more and are usually less expensive. To hire a licensed tradesperson is not feasible and hotels usually will not compete on a salary basis as it could cost as much as two or three times more what they would normally pay. The tradesperson would have little versatility outside their specific training and would only be suited to a larger hotel that had a sufficient amount of work to keep them fully occupied in that particular trade.

It would make no sense to hire an electrician for $75,000 a year unless that person would have sufficient volume of electrical work ($75,000 +) to make it cheaper to have one on staff. More often than not, if a licensed trade person is working for you it is only because they are between jobs and will leave when there is an opening elsewhere for their skills. For the complexities of a building and its systems it normally takes a good year and sometimes more to learn where everything is and how everything works. From valve locations, breakers, systems layout to operating procedures. Seasonal layoffs should never be considered for a couple of reasons; one, a year or more has been spent in training the individual who may permanently leave.

The positions of the Director of Engineering or Chief Engineer or Maintenance Manager or by whatever that position is called, is usually certified, as well as the assistant position. Some of the major hotels make it mandatory. The position should only report to the General Manager and is a executive committee member. There are properties where the reporting line of the Director of Engineering is to a Rooms Division manager, or other; which defies logic.

Engineering is a department with a function of it's own and an engineering manager has to insist that the Engineering Department comes first! The building comes first. The guest comes first. Engineering has responsibility of all departments including those areas – boiler rooms, mechanical rooms, all behind the scenes, that a rooms division could never fathom. Rooms can represent a small piece of the pie when compared to food and beverage and the building mechanics. Engineering in some instances should only report to a corporate engineering position who's neutrality would ensure that budget funds are funnelled to the building and the assets.

The administrative assistant given today's phenomenal amount of paperwork, records keeping, parts ordering, purchase orders, inventory, payroll and job assignment and dispatch is an essential full time position. Scheduling of work will enable response to issuing departments on a timetable.

This position reports only to the Director of Engineering. The assistant Director of Engineering, or assistant maintenance manager, again, by whatever term is used must be able to make instant decisions and operate the department effectively. This position has full authority over the departments operation and the shift engineers and engineers. The position reports to the Director of Engineering and in absence, to the General Manager.

The shift engineers are normally the "runners" that carry the radio or pager and their primary function is to respond to the day to day maintenance requests generated by the housekeeping department or PBX, or those that may be assigned to them and it is emphasized written maintenance requests depending on the nature of the request. A direct verbal request by a guest is given first priority and is paged. Fire or flood is paged.

All else is to be written on a maintenance request form that is then distributed or assigned by the administrative assistant. The nature of the frequent spontaneous requests by the shift engineers especially at night when they are by themselves, should not be assigned tasks such as painting or projects of a long duration.

The engineers, are those general workers whose skills are utilized by the assistant director of engineering for those jobs outside the scope of the shift engineers requiring longer time to complete or are more extensive. Staffing levels in the "crisis mode" should determine that it is maintain only and that projects or wishes or to create what never existed is costed out to appropriate outside trades. To do otherwise is detrimental to the property.

ATTRIBUTES AND QUALITIES OF HOUSEKEEPING STAFF

Honesty

This is a very essential attribute for housekeeping staff, especially Room Attendants, who have access to all guest rooms. Guest belongings, sometimes invaluable are often found lying around in the room. The temptations to thieve are great.

It is only the personal quality of discipline and integrity that checks these temptations:

- *Eye for Detail*: It is one of the greatest qualities that house keeping staff must have. It is with this quality that the finer aspects of housekeeping are taken care of and it is what determines a good service from an average one. This quality enables housekeeping staff to take into consideration the minutest details.
- *Co-Cooperativeness*: Housekeeping staff needs to be co-operating with other departments to achieve more efficiency.
- *Briefing and Scheduling of Staff*: Briefing is that process at the beginning of a work shift which is provided by management to facilitate a two-way communication between management and staff.

It is the one time during a shift that all housekeeping staff are together to share information and feelings before they disperse to their work areas.

– Briefing Schedule:

i Personal hygiene and grooming.

ii Any new policies and procedures introduced by managcl1lenL must be made out and explained to the staff.

iii At n briefing the duties or each staff member and the areas of accountability are explained. This would mean that staffs are assigned a floor and allotted their number of rooms. The staffs likewise, are told which floors or public areas they are assigned to for cleaning. They are also told which supervisor would be in charge.

iv Briefing is a time which can be used as a training opportunity. Simple tasks may be demonstrated so that they can be practiced under supervision at their work place.

CLEANING A ROOM

Prior to reporting on a floor the room attendant already knows the status of a room in her given lot of rooms. The room attendant can prioritize room to be attended to first on the basis of immediate needs. Before entering the room knock at the door firmly with the index finger knuckle announcing clearly" Housekeeping".

When there is no answer, repeat the knock after ten seconds announcing yourself as before. If there is still no answer open the door and knock announcing inside the room "Housekeeping". When there is no reply and one is relatively sure that there is no one in, open the door wide and keep it that way till the entire cleaning cycle in the room is complete.

ROOM CLEANING PROCEDURE

- And centre sashes or windows, close windows.
- Arrange furniture if necessary
- Check the maintenance requirements and report to the department head.
- Clean all the surfaces in single circular motions with a dry cloth. Use a hand dust pan to collect any unwanted matter on the surface without lifting dust in the air Ensure that all surfaces are spotlessly clean. Pay special attention to nooks and corners especially those points that may not obviously be visible to the guests eye.
- Clean lamp shades with a clean dry duster.
- Clean mirror with a dry cloth.
- Clean the bath room.
- Clean the ceiling and air-conditioning vents for cobwebs.

- Collect all loose papers or magazines and stack them neatly on the desk.
- Disinfect telephone mouthpiece with Dettol. Wipe balance of the telephone with a damp cloth, check phone for the dial tone.
- Dust both sides of all room doors, baseboards, window sills, inside and out, bottom
- Dust closet, shelves, hangers and rods. Brush the closet floor.
- Have a last look at the room referring to the checklist for completion of work.
- Switch off the room air-conditioner. Draw all curtains and open the windows for airing the room.
- Switch on the air-conditioning.
- Turn the mattress side-to-side on succeeding days followed by end-to-end turning. Smooth out mattress to air it.
- Use a stiff upholstery brush or vacuum cleaner on upholstered furniture arms, backs and seats.
- Wash the floors.

CLEANING A BATHROOM

- Clean mirror first with dry cloth then with glass cloth and finally with dry cloth.
- Clean the ceiling and air-conditioning vents for cobwebs.
- Cleaning activity starts from the ceiling downwards to the floor.
- Collect all trash in bathroom waste basket and deposit in trash hamper of the maids-cart.
- Finally close the windows shut all lights and close the bathroom doors.
- Floors are cleaned from the wall farthest to the door to the exit.
- Open all exhaust vents.
- Scrub the floor with the prescribed mop and ensure it is dry
- Scrub the toilet bowl and bidet using the special brush or mop and the prescribed sanitizer. The inner rim should be cleaned. Ensure it is dry and spotless inside. Clean the WC from the outside with a sponge till it is sparkling find dry. Clean the lid and toilet seat of the toilet bowl dry and close them.
- Scrub to dry the area next to the wash basin.
- Wipe down tile walls using a sponge or damp cloth. Follow with a dry cloth ensuring that tiles are free of water marks.
- Wipe dry the shower curtain with a sponge.
- Wipe off light bulbs and shades with dry cloth. Check that all bulbs are working.

DIRTY DOZEN

- Air-conditioning ducts and diffuser grills. Under bathroom counters.

- Area above racks
- Behind the WC bowl- the s-trap.
- Beneath the table
- Faucet nozzle filter
- In the toilet roll niche
- Interior surface of drawers
- Rear surface of doors
- Toilet vents
- Top of the door edges and ceiling.
- Top of the picture frames

ROOM MAINTENANCE PROCEDURE

As hose keeping has contact with all rooms and public areas practically in every shift, it is they who detect report and ensure the completion of all maintenance work. This requires close co-ordination with the engineering department.

WEEKLY CLEANING PROCEDURE

In addition to daily cleaning routine, a room attendant normally has some cleaning chores that are of a time-consuming nature. Such items may sometimes be beyond the physical capacity and need the assistance of a skill worker.

Such tasks are:

- Cleaning of window panes
- Polishing of brassware
- Scrubbing of balconies and terraces
- Scrubbing of bathroom tiles
- Vacuuming of under heavy furniture.

MANAGEMENT CONTROL AND STAFFING

Although there is a tendency to want a "bright line" to define businesses as small, medium-size or large, this guidance does not provide such definitions. It uses the term "smaller" rather than "small" business, suggesting there is a wide range of companies to which the guidance is directed.

The focus is on businesses that have many of the following characteristics:

- Fewer lines of business and fewer products within lines
- Concentration of marketing focus, by channel or geography
- Leadership by management with significant ownership interest or rights
- Fewer levels of management, with wider spans of control
- Less complex transaction processing systems and protocols
- Fewer personnel, many having a wider range of duties
- Limited ability to maintain deep resources in line as well as support

staff positions such as legal, human resources, accounting and internal auditing.

None of these characteristics by themselves is definitive. Certainly, size by whatever measure - revenue, personnel, assets, or other - affects and is affected by these characteristics, and shapes our thinking about what constitutes "smaller."

Costs and Benefits

Management and other stakeholders of public companies, particularly smaller ones, have focused great attention on the cost of complying with Section 404, with less attention given to the associated benefits. Although it may be difficult to measure impacts associated with inaccurate financial reporting, market reactions to corporate misstatements clearly signal that the investment community does not readily tolerate inaccurate reporting, regardless of company size. In that respect and with other benefits described below, effective internal control adds significant value.

Among the most significant benefits is the strengthened ability of companies to access the capital markets, providing capital which drives innovation and economic growth. Other benefits include reliable and timely information supporting management's decision-making, consistent mechanisms for processing transactions across an organization enhancing speed and reliability, and ability to accurately communicate business performance with partners and customers.

Meeting Challenges in Attaining Cost-Effective

Internal Control

The characteristics of smaller companies provide significant challenges for cost-effective internal control. This particularly is the case where managers view control as an administrative burden to be added onto existing business systems, rather than recognizing the business need and benefit for effective internal control that is integrated with core processes.

Among the challenges are:

- Obtaining sufficient resources to achieve adequate segregation of duties
- Management's ability to dominate activities, with significant opportunities for management override of control
- Recruiting individuals with requisite financial reporting and other expertise to serve effectively on the board of directors and audit committee
- Recruiting and retaining personnel with sufficient experience and skill in accounting and financial reporting
- Taking management attention from running the business in order to provide sufficient focus on accounting and financial reporting

- Maintaining appropriate control over computer information systems with limited technical resources.

While all companies incur incremental costs to design and report on internal control over financial reporting, costs can be proportionally higher for smaller companies. Yet despite resource constraints, smaller businesses usually can meet this challenge and succeed in attaining effective internal control in a reasonably cost-effective manner. This is accomplished in a variety of ways, outlined in this guidance, many of which already exist today in smaller companies and for which management can "take credit" in considering internal control effectiveness.

Wide and Direct Control from the Top

Many smaller businesses are dominated by the company's founder or other leader who exercises a great deal of discretion and provides personal direction to other personnel. While key to enabling the company to meet its growth and other objectives, this positioning also can contribute significantly to effective internal control over financial reporting. In-depth knowledge of different facets of the business - its operations, processes, array of contractual commitments and business risks - enables its leader to know what to expect in reports generated by the financial reporting system and to follow up as needed when unanticipated variances surface. A related downside in terms of ability to override established control procedures can be addressed with specified protocols.

Effective Boards of Directors

Smaller hotels typically have relatively straightforward business operations with less complex business structures, enabling directors to gain more in-depth knowledge of business activities. Directors may have been closely involved with the company during its evolution and have a strong historical perspective. Coupled with what often is exposure to and frequent communication with a wide range of managers, this assists the board and its audit committee in performing oversight responsibilities for financial reporting in a highly effective manner.

Compensating for Limited Segregation of Duties

Resource constraints may limit the number of employees, sometimes resulting in concerns regarding segregation of duties. There are, however, actions management can take in order to compensate for potential inadequacy. These include managers reviewing system reports of detailed transactions; selecting transactions for review of supporting documents; overseeing periodic counts of physical inventory, equipment or other assets and comparing them with accounting records; and reviewing reconciliations of account balances or performing them independently. In many small companies managers already are performing these and other procedures supporting reliable reporting, and credit should be taken for their contribution to effective internal control.

Information Technology

The reality of limited internal information technology resources often can be dealt with through use of software developed and maintained by others. These packages still require controlled implementation and operation, but many of the risks associated with in-house developed systems are avoided. Typically there is a limited need for Programme change controls, inasmuch as changes are done exclusively by the developer company, and generally a smaller company's personnel lack technical expertise to make unauthorized modifications.

Such commercially available packages also bring advantages in the form of embedded facilities for controlling which employees can access or modify specified data, performing checks on data processing completeness and accuracy, and maintaining related documentation. Further advantage can be gained by utilizing software that comes with a variety of built-in application controls that can improve consistency of operation, automate reconciliations, facilitate reporting of exceptions for management review, and support proper segregation of duties. Smaller companies can take advantage of these capabilities, ensuring "flags" or "switches" are properly set to take advantage of the software's capabilities.

Monitoring Activities

The monitoring component is an important part of the Framework, where a wide range of activities routinely performed by managers in running a business can provide feedback on the functioning of other components of the internal control system. Management of many smaller businesses regularly perform such procedures, but have not always taken sufficient "credit" for their contribution to internal control effectiveness. These activities, usually performed manually and sometimes supported by computer software, should be fully considered in designing and assessing internal control. From a different perspective, there is another way monitoring activities can promote efficiency.

After the first year of assessing and reporting on internal control, many companies repeated the assessment process in year two with little if any cost savings. A different approach, however, can be taken to promote efficiency. By focusing on monitoring activities already in place or that might be added with little additional effort, management can identify significant changes to the financial reporting system since the prior year, thereby gaining insight into where to target more detailed testing. While for effective internal control all five components must be in place and operating effectively and some testing of each component is necessary, highly effective monitoring activities can both offset certain shortcomings in other components and sharpen targeting of assessment work with resulting overall efficiency.

Achieving Further Efficiencies

In addition to considering the above, companies can gain additional efficiencies in designing and implementing or assessing internal control by focusing on only those financial reporting objectives directly applicable to the company's activities and circumstances, taking a risk based approach to internal control, right sizing documentation, viewing internal control as an integrated process, and considering the totality of internal control. The COSO Framework recognizes that an entity must first have in place an appropriate set of financial reporting objectives.

At a high level, the objective of financial reporting is to prepare reliable financial statements, which involves attaining reasonable assurance that the financial statements are free from material misstatement. Flowing from this high level objective, management establishes supporting objectives related to the company's business activities and circumstances and their proper reflection in the company's financial statement accounts and related disclosures. These objectives may be influenced by regulatory requirements or by other factors that management may choose to incorporate when setting its objectives. Efficiencies are gained by focusing on only those objectives directly applicable to the business and related to its activities and circumstances that are material to the financial statements.

Experience shows that this can be most efficiently accomplished by beginning with a company's financial statements and identifying supporting objectives for those business activities, processes and events that can materially affect the financial statements. In this way, a basis is formed for giving attention only to what is truly relevant to the reliability of financial reporting for that company.

Focusing on Risk

While management considers risks in several respects, its overarching consideration is the risks to key objectives, including the risks to reliable financial reporting. Risk-based means focusing on quantitative and qualitative factors that potentially affect the reliability of financial reporting, and identifying where in transaction processing or other activities related to financial statement preparation something could go wrong. By focusing on key objectives management can tailor the scope and depth of risk assessments needed. Often risk is considered in the context of initially designing and implementing internal control, where risks to objectives are identified and analyzed to form a basis for determining how the risks should be managed. Another is in the context of assessing whether internal control is effective in mitigating risks to objectives. In the context of assessing internal control effectiveness, there sometimes is a tendency to consider internal control using generic lists of controls appropriate to a "typical" organization. While these tools in questionnaire or other form may be useful, an unintended result is that management sometimes focuses on "standard" or "typical" controls that simply are not relevant to the company's financial reporting objectives or risks associated with those objectives.

A related problem encountered is starting assessments with the details of accounting systems and documenting them in extreme depth without recognizing whether the entirety of processes are truly relevant to achieving reliable financial reporting. This is not to say that such approaches cannot be useful, as they can be. However, whatever approach is followed, efficiencies are gained when attention is directed to the objectives management has established specific to the company's business activities and circumstances.

Right-Sizing Documentation

Documentation of business processes and procedures and other elements of internal control systems is developed and maintained by companies for a number of reasons. One is to promote consistency in adhering to desired practices in running the business. Effective documentation assists in communicating what is to be done, and how, and creates expectations of performance. Another purpose of documentation is to assist in training new personnel and as a refresher or reference tool for other employees. Documentation also provides evidence to support reporting on internal control effectiveness. The level and nature of documentation varies widely by company. Certainly, large companies usually have more operations to document, or greater complexity in financial reporting processes, and therefore find it necessary to have more extensive documentation than smaller ones.

Smaller companies often find less need for formal documentation, such as in-depth policy manuals, systems flowcharts of processes, organization charts, job descriptions, and the like. In smaller companies, typically there are fewer people and levels of management, closer working relationships and more frequent interaction, all of which promotes communication of what is expected and what is being done. A smaller business, for example, might document human resources, procurement or customer credit policies with memoranda and supplement the memoranda with guidance provided by management in meetings. A larger company will more likely have more detailed policies (or policy manuals) to guide their people in better implementing controls.

Questions arise as to the extent of documentation needed to deem internal control over financial reporting as effective. The answer is, of course, it depends on circumstances and needs. Some level of documentation is always necessary to assure management that its control processes are working, such as documentation to help assure management that all shipments are billed, or periodic reconciliations are performed. In a smaller business, however, management is often directly involved in performing control procedures and for those procedures there may be only minimal documentation because management can determine that controls are functioning effectively through direct observation.

However, there must be information available to management that the accounting systems and related procedures, including actions taken in connection with preparation of reliable financial statements, are well designed, well understood, and carried out properly.

When management asserts to regulators, shareholders or other third parties on the design and operating effectiveness of internal control over financial reporting, management accepts a higher level of personal risk and typically will require documentation of major processes within the accounting systems and important control activities to support its assertions. Accordingly, management will review to determine whether its documentation is appropriate to support its assertion. In considering the amount of documentation needed, the nature and extent of the documentation may be influenced by the company's regulatory requirements. This does not necessarily mean that documentation will or should be more formal, but it does mean that there needs to be evidence that the controls are designed and working properly.

In addition, when an external auditor will be attesting to the effectiveness of internal control, management will likely be expected to provide the auditor with support for its assertion. That support would include evidence that the controls are properly designed and are working effectively. In considering the nature and extent of documentation needed by the company, management should also consider that the documentation to support the assertion that controls are working properly will likely be used by the external auditor as part of his or her audit evidence.

There may still be instances where policies and procedures are informal and undocumented. This may be appropriate where management is able to obtain evidence captured through the normal conduct of the business that indicates personnel regularly performed those controls. However, it is important to keep in mind that control processes, such as risk assessment, cannot be performed entirely in the mind of the CEO or CFO without some documentation of the thought process and management's analysis.

Many of the examples contained later in this guidance illustrate how management can capture evidence through the normal course of business. Documentation of internal control should meet business needs and be commensurate with circumstances. The extent of documentation supporting design and operating effectiveness of the five internal control components is a matter of judgment, and should be done with costeffectiveness in mind.

Where practical, the creation and retention of evidence should be embedded with the various financial reporting processes.

Viewing Internal Control as an Integrated Process

It is useful to view the Framework's five internal control components as comprising an integrated process, which indeed internal control is. A process perspective highlights the interrelationship of the components, and recognizes that management has flexibility in choosing controls to achieve its objectives and that an organization can adjust and improve its internal control over time. As noted, the internal control process begins with management setting financial reporting objectives relevant to the company's particular business activities and circumstances.

Once set, management identifies and assesses a variety of risks to those objectives, determines which risks could result in a material misstatement in financial reporting, and determines how the risks should be managed through a range of control activities.

Management implements approaches to capture, process and communicate information needed for financial reporting and other components of the internal control system. All this is done in context of the company's control environment, which is shaped and refined as necessary to provide the appropriate tone at the top of the organization and related attributes. These components all are monitored to help ensure that controls continue to operate properly over time.

The Totality of Internal Control

Each of the five components of internal control set forth in the Framework is important to achieving the objective of reliable financial reporting. Determining whether a company's internal control over financial reporting is effective involves a judgment. Internal control has five components that work together to prevent or detect and correct material misstatements of financial reports.

When the five components are present and functioning, to the extent that management has reasonable assurance that financial statements are being prepared reliably, internal control can be deemed effective. While each component must be present and functioning, this does not mean, however, that each component should function identically or even at the same level in every company.

Some trade- offs may exist between components. Accordingly, effective internal control does not necessarily mean a "gold standard" of control is built into every process. A deficiency in one component might be mitigated by other controls in that component or by controls in another component strong enough such that the totality of control is sufficient to reduce the risk of misstatement to an acceptable level.

COMMUNICATION

The most disruptive method of communication for maintenance requests is VERBAL. Normally when an engineer is sighted on route to a job site it inevitably happens that someone "Could you fix this?"

I suppose it's normal for everyone to take the easiest route or the path of least resistance. When an engineering person is on route to a job they generally have brought the tools and materials for that particular job and are while on route forming a plan of attack in troubleshooting. I recall sending an individual on a job that would have taken thirty minutes including travel time, to come back an hour and a half later because he was interrupted with other jobs while on the way. Verbal requests should not only be avoided, they should be refused.

The best way of communicating maintenance requests has always been to fill out the appropriate maintenance request form and submit for action. Each area department head should inspect their areas daily, making out request forms as they go. Managers work in their area every day but seem oblivious to deficiencies. It is not nor should it be the responsibility of the engineering department to inspect or maintain areas that are managed by others.

Walkthroughs are another good method of keeping on top of the property's condition. A walkthrough should be conducted monthly of all public or common areas. Public or common areas are those areas of the building that do not specifically come under the jurisdiction of any one department or department head; such as lobby, grounds, public washrooms.

If walkthroughs are to be conducted of a restaurant or lounge or meeting room etc., the department head responsible should be held accountable for any deficiency and be able to produce a copy of the maintenance request form for that particular item. If the question is one of cleanliness, then again show a request of the housekeeping department to action. Too often, engineering will get a request for a burnt light or paint touchup just minutes before the guest arrives.

They usually are the ones to call ten minutes before a meeting starts to report a critical light burnt out or a piece of equipment not working. Meeting rooms will have holes poked into the ceiling or walls, doors knocked off their hinges. We have had scrapes in walls repaired only to see them damaged again within minutes. All hotels seem to have the same common challenge with the banquet department. In their defense we have observed with banquets that it may be a staffing issue where part timers are only called in for the last minute for functions and they really don't care. Regular staff are too few to handle equipment properly as we see many a banquet person moving an eight-foot table by themselves and of course smacking into doors and walls. We never see supervisors "supervising" or inspecting vacant meeting rooms.

Lists of actions due to inspections are also good, however it then makes it incumbent on the engineering department to then write up maintenance request forms for assignment. The maintenance request form is one of the most essential tools for which the engineering department operates. They are used to track trends, monitor inventory and labour and to ensure that things are not forgotten. Completed maintenance request forms should be sorted by type such as plumbing, electrical etc. to indicate trends and frequencies. They can then be actioned in an attempt to eliminate repeating problems.

A good example of studying trends towards a solution is a hotel where I had started to work and it was mentioned to me that all guest room fan coil units leak condensation in the summer when the air conditioning is on. Too late to investigate and repair all four hundred and fifty units, we set up a room layout template and proceeded to chart each report of a leaking air conditioning unit during the summer season.

We would normally have liked to pre-empt any guest complaint but as this situation was happening for the previous twenty-five years that one more season wouldn't hurt. The survey indicated that 25% of the fan coil units had leaked and resulted in many repeat complaints exaggerating the extent of the problem. Unfortunately more that one hundred units were leaking but it went back to a construction deficiency where all the drain lines of these units were sloped uphill.

The fault was not only with the plumbers however; the drywall installers pushed up on the metal studs pushing up on the unit drain lines. The plumbing error is where they measured from the ceiling concrete slab to slant the drain line but the slab they measured from was poured on a slope as well. Engineering had one person of each shift who did nothing but drain these condensation pans daily to help prevent their leaking. They did this for twenty-five years! Now that the drains have been corrected and the problem resolved the engineers can go on to other things. Tracking request history is important.

BUDGETS

Budgets by and large are an interesting vehicle for fiscal manipulation. The engineering budget is split into two categories, heat light and power, and repair and maintenance. Depending on the location of the hotel the heat light and power budget might consume 4% or more of sales revenue with repairs and maintenance at about 5 or 6%.

The combined average being about 10% of sales revenue. Note that a renowned consulting group determined, albeit 1991, that of full service hotels over 200 rooms and an average rate of $75.00 or more; it would cost about 10.3% of revenue. It should be understood that HLP consumptions and costs are variable due to weather, room occupancy, restaurant and banquet covers, market price volatility. Predictability can only be assumed, however, baselines for utility consumption can be established to provide a relatively accurate consumption pattern for billing units. Regression analysis is one such method.

Keeping records of all utilities, heating degree-days, cooling degree-days, guests in house, covers, will provide background information to weigh against billing unit consumption. Meter information should be gathered on a daily basis to quickly diagnose any anomaly in consumption such as major leaks or equipment malfunction. The general ledger, chart of accounts will indicate each utility, i.e.; electricity, natural gas, steam, water and sewage etc. Caution should be exercised when gathering utility history from P&L statements as these statements have sometimes gone through numerical gymnastics. I once had a utility budget pared down by a controller telling me to just say, "tell them the weather changed."

The repair and maintenance portion, R&M covers the balance of the engineering expenses such as labour, building, mechanical equipment repairs, kitchen repairs, uniforms and on and on, covering almost all repair contingencies. What must be understood with any budget is that it is a guide only. Engineering budgets are best replicating historic data for that particular property. Zero-based budgeting is not possible, or at the least will not be accurate at year-end. When budgets are made it is only a foggy view of the next fiscal year.

An unexpected pump failure could cost $10,000.00 to name only one incident or the cost of natural gas go up 150% in one month. There are some hotels attempting at monthly forecasts that as a tool may arrive at some idea on how achievable the budget might be next month. Engineering forecasts are best kept to the weather. Inevitably once the engineering manager submits the annual budget it is often "massaged" to placate corporate offices.

The end result of any budget is a reflection of management's commitment to the level of maintenance they would like to see in their property.

General Considerations

An agency, to serve well, can afford to deliver only the service that each client pays for. In actual practice, many agency services are performed for the commission received from the sale of advertising space and materials. Agencies which have no method by which to determine the cost of serving each account are likely to "rob Peter to pay Paul." In such cases, the policy-making executives see only an operating statement which indicates that the agency made or lost money. Such operating statements do not show what it has cost to serve each account or what the income from each account has been.

A budget which simply forecasts the total revenue by classes and the total costs and expenses by type is of little use in advertising agency management. Such a budget could be compared with the budget of a manufacturing concern that does not segregate the income from various products or the costs applying to the manufacture and sale of each product. There are those who suggest that the advertising agency budget be segregated so as to show departmental costs; however, departmental costs are of little importance compared with the cost of serving each client. In some businesses, the steps in the manufacturing processes can be segregated within the departments of the manufacturer's plant. Departmental costs become of value in such cases. In the advertising agency business, there is no standard for grouping costs within departments.

For example, the copy cost could be large on one account; on another, the art cost could exceed copy cost; and on a third, contact cost could easily be the largest element. There is no scientific method for allocating gross revenue to the various departments within the agency, but it is relatively simple to determine each element of cost entering into serving one particular client.

It is impossible to prepare accurate budgets without first having established a cost-accounting system. No forecast of future operations can be accurately drawn without a knowledge of past operations in connection with similar types of transactions. Budgeting and cost accounting, therefore, are inseparable partners and must be used together.

A properly established cost-accounting system will furnish periodic statements showing separately the results of the agency's operations with each client. Such cost-accounting statements will show each of the sources of income, including, for example, commission received from newspaper space, magazine and trade-paper space, outdoor advertising, radio time, radio talent, advertising materials, service fees and miscellaneous items. The statement will show the various costs incurred in serving each client.

These costs are broadly divided into direct and indirect costs. Included among the direct expenses are creative and other direct salaries. These salaries include the cost of the time devoted to the account by creative people and others who spend time directly on clients' accounts, performing such services as contacting, planning, copy preparation, art direction, research, media selection and buying, production and publicity. Other direct expenses comprise those expenses that are incurred directly in connection with serving a particular client's account. They include such items as traveling, research, enter-So training and advertising materials purchased to serve a particular client which cannot be billed to the client. In this last category might appear such an item as resetting type because of an error made by the agency.

Included among the indirect expenses are indirect salaries. These include salaries paid to agency employees who do not work directly on any one account. Work performed in the following categories is generally included in this classification: stenography, typing, ordering, billing, accounting and administrative work. Other indirect expenses include all of the expenses of the agency that are incurred in its general operation, but which are not specifically incurred in connection with servicing particular clients. This classification includes such items as rent, light, local telephone, general travel, general entertaining, dues and subscriptions, stationery and supplies and the like.

The proper cost-accounting system will enable the agency to segregate its costs and expenses by clients and to segregate the costs and expenses on each account in accordance with the preceding formula. Because the advertising agency business lends itself particularly well to cost accounting, costs and expenses can be segregated properly with a minimum of effort, provided that the accounting and cost-accounting system is designed with this in mind. The form of the cost-accounting statements, to be of greatest use, must be in exactly the same form as the budget. There is no one ideal form. The type of statement to be used will depend somewhat on the requirements of the people who are going to work with the statements. The statements should be in such form that management can clearly understand the figures. The budget and the cost-accounting statements are intended to accomplish two principal objectives:

1. To show management how its policies are expected to work out.
2. To indicate to management how well the organization is carrying out its policies.

In other words, the budget is intended to show what will happen if the organization does what management directs, and the cost-accounting statement is intended to show whether the organization was able to do these things. No agency should attempt to prepare a budget or forecast until it has first established an adequate cost-accounting system. A forecast is not simply a schedule showing what business an agency can expect to do in the future; rather, it is a detailed report showing not only what business the agency is expected to do for a period of time, but showing as well the cost of transacting that business. The means for preparing an agency budget are well established. Following is an analysis of them.

MANAGING BUDGET

Budget generally refers to a list of all planned expenses and revenues. A budget is an important concept in microeconomics, which uses a budget line to illustrate the trade-offs between two or more goods. A personal budget is among the most important concepts of personal finance. In a personal or family budget all sources of income (inflows) are identified and expenses (outflows) are planned with the intent of matching outflows to inflows (Making ends meet). There are a wide variety of personal budgeting methods and tools that can be employed to help individuals and families with the budgeting process. Also the level of planned finance available to a person, corporation or government, as set by a certain person.

The budget of a government is a summary or plan of the intended revenues and expenditures of that government. In the United States, the federal budget is prepared by the Office of Management and Budget, and submitted to Congress for consideration. Invariably, Congress makes many and substantial changes. Nearly all American states are required to have balanced budgets, but the federal government is allowed to run deficits. In the UK the budget is prepared by the Chancellor of the Exchequer, the second most important member of the government, and must be passed by Parliament. The Parliament seldom makes changes to the budget.

The budget of a company is compiled annually. A finished budget usually requires considerable effort and can be seen as a financial plan for the new financial year. While traditionally the Finance department compiles the company's budget, modern software allows hundreds or even thousands of people in the various departments (operations, human resources, IT etc) to contribute their expected revenues and expenses to the final budget.

If the actual numbers delivered through the financial year turn out to be close to the budget, this will demonstrate that the company understands their business and has been successfully driving it in the direction they had planned. On the other hand, if the actuals diverge wildly from the budget, this sends out an 'out of control' signal and the share

Cost-plus pricing is a pricing method commonly used by firms. It is used primarily because it is easy to calculate and requires little information. There are several varieties, but the common thread in all of them is that you first calculate the cost of the product, then include an additional amount to represent profit. Cost-plus pricing is often used on government contracts, and has been criticized as promoting wasteful expenditures.

Calculating Price Using the Cost-plus Method

There are several ways of determining cost, and the profit can be added as either a percentage markup or an absolute amount. One example is:

P = (AVC + FC%) * (1 + MK%)

where:

- P = price
- AVC = average variable cost
- FC% = percentage allocation of fixed costs
- MK% = percentage markup

For example: If variable costs are 30 yen, the allocation to cover fixed costs is 10 yen, and you feel you need a 50% markup then you would charge a price of 60 yen:

P = (30 + 10) • (1 + 0.50)

P = 40 • 1.5

P = 60

An alternative way of doing a similar calculation is:

P = (AVC + FC%)/ (1 " MK%)

To make things simpler, some firms, particularly retailers, ignore fixed costs and just use the purchase price paid to their suppliers as the cost term.

They indirectly incorporate the fixed cost allocation into the markup percentage. To simplify things even further, sometimes a fixed amount is applied rather than a percentage. This fixed amount is usually determined by head-office to make it easy for franchisees and store managers. This is sometimes referred to as turnkey pricing.

Another variant of cost plus pricing is activity based pricing. This involves being more careful in determining costs. Instead of using arbitrary expense categories when allocating overhead, every activity is linked to the resources it uses.

Cost will need to be recalculated and the percentage markup will likely need to be adjusted as the product goes through its life cycle.

This is sometimes referred to as product life cycle pricing, although it is seldom done deliberately or in a planned and organized manner. Price skimming and penetration pricing are also types of product life cycle pricing but they are demand based pricing methods rather cost based.

Advantages of Cost-plus Pricing:

1. Easy to calculate
2. Minimal information requirements
3. Easy to administer
4. Tends to stabilize markets - insulated from demand variations and competitive factors
5. Insures seller against unpredictable, or unexpected later costs
6. Ethical advantages

Disadvantages:

1. Tends to ignore the role of consumers
2. Tends to ignore the role of competitors
3. Use of historical accounting costs rather than replacement value
4. Use of "normal" or "standard" output level to allocate fixed costs
5. Inclusion of sunk costs rather than just using incremental costs
6. Ignores opportunity costs
7. Contractors may not focus on performance because the cost is always covered by the client

In microeconomics, Production is simply the conversion of inputs into outputs. It is an economic process that uses resources to create a commodity that is suitable for exchange.

This can include manufacturing, storing, shipping, and packaging. Some economists define production broadly as all economic activity other than consumption. They see every commercial activity other than the final purchase as some form of production. Production is a process, and as such it occurs through time and space. Because it is a flow concept, production is measured as a "rate of output per period of time".

There are three aspects to production processes:

1. The quantity of the commodity produced,

2. The form of the good produced,
3. The temporal and spatial distribution of the commodity produced.

A production process can be defined as any activity that increases the similarity between the pattern of demand for goods, and the quantity, form, and distribution of these goods available to the market place.

A production process is efficient if a given quantity of outputs cannot be produced with any less inputs. It is said to be inefficient when there exists another feasible process that, for any given output, uses less inputs. Some economists (in particular Leibenstein) use the term X-efficiency to indicate that production processes tend to be inherently inefficient due to satisficing behaviour. The "rate of efficiency" is simply the amount of (or value of) outputs divided by the amount of (or value of) inputs. If a production process uses 50 units of input (or $5000 worth of inputs) to produce one unit of output it is more efficient than a process that uses 55 units of input (or $5500 worth of inputs) to produce the same level of output. It is said to be 10% more efficient ({55-50}/50=1/10=10%).

The inputs or resources used in the production process are called factors by economists. The myriad of possible inputs are usually grouped into four or five categories.

These factors are:

- Raw materials (natural capital)
- Labour services (human capital)
- Capital goods
- Land

Sometimes a fifth category is added, entrepreneurial and management skills, a subcategory of labour services. Capital goods are those goods that have previously undergone a production process. They are previously produced means of production. Some textbooks use "technology" as a factor of production.

In the "long run" all of these factors of production can be adjusted by management. The "short run" however, is defined as a period in which at least one of the factors of production is fixed. A fixed factor of production is one whose quantity cannot readily be changed. Examples include major pieces of equipment, suitable factory space, and key managerial personnel. A variable factor of production is one whose usage rate can be changed easily. Examples include electrical power consumption, transportation services, and most raw material inputs. In the short run, a firm's "scale of operations" determines the maximum number of outputs that can be produced. In the long run, there are no scale limitations.

The total product (or total physical product) of a variable factor of production identifies what outputs are possible using various levels of the variable input. This can be displayed in either a chart that lists the output level corresponding to various levels of input, or a graph that summarizes the data into a "total product curve". The diagram shows a typical total product curve. In this example, output increases as more inputs are employed up until point A. The maximum output possible with this production process is Qm. If there are other inputs used in the process, they are assumed to be fixed.

The average physical product is the total product divided by the number of units of variable input employed. It is the output of each unit of input. If there are 10 employees working on a production process that manufactures 50 units per day, then the average product of variable labour input is 5 units per day.

The average product typically varies as more of the input is employed, so this relationship can also be expresses as a chart or as a graph. A typical average physical product curve is shown (APP). It can be obtained by drawing a vector from the origin to various points on the total product curve and plotting the slopes of these vectors.

The marginal physical product of a variable input is the change in total output due to a one unit change in the variable input (called the discrete marginal product) or alternatively the rate of change in total output due to an infinitesimally small change in the variable input (called the continuous marginal product). The discrete marginal product of capital is the additional output resulting from the use of an additional unit of capital (assuming all other factors are fixed). The continuous marginal product of a variable input can be calculated as the derivative of quantity produced with respect to variable input employed. The marginal physical product curve is shown (MPP). It can be obtained from the slope of the total product curve.

Because the marginal product drives changes in the average product, we know that when the average physical product is falling, the marginal physical product must be less than the average. Likewise, when the average physical product is rising, it must be due to a marginal physical product greater than the average. For this reason, the marginal physical product curve must intersect the maximum point on the average physical product curve.

MPP keeps increasing till it reaches its maximum. Up until this point every additional unit has been adding more value to the total product than the previous one. From this point onwards, every additional unit adds less to the total product compared to the previous one. But the average product is still increasing till MPP touches APP. At this point, an additional unit is adding the same value as the average product. From this point onwards, MPP starts to reduce and so does APP because every additional unit is adding less to APP than the average product. But the total product is still increasing because every additional unit is still contributing positively. Therefore, during this period, both, the average as well as marginal products, are decreasing, but the total product is still increasing. Finally we reach a point when MPP crosses the x-axis. At this point every additional unit starts to diminish the product of previous units, possibly by getting into their way. Therefore the total product starts to decrease at this point. This is point A on the total product curve.

Diminishing returns can be divided into three categories:

1. Diminishing Total returns, which implies reduction in total product with every additional unit of input. This occurs after point A in the graph.
2. Diminishing Average returns, which refers to the portion of the APP curve after its intersection with MPP curve.
3. Diminishing Marginal returns, refers to the point where the MPP curve starts to slope down and travels all the way down to the x-axis and beyond. Putting it in a chronological order, at first the marginal returns start to diminish, then the average returns, followed finally by the total returns.

These curves illustrate the principle of diminishing marginal returns to a variable input (not to be confused with diseconomies of scale which is a long term phenomenon in which all factors are allowed to change). This states that as you add more and more of a variable input, you will reach a point beyond which the resulting increase in output starts to diminish. This point is illustrated as the maximum point on the marginal physical product curve.

It assumes that other factor inputs (if they are used in the process) are held constant. An example is the employment of labour in the use of trucks to transport goods. Assuming the number of available trucks (capital) is fixed, then the amount of the variable input labour could be varied and the resultant efficiency determined. At least one labourer (the driver) is necessary. Additional workers per vehicle could be productive in loading, unloading, navigation, or around the clock continuous driving. But at some point the returns to investment in labour will start to diminish and efficiency will decrease. The most efficient distribution of labour per piece of equipment will likely be one driver plus an additional worker for other tasks (2 workers per truck would be more efficient than 5 per truck).

Resource allocations and distributive efficiencies in the mix of capital and labour investment will vary per industry and according to available technology. Trains are able to transport much more in the way of goods with fewer "drivers" but at the cost of greater investment in infrastructure. With the advent of mass production of motorized vehicles, the economic niche occupied by trains (compared with transport trucks) has become more specialized and limited to long haul delivery.

There is an argument that if the theory is holding everything constant, the production method should not be changed, i.e., division of labour should not be practiced. However, the rise in marginal product means that the workers use other means of production method, such as in loading, unloading, navigation, or around the clock continuous driving. For this reason, some economists think that the "keeping other things constant" should not be used in this theory.

The total, average, and marginal physical product curves mentioned above are just one way of showing production relationships. They express the quantity of output relative to the amount of variable input employed while holding fixed inputs constant. Because they depict a short run relationship, they are sometimes called short run production functions. If all inputs are allowed to be varied, then the diagram would express outputs relative to total inputs, and the function would be a long run production function. If the mix of inputs is held constant, then output would be expressed relative to inputs of a fixed composition, and the function would indicate long run economies of scale.

Rather than comparing inputs to outputs, it is also possible to assess the mix of inputs employed in production. An isoquant relates the quantities of one input to the quantities of another input. It indicates all possible combinations of inputs that are capable of producing a given level of output.

Rather than looking at the inputs used in production, it is possible to look at the mix of outputs that are possible for any given production process. This is done with a production possibilities frontier. It indicates what combinations of outputs are possible given the available factor endowment and the prevailing production technology.

You can use a lot of labour with a minimal amount of capital, or you could invest heavily in capital equipment that requires a minimal amount of labour to operate, or any combination in between. For most goods, there are more than just two inputs. For example in agriculture, the amount of land, water, and fertilizer can all be varied to produce different amounts of a crop. An isoquant, in the two input case, is a curve that shows all the ways of combining two inputs so as to produce a given level of output. In the three input case it will be a surface. Iso is Latin for equal and quant is short for quantity. Movement along an isoquant depicts a constant rate of output, but a changing input ratio. A unique isoquant can be constructed for every level of output, and a family of isoquants can be created to represent various output levels. Isoquants further from the origin represent greater amounts of output. Isoquants are usually considered to be everywhere dense, meaning an infinite number of them could be plotted in any two input space.

A typical isoquant is illustrated in the diagram to the right. At point A in the diagram Ka units of capital are combined with La units of labour to produce 100 units of output. It is downward sloping, convex to the origin, and non-intersecting (additional isoquants, not shown, would be drawn parallel to this one). A complete isoquant is actually a closed curve, but only the "down sloping to the right" portion makes economic sense. The upward sloping parts of isoquants, for example, indicate that that level of output could be produced by less of both inputs so this section is of little interest to decision makers. The economic section of the isoquants is defined by a pair of lines called ridge lines.

The "downward to the right" slope of the economic region of an isoquant is due to the possibility of substituting one input for another in the production process while keeping the level of output constant.

Isoquants are typically convex to the origin reflecting the fact that the two factors are substitutable for each other at varying rates. This rate of substitutability is called the "marginal rate of technical substitution" (MRTS) or occasionally the "marginal rate of substitution in production". It measures the reduction in one input per unit increase in the other input that is just sufficient to maintain a constant level of production. For example, the marginal rate of substitution of labour for capital gives the amount of capital that can be replaced by one unit of labour while keeping output unchanged.

To move from point A to point B in the diagram, the amount of capital is reduced from Ka to Kb while the amount of labour is increased only from La to Lb. To move from point C to point D, the amount of capital is reduced from Kc to Kd while the amount of labour is increased from La to Lb. The marginal rate of technical substitution of labour for capital is equivalent to the absolute slope of the isoquant at that point (change in capital divided by change in labour). It is equal to 0 where the isoquant becomes horizontal, and equal to infinity where it becomes vertical.

The opposite is true when going in the other direction. In this case we are looking at the marginal rate of technical substitution capital for labour (which is the reciprocal of the marginal rate of technical substitution labour for capital). It can also be shown that the marginal rate of substitution labour for capital, is equal to the marginal physical product of labour divided by the marginal physical product of capital. In the unusual case of two inputs that are perfect substitutes for each other in production, the isoquant would be linear (linear, a straight line, with a function $y = a - bx$). If, on the other hand, there is only one production process available, factor proportions would be fixed, and these zero-substitutability isoquants would be shown as horizontal or vertical lines.

SCHEDULED MAINTENANCE

A plan to do maintenance work in the future is usually of two types and that is scheduled maintenance and preventive maintenance. Scheduled maintenance is that type of work that requires longer durations to complete, planning of manpower and tools and materials required, co-ordination with other trades and possibly outside contractors. The timely replacement or maintenance on a major piece of equipment could involve shut downs of other departments or blocks of guest rooms. Projects such as building of walls or complete painting of areas could also come under scheduled maintenance. Indeed, any project requires scheduling and planning.

Preventive Maintenance, as it's name implies is the intent to perform timed inspections, minor adjustments, lubrication based on manufacture's recommendations with the ultimate goal of preventing unscheduled breakdowns and prolonging the life and efficiency of the equipment. During the course of the inspection if it is determined that major work may be required, then work orders are generated to schedule the maintenance. Room Maintenance, both guest and meeting rooms again follows the above with inspections and generating work orders to schedule and correct deficiencies. The frequency of inspections should be determined to happen sometime before the area slow periods.

If guest rooms occupancy is peak in summer then schedule the inspection just prior to the downturn as it will give time to order necessary materials and schedule the labor to accomplish the tasks. The importance of inspections cannot be over emphasized because I have yet to see room attendants or banquet staff adequately report deficiencies. Breakdown maintenance can be both negative and positive. Negative if it has an impact on guest comfort, safety, or is detrimental to the smooth flow of production that keeps other departments operational.

Breakdowns can be very expensive if it happens after hours and outside contractors are required, or if say the main chiller shuts down and all your guests walk out. Positive as you would not want to spend $100 a year on preventive maintenance on a blender worth $50. Also, in maintenance repairs don't waste $20 worth of time to repair something only worth $10.00. Contract maintenance is mandated in some instances such as for elevator service, kitchen hood exhaust cleaning and fire systems. The reasoning behind this is to ensure that the work is performed by qualified technicians, and may also require licenses and special knowledge. Local regulations and insurance companies usually require these contracts. It also serves the purpose of making sure the work gets done irregardless of budget restraints. Maintenance contracts or contracting out is almost always necessary to complement an engineering department that is undersized.

HIRING

The hiring of engineering management personnel is unfortunately processed by persons without a technical and mechanical background. The difficulty with some properties is that they may not have the corporate resources to use a engineering person on staff, either at head office or a similar hotel in a chain. The benefit of experience and certification in property and hotel operation is apparent.

Often, again for the sake of the bottom line engineering management are hired based on little experience and know-how to save on dollars. There are some instances where power engineering 4th class or higher is required to satisfy boiler and pressure vessel regulations, however these only form the minimum entry level requirements of power plants in lumber mills and power process industries and may be necessary if the building has equipment with heating surfaces and refrigeration exceeding normal capacity.

EMPLOYMENT TRAINING

General

The efficiency and economy with which any department will operate will depend on the ability of each member of the organization to do his or her job. Such ability will depend in part on past experiences, but more commonly it can be credited to the type and quality of training offered. Employees, regardless of past experiences, always need some degree of training before starting a new job. Small institutions may try to avoid training by hiring people who are already trained in the general functions with which they will be involved. However, most institutions recognize the need for training that is specifically oriented towards the new experience, and will have a documented training programme.

Some employers of housekeeping personnel find it easier to train completely unskilled and untrained personnel. In such cases, bad or undesirable practices do not have to be trained out of an employee. Previous experience and education should, however, be analysed and considered in the training of each new employee in order that efficiencies in training can be recognized. If an understanding of department standards and policies can be demonstrated by a new employee, that portion of training may be shortened or modified. However, skill and ability must be demonstrated before training can be altered. Finally, training is the best method to communicate the company's way of doing things, without which the new employee may do work contrary to company policy.

First Training

First training of a new employee actually starts with a continuation of department orientation. When a new employee is turned over to the housekeeping or environmental services department, orientation usually continues by familiarizing the employee with department rules and regulations. Many housekeeping departments have their own department employee handbooks.

For an example, which contains the housekeeping department rules and regulations for Bally's Casino Resort in Las Vegas, Nevada. Compare this handbook with that of the generic handbook. Although these handbooks are for completely different types of organizations, the substance of their publications is essentially the same; both are designed to familiarize each new employee with his or her surroundings. Handbooks should be written in such a way as to inspire employees to become team members, committed to company objectives.

A Systematic Approach to Training

Training may be defined as those activities that are designed to help an employee begin performing tasks for which he or she is hired or to help the employee improve performance in a job already assigned. The purpose of training is to enable an employee to begin an assigned job or to improve upon techniques already in use. In hotel or hospital housekeeping operations, there are three basic areas in which training activity should take place: skills, attitudes, and knowledge.

Skills Training

A sample list of skills in which a basic housekeeping employee must be trained follows:

- *Bed making*: Specific techniques; company policy
- *Vacuuming*: Techniques; use and care of equipment
- *Dusting*: Techniques; use of products
- *Window and mirror cleaning*: Techniques and products
- *Setup awareness*: Room setups; what a properly serviced room should look like
- *Bathroom cleaning*: Tub and toilet sanitation; appearance; methods of cleaning and results desired
- *Daily routine*: An orderly procedure for the conduct of the day's work; daily communications
- *Caring for and using equipment*: Housekeeper cart; loading
- *Industrial safety*: Product use; guest safety; fire and other emergencies

The best reference for the skills that require training is the job description for which the person is being trained.

Attitude Guidance

Employees need guidance in their attitudes about the work that must be done. They need to be guided in their thinking about rooms that may present a unique problem in cleaning.

Attitudes among section housekeepers need to be such that, occasionally, when rooms require extra effort to be brought back to standard, it is viewed as being a part of rendering service to the guest who paid to enjoy the room.

Carol Mondesir,1 director of housekeeping, Sheraton Centre, Toronto, states that:

- A hotel is meant to be enjoyed and, occasionally, the rooms are left quite messed up. However, as long as they're not vandalized, it's part of the territory. The whole idea of being in the hospitality business is to make the guest's stay as pleasant as possible. The rooms are there to be enjoyed.

Positive relationships with various agencies and people also need to be developed.

The following is a list of areas in which attitude guidance is important:

- The guest/patient
- The department manager and immediate supervisor
- A guestroom that is in a state of great disarray
- The hotel and company
- The uniform
- Appearance
- Personal hygiene

Meeting Standards

The most important task of the trainer is to prepare new employees to meet standards. With this aim in mind, sequence of performance in cleaning a guestroom is most important in order that efficiency in accomplishing day-to-day tasks may be developed.

In addition, the best method of accomplishing a task should be presented to the new trainee. Once the task has been learned, the next thing is to meet standards, which may not necessarily mean doing the job the way the person has been trained. Setting standards of performance is discussed in Chapter under "Operational Controls."

Knowledge Training

Areas of knowledge in which the employee needs to be trained are as follows:

- Thorough knowledge of the hotel layout; employee must be able to give directions and to tell the guest about the hotel, restaurants, and other facilities
- Knowledge of employee rights and benefits
- Understanding of grievance procedure
- Knowing top managers by sight and by name

Ongoing Training

There is a need to conduct ongoing training for all employees, regardless of how long they have been members of the department.

There are two instances when additional training is needed:

- The purchase of new equipment, and
- Change in or unusual employee behaviour while on the job.

When new equipment is purchased, employees need to know how the new equipment differs from present equipment, what new skills or knowledge are required to operate the equipment, who will need this knowledge, and when. New equipment may also require new attitudes about work habits. Employee behaviour while on the job that is seen as an indicator for additional training may be divided into two categories: Events that the manager witnesses and events that the manager is told about by the employees. Events that the manager witnesses that indicate a need for training are frequent employee absence, considerable spoilage of products, carelessness, a hig

Events that the manager might be told about that indicate a need for training are that something doesn't work right something is dangerous to work with, something is making work harder. Although training is vital for any organization to function at top efficiency, it is expensive. The money and man-hours expended must therefore be worth the investment. There must be a balance between the dollars spent training employees and the benefits of productivity and high-efficiency performance. A simple method of determining the need for training is to measure performance of workers: Find out what is going on at present on the job, and match this performance with what should be happening. The difference, if any, describes how much training is needed.

In conducting performance analysis, the following question should be asked: Could the employee do the job or task if his or her life depended on the result? If the employee could not do the job even if his or her life depended on the outcome, there is a deficiency of knowledge. If the employee could have done the job if his or her life depended on the outcome, but did not, there is a deficiency of execution. Some of the causes of deficiencies of execution include task interference, lack of feedback and the balance of consequences.

If either deficiency of knowledge or deficiency of execution exists, training must be conducted. The approach or the method of training may differ, however. Deficiencies of knowledge can be corrected by training the employee to do the job, then observing and correcting as necessary until the task is proficiently performed. Deficiency of execution is usually corrected by searching for the underlying cause of lack of performance, not by teaching the actual task.

Training Methods

There are numerous methods or ways to conduct training. Each method has its own advantages and disadvantages, which must be weighed in the light of benefits to be gained. Some methods are more expensive than others but are also more effective in terms of time required for comprehension and proficiency that must be developed. Several useful methods of training housekeeping personnel are listed and discussed.

On-the-job Training

Using on-the-job training, a technique in which "learning by doing" is the advantage, the instructor demonstrates the procedure and then watches the students perform it.

With this technique, one instructor can handle several students. In housekeeping operations, the instructor is usually a GRA who is doing the instructing in the rooms that have been assigned for cleaning that day. The OJT method is not operationally productive until the student is proficient enough in the training tasks to absorb part of the operational load.

Simulation Training

With simulation training, a model room is set up and used to train several employees. Whereas OJT requires progress towards daily production of ready rooms, simulation requires that the model room not be rented. In addition, the trainer is not productive in cleaning ready rooms. The advantages of simulation training are that it allows the training process to be stopped, discussed, and repeated if necessary. Simulation is an excellent method, provided the trainer's time is paid for out of training funds, and clean room production is not necessary during the workday.

Coach-Pupil Method

The coach-pupil method is similar to OJT except that each instructor has only one student. This method is desired, provided that there are enough qualified instructors to have several training units in progress at the same time.

Lectures

The lecture method reaches the largest number of students per instructor. Practically all training programmes use this type of instruction for certain segments. Unfortunately, the lecture method can be the dullest training technique, and therefore requires instructors who are gifted in presentation capabilities. In addition, space for lectures may be difficult to obtain and may require special facilities.

Conferences

The conference method of instruction is often referred to as workshop training. This technique involves a group of students who formulate ideas, do problem solving, and report on projects. The conference or workshop technique is excellent for supervisory training.

Demonstrations

When new products or equipment are being introduced, demonstrations are excellent. Many demonstrations may be conducted by vendors and purveyors as a part of the sale of equipment and products. Difficulties may arise when language barriers exist. It is also important that no more information be presented than can be absorbed in a reasonable period of time; otherwise misunderstandings may arise.

Training Aids

Many hotels use training aids in a conference room, or post messages on an employee bulletin board. Aside from the usual training aids such as chalkboards, bulletin boards, charts, graphs, and diagrams, photographs can supply clear and accurate references for how rooms should be set up, maids' carts loaded, and routines accomplished. Most housekeeping operations have films on guest contact and courtesy that may also be used in training. Motion pictures speak directly to many people who may not understand proper procedures from reading about them. Many training techniques may be combined to develop a well-rounded training plan.

Development

It is possible to have two students sitting side by side in a classroom, with one being trained and the other being developed. Recall that the definition of training is preparing a person to do a job for which he or she is hired or to improve upon performance of a current job. Development is preparing a person for advancement or to assume greater responsibility. The techniques are the same, but the end result is quite different.

Whereas training begins after orientation of an employee who is hired to do a specific job, upon introduction of new equipment, or upon observation and communication with employees indicating a need for training, development begins with the identification of a specific employee who has shown potential for advancement. Training for promotion or to improve potential is in fact development and must always include a much neglected type of training—supervisory training.

Many forms of developmental training may be given on the property; other forms might include sending candidates to schools and seminars. Developmental training is associated primarily with supervisors and managerial development and may encompass many types of experiences. The various developmental tasks that the trainee must perform over a period of 12 months. Development of individuals within the organization looks to future potential and promotion of employees. Specifically, those employees who demonstrate leadership potential should be developed through supervisory training for advancement to positions of greater responsibility.

Unfortunately, many outstanding workers have their performance rewarded by promotion but are given no development training. The excellent section housekeeper who is advanced to the position of senior housekeeper without the benefit of supervisory training is quickly seen to be unhappy and frustrated and may possibly become a loss to the department. It is therefore most essential that individual potential be developed in an orderly and systematic manner, or else this potential may never be recognized. Even though there will be times that the trainee may be given specific responsibilities to oversee operations, clean guestrooms, or service public areas, advantage should not be taken of the trainee or the situation to the detriment of the development function.

Development of new growth in the trainee becomes difficult when the training instructor or coordinator is not only developing a new manager but is also being held responsible for the production of some aspect of housekeeping operations.

RECORDS AND REPORTS

Whether you are conducting a training or a development programme, suitable records of training progress should be maintained both by the training supervisor and the student. Periodic evaluations of the student's progress should be conducted, and successful completion of the programme should be recognized. Public recognition of achievement will inspire the newly trained or developed employee to achieve standards of performance and to strive for advancement.

Once an employee is trained or developed and his or her satisfactory performance has been recognized and recorded, the person should perform satisfactorily to standards. Future performance may be based on beginning performance after training. If an employee's performance begins to fall short of standards and expectations, there has to be a reason other than lack of skills. The reason for unsatisfactory performance must then be sought out and addressed. This type of follow-up is not possible unless suitable records of training and development are maintained and used for comparison.

HOSPITALITY MAINTENANCE AND ENGINEERING

Interest in employment, now the preserve of many individuals, but not all, in western economies, derives from the fact that'Work dominates the lives of men and women ... the management of employees both individually and collectively remains a central feature of organisational life'. Before beginning an examination of employment relations in the HI, it is useful to outline the historical development of employment relations and their relevance as a field of study, thereby introducing the reader to some of the key terms used throughout the book.

Hyman academic interest in employment relations was prompted when the potential stability of social order was put under threat by militant behaviour among a growing number of unionized industrial manual workers, who were no longer prepared to tolerate very bad terms and conditions of employment.

This challenge to social order, which began in the late nineteenth century, was met by two responses. First, the social welfare reformers, in keeping with their predecessors who had successfully campaigned for health and safety legislation earlier in the nineteenth century, urged legal intervention to improve the conditions under which work was performed and the terms under which it was undertaken. They achieved limited success, notably the introduction of minimum wages in four manufacturing industries in 1906. The second and main response, which was to characterize public policy on employment relations until 1979, was that voluntary collective bargaining provided the best means to secure order within employer-employee relations. Collective bargaining is a process whereby employers and trade unions negotiate the substantive terms and conditions of employment, such as pay and hours of work, and procedural agreements that facilitate the resolution of disputes between the parties.

Industrial relations, the term in usage at the time, focused on the institutions of collective bargaining in fixing these'rules' of employment, largely within male-dominated manufacturing environments. Collective agreements were not legally enforceable. While public services such as the health service, the railways and the coal mines came to assume importance in industrial relations following the mass nationalization programme after the Second World War, private services remained the'Cinderella' of British industrial relations. Even though the growth of private services such as retailing and hospitality opened up more employment opportunities for women, whose main work opportunities had been in domestic service in the earlier part of the century, unregulated, female service work was deemed not to be part of industrial relations.

Even so, the lack of collective bargaining arrangements prompted the Labour government to extend the scope of minimum wage legislation to embrace these sectors. Thus in 1945 the newly named wages councils, a form of'state-sponsored' collective bargaining, were able to fix remuneration and paid holidays for many'unprotected' workers in private services.

COLLECTIVE CONSENSUS AND A MORE ACTIVE STATE

Greater state intervention in employment matters was a response by both Conservative and Labour governments to the mounting economic difficulties of the 1960s, *e.g.* statutory and voluntary incomes policies. State intervention also constituted a response to the perceived failure of voluntary collective bargaining to provide an effective regulatory mechanism for social order and social welfare, notably to protect the interests of the low-paid, many of whom were women. This perceived breakdown prompted the government to appoint a Royal Commission in 1965, the Donovan Commission, to investigate the state of employer-worker relations, in order to recommend how the'system' could be reformed.

The Donovan prescription sought to maintain voluntarism, and placed the onus on employers to improve the rules of employment, and to introduce more formal procedures for the resolution of disputes. Donovan's prescription was not universal, because it could not be applied to large parts of private services comprising small, informally managed, non-union workplaces, where female and part-time employment was concentrated.

A different approach based on legal intervention in employment relations began to develop, based on employment protection for individual employees. Early employment protection rights of the 1960s included the right to a written statement of terms and conditions of employment, statutory redundancy pay and equal pay. Workers lacking the protection of a trade union and with no recourse to formal workplace procedures could resolve an employment dispute, which is those in scope of the law, by going to an industrial tribunal.

The 1970s represented a significant turning point for legal intervention in employment relations. Britain joined the European Economic Community in 1972. This heralded the start of a wide-ranging programme designed to establish a floor of new rights relating to matters including unfair dismissal, maternity leave, sex and race discrimination and health and safety at work. The main beneficiaries were to be those working in private services. Events of the 1980s and early 1990s effectively killed the model of voluntary collective bargaining. In pursuit of an overriding objective to deregulate the labour market and employment, successive Conservative governments systematically dismantled institutions deemed to interfere with the free working of the labour market, notably the trade unions and wages councils. Paradoxically, in spite of the government's antipathy to the EU's social action programme and subsequent opt out of the social chapter, the EU continued to influence British employment relations in a significant way. Rulings from the European Court of Justice obliged Britain to introduce new legislation, *e.g.* the transfer of undertakings or the amendment of existing legislation relating to equal pay and sex discrimination.

The floor of employment rights was both strengthened and extended. Managers reasserted the right to manage increasingly flexible and non-standard workers under the banner of'managerialism', in workplaces that might be labelled'bleak houses'. An alternative version of management thinking stressed the benefits of'commitment' over'control'. Both approaches came to signify the two variants of HRM.'Soft' HRM emphasized fostering commitment, improving quality and developing the human resource, whereas'hard' HRM was contingent and calculating in its utilization of the human resource.

If organizations were to survive the effects of adverse economic conditions, globalization and increasing competition, the imperative was to integrate HRM within business strategy. The impact of HRM on industrial relations was widely debated. Other key issues in the wider academic debate included the extent of continuity and change in industrial relations, the sharp decline in trade union membership, the impact of deregulation and whether employment relations could be re-regulated.

NEW LABOUR: NEW HOPE?

By the mid-1990s individual relationships were catapulted firmly to the forefront of analysis of the employment relationship. Recognition of this change had been apparent from WIRS in 1990, perhaps most notably within the HI. HI managers are free to exercise a high degree of managerial prerogative in the absence of unorganized labour, termed'unbridled individualism'. The election of a Labour government for the first time in nearly 20 years in 1997 raised expectations that there would be a new agenda for employment relations, although Heery's assessment was that'it is extremely doubtful whether New Labour will issue in a new industrial relations'. New Labour's stakeholder economy is based on fairness and partnership. Fairness at work is to be achieved in two ways.

The government signed up to the EU social chapter and set about introducing a new floor of minimum employment standards, including a National Minimum Wage, and family-friendly measures. Social partnership between employers and workers is designed to foster a more consensual and cooperative relationship between employers and employees. The Low Pay Commission whose first task was to recommend the initial rate of the NMW, provides an early manifestation of social partnership comprising employer, worker and independent representatives. Although many of the Conservatives' trade union reforms remain in place, the introduction of statutory trade union recognition procedures might help reverse the steep decline in trade union membership.

By the time of WERS in 1998 the system of collective representation had crumbled'to such an extent that it no longer represented the dominant model'. In reality employment relations could conform to different and diverse patterns. Private service establishments employing 25 or more employees were numerically more important than private sector manufacturing and the public sector put together. Their share of employment increased from 26 per cent in 1980 to 44 per cent in 1998, reinforcing the point that alternative ways to view and reform employment relations were long overdue, particularly in circumstances of'bleak house' or'black hole' employment. Although we find these terms wanting in respect of the HI, they highlight the relevance of the industry as a unit of analysis. Consequently we shall show how these types of workplaces throw up major problems for employment relations reform.

Agenda for the Twenty-first Century

In calling for a new industrial relations paradigm, Ackers now argues that the new problem of social order focuses on links between employment and society, and that such a link provides an explicit ethical framework for policies like social partnership.

He rejects the traditional industrial relations notion of workers as unattached individuals in their out-of-work lives, and argues that industrial relations can no longer ignore issues of work-life balance and corporate social responsibility. Indeed social concerns underpin'Fairness at Work' and the'Welfare to Work' programme, and family-friendly issues are a new addition to WERS.

Hence a new definition of industrial relations as neo-pluralism: Employment relations are the study of the social institutions involved in the normative regulation of the employment relationship and business's interaction with other stakeholders in society. Thus Ackers rejects as inappropriate Kelly's industrial relations paradigm for the twenty-first century, which derives from a redefinition of Marxism based on socialism, workers' mobilization, economic militancy and strikes, and organized labour. Edwards identifies three pressing issues in contemporary employment relations:'high commitment' or'high involvement' work systems, the international context and economic performance.

The first, although interesting, is very rarely found anywhere in Britain. Its alternative of'low skills' and'low wages' strikes right at the heart of much hospitality employment. This links to economic performance, where the absence of collective bargaining is likely to have contributed to income inequality and the perpetuation of low pay in the HI, although pay may be subsidized by the state through social security and taxation.

The further subsidy of low pay through tips as a defensible employment practice is a matter of conjecture. We shall also explore if particular employment relations practices can be linked to successful performance outcomes. The international context and its implications for employment relations in the HI are considered below and in subsequent chapters.

A fourth pressing issue can be added. Employment relations discourse needs to recognize that prejudice and bias have been built into much of the theoretical and practical analysis, thus distorting its perspective. Gender is not the only example, but may be the most obvious. In spite of an increasing interest in what may be described as'women's issues', such as (un)equal pay and employment opportunities, family-friendly policies and sexual harassment, one major barrier to understanding employment relations is an assumption that they are gender neutral. The argument is that adding women's issues to the agenda is simply not good enough. Management, trade unions and the state are not gender neutral, and therefore we need to recognize the gendered characteristics of the employment relationship and work and integrate this into our understanding of the field of employment relations. Other'omissions' include age, ethnicity and the role of customers.

We shall explore these issues throughout the book where it is possible or relevant to do so. All these issues were placed under review in The Future of Work Programme launched by the ESRC in 1998. The Programme has supported 27 projects designed to rectify gaps in our understanding and improve the quality of information available to the policy-makers in the UK. Topics under investigation have included the future of unskilled work, business re-engineering and performance, the changing position of ethnic minorities and women in the labour market, the future for trade unions and the changing nature of the employment relationship.

EMPLOYMENT RELATIONS IN THE HOSPITALITY INDUSTRY

Three terms denote the relations between managers and workers in the employment relationship-industrial relations, employee relations and employment relations. These terms are often used interchangeably, but can also convey subtle differences of meaning. They may coincide with other fields of academic enquiry and practical activity concerned with'people management', namely personnel management and HRM. Edwards provides an insightful analysis of the employment relationship, taking as his starting point the distinction made by Fox and Flanders between market relations and managerial relations. At the root is an economic exchange between capital and labour, in which the price of labour is set as a contract of employment. In this economic exchange between the buyer and seller of labour, the parties do not share equal power resources.

In common law the employer has the right to command and the employee has a duty to obey. The commodity at the heart of the bargain is the worker's labour power. The employer will seek to maximize control over that'labour process' in order to generate a surplus as profit. The employment relationship, as an exchange and in recognition of its broader context, has also been termed the effort-reward bargain:'an economic, social and political relationship, for which employees provide manual and mental labour in return for rewards allotted by employers'. Labour only becomes useful if it can be persuaded by management to work, but this is only the beginning. Workers must demonstrate commitment, continue working to the required standards, and not deviate from those standards.

In other words workers must follow'rules', otherwise management may need to deploy corrective or punitive measures via the disciplinary procedure. Bonamy and May argue that a weakening of employment relationships since the 1970s has given rise to the emergence of employment as a service relationship.

This relationship demands increased recognition of the professional qualities of the'autonomous' worker, which poses problems of incompatibility with an employment contract built upon subordination. Pay is determined by time worked, whilst idle time due to poor organization and absenteeism is reduced.

This is manifested in new forms of employment contract, externalization of employment to agencies and the sub-contracting of activities. Edwards notes that, if we were starting from scratch, 'employment relations' might be the best label.

Employment relations do not rule out all variants within the employment relationship including:

- Trade unions and formal collective bargaining;
- Individually based management/workforce relations conducted informally;
- Managerialism;
- More democratic and highly participative non-union relations;
- Men, women and disadvantaged groups;
- Employees and workers, including atypical workers and the self-employed.

Further:

- Employment relations is the main term used in the WERS sourcebook;
- Industrial tribunals have been renamed employment tribunals;
- The cornerstone of New Labour's industrial relations policy is the Employment Relations Act 1999.

A necessary departure for this book, as noted earlier, is to relocate the nexus of the employment relationship to include a relatively ignored third actor in the employment relationship-the customer. The notion of the customer in the employment relationship has been increasingly incorporated into the sociology of work, but less so in employment relations. Front-line workers, such as receptionists and servers in bars and restaurants, have to serve two'masters': their superior manager and the customer. Individual workers can have a simultaneous and coterminous employment relationship with the organization and the customer.

Organizations in services are best seen as inverted pyramids, with most workers in direct customer contact. Direct service workers engage directly with customers in an exchange that carries both economic and social connotations. Their ability to deliver successfully hinges upon a social relationship with indirect service workers, whose actions are also instrumental to the provision of good customer service, *e.g.* an enjoyable meal or clean bedrooms. Indirect service workers are not in regular customer contact, so customer influence may be more economic than social. Hence, customers cannot be excluded from an analysis of the employment relationship.

An earlier definition has been revised:

- Employee relations in hotels and catering are about the management of employment and work relationships between managers and workers and, sometimes, customers; it also covers contemporary employment and work practices.
- Before exploring the facets of the employment relationship, we need to outline why our attitude towards things influences the way in which we see any given situation, and how it.
- Triplets watch a local football match from adjoining seats, getting an almost identical view of the game. The result is United 5 City 1. One triplet is deliriously happy, the second feels very low, while the third is able to provide a balanced analysis of events, conceding that the result was a fair one, although two of United's goals were the result of dubious refereeing and City deserved more than a single goal.
- Why did their particular attitude affect their view of the game?

Fox proposed two frames of reference as a means by which'the problems of industrial relations can be seen realistically and laid more open to solution'. The unitary perspective is a'management ideology' built on the belief that everyone in the organization shares the same goals, and that'conflict' is pathological and derives from deviance. Trade unions are seen as an intrusion, competing with management for worker loyalty.

Fox's main argument was that the unitary perspective was a naive and unrealistic frame of reference that might'distort reality and thereby prejudice solutions'. Yet in reality many managers do perceive their organizations in unitary terms, regarding themselves as the sole source of authority. Unitarism has underpinned the'human relations school' of management, including Mayo, Likert, McGregor, Schein and Herzberg, and reasserted itself in'managerialism' and HRM. Fox suggested that the more realistic approach to managing people was to recognize that organizations are pluralistic, comprising various groups, each with their own basis of authority and sets of interests. The'rules' of employment are not just the preserve of management. A new pay rate set by management will not necessarily be seen as fair by workers, creating an issue of potential dispute. Therefore conflict or differences between individuals and groups are inevitable. Management should recognize this inevitability, and find the ways and means to regulate such differences. An institutional approach-collective bargaining between employers and trade unions, and the development of formal procedures to deal with disputes about pay, grievances and discipline-was considered to be the most appropriate solution. However, this is flawed to the extent that it implies both parties to the bargain have equal power resources at their disposal.

Later Fox revised his thinking and added a third perspective of radicalism, prompted by a wave of'shop floor' discontent and'wildcat' strikes at workplace level. Such worker behaviour was perceived as a reaction against exploitative and oppressive employers whose sole aim was to maximize profit. Conflict was caused by the economic disparity of society as a whole, with the principal disparity between capital and labour-employers who own and manage the means of production and workers who have their capital to sell.

This view underpins the labour process approach. This approach stresses the contradiction of managerial goals, with regulation and control having to be balanced by the need to gain workers' consent. Even today Edwards argues that unitarism cannot be written off as naive and outdated any more than radicalism because of the apparent disappearance of discontent. Ackers' neo-pluralism refocuses the employment relationship beyond the workplace by connecting the old pluralist and voluntary frames of reference with new questions raised by contemporary society. The health of society is put first, encouraging industrial relations policy initiatives that are driven by social concerns, not just a business agenda. Further he argues that the employment relationship bears hidden ethical considerations of trust and responsibility in relation to human beings. As we shall show, both managers and workers in a variety of work and employment situations in the HI do see their workplaces in unitary terms, but this does not necessarily infer the absence of conflict.

Areas of potential dispute, conflict and difference do exist between managers and workers, between managers and other managers, and between workers and customers, demonstrating that workplaces are pluralistic. In cases where workers'fiddle' or'pilfer' from their employer, the nature of their behaviour is more in keeping with a radical perspective.

Thus it is possible to observe facets of unitarism, pluralism and radicalism in the same employment relationship in which management, for the most part, remains the more powerful. Even so, areas of common interest self-evidently exist otherwise all these relationships would break down. Consent provides the basis for resolving conflict and achieving cooperation. Cooperation is built on trust between individuals engendered at workplace level rather than through elaborate organizational mechanisms. Yet securing workers' consent is neither a straightforward nor certain process. Therefore, a mix of overt and covert conflict and cooperation underpins all employment relationships and, as we shall argue, workplace harmony owes more to pragmatic acceptance and accommodation among the parties in the employment relationship than to ideological belief.

THE RULES OF EMPLOYMENT AND POWER RELATIONS

We have already noted that the employment relationship is underpinned by rules, hence the continuing validity of Clegg's definition of industrial relations as'The study of the rules governing employment' which Edwards explains in more detail: This does not limit the subject to the collective relations between managements and trade unions, for a rule can derive from other sources, and there are rules governing non-union groups; nor does it restrict analysis to one sector, for it covers all paid forms of employment. A rule is a social institution involving two or more parties which may have its basis in law, a written collective agreement, an unwritten agreement, a unilateral decree or merely an understanding that has the force of custom. In non-union settings, as much as union ones, rules determine rates of pay, hours of work, job descriptions and many other aspects of employment. The subject is about the ways in which the employment relationship is regulated. To regulate means to control, to adapt or adjust continuously or to adjust by rule.

MANAGERIAL ISSUES

While rules may be the substantive rules of employment, *e.g.* pay and conditions of employment, implicit in the notion of rules affecting people is the concept of behaviour. Management's job is to control and direct workers' behaviour to perform work to the desired standards, and thereby ensure that the rules of employment are adhered to.

Four key issues arise:

1. Rules are not always absolute and may be gendered.
2. Managerial control of workers' behaviour is underpinned by a power relationship.

3. This power relationship is unequal and may be gendered.
4. Managers have a choice of means to maximize control.

The first point is that one should caution against perceiving rules in too absolute a sense. At one end of the spectrum rules embodied in the law of the land provide a good example of formal rules. Any breach may incur very severe penalties, *e.g.* health and safety. In a workplace setting rules in practice may derive from informal understandings that can in one set of circumstances be interpreted by the worker as a permissive concession or in a different set of circumstances as something to be observed at all costs. Strawberries as a worker's perquisite during the Wimbledon lawn tennis championship are a good example. Experienced workers know that taking home unwanted strawberries is'permitted' during busy periods. When fewer staff are needed, increased managerial surveillance will be deployed to dismiss staff caught in possession of company property.

Rule-learning is part of what Polanyi refers to as'tacit skills'. As argued elsewhere:

Tacit skills, such as learning to deal with customers, are learnt in and through the very act of doing, often involving trial and error and not from following a body of procedurally-designed rules. They are seen as an interpretive achievement of the user as to how the'rules' fit the task in hand. By mastery of the rules comes the power to extend them. This example embracing the customer provides a developmental point to Edwards' observation that rule-making is difficult, and that rules have to be interpreted in action for them to have any real meaning. Specifically in the labour contract this is because the worker's ability to work is only realised as useful labour in the course of carrying out that work, hence'a rule is a complex social institution'.

In service work physical appearance and'personality', or'aesthetic labour', are an implicit part of the employment contract. Only female flight attendants, not their male colleagues, are subjected to regular weigh-ins to ensure they comply to specified weight: height ratios. This demonstrates clearly how a rule may be gendered. The second point to note is that the very essence of management seeking to control workers' behaviour is underpinned by a power relationship.

Power is the capacity to pursue one's own interests individually and collectively, involving the capacity to oppose the actions of others and to pursue one's own objectives, and is embedded in continuing relationships. This does not mean power has to be exercised by either party in an overt sense. The threat of power may be sufficient to maintain broadly consensual employment relationships, such that any disputes or differences are resolved amicably without recourse to either party seeking to deploy sanctions against the other. The third point assumes a power inequality in the employment relationship. Self-evidently an employer is more powerful than an individual worker. The employer's ability to terminate a worker's services is likely to be more detrimental to the worker than to the employer, in spite of employment protection legislation.

Yet the individual behaviours of workers, such as high labour turnover, may be detrimental to an employer, even though they are not concerted. When workers combine collectively, with or without the backing of a trade union, there is some tilt in the balance of power, because collective sanctions may be imposed against the employer. Ultimately the outcome of the process by which each side seeks to gain concessions will depend on the relative power of the parties. For example, a plentiful supply of suitable workers in the labour market makes existing workers more readily dispensable and replaceable on the employer's terms. The opposite would be true for workers with scarce skills who can command high wages.

As Wajcman argues, gender relations are power-based and women's subordination in the workforce and workplace owes as much to trade unions as it does to managers. Spradley and Mann provide a graphic account of how the subordination of one group of female workers was brought about by another group of male workers who were the custodians of the male proprietor's trust.

The male bartenders controlled the orders, and sought to make the cocktail waitresses' job difficult by giving orders in an inconsistent and confusing way. Any mistakes became the waitresses' responsibility, even if they had been caused by the bartenders. Such was the power of the bartenders that pleasing them became more important than pleasing the customers. The fourth point is that managers have a choice of means to maximize control over workers. Friedman's'direct control' is a variant of Taylorism. Management is responsible for planning, designing and organizing the labour process, while cheap, unskilled workers perform standardized, simple repetitive tasks. Fast food is a good case in point, and also epitomizes McDonaldization, a social critique of how contemporary society and culture are being shaped by rationalist scientific management. While Taylorism sought to control the organization of work, McDonaldization is based on rationalization, replication, standardization of products and service, and quantification. In this low trust strategy worker behaviour is controlled through the use of standardized scripts in the service encounter.

In Friedman's alternative of'responsible autonomy', a high trust approach, managers delegate control to relatively privileged skilled workers who may already have elements of job control and discretion. The objective is to get workers to identify with the competitive aims of the organization so they will behave responsibly with minimum supervision. An obvious example of where such an approach might be used is in a luxury hotel, but it is also associated with empowerment and much customer-service work. As we shall argue and implied in the example of cocktail waitresses, these and other similar approaches including'hard' and'soft' HRM provide a useful framework for analysis, but are not necessarily alternatives.

The history of hotel internationalization has been characterized by American chains that secure control and integration through highly standardized procedures and manuals of operational procedures. Yet a'soft' focus on the service encounter as the driver of competitive advantage necessitates developing a culture of customised service. Mass customization illustrated by Burger King's have it your way' slogan as a challenge to McDonald's hold on the market is proposed as an alternative paradigm to McDonaldization.

WORKERS AND CUSTOMERS

Other tensions within the employment relationship impinge upon the rules of employment and power relationships. If management is about the achievement of organizational goals through people it can be argued that managers will be successful to the extent that these goals coincide with the aims and aspirations of those people, be they workers or customers. This'matching' of broadly reciprocal needs between employers and workers may be referred to as a'psychological contract', or set of contracts. It suggests managers and workers can share goals, but this is not at all straightforward. There is not a necessarily clearcut distinction between boss and worker, or a'them and us' scenario. Further we must also account for a psychological contract with customers.

Two key points are noteworthy:

1. Organizations comprise people and are, therefore, social organizations.
2. People, as social animals, may behave in unpredictable ways.

Workers

Human beings do not necessarily behave consistently or predictably, even in the same sets of circumstances. People are citizens and customers as well as employees, and these multiple identities bring different and sometimes conflicting expectations of the organization.

This makes the management of the employment relationship an uncertain process within which there is a blend of contradictory principles around the need to control and to gain the consent of workers. Workers may seek to regain control individually or collectively when they perceive that management has operated outside the rules. At that point workers' consent has been withdrawn and management will need to find ways to restore order and regain consent. In Lucas workers' individual response to organizational rules is seen in three main ways-to conform or be deviant in employment, or to terminate their employment. These responses are similar to Marchington's'getting on','getting by' and'getting back'. These are behaviours deployed in circumstances where customer care and service quality are dependent on workers' use of their tacit skills, which contain both technical and attitudinal elements. Limiting the definition of tacit skills to employer-employee relations is too narrow. Marchington overlooked how workers exhibit their tacit skills in ways other than in respect of their relationship with the employer, notably the customer. The point that'getting back','getting by' and'getting on' are as much resistance strategies in the labour process as coping mechanisms is developed.

At workplace level personal relationships are likely to be closely connected to morale and success. Managers often'muck in' when required. In small workplaces the existence of a single leader, often the owner, may serve to inspire loyalty from the workforce, but it is not a one-way process, as workers' respect has to be earned. Is it realistic to suggest that Mina, Jo and Sadie, who wait on table in the restaurant, share all the same goals as their boss? The hotel may not be doing very well, so there may be mutual concern for the survival of the business. Yet these ladies' main goal may be to serve their customers cheerfully and effectively, while at the same time enjoying some social banter among themselves and with their customers in the process of earning a reasonable wage.

Customers

Within the triadic employment relationship a simultaneous and coterminous relationship with the organization and the customer directly impinges on how workers carry out their work, and such interactions may be rewarding or stressful. The consequent effect on workers' performance may have positive or negative implications for the rules of employment: what they can earn, their prospects of promotion or actually keeping their job. Unequivocally the worker-customer relationship affects the rules governing employment and workplace behaviour. But so do employer-customer relationships, hence the employment relationship embodies a triadic set of power relations.

This relationship embodies a socio-economic exchange, and is not simply an economic exchange around the price of labour. Fox provides a useful starting point, since he noted that organizations are social organizations and how people behave is a crucial issue in the employment relationship. Even Edwards' point that'a rule is a complex social institution' does not adequately encapsulate our position. The main justification for widening the scope of this relationship derives from the fact that the service encounter is the interaction of the producer and consumer of services, and is a more complex phenomenon where financial considerations are interwoven with social ones. In hospitality the social function of service work derives from the provision of a'home away from home'. The service encounter entails'emotion work'-the assumption of a social-self, which effectively masks the individual's own personal dispositions to act, including the need to smile and be pleasant in an uninvolved way. We have already noted that'aesthetic' and sexual labour may also be inherent in service work. It is the'normalizing' social role of service labour that distinguishes it from other wage labour. Service work cannot be understood in terms of economic rationality alone.

Examination must be based on the supposition that service work is the intended outcome of a necessarily social process in which some social interaction occurs between one or more producers and one or more consumers. The relations between three groups of people-managers, workers and customers-embody the potential for contradiction between, on the one hand, uncertainty, unpredictability, conflict and difference and, on the other hand, consent, team effort and concerted performance.

The practical benefit this book seeks to convey accrues from an understanding of the nature and scope of the rules of employment in this triadic employment relationship, and how it is regulated, primarily at workplace level.

THE EMPLOYMENT RELATIONSHIP IN A WIDER CONTEXT

This chapter concludes by considering some key external contextual influences on workplace employment relationships at two levels-internationally and, in more detail, nationally in Britain.

The International Context

The national context of British employment relations increasingly needs to be understood within a much wider international context.

Three international dimensions have particular resonance for this book:

- International competition has created more open economies that have attracted investment from foreign-owned businesses. For example the French-owned groups Accor and Envergure have respectively opened hotels within their Novotel and Campanile brands in the United Kingdom.
- On a larger scale American multinational corporations have created world brands. McDonald's, Burger King, KFC and Marriott are among those that are now household names in many countries across the world.
- Spin-offs from European integration, especially on employment law in Britain, have provided an important underpinning to the employment relationship in the HI.

Foreign investment and MNCs are clearly important factors underpinning the expansion of hospitality and tourism not only in Britain but also in developing countries. Examples of'better' employment practices, in so far as they may exist in the British HI, have been associate served employment relations practice in the British HI, but the similarity has been overstated.

The United States has substantially more legal regulation than Britain, which has benefited American HI workers, while the trade unions are not entirely powerless-issues we highlight in later chapters. The European model based on social partnership designed to forge a common agenda between capital and labour is considerably more diverse and different across the member states than is often acknowledged. While we cannot expect it to reflect current developments in HI employment relations in most British workplaces, it has not necessarily produced wholesale benefits for HI workers across the EU either.

The British experience is not necessarily mirrored in other countries across the world. Differences in other countries' institutional arrangements and cultural considerations are among the factors that will affect their employment relations systems. Detailed comparison with other countries is beyond the scope of this book, but key instances of international employment relations within hospitality and tourism are cited throughout the remaining chapters.

THE BRITISH CONTEXT

Workplace employment relationships cannot be immune from wider economic, social, legal and political contextual influences. Contemporary examples, which may be influential in Britain today. The distinctions between these sets of influences are not always clear-cut as they can be interrelated.

The State

Although we have already touched upon some aspects of the state's interest in employment relations, we need to examine its role in a little more detail. The state is not a single or cohesive body, and comprises a number of institutions that have an interest in the employment relationship, whose objectives do not necessarily coincide. Parliament is the legislature, government ministers form the executive, the judiciary enforces the law, and civil servants are the administrators.

The state sponsors specialist agencies in the field of employment, and has done so since the end of the nineteenth century. Three government departments impinge on employment relations within a much wider brief. The most important is the DTI, which has overall responsibility for employment relations, small firms and competitiveness. The Employment Relations directorate is responsible for developing policy and legislation affecting individual workers and trade unions, EU legislation, promoting partnership and best practice, regulation of employment tribunals and the dates of public holidays. The DTI publishes consultation documents, research papers, practical guidance on how to implement employment legislation and regulations, and codes of practice on matters such as picketing.

The Department for Education and Skills is responsible for developing the skills of young people and adults. he Department for Work and Pensions delivers support and advice in areas of work and work-related benefits, including New Deal, sickness and accidents at work, and retirement. Although publicly funded, other state agencies and bodies are independent of government because they are controlled and managed by their own executive. The main institutions discussed later in the book are ACAS, the Central Arbitration Committee and employment tribunals. The Equal Opportunities Commission, Commission for Racial Equality and Disability Rights Commission each have overall responsibility for specific types of anti-discrimination or equal opportunities legislation.

The Health and Safety Commission and Health and Safety Executive have responsibility for health, safety and welfare legislation. Their roles include the publication of codes of practice.

Other bodies assist with the enforcement of minimum employment standards. The Inland Revenue's powers include obtaining information from employers, issuing enforcement notices requiring employers to pay the NMW and imposing penalties on employers not observing the NMW. Environmental Health Officers are responsible for the enforcement of health and safety standards. Many other institutions, some of which may have a political bias, offer a mixture of fact and opinion on employment relations. National bodies, which take either an employer or management view, include the Confederation of British Industry, the Institute of Directors, and the Chartered Institute of Personnel and Development. The British Hospitality Association, Restaurant Association, the British Beer and Pub Association the Hotel, Catering and International Management Association and the British Institute of Innkeeping are specific to the HI. The HtF, formerly the HI's National Training Organisation is recognized by government as the employer-led voice on all issues relating to hospitality training, education and qualifications.

The HtF also carries out research, and produces useful statistical information about the labour market. The Trades Union Congress Institute of Employment Rights and the Low Pay Network serve to defend workers' interests. The HCIMA can also be regarded as having a worker perspective since, as the professional body of hospitality managers; it serves to defend their interests as well as disseminating good management practice. Three large unions have special sections for hospitality workers: the General, Municipal and Boilermakers' Union, the Transport and General Workers Union and the Union of Shop, Distributive and Allied Workers. The National Association of Licensed House Managers was self-standing for many years, but has recently become part of the TGWU.

2

The Hotel Development Process

INTRODUCTION

The ability to add value and to create a sustainable hotel project ultimately starts from the first brush on paper and opportunities for this are all the way through to the final touch of paint on the finished product.

The crisis has had a huge impact on all real estate development, including hotels. But due to the gap between hotel supply and demand across the country there remains great opportunities for hotel projects.

Hotels are typically more complex to develop compared with other asset classes, as their design is tailored to the brand operating the business.

The design of these can also have an impact on the overall profitability of the hotel operation, as design deficiencies affect the operation of a hotel and ultimately have a negative impact on the bottom line — and hence asset value.

In order to reduce the risk of developing a hotel, which may not be commercially successful, it is important to seek advice from a hospitality consultant, who will ultimately act as the commercial conscience of the developer.

At the start of the development, prior to building and design stage, the most important question to answer is "is the project viable?" Demand and supply factors for the hotel project need to be identified in order to understand the dynamics of the future operation — to basically understand who will be the target audience for the hotel and build for that. A developer needs to have an understanding of the estimated cash-flow income of the future operation from the opening day of the hotel. This will then provide any potential investor with a comfort level that debt can be serviced from the operation.

When hotels are part of a wider scheme, the design and development of the hotel needs to be in line with the overall development vision of the scheme. In a resort environment, it is important to understand the relationship between hotel, golf, spa, residential and other facilities, and in an urban mixed-use scheme. The hotel will, more often than not, be managed by a professional hotel operator. It is always of benefit to ask a consultant to run a competitive tender processes (be it tailored or to the wider market) when looking for a hotel company to manage your property, as this provides the opportunity to drive the process in order to achieve the best commercial deal terms available in the market. These contracts typically run for 15-25 years and key terms agreed at the beginning will have a major impact going forward.

Hotels are particularly sensitive to market changes, economic downturns and to alterations in supply and demand — for example when competitive hotels open up next to your own hotel this can severely impact performance. It is better to have all advice and information prior to decisions being taken on concept, design, architecture style, number of rooms, size of facilities, star classification and so on — to avoid the need to either redo all the aforesaid or to face the possibility of building a hotel which no operator wants to manage or which will not be commercially viable.

THE ART AND SCIENCE OF OPENING A HOTEL

PRE-OPENING STAFF PLAN

The pre-opening staffing begins with an organizational chart with all positions. Once the titles and staff counts by position are finalized, then spreadsheets are created to include the position titles, start dates, pay rates, bonus, transfer allowances, and number of full-time equivalents (FTEs) for all positions.

The pre-opening staff plan is a comprehensive document that states who is hired, when they start, how much they are paid, and whether or not they are allocated a relocation allowance and benefit costs. Each of these pieces is used to build the pre-opening staff plan budget. If hiring has already begun and the opening date changes, the budget must be amended. Hiring a position that does not conform to the plan, such as bringing on a renowned chef one month earlier than planned, also requires the budget be modified.

PRE-OPENING BUDGET

The OPM develops and manages the preopening budget.This budget typically consists of three major categories; labour cost (40 per cent), sales and marketing efforts (40 per cent), and miscellaneous (20 per cent).

The labour cost is taken directly from the pre-opening staff plan. Sales and marketing activities comprise advertising, collateral, public relations, and travel to see clients.

Rounding out the budget are all of the miscellaneous items. These include office space rental before moving into the hotel, utilities (power, water, Internet, and telephone), human resources recruitment (ads, headhunters, drug testing, etc.), training materials, association dues, and licenses and permits (business, liquor, sales tax collection, etc.). If the hotel opening date is delayed for any reason, the pre-opening budget is affected. Additional costs include labour, office rent, utilities, and marketing efforts. If the opening date changes within three weeks of the original plan, major costs are encountered, as most of the staff is already hired.

OPERATIONAL SUPPLIES AND EQUIPMENT (OS&E)

The largest and most complex aspect of the OPM's responsibility is specifying, quantifying, and budgeting for the operational supplies and equipment (OS&E) list.This budget typically pencils out to $8,000 to $10,000 per guest room for a typical four-star property. The list of goods typically exceeds 2,500 line items. Add a little more for a full-service resort; deduct a little for an in-city business hotel.

The OS&E comprises all of the items that are not nailed down, with the exception of the furniture, fixtures, and equipment (FF&E). The FF&E is typically specified and ordered by the interior designer. Typical guest room items include bedding (frames, box springs, mattresses, mattress pads, sheets, pillows, pillowcases, towels, etc.), clock radios, hangers, laundry bags, laundry tickets, iron, ironing board, ironing board organizer, luggage rack, guest amenities (soap, shampoo, lotion, etc.), hair dryer, shower curtains, and shower curtain hooks.

Housekeeping equipment includes vacuums (guest room and wide-area units), carpet shampooers, carpet extractors, housekeeper carts, laundry bins, garbage trucks, valet delivery carts, and shelving, to name a few of many items. Housekeeping must also keep an inventory of guest request items including humidifiers, dehumidifiers, cribs, high chairs, rollaway beds, bedboards, spare pillows, towels, amenities, refrigerators, laundry soap, and so on.

HOTEL PRICING ON THE WEB

Recent studies have shown that online travel purchasers tend to be price driven. For example, according to Yesawich, Pepperdine and Brown, almost 6 out of 10 leisure travellers now actively seek the "lowest possible price" for travel services. Similarly, a recent Forrester Research study found that 66% of all buyers used an online discount in the past 12 months to buy travel online, and a study by the Joint Hospitality Industry Congress found that there is a real expectation among consumers that Internet prices will be lower than those in the "bricks and mortar" world. Such a perception has developed for several reasons.

First, many of the most wellknown Internet retailers compete with traditional outlets based, to a large extent, on price. As a result, there is an assumption among Web users that the same is true for travel products. Secondly, many consumers are aware of the lower distribution costs associated with Web channels. As Jack Geddes, Managing Director Sales and Marketing Asia, Radisson Hotels Worldwide, has pointed out "Consumers now understand that suppliers are cutting costs through this channel and expect savings to be passed onto them, as well as being rewarded for making the booking themselves".

Such expectations are being reinforced by the budget airline sector, which offers significant discounts for online bookings. Companies such as EasyJet, RyanAir, and Buzz estimate that by avoiding telesales and travel agents, they can make savings of up to 30%—which they pass on to customers in the form of lower fares. Lastly, many hotels use the Web to sell last minute deals—packages at relatively low prices but with short lead times. While such promotions can help dispose of distressed inventory, they have also resulted in the public associating rooms sold over the Internet with cheaper prices.

These factors have combined to make consumers associate online booking with good value. However, in the case of hotel own branded Web sites, industry practice seems to be the opposite of theory. In their 1999 survey, O'Connor and Horan found that, in the majority of cases, rates obtained over hotel Web sites were significantly higher than those obtained by contacting the hotel company's Central Reservations Office. Often the rate quoted by the company's Web site was substantially higher, despite the associated lower cost of distribution.

However, this study was limited in that it only focused on direct sales over hotel chains' own branded Web sites. Hotel electronic distribution is rapidly evolving and a large number of other online consumerfocused channels are now available, with most chains using multiple routes to get their product to the consumer. The availability of so many alternative points-of-sale poses some interesting questions.

Is there consistency between the rates and availability being offered over alternative channels? Research has shown that consumers shopping for travel online almost always check more than one site before purchasing. Jupiter Media Metrix, for the hotel product 10% of bookers visit one site, another 43% visit two or three sites, and 22% visit four or more sites. Online purchasers have become increasingly intolerant of inconsistent information, and may react to disparate rates on different channels by purchasing from the company's competitor. Furthermore, if rates are not consistent across channels, is any particular route consistently cheaper? And lastly, if rates are different over alternative channels, is the pricing strategy logical from both the consumer's and the hotel's perspective?

METHODOLOGY AND LIMITATION OF THE STUDY

Hotel Internet use have been limited. Murphy focused on rating the content of hotel Web sites, while Van Hoof and Combrink attempted to measure managers' perceptions of, and attitudes towards, the Internet. Web reservations facilities were investigated in detail in a prior paper by the author. However, the issue of pricing over multiple simultaneous travel distribution channels does not appear to have been the subject of extensive systematic research to date. The objectives, therefore, of this study were to analyse the rates being offered to consumers over hotel electronic distribution channels and to subsequently identify the pricing strategies being used by the hotel companies.

Obviously, an exhaustive analysis of the rates being offered by all hotels would be impossible. However, as the use of both technology and electronic distribution has in the past been lead by the major international hotel chains, an analysis of their efforts was thought to be indicative of developments in the field. As a result, it was decided to focus the study on the Behaviour of the top 50 international hotel brands.

While this strategy means that the findings are not representative of the industry as a whole and thus the results not generally applicable, it does allow an accurate benchmark of trends as they currently stand to be established. The companies were chosen based on the ranking of the top 50 hotel brands published in *Hotels* magazine in July 2000. Two companies were removed from the listing as they are in effect resorts, only distribute their rooms as part of packages, and thus their products are not directly comparable. Furthermore, three companies neither offered online reservations facilities on their own Web site nor were they listed on any of the other channels studied. Thus, the results reflect the findings for 45 hotel brands for which consistent data could be found.

Five major types of electronic B2C distribution channels were identified from the literature and leading examples of each category selected for inclusion in the study. In addition to the chain's own Web site, these included channels that draw their data/ reservations engine from the Global Distribution Systems; those that are based upon the databases/reservation engine of the Switch companies; and pure Web-based channels that require their inventory/ reservations database to be maintained online.

While not collectively exhaustive, these represent the majority of the non-direct-to-hotel reservations. Omitted from the study were the "nameyour- price"/"auction" style Web sites, which, due to their bidding pricing structure, were not comparable and thus could not be included. Voice channels were also incorporated into the study for comparison purposes by analysing the rates offered by the toll-free number to the Central Reservations Office (CRO). Data were collected by iteratively reserving a double room for specified dates in a selected property from each of the brands using each of the distribution channels. Where the product requested was available on the system, both the number of rates displayed and the lowest rate available were recorded for analysis. The hotel company's Central Reservation Office was subsequently telephoned and the same product requested.

In the latter case, the first rate quoted by the telesales agent was recorded. This process was repeated for five sets of alternative dates to reduce the possibility of error due to systems malfunctions or other exceptional circumstances. The order in which the channels were polled was also varied to minimize the effect of yield management systems.

GLOBAL VIEWS OF SERVICE QUALITY AND EFFECTIVENESS MANAGEMENT

In addition to service encounter models, more global views of the management of service performance have been addressed. Bowen and Lawler stress that decisions concerning how to manage service employees should be based on five contingency factors. They state that an organization should consider its basic business strategy, the nature of the relationship to the customer, business environment, and types of managers and employees.

Thus, management of services is based on a set of variables that constitute settings in which service encounter perceptions are formed. Singh and Deshmukh advocate the application of Total Quality Management principles to the management of services. They stress that TQM is a systems approach to organizations in which every element interacts with every other element. Like Bowen and Lawler, they argue that service quality is not simply a function of what the manager wants the employee to do, or what the customer perceives, or how well trained the employee is.

The success of a service organization is predicated more on the interaction of many its aspects. One systems approach to achieving service quality and effectiveness is found in Hauser's and Clausing's "house of quality." Applying the "house of quality" to the service encounter, Fitzsimmons and Fitzsimmons show how marketing, design, engineering and manufacturing must be coordinated in order to actually meet the customer's desires.

A global or systemic view is critical in managing an organization's adoption of a technology, particularly when that adoption directly involves the organization's operations. The manufacturing management literature of the 1980's and early 1990's, for example, is replete with discussions that advocate this perspective. This is so because its contributors found that the repercussions of introducing a new technology into a manufacturing concern ran through virtually every aspect of that concern's organizational structure. They further found that unless that concern accommodated the adoption of its new technology by reorganizing itself so as to effectively exploit its new technology's capabilities, the end result was far more likely to be counterproductive and deleterious than beneficial. Both Sciulli and Rodger and Paper argue that what has been said about manufacturing organizations and their adoption of new technologies holds true for service organizations as well, and their adoption of IT, in particular in both the banking and healthcare industries. Their argument is in part supported by the work of a committee of the National Academy of Sciences that identified a phenomenon that it labeled the "information technology paradox."

This paradox refers to the lagging growth in service sector productivity when compared to the growth in investments in service sector IT. The committee provided a list of several explanations for this paradox. At the top of its list was the mismanaged employment of information technology. It does not however, discount the importance of the service encounter, that is, the interaction between customers and customer contact personnel. Rather, it regards successful service encounters as resulting from a coordinated convergence of organizational factors; customer contact personnel training, job design, the reward/punishment system, empowerment, and the manner in which IT is integrated with the rest of these factors forming an organizational infrastructure supporting those encounters.

By rigorously analysing service operations and the encounters they produce as a function of the effectiveness with which technology and its adoption are managed, it may be possible to discover a basis for identifying types of service failures resulting from infrastructure design flaws integrating IT.

USEFUL CONSTRUCTS AND GUIDES

Although each pricing decision is unique, some constructs and concepts are useful in analysing pricing situations. The models of market structure, concepts of costs, demand concepts and the company philosophy of followership or leadership, are very helpful. With full knowledge of them, a "right price" can be established. But decision makers are confronted with incomplete or outdated information. The reasoning process they employ considers answers to two kinds of questions. First is "what if" or conditional reasoning. They assess possible courses of action, and the probable consequences of each. For example, if I change prices to A, what is the probability that competitors will meet the change, will not meet it, or will meet it partially, and what will be the consequences of each competitive reaction?

Second, there is a consideration of the relationship of price changes to changes in the other aspects of the marketing programme, advertising, distribution channels, product packaging, and personal selling. Prices may also be established through research. Various prices may be tested in limited areas and the "best" price selected. Research of customers' opinions and reactions to products is often sought as a basis for price. Sometimes products are tailored to meet predetermined price points, and product quality is changed so that prices can be maintained and product-line requirements and distributors' price points met. Although price is not merely the result of costs, price-cost factors are accorded major consideration. Moreover, since price affects volume, volume affects costs, and costs affect prices, the pricing decision is a circular one. Also, a variety of cost concepts may be applied. Prices can be based on total costs, average, or variable costs. The last basis leads to a marginal approach to costs. The major contribution of economic reasoning to the consideration of costs is the idea of marginal cost. Businessmen tend to rely more on an average cost approach to pricing than on a marginal approach.

Average costs, which are rarely pertinent to an optimal decision, satisfy the desire to "cover our costs and make a profit." In reality, this reliance on average costs can lead to a decision that can actually reduce sales, increase costs, and reduce profits. However, some executives advocate that sunk costs should be ignored. They are not affected by current decisions-nothing can be done about them. Yet it is also recognized that over the long run, they must be covered. A consideration of the impact of sales volume on costs provides a useful train of thought. For instance, price theory suggests a U shape for average costs-they decline to a point with increasing volume, reach their minimum, and then increase as volume increases.

This seems to make sense, since the concept introduces the notion of economies of scale and the impact of capacity on costs, indicating that volume beyond a certain point may increase costs. In addition to cost factors, pricing decisions in basic industries are greatly influenced by governmental considerations. Some industries such as steel are treated like public utilities and, sensitive to governmental reaction, must justify price increases. Although no laws exist that require governmental approval of price increases in these industries, such increases are judged as to their being warranted. A variety of pricing practices are of particular concern to certain industries.

For example, bidding is significant in defence marketing, hedging in commodity marketing, markdown in fashion merchandise, dumping in international marketing, price deals in food marketing, and loss leaders and discounting in retailing. In formulating marketing strategy, we have dealt with only the broader relationships of pricing to selected elements in the marketing mix. Price decisions in specific situations require both experience and practical knowledge. Theory alone will not suffice. In fact, where pricing is of critical concern, pricing specialists become necessary.

PRICING INFLUENCES

Since prices have great impact on both revenue and competitive reactions, pricing policies are usually determined at a high executive level. The pricing task involves not only a maze of variables but also conflicting situations. Conflicts exist among manufacturers and distributors, retailers and wholesalers, and consumers and retailers. For example, intermediate and ultimate customers weigh the prices they pay, competitors are influenced and react, suppliers watch margins carefully, financial institutions consider the impact on stock, and the government assesses competitive implications. Among the present and future external factors that influence pricing policy are number and concentration of competitors, the degree of competition, profitability, ease of entry, product heterogeneity, size, legal aspects, channels of distribution, elasticity of demand, total industry demand, kind and size of buyers, and spatial forces.

But basically these are handled through consideration of anticipated cost-revenue relationships. For in the long run, prices are constrained at their upper bound by market reaction and competition and at their lower bound by costs full or incremental. The latter are most significant in the immediate term, whereas total costs reflect a long-run situation. Prices may also be the result of competitive conditions such as total collusion or "cutthroat" competition. Either is unlikely for any protracted period of time, however-the former for legal reasons and the latter for economic considerations. Although precise cost information cannot be obtained, it is even more difficult to gain information about consumer reactions to prices. The latter is obtained from surveys, experiments, and observation. For example, consider the cost-price relationships of an automobile with its thousands of parts. What are the actual materials and labour costs of each? What is the overhead burden and how should it be spread? How are joint costs to be allocated? How many autos can be sold at each price? What are the price interrelationships among items of a product line? These are difficult problems to face.

But such costs, particularly increased costs, are price factors and the cost-price spiral is widely recognized. Also, as prices increase, sales may decline, which often results in increasing costs, since fixed costs are spread over fewer units. In reality, cost accounting of the marginal variety, which is advocated as a basis for pricing, is not often used. Both the ambiguity of costs and the difficulty of deriving the data make this impractical. In practice, the relationship of actual costs to prices may be rather loose, and in fact the prices of finished goods and raw materials or components can move in different directions. Prices should be based on both costs and market influences. In essence, maximum prices are governed by market factors and minimum prices by costs, and as they change, so should prices. The tendency exists, however, to maintain prices once they have been established. It should be noted that it is not the actual price or price change that is so significant, but rather the customer's perception and interpretation of these changes.

PROBLEMS IN SETTING PRICES

What are the major problems in establishing prices? First, costs cannot be determined precisely. Second, management must deal with expectations-expected demand, expected costs, and the maximization of expected profits. This is particularly true of new products. Although cost estimates are more reliable than demand estimates, both are subject to wide error. They are based on the patterns of past data, which may deviate widely in the future, especially demand data, which incorporate a host of unpredictable market forces. Pricing must also be viewed from the perspective of a company's total product line, since products have complementary and competitive demands, joint and common costs, and by-products. Sometimes the demand for product A influences the demand for product B. This relationship is termed the cross elasticity of demand, with a negative cross elasticity referring to products that are complementary, a positive cross elasticity to substitutable products, and a zero cross elasticity to unrelated products. For example, an increase in the demand for pizza will increase the consumption of certain cheeses, while a large increase in the use of a company's brand R detergent may decrease the use of its brand S detergent.

Since market situations confronting products within a line differ, sellers have varying degrees of discretion in setting prices for particular items in a line, and should consider products both as separate entities and as members of a product set. Cost-plus pricing or uniform markups ignore individual product acceptance, market demands, and competitive conditions. In reacting to competitors' price changes, a company can sit tight, meet the change, or modify its own price or other elements of its marketing mix. Where customers consider not only price, but also availability, delivery, quality, service, and reliability, sensitivity to price diminishes.

When products are not homogeneous, companies have wider latitude in pricing situations. But when products are homogeneous and a price is cut, competitors may have to meet the reduction. Companies have the choice of following a price rise or not. Executives should study the reasons for price changes, their temporary and permanent effects, the impact on profits and. market share, likely industry response, and the alternatives available, before making decisions. Both purchasing situations and the decentralization of authority affect pricing policies. Prices may vary by the quantity purchased, and the purchaser's geographic area, trade position, and the functions he performs, as well as by the method and timing of purchases. In large, decentralized companies featuring profit-centre accounting, intra company pricing and transfer pricing, can influence product prices and raise significant conflicting problems. In some industries price changes in basic commodities occur frequently. Can computer programmes be developed to spell out the decision maker's thought processes in reacting to price changes? After studying a pricing executive in action over a period of time, one researcher developed a flow-chart programme that quite accurately predicted price reactions.

The programme included such information as personal biases and organizational influences in price reactions as well as market shares, anticipation of competitors' reactions, and intentions of the district office. The computer programme provided a simulation of the price-reaction process. Pricing policies are sometimes charged with emotion. Monopoly prices, price determination, and administered pricing are among the terms evoking emotional reaction. Also, the practice of price-cutting is often viewed with disdain or as an unethical practice by others in an industry, even to the point of indicating shoddy merchandise and service. Typically, new products have a monopoly position for a period a degenerative monopoly position.

Eventually competitors will develop competing and even improved products. The pricing executive must decide whether to charge relatively high or low initial prices, and the marketing consequences and related strategies are quite different in each situation. Obviously, regardless of economic models, it is difficult to establish an optimum price because demand and costs change over time.

The attention usually settles on current profit maximization rather than on the long-run maximization; the whole life cycle of a product and the total product line, rather than a single item, must be considered in pricing; and price must be considered from the perspective of the total marketing mix. Where products are relatively homogeneous; several large firms constitute a significant part of the market; and buyers are well informed, then estimates of buyer reaction become a significant aspect of the pricing picture. So do competitive reactions that may be ferreted out by the use of marketing intelligence. Studies of what competitors have done in the past, coupled with detailed analyses of the current competitive situation, may furnish guides on what they are likely to do. This reasoning process, utilizing subjective probability estimates, can provide decision makers with good guides for contemplated price changes. A specific illustration is seen in the following example: Since early 1955, the Everclear Plastics Company had been producing a resin called Kromel, basically designed for certain industrial markets.

In addition to Everclear, three other firms were producing Kromel resin. Prices among all four suppliers were identical; and product quality and service among producers were comparable. Everclear's current share of Kromel industry sales amounted to 40%. Four industrial end uses comprised the principal marketing area for the Kromel industry. These market segments will be labeled A, B, C, and D. Three of the four segments were functionally dependent in segment A in the sense that Kromel's ultimate market position and rate of approach to this level in each of these three segments was predicated on the resin's making substantial inroads in segment A. The Kromel industry's only competition in these four segments consisted of another resin called Verlon, which was produced by six other firms. Shares of the total Verlon-Kromel market currently stood at 70% Verlon industry, and 30% Kromel industry.

Since its introduction in 1955, the superior functional characteristics per dollar cost of Kromel had enabled this newer product to displace fairly large poundages of Verlon in market segments B, C, and D. On the other hand, the functional superiority per dollar cost of Kromel had not been sufficiently high to interest segment A consumers. While past price decreases in Kromel had been made, the cumulative effect of these reductions had still been insufficient to accomplish Kromel sales penetration in segment A. In the early fall of 1960, it appeared to Everclear's management that future weakness in Kromel price might be in the offing. The anticipated capacity increases on the part of the firm's Kromel competitors suggested that in the next year or two potential industry supply of this resin might significantly exceed demand, if no substantial market participation for a Kromel industry were established in segment A. In addition, it appeared likely that potential Kromel competitors might enter the business, thus adding to the threat of oversupply in litter years.

Segment A, of course, constituted the key factor. If substantial inroads could be made in this segment, it appeared likely that Kromel industrial sales growth in the other segments not only could be speeded up, but that ultimate market share levels for this resin could be markedly increased from those anticipated in the absence of segment A penetration. To Everclear's sales management, a price reduction in Kromel still appeared to represent a feasible means to achieve this objective, and perhaps it could still be profitable to Everclear. However, a large degree of uncertainty surrounded both the overall attractiveness of this alternative, and under this alternative the amount of the price reduction which would enable Kromel to penetrate market segment A.

BUSINESS STRATEGY

Organizational strategy begins wish the organization's mission statement that identifies what service the organization provides. This implies an interaction between the target market segment and the service provided and an interaction between technology and personnel employed to produce and deliver the service and how the service package is designed.

The design of a job consists of what customer encounter personnel are expected to do based upon their skills and qualifications and organizational constraints. These expectations cannot, however, be divorced from the technology through which customer encounter personnel act. A service is produced as a response to an existing market that it can opportunistically enter, as an instrument that calls new kinds of markets into being, or as a combination of both.

The Internet auction company, eBay, is a recent example of such a combination. On-line auctioning existed prior to eBay's appearance. However, eBay took on-line auctioning several steps beyond what already existed to an interactive environment and redefined customer expectations. As a result, eBay has virtually monopolized the on-line auctions industry and has dramatically expanded the industry's market in which it is the dominant player, attracting new customers while holding its old ones. The nature of services is such that their production and consumption is simultaneous.

Consequently, the production and delivery of a service constitute its encounter with the customer whose expectations are standards against which the efficacy of the service is evaluated. How the production and delivery of the service are designed into the service package is therefore, critical. The technology selected for the service package plays a part in that design. On the one hand, the service package is first designed to which a suitable and available technology is then attached. Such is the case, for example, with fast foods where IT systems are employed to open transactions and communicate customer orders to the back room. IT may be employed in the back room to monitor operations and bring the transactions to a close.

On the other hand, technology may restrict how decision makers would like to design their service packages or it can open up the design of a package so as to include heretofore infeasible possibilities by which competitive advantages can be pursued. Such is the case, for example, in tele radiology. Recent developments in IT and standardization in the way imaging equipment generates its images has made it technologically possible to physically decouple radiologists from the images they must read. As a result, access to radiological services has become decidedly more timely and widespread for potential customers than heretofore thought possible.

Such developments have created opportunities to redesign the initial service package and revise customer expectations by reinforcing initial diagnoses with second and third opinions and exploiting subspecialization skills while at the same time, reducing the turn-around time to patient consultation.

SERVICE PACKAGE DESIGN

The widely accepted means of categorizing service organizations is through the use of typologies. One of the most widely used typologies is Lovelock's that strategically profiles a service package. Of particular interest to the authors of this Study is Lovelock's typology that juxtaposes customization of services with exercise of judgement and discretion by customer contact personnel in meeting individual customer needs.

A barber, for example, is expected to provide the customer more customised services than a home pest exterminator who has a finite set of programme modules from which to select and much less judgment to exercise. Like the barber, an attorney also performs a customised service but the attorney must use and exercise judgement and discretion that exceeds the judgment and discretion a barber uses and exercises and certainly exceeds the judgment and discretion the home pest exterminator must use and exercise. It is expected that similar services will position themselves similarly in Lovelock's typologies.

Technological innovations in service production and delivery can, however, lead to typological repositionings of a service operation and a consequent revision and redesign of its profile and service package. One must assume that such redesign of the service package is done to derive some competitive advantage or at least prevent the service operation from being competitively disadvantaged. The various technologies an organization chooses to employ therefore interact with all the typologies that strategically profile it and contribute to the design of the organization's service package.

The specific interaction between the employment of IT and the extent to which customer contact personnel are empowered or not empowered to use and exercise judgment and discretion to meet customer needs during the service encounter is this study's object of analysis. Working down the main diagonal of Lovelock's typology of customization and discretion, the more standardized the service, the less use and exercise of judgement and discretion by customer contact personnel is necessary.

The more customised the service, the more use and exercise of judgement and discretion by customer contact personnel is necessary. In most cases customer contact personnel are the sole points of contact customers have with an organization providing them the service they seek. Their evaluations of it and decisions about future patronization of it are largely determined by how customer contact personnel manage to present the organization during service encounters.

Thus, how the judgment and discretion customer contact personnel are empowered or not empowered to use and exercise and the IT they employ interact in the design of the service encounter can be decisive if the organization is to attract and hold its customers. The extent of judgment and discretion customer contact personnel are expected to use and exercise understandably varies from service to service. However, what about situations that do not precisely conform to a given service for which the technology has been designed? Judgment and discretion used and exercised by customer contact personnel in such situations is important for at least two reasons. First, decisions including judgment and discretion or the lack of them may affirm or contradict organizational objective or policies.

Furthermore, unacceptable decisions issuing there from will result in positive or negative encounters from the customer's viewpoint. These decisions may be particularly important in achieving a service recovery when a service failure has occurred or is imminent. A service operation employs IT in order to increase and improve service efficiency and effectiveness in a way that is consistent with its competitive strategy. Fitzsimmons suggests that IT accomplishes this by creating another entry barrier, generating revenue, creating a database upon which empirically based decisions can be made, and enhancing productivity. Customer contact personnel draw on and contribute to such a resource when they access IT to support their service encounter activity.

Their access to the IT system can, however, vary. They may be restricted with respect to the range of information they can browse. They may also be restricted with the respect to the range of information they can input. Fast food customer contact personnel can browse virtually no range of information and the range of information they input into the system is restricted to the orders they take. Their job can be characterized as being almost completely circumscribed by the technology associated with their job. A customer wants, for example, a taco with allowable modifications.

A predetermined closed set of intermediate steps is synchronic with the outcome. The employee merely selects predetermined and technologically constrained choices, as one would push a stop or start button on a machine. Airline ticket counter personnel must, on the other hand, be able to browse routings, schedules, and ticket information for the entire industry in order to input the orders they take. The outcome of the order is something separate from the subset of intermediate steps that achieve it. Airline ticket counter personnel must create that subset.

They use IT to expedite the construction and creation of that subset. The IT they employ does not therefore, so nearly circumscribe their jobs as with the fast food order taker. Job design for service employees has been categorized as a "production line" approach or an "empowerment" approach. The production line approach, as its name implies, is based on a Tayloristic view. It is based on four tenets — simple tasks, clear division of labour, substitution of equipment and systems for employees, and little decision-making discretion of employees. This design seeks to gain customer satisfaction through efficiency, consistency, and low costs.

The empowerment approach, on the other hand, allows employees to make decisions that in the production orientation would be reserved for higher-level management. In such settings, jobs are less simple and more broadly defined and employees are given more latitude. In order for employees in such a design to be effective, they must have access to needed information, knowledge about how to use the information, and sufficient power to meet customer requests during the service encounter. The production line approach gains its low costs through consistency, which can be translated into lack of personal service.

This means that as the service encounter is standardized, the choice of actions possible by the service provider is limited. Attempts to provide personalized service in such a setting would drive up costs and violate the competitive advantage of the firm. In addition, while the customer receiving the personal service may be more satisfied, other customers who are receiving slower service because of it may be disgruntled. The empowerment design is slower, less efficient and more expensive to operate. It requires careful selection and extensive training of employees.

This design could put a firm at a competitive disadvantage from a cost standpoint servicing encounters of a routine form. Companies must clearly define their business strategy and know the environment and the customer base they pursue in making a decision concerning job design for their employees.

MAKING HOTEL SUCCESSFUL

Even when the U.S. economy was growing and prosperous, the hotel under its previous owner did not succeed in servicing its debt. Now, because of the current recession, its financial picture is even more bleak. As the hotel's new lender-owner, you may decide to retain it in your bank's portfolio, or to find a buyer on suitable terms as soon as possible (a period surely measured in months, and perhaps in years, due to the depressed condition of the hospitality marketplace).

Purchasers of hotels typically base the purchase price on the property's income stream, applying a capitalization rate to the cash flow before debt service. If the cash flow is a negative number, how can you make the hotel pay its own way? Evaluate management. We assume that the hotel you've taken back has management already in place-an in-house management team or representatives of a professional management firm engaged by the previous owner.

Begin by evaluating the basic documents that the management should have prepared as a guide to the hotel's focus and direction:

- The current-year marketing plan, which characterizes the hotel's customers and sets forth a strategy for securing their business.
- The current-year budget, which estimates the revenue and expense dollars.
- A long-range business plan, which projects the marketing and budget picture, ideally for three to five years into the future.
- A capital facilities plan, which anticipates any expansions or renovations the property may require.
- The operations manual, which outlines the duties of employees and sets standards for their performance.

Next, try to determine whether the manager and key department heads are actually using the plans. Those plans should be living documents. Increase revenue. In times like these, many hoteliers are tempted to save money by cutting back on marketing, but that is the worst thing to do. To put more bodies in the beds, you need creative marketing.

For instance, if your hotel has focused in the past on international leisure travellers, it has been especially hard-hit in recent months by the combination of worldwide recession and Middle East war.

As the threat of war mounted, your hotel should have been targeting domestic tour groups, corporate business, and frequent individual travellers. Your hotel may also have to reduce its room rates to a more competitive level, then increase the volume of business enough to generate a profit. How sophisticated is your hotel's marketing plan? It should begin with knowledge of the existing customer base. Many luxury hotels maintain a detailed guest history which allows them to respond to the specific whims and desires of each repeat guest, but even an economy property should maintain a guest tracking system that provides demographic data on the guests as well as the origin of their reservations.

Control expenses. Your hotel may be losing money because its expenses exceed its revenues.

A recession is a good time to take a fresh look at every conceivable expense. Most people want to start with wages and benefits, because payroll constitutes the largest single expense category. The hotel should trim its payroll where it can, but it must not cut back so far as to compromise service. Examine your hotel's contracts with outside vendors.

Get competitive quotes from at least three sources, then negotiate with the suppliers of:

- Goods used in the hotel, including food and beverage items, cleaning supplies, and office supplies;
- Outside contract services such as pest control, pool cleaning, linen and laundry, and maintenance of indoor plants and outdoor landscaping; and
- Maintenance contracts on major equipment such as the climate-control system, computers, and elevators.

Evaluate your hotel's preventive maintenance programme. In the short run you can save money by deferring maintenance, but letting the physical plant and equipment deteriorate will cost you more in the long run for repairs or replacement. What's more, breakdowns seem inevitably to occur at an inconvenient hour, creating emergencies when workers charge a premium for their time. Manage to quality standards. Service quality is particularly important in a recessionary economy, when you can't afford to lose a single guest.

Five ways exist to monitor quality:

- Personal inspection-You or your designated in-house hospitality executive should visit the property at regular intervals to observe and ask questions.
- Franchise inspections-If your hotel has a franchise, the franchise company will send inspectors to the property to assess its compliance with their company's quality standards.
- In-house market research-You can hire a market research firm to interview guests on a random basis during their stay or as they depart.
- Secret-shopper programmes-I use these programmes myself on my clients' behalf, and I recommend them to every absentee owner. Secret-shopper programmes can test the honesty of the staff and quality of service.
- Guest comment cards-While most comments reflect only the best and worst aspects of the guest experience, you should receive a summary of these cards at least every month and review the most egregious complaints with the hotel manager.

The keys to maintaining standards with lean staff are flexible staffing and cross-training. If the hotel has an extra clerk at the front desk when the dining room needs an extra server, that clerk should be able to fill in. As an owner, you should receive regular reports which allow you to track the relationship between staffing levels and the volume of business, and training reports that show who has learned what. Don't assume that hiring a management firm absolves you of the need to be an active owner. You must still hold the firm accountable.

Obtain assurances from each candidate firm that you will have veto power at all times over any manager or key department head the firm assigns to your property. If one of these individuals isn't fitting in, you want the right to have the management firm remove and replace that person rapidly.

The new world of appraisals set in motion by the Financial institutions Reform, Recovery and Enforcement Act continues to evolve. Meanwhile, the industry nears the July 1 deadline for states to have functioning licensing and certification programmes. Significant deliberations have been in the works on several fronts.

To recap them:

- The Federal Financial Institutions Examination Council Appraisal Subcommittee, which has the power to extend the July 1 deadline on a state-by-state basis, has been considering a petition to grant more time to all states. Late last year the ABA and state bankers associations asked the subcommittee to grant a blanket extension to Dec. 31.

  While many states have passed laws setting up systems to address requirements of FIRREA, putting the systems in place and using them to qualify appraisers is a time-consuming task.
- The Federal Reserve Board has been reviewing comments on its proposal to cut the de minimis level for institutions it regulates to $50,000 from $100,000. While doing so would put the Fed in synch with the Comptroller's Office and FDIC, bankers have urged the agency to leave the limit where it stands.
- The Appraiser Qualifications Board was set to meet in late March to consider public comments and make a final decision on a restructuring of appraiser categories.

The board is part of the Appraisal Foundation, a private standards setting body with which the Exam Council's subcommittee works and to which states and the appraisal industry look for guidance. Late last December, the board proposed to expand to three categories the original two-category system of appraiser qualifications it envisioned under FIRREA. The board learned that in some states with significant quantities of high-priced homes, its original categories would have barred qualified residential appraisers from properties they are capable of appraising.

To remedy this, the board proposed creating three qualification levels-two certified and one licensed. Some changes in the latter category caused ABA to object, though it endorsed most other aspects of the proposal. For its part, in late January the Exam Council's Appraisal Subcommittee announced that it would be willing to accept a three-tier system in those states that considered it necessary for their real estate markets. The subcommittee noted that its agreement was general in nature and not a judgment on the qualification board's specific proposal. The government body also set several conditions for its actual approval.

SUCCESSESFULLY GROWTH OF HOTEL AND MOTEL

Everywhere in North America, suburbanization has caused a relative and, in many cases, absolute decline of downtown areas. The effect on the downtowns of small metropolitan regions (small-metro downtowns) has been particularly severe, for they possess fewer assets than those of larger metropolitan regions to resist the effects of suburban development. This identifies the few healthy small-metro downtowns in order to draw lessons that can aid the other downtowns within this urban size category, all of which are struggling. Our study concentrated on downtowns of North American metropolitan regions with populations between 100,000 and 500,000. There are 177 metropolitan statistical areas in the U.S. and 25 census metropolitan areas and census agglomerations in Canada in this size range (excluding U.S. primary statistical areas that are part of consolidated metropolitan statistical areas, all with populations exceeding our threshold). In the U.S., these metropolitan areas have a total population of 40.8 million, roughly one of every seven Americans. Small Canadian metropolitan regions register an overall population of 5.08 million, which represents about one sixth of this country's population.

Our objectives in this study were fourfold: (I) identify successful small-metro downtowns across the U.S. and Canada; (2) explore reasons for their success; (3) from their experience, draw lessons for less successful downtowns; and (4) generate information on a category of downtowns that has been neglected in the literature. To meet these objectives, we surveyed planners and other urban professionals from the United States and Canada who have an interest in downtown revitalization. Respondents were first invited to define what are, in their opinion, the features that contribute to the well-being of successful small-metro downtowns. Then, they were asked to identify successful ones and justify their selections. As expected, we found that few such downtowns were perceived as successful.

And these districts nearly always cumulate advantages that are exceptional among small-metro downtowns—close proximity of a university, a state capital (in the U.S.), or provincial legislature (in Canada); a strong historical character; and a powerful tourist appeal. The article closes with a discussion of the implications of these findings for the vast majority of these downtowns, which are in a poor state of health. This latter part of the article is based on interviews with informants from the cities whose downtowns were selected in the survey.

DOWNTOWN DECLINE AND REVITALIZATION EFFORTS

In downtowns across North America, whether in large or small metropolitan regions, attempts at revitalization can be grouped into three phases. The first phase concentrated on adaptation to automobile accessibility, the second on head-on competition with suburbs, and the third on the accentuation of a distinct core area identity. Early strategies of the 1950s and 1960s aimed at maintaining the preeminence of the downtown within a changing transportation environment. Planners sought to preserve or restore the dominant position of the downtown by replacing or complementing transit accessibility focused on the core area with similarly advantageous automobile-oriented access patterns. Radial expressways and widened arterial roads were meant to channel flows of cars towards downtowns, increasingly well provided with parking space.

It soon became clear, however, that accessibility alone would not safeguard the primacy of central business districts.

Policymakers became convinced that to stem the retail hemorrhage towards the suburbs, downtowns had to gloss their image and embrace suburban shopping formulas. This phase, which ran from the late 1950s into the early 1980s, consisted largely of attempts at ridding CBDs of eyesores and tailoring downtown shopping to the tastes of the day.

Sectors seen as blighted or merely obsolete were razed with the hope of replacing them with up-to-date developments apt to fuel downtown growth. This was also the time when indoor retail malls, an already well established suburban shopping formula, were introduced in CBDs. This strategy was grounded in the assumption that by replicating conditions found in suburban shopping centres, downtown areas could compete successfully with suburbs.

The 1970s marked a radical departure from earlier approaches to downtown revitalization. The shift was induced by a growing recognition of the ineffectiveness of previous efforts at reversing CBD decline. In fact, earlier revitalization attempts were often held responsible for downtowns' downward spiral. For example, in small-metro downtowns, most enclosed retail malls were economic failures, and even prosperous malls tended to generate little retail activity beyond their walls. Also fueling the 1970s transformations were public expenditure cutbacks, the opening of planning to public participation, and a rediscovery of the merits of pre-World War II built environments, most notably the traditional pedestrian-oriented retail street.

Increasingly, planning interventions emphasized preservation or enhancement of the uniqueness of the physical features of downtowns within rapidly suburbanizing metropolitan regions and the targeting of markets where CBDs enjoyed competitive advantages. This reorientation signaled a mounting sentiment that downtowns could no longer compete with the suburb on its own terms and that their salvation rested instead on their distinction from the suburban realm in terms of the nature of their activities, a more compact built environment, and the predominance of pedestrian movement for intradowntown journeys. The post-1970s attempts at revitalization did not, however, mark a clear break with previous efforts. Large redevelopment projects continued to be a mainstay of revitalization strategies. While redevelopment projects did not lose their allure, the process leading to this outcome underwent transformations. With the demise of large, federally funded urban renewal programmes, reliance on partnership-based approaches gained in popularity.

Projects included, for example, convention centres, professional sport venues, and aquariums. Meanwhile, in downtowns, or portions thereof, that were not subjected to redevelopment, increased importance was given to the preservation of the traditional built environment and its occupation by activities targeting markets congruent with the attributes of core areas—festival places and hospitality and recreational establishments.

In small metropolitan areas, there was a lag in the succession of these phases due to the tendency for revitalization strategies to be first devised and tested in larger metropolitan regions (urban renewal in Pittsburgh, Philadelphia, and New Haven in the late 1940s and in the 1950s, for example). Moreover, the impact of these phases was attenuated in small-metro downtowns by a lesser availability of public- and private-sector resources.

The foremost consequence of limited resources was a weaker involvement in urban renewal and a resulting preservation of much of these CBDs' traditional built environment. Another effect was a tendency in all phases to rely on small- rather than large-scale interventions. Small-metro downtowns deserve distinct treatment because the circumstances they face are different from those encountered by CBDs of smaller urban areas or of larger metropolitan regions. They are more complex than downtowns of small urban areas (with less than 100,000 residents) and thus require more diversified revitalization strategies. In small urban area downtowns, the problem is often one of main street revival and can lend itself to targeted remedies such as the introduction of a farmers' market, an unusual attraction (such as the carousel in Mansfield, OH), or the adoption of a theme for the street.

At the same time, small-metro downtowns are more often in a state of decline than those of large metropolitan regions. While large-metro downtowns that perform poorly on all fronts (employment, retail, services, housing) are the exception, the opposite holds true for small-metro CBDs. One reason for this discrepancy is the absence in small-metro downtowns of assets widely distributed among their large-urban-area cousins, such as important employment and retail concentrations, world-class attractions, and elaborate public transit networks. Another factor of decline among these CBDs is the higher decentralization propensity of small-metro downtowns due to their limited critical mass, their near total dependence on the automobile, and the relative ease with which different destinations, including peripheral ones, can be reached from anywhere within these metropolitan regions. With the expectation of poor health generally among small-metro CBDs, we engaged in a study purporting to identify the exceptional ones that are vital, with the intention of drawing lessons that can be of use to less successful CBDs. The study relied on a two-pronged methodology. The first phase consisted of an Internet survey.

Emails with a link to the Internet survey form were sent to the 1,076 persons in our sample: 371 (34.5%) to university planning, urban studies, and urban geography faculty members; 503 (46.8%) to planners employed by the central cities of small metropolitan regions; and 202 (18.8%) to professionals with a possible interest in downtown revitalization who are associated with government agencies (such as regional HUD offices) and economic development and research institutes with an urban focus. This sample was not constructed with a probabilistic objective, but rather in a fashion that would maximize the information on small-metro downtowns across the continent. Of the sent emails, a total of 859 reached their destination (217 were undeliverable). The number of answered questionnaires after two reminders was 295—a 34.4% response rate.

As do all surveys, this one reflects the values of its respondents. Far from being a challenge to the validity of its findings, we see the expression of these values as an important contribution of our survey. The values it picks up are indeed those of people who are among the best informed on the state of downtowns. Its respondents are also active in the framing and deployment of downtown revitalization strategies and in the advancement of knowledge on downtowns. Directly or indirectly, their values thus become embedded in downtown revitalization policies. Moreover, in most cases these values have been influenced by firsthand experience of downtowns and past revitalization efforts. Respondents answered the three-question survey on a Web site. Question 1 listed 19 factors potentially influential in the success of small-metro CBDs. Respondents were invited to rate each factor on a scale of 1 to 4, from 1 = very important to 4 = not important at all. Comments were solicited at the end of this question.

The Web site used information about a respondent's state or province to generate, in question 2, a list of all small metropolitan areas in their region, defined as their home state or province and contiguous states or provinces. Respondents were asked to rate each downtown within their region. The adoption of this approach was based on the view that, contrary to the knowledge of downtowns of large metropolitan regions, which is continental or global in scope, awareness of those of small-metro downtowns is mostly regional. Space was provided for comments on each CBD. Respondents were also offered the opportunity to rate small-metro downtowns within their own region that were not listed in question 2. Because our roster included only the names of metropolitan regions with a 100,000-500,000 population, respondents readily used the space reserved for unlisted downtowns and for comments on enumerated metros to single out the successful downtown within multicentreed metropolitan regions.

In question 3, respondents were asked to mention and comment on any successful small-metro downtown, irrespective of its regional location in North America. There was no limit on the number of downtowns that could be identified as very successful or successful in question 2's list, in the space made available in question 2 for additional downtowns within the region of a respondent, or across the continent in question 3. The second phase of the study consisted of interviews with urban professionals (mostly planners) from the urban areas identified in the survey.

These interviews were intended to cast additional light on the conditions accounting for the healthy state of the selected downtowns, including the revitalization strategies deployed there. We carried out 10 face-to-face and 24 telephone interviews. Two more respondents answered our questions in writing. There was a great deal of agreement among survey respondents about the important attributes of successful downtowns. Together, factors believed to account for the success of small-metro CBDs rated as "very important" by at least half the respondents evoke features of traditional pre-World War II downtown areas: an active, street-oriented retail scene; cultural activities; concentrations of jobs; and a pedestrian-friendly environment with busy sidewalks.

The "important" category adds a further characteristic associated with traditional downtowns: Well preserved neighbourhoods indeed constitute a significant component of traditional downtowns. The other factors ranking high in the "important" category can be perceived as amenities and activities likely to attract and retain people in downtown areas—historical character, distinctive architecture, green space, civic events, and tourist activities. For 18 of the 19 factors listed in the questionnaire, the sum of the "very important" and "important" ratings exceeds 50%. The exception is the presence of an indoor retail mall, which was rated in these two categories by less than one quarter of respondents. This negative attitude towards indoor malls is consistent with the attachment to the traditional perception of downtowns and with the resistance to attempts at bringing downtowns closer to suburban development norms expressed in the choice of many factors categorized as "very important."

Anti-mall sentiments can thus be construed as a commitment to the preservation of the distinctiveness of downtowns within the contemporary urban environment. Another explanation may be the abovementioned failure of most of these malls. When asked for other factors (i.e., factors not listed by us in question 1), many respondents emphasized the importance of a resident population and of a wide variety of land uses to assure 24-hour activity.

Another common response was the need to find a market niche for downtowns. Some mentioned the importance of distinctive, often locally owned shops apt to create a retail environment that departs from the one produced by chains found in the suburbs. Others stressed the role that food, entertainment, and the arts can play in this regard.

But the most frequently voiced comment concerned the need to properly blend and integrate the identified success factors. Numerous respondents observed that more important than the presence of individual activities is how they interact. In this same vein, many comments concerned the role of small-scale developments, short blocks, and judicious urban design in maximizing pedestrian-based synergy between downtown activities.

Certain attributes are disproportionately present among these downtowns. Seven of them have a large university that is either in or adjacent to the CBD. In five more cases, while not immediately downtown, a university is located within 2 miles of this district; and in two additional cities, Savannah, GA, and Asheville, NC, there is a smaller college in or close to the CBD. Moreover, five of the selected downtowns host a state capital or provincial legislature. Another common feature among selected downtowns is their historical character. It is noteworthy that virtually none of the chosen CBDs have undergone a profound alteration of their traditional built environment resulting from redevelopment initiatives. This is due to avoidance of or limited reliance on urban renewal in most selected downtowns and a celebration of this historical flavor. (One exception is downtown Boise, ID, where several blocks were torn down to make way for a regional mall, which never materialized.)

Older, architecturally significant buildings have been restored and parts of these CBDs have received historical district designations. In fact, historical flavor has turned many of these downtowns into major tourist destinations. The importance of tourism can be gauged by the presence of unusual concentrations of hotel/motel rooms. Most of the 19 downtowns register a high ratio of hotel/motel rooms to central-city population. Asheville and Santa Fe have 70 rooms per 1,000 residents, and all but three of the remainder have at least 20 rooms per 1,000 residents. For comparison, central cities within metropolitan regions with a modest visitor orientation register scores in the 5-10 per 1,000 range. For example, the ratio is 6 in Kitchener, ON; 8 in Flint, MI; and 9 in Columbus, GA, and Regina, SK.

Nearly all selected downtowns are further advantaged by the easy accessibility of natural amenities, generally bodies of water, untarnished by defacing developments such as waterside freeways. These amenities have usually been the object of restoration projects intended to enhance their appeal and accessibility, ranging from the creation of large waterfront parks, as in Chattanooga, TN, to the naturalization of the banks of the San Luis Obispo, CA, creek. As indicated, all chosen downtowns share the presence of continuous street-oriented retail facades. This characteristic is hardly specific to successful downtowns, however. By virtue of its age, this built form is found in most downtowns, whether they are successful or not. But the successful CBDs are distinguished from other such areas by the occupation of street-facing premises by well patronized retail and hospitality establishments and by high levels of pedestrian movement. Chosen downtowns were able to substitute activities targeting niche markets for mainstream retail activity, which historically had dominated these districts but in most cases plummeted in the face of suburban competition.

Department and chain stores have generally been replaced with boutiques, restaurants, bars, cultural activities, and entertainment. The adaptation of these activities to downtown markets—the university community, government employees, and tourists, for example—is a factor of synergy within downtown areas, as is the pedestrian friendliness of their street-level environment.

The quality of walking space receives considerable attention in downtowns chosen in the survey. Six of the selected downtowns possess a pedestrian mall, a rare occurrence in contemporary North America, and number ban parking lots. In summary, in addition to a pedestrian-hospitable environment, all highly rated CBDs possess at least one of the following assets: a university that is in or close to downtown; presence in a metropolitan region with a strong visitor orientation; a well preserved historical district; and a state capital or provincial legislature. In justifying their selection of successful downtowns, respondents also alluded to the presence of cultural activities—art galleries and live entertainment—and natural amenities.

Yet for all their shared features, downtowns selected in the survey present many differences. If all these downtowns are perceived as historically rich relative to the remainder of their metropolitan regions, some of them, Chattanooga, TN, and Savannah, GA, in particular, possess an exceptional historical character. The markets they cater to represent another difference among downtowns chosen in the survey. While most draw several markets, in some places activities are narrowly focused on university students. This is the case in Athens, GA, and State College, PA. Downtown State College, for example, contains 42 bars and 50 fraternity houses. These downtowns are further differentiated by the extent to which they have suffered the retail assault of the suburbs.

In a few instances, thanks to the underdevelopment of suburban retail establishments or the long distance from the downtown of large suburban shopping concentrations, downtowns were able to retain some mainstream shopping. This happened, for example, in Kingston, ON, Santa Barbara, CA, and Rochester, MN. Finally, a few downtowns—Victoria, BC, and Madison, WI, for example—break from the ranks by posting relatively high public transit patronage.

Answers to question 3, where respondents were asked to name successful small-metro downtowns irrespective of their location in North America, added five CBDs to our list. These are downtowns that were mentioned by a minimum of three respondents, had not been selected in the previous question and approximated our size criteria. All enjoy the presence of a nearby university campus. Portland, ME, and Knoxville, TN, feature well restored historical centres that are popular with tourists. Boulder, CO, has created a downtown pedestrian mall, and downtown Lincoln, NE, is the site of the state capital. Question 3 findings thus confirm those of question 2.

At first glance, observations from this study do not seem to be of much use to the majority of small-metro CBDs, which did not make the list of successful downtowns. It indeed appears that only those downtowns blessed with extraordinary assets that do not lend themselves easily to duplication (such as core area university campuses, seats of government, or exceptional historical character) can aspire to be successful.

But closer examination reveals that extensive efforts were made to revitalize these successful downtowns, which served to create or enhance some of their advantages or to extend the benefits of existing assets. After all, these are not the only downtowns with a built environment that is distinctive within its metropolitan region or with historical merit. Moreover, it is not unusual to find deteriorated downtowns with universities or government employment close by. Somehow, these less successful downtowns have not been able to take advantage of such features to the same extent as those picked by our survey respondents.

Comments from the survey and subsequent interviews reveal six categories of measures used in successful downtowns. Note that none of the downtowns relied on the full roster of revitalization measures and, indeed, that a number of CBDs made very little use of any of them. In the first category we find initiatives intended to stimulate development, such as public-sector financial support to private investments in the form of tax increment financing, loan guarantees, and different forms of incentive funding. Within this category also fail public-sector involvement in land assembly and brownfield rehabilitation. The second category groups different types of streetscape, urban furniture, facade improvement programmes, and the introduction of public art.

The third category includes the erection of public buildings such as convention centres, courthouses, and municipal offices. The next group deals with transportation and parking issues. We find under this rubric traffic calming measures, the creation of pedestrian malls, the provision of municipally run parking, as well as control—occasionally banning—of parking lots. The fifth category concerns the restoration of natural amenities, essentially waterfronts, and the opening of pedestrian-friendly corridors to these sites. And the final category groups efforts at increasing the visibility of the downtown through marketing and event programming.

While most of the selected downtowns enjoy the active involvement of a vast array of organizations, including the planning department, the chamber of commerce, downtown business associations, citizen organizations, private foundations, and arts groups, in other downtowns organizational support is virtually absent. This is the case in downtown Victoria where, since the dissolution of the Business Improvement Area for lack of interest on the part of property owners, the planning department is pretty much alone in fending for the downtown area. We now briefly explore how listed measures and the involvement of different organizations congealed into revitalization strategies. To this end, we rely on the content of interviews to picture the strategies adopted by three of our downtowns—Asheville, NC, Chattanooga, TN, and Kingston, ON—chosen for their representation of different types of approaches. Asheville, NC. Following the 1972 opening of a regional shopping mall in the suburbs, downtown Asheville entered a cycle of decline that lasted into the 1980s. Many buildings were boarded up and remaining businesses were often left struggling.

This situation prompted a broad collaborative approach involving the City Development Office, whose primary function is to assure downtown revitalization; the Downtown Commission appointed by the city; the Downtown Association, which is responsible for programming and retail marketing; the Arts Council; and strong merchant and resident organizations. From the mid 1980s, downtown issues assumed a prominent position on the municipal political scene and mobilized multiple interest groups. Since then, local government support for downtown revitalization initiatives has been unwavering, with the exception of a hiatus in the early 1990s when municipal leadership was taken by suburban interests for one term.

Asheville has relied on a variety of financial inducements to stimulate private investment in its downtown, and thereby bolster the commercial and residential function of the district and the rehabilitation of historic buildings. For example, loan guarantees from the municipal administration allowed the restoration of 11 adjacent historic buildings and the erection of a parking structure. Overall, the revitalization of downtown Asheville was not so much the outcome of a few major projects as that of numerous local entrepreneurial initiatives and small-scale improvements to the built environment. Chattanooga, TN. In Chattanooga, as in Asheville, interest in the downtown was triggered by the severe damage caused by suburban retail development. Downtown Chattanooga lost its department and chain stores to the regional mall, but was able to preserve its office employment base.

The revitalization process was initiated in the early 1980s by three distinct initiatives: one focusing on urban design, the second on the waterfront, and the third on the promotion of specific projects in the CBD. The Chattanooga approach to downtown revitalization parallels characteristics of the "urban regime" model documented within large metropolitan regions. This model involves the presence of stable alliances, driven by private economic interests with the means to carry out their own revitalization efforts. The Lyndhurst Foundation, set up by a pioneer of the Coca-Cola bottling business, has played a leading role in launching and funding downtown renewal initiatives. What is more, banks have been active in the renovation of historic buildings. Like Asheville, Chattanooga has made extensive use of public funding support to leverage private investment in the downtown and has taken a multipronged approach to revitalization. But more than most other downtowns selected in the survey, Chattanooga has relied on large projects.

This is the case of Warehouse Row, consisting of the restoration of eight historic warehouses; Charleston Place, which includes a hotel, conference centre, 30 stores, and an athletic club; the Tennessee Aquarium; and the $120 million waterfront plan presently being implemented. This plan involves the creation of public parks, streets, and the expansion of a museum and the aquarium. The revival of Downtown Kingston began in the late 1960s when railroad lines and derelict industrial structures along Lake Ontario made way for a park, marina, hotels, and luxurious apartment buildings. Along with the failure of a downtown shopping mall proposal and citizen mobilization against threats to historic structures, this concentration of new developments on the waterfront contributed to the preservation of downtown Kingston's traditional built environment. In comparison to Asheville, Chattanooga, and many other downtowns selected in the survey, the last decades have witnessed little public sector intervention in downtown Kingston.

After involvement in waterfront redevelopment, public sector efforts were pretty much confined to streetscape beautification and an upgrading of the downtown's urban furniture. Still, the district remained healthy and even held on to some of its mainstream retail activity, thanks to the distance of the regional mall from the downtown and a large close-by population. In addition, the Business Improvement Area is effective in marketing the downtown and recruiting new stores to fill empty premises. And with different community organizations using the downtown as a venue for their events, there are activities programmed over all summer weekends. Asheville and Chattanooga mirror the high level of interventionism shared by most successful downtowns identified in the study. Kingston, on the other hand, figures among selected downtowns where public sector involvement has been lowest.

The contrast between these downtowns can be interpreted as a consequence of differences in the severity of threats confronting them. Again, in a fashion that is common to most downtowns rated as successful in the survey, Asheville's and Chattanooga's revitalization efforts were reactions to manifest signs of downtown decline in the wake of advancing retail suburbanization. Kingston, on the other hand, is more representative of the minority of successful downtowns where damage inflicted by suburbanization was limited. Many interviewees and a number of comments made in the survey stress the fragility of vital downtowns.

They underscore the need for constant vigilance to safeguard the health of these districts, and thus the importance of durable political support and stable downtown alliances. Sustained mobilization around downtown issues is needed to secure municipal government interest in downtown matters and willingness to tailor interventions to CBD realities. Downtowns indeed require a different approach to planning and development from the remainder of their metropolitan regions, most particularly suburban areas. Financial incentives are frequently necessary to lure investments to the core, and in contrast to most other parts of metropolitan areas, the vitality of downtowns demands an environment that is stimulating for pedestrians. But the risk always looms that the special needs of downtowns will be overlooked by city councils, especially if they are dominated by pro-suburban interests. The outcome could then be extreme difficulty in attracting investments and, over time, a less distinctive built environment.

In addition, despite the stabilizing effect of universities and government, the replacement of mainstream by specialized retailing and heavy reliance on hospitality and tourism make the downtowns selected in the survey acutely sensitive to economic cycles. Less capable than mainstream suburban retail to withstand recessions, the economies of successful downtowns risk being devastated by a severe downturn. These downtowns would then require economic rebuilding strategies to take advantage of the subsequent recovery. Successful downtowns must also constantly stay on top of the frequent fashion shifts characteristic of their niche retail markets and of the hospitality and entertainment sectors.

When considering the duplication potential of lessons drawn from our selected downtowns, we must keep in mind that these are the bright stars in the constellation of small-metro downtowns, and that it is unrealistic to expect a generalization of their level of performance across CBDs of similar size urban areas. There are obviously wide variations in the extent to which such downtowns can benefit from the experience of their successful counterparts. For example, many lessons from the downtowns chosen in the survey are pertinent to other downtowns where the traditional built environment is still in place. In contrast, such lessons are of little relevance to those downtowns where the pre-World War II layout has been severely compromised.

Still, the situation for small-metro downtowns is not as somber as it was in the earlier phases of suburbanization, when the lure of the periphery was fuelled by generalized aspiration for a car-oriented lifestyle. For the many individuals for whom this lifestyle has since lost its luster, the traditional layout of downtowns can be attractive, provided these districts contain activities adapted to their needs and preferences. Demographic trends are also in part favourable to downtown areas. The prevalence of small, predominantly childless households in downtowns and surrounding neighbourhoods has long been documented. The bulge of aging baby boomers, some of whom are ready to trade their suburban homes for smaller dwellings in a pedestrian-friendly area, provides ample potential residents for core areas. This is also the case for the growing proportion of childless households in all age categories.

What is more, interest in downtowns may be bolstered by present-day environmental and economic development thinking. The compact and pedestrian-oriented characteristics of downtown areas are consistent with smart growth principles presently in vogue. Downtown revitalization figures prominently among measures that the smart growth movement advances to contain urban sprawl and reduce automobile dependence. From an economic development perspective, lively, entertainment- and culture-rich downtowns are depicted as appealing to the "creative class," broadly defined to include people engaged in professional, product development, entrepreneurial, artistic, and management occupations. According to the perspective expounded by Richard Florida, the creative class assumes a leading role in economic growth.

This view therefore implies an enhanced ability on the part of metropolitan regions possessing a healthy downtown to attract members of the creative class and thereby enjoy resulting economic rewards. Revealingly, metropolitan regions whose downtowns were selected in our study figure prominently among urban areas in their size category posting a high presence of the creative class. The foremost generalizable lesson that can be distilled from our selected downtowns is disarmingly simple: Their success can be attributed to an ability to attract people and assure that they remain in their midst to pursue many of their activities. Chosen CBDs possess magnets (a university, government presence, historical character, and specialized retail establishments) and provide reasons for people to spend time downtown.

Selected downtowns indeed offer a synergy-rich environment consisting of activities that are well adapted to core-area markets and are set within a pedestrian-hospitable environment. In reality, however, it is difficult to distinguish between magnet and retention features, because the presence of many people and of the activities they support itself adds to the allure of downtown areas. If typical small-metro downtowns cannot improvise the university campus, seat of government, or exceptional historical character commonly found in the downtowns selected in our survey, they can nonetheless make efforts to draw employment and, perhaps with most promise, new housing. Lessons from successful downtowns underscore the need for strategies that are both multipronged and well coordinated. In typical small-metro downtowns, revitalization strategies would at once need to attract employment and housing and create an environment that is hospitable to downtown workers and nearby residents.

Ideally, such an environment will possess historical flavor and lively street life, two characteristics that will differentiate it from the suburbs. It will also harbor retail and services that are suited to the needs and tastes of people who are attracted downtown. For example, to cater to the needs of nearby residents and encourage further housing development, a downtown must provide a variety of food outlets. Given the nature of the markets they are susceptible to lure, success for typical small-metro downtowns is a function of their ability to provide activities and settings that are unique within their metropolitan regions. These downtowns should attempt to launch a virtuous cycle whereby the attainment of a critical mass of users and activities within a distinct environment will make them attractive to a growing number of visitors. This type of cycle is a major factor in the success of the downtowns selected in the survey.

Our research findings are generally in accord with the transition over the last decades in the perception of the role of downtowns and of appropriate revival interventions. They resonate with the recent literature's emphasis on the preservation and enhancement of the traditional layout and historical character of downtowns. Our results also mirror the importance recent writings give to people places, pedestrian connectivity, variety of land uses, and, generally, quality of life within downtown areas. Likewise, many of our selected downtowns have adopted revitalization strategies that are consistent with those documented in recent writings. These strategies are inclusive, drawing on diverse constituencies such as property owners, merchants, residents, governments, and historic preservationists and rely extensively on private/public sector partnerships.

Yet, findings from our research are occasionally at variance with the literature. This is mostly a consequence of the scant coverage it gives to downtowns belonging to metropolitan regions with populations of 100,000-500,000. Whereas the revitalization strategies of large-city downtowns can benefit from extensive public transit systems, national- and world-scale attractions, the enduring presence of mainstream retail, large office space concentrations, and the key role of big corporations, most CBDs of small metropolitan regions cannot count on such advantages.

This explains in large part the differences between our findings and previous literature depictions of large-metro downtown revitalization strategies. More than those of their larger counterparts, successful downtowns of small metropolitan regions tend to target niche markets, make use of small- rather than large-scale revitalization interventions, and rely on the public sector.

The results of this research were not surprising insofar as they confirm the observation that the vast majority of small-metro downtowns have not recovered from the severe damage inflicted by suburbanization. Findings also mirror the conceptual turn that has run through the planning profession over the last decades. The emphasis of revitalization strategies on features of traditional downtowns, such as street-oriented and pedestrian-friendly environments, is in agreement with current thinking within the planning profession. The assets respondents associate with a successful downtown paint the picture of the traditional downtown, harking back to the pre-1950 period. This depiction is consistent with the present popularity of built environment preservation and new urbanism within the planning community. The usefulness of these findings lies in lessons derived from the downtowns identified as successful, which can be of aid to ailing CBDs. The proposals generated by this research stress the need to emphasize the distinction of downtowns from the suburban realm.

First, this type of revitalization strategy should involve an accentuation of historical character and street-level activity, two features that distinguish these districts from suburban-type developments. Second, with the irrevocable loss of mainstream retail activity to the suburbs, downtown revival strategies are compelled to capitalize on the few markets where this sector holds a comparative advantage over suburban locales.

Acknowledgements We acknowledge financial support from the Waterloo Community-University Research Alliance and thank the planners who answered our questionnaire and who agreed to be interviewed. We are also grateful to the anonymous referees for their helpful comments. Because of the limited literature on small-metro downtown revitalization and considerable overlapping in the nature and sequence of revitalization phases in both large and small metropolitan region downtowns, the following four paragraphs draw on writing pertaining to both categories of downtowns.

The sample was constructed from several sources: rosters of both the American Institute of Certified Planners and the Canadian Institute of Planners; the Web sites of North American university planning, urban studies, and geography departments and programmes; and the Web sites of organizations involved in downtown revitalization and urban research in the U.S. and Canada. All identified academics were included in our sample. As regards planners employed by small-metro central cities, two names were incorporated in the sample from those administrations with less than seven accredited planners, and where there were more than seven planners, every fourth name was added to our list. All professionals with a possible interest in downtowns who are associated with government agencies or economic development or research institutes with an urban focus were surveyed.

The presence of a retail mall was rated as "not important at all" by 33.9% of respondents, by far the highest score within this category. The second highest factor rated as "not important at all"—abundant parking—was selected by a meager 5.4% of respondents. Irrespective of the 20% rule, cores that were placed in either of the two categories by less than four respondents were not included. The few cases where the 20% threshold was attained with less than four citations are due to a strong reliance on the "don't know" option. The important proportion of tourist- and university-oriented downtowns within those given highest rankings could be interpreted as an artifact of the method used in this research. The presence of academics in the sample would favour the reporting of downtowns with a university, because of the evident familiarity of this group of respondents with such CBDs.

And tourist destinations are obviously better known by everyone, including our respondents. Two features of the methodology reduce the likelihood of such biases, however. First, academics amounted to only a little above a third of our sample.

Second, and most importantly, to assure that as many downtowns as possible would qualify as successful, we set low thresholds—citation by 20% or more for the cores on the regional lists and three mentions or more for the continent-wide selection. The only selected downtown that does not fully share the historical features and intense street orientation of the highly rated core areas is that of Rochester, MN, where the main focus has been on a modernization of the downtown through the building of an indoor mall and of a skyway and underground passageway system. The hotel/motel room to central-city population ratio was calculated from American Automobile Association and Canadian Automobile Association tour book hotel/motel directories.

This method somewhat underestimates the presence of hotel/motel rooms, because the directories exclude lower-end facilities. In the case of Burlington, VT, the central city was combined with a suburb. This is because while close to City of Burlington boundaries, this metropolitan area's main concentration of hotel and motel rooms is in South Burlington. There are two explanations for the exceptional presence of pedestrian malls in these downtowns. First, by virtue of their success, we can assume that some of the downtowns selected in the survey are among those that have been most engaged in revitalization efforts, one form of which was the creation of a pedestrian mall.

Second, and perhaps most importantly, these downtowns are among the few that can generate sufficient numbers of pedestrians and activities to bring malls to life, thanks in large part to the presence of tourists and university students. Elsewhere, the use of pedestrian malls as instruments of revitalization has generally failed lamentably. In Rochester, MN, the Mayo Clinic and the Methodist Hospital attract many visitors—patients and their families—which explains the high hotel/motel room to resident ratio. Rochester ranks fifth in this regard among core areas. Moreover, the Mayo Clinic, with its intense medical research activity, maintains with downtown

Rochester a relationship that recalls the one prevailing between centrally located universities and their downtown areas. Respondents listed a total of 170 downtowns in question. These, only 17 were part of metropolitan regions that come close to our size criteria and were mentioned by at least three respondents. Twelve of these downtowns were also ranked highly in question 2, thus lending additional credence to this question's regional selections. Of the five additional downtowns mentioned in answers to question 3, two had been listed as options in the previous question, but had not been selected by a sufficient proportion of respondents from their home region to be included among successful CBDs. Of the remaining three downtowns, one was excluded from question 2's options because the population of its metropolitan region is slightly above the 500,000 limit. The other two are part of larger consolidated census metropolitan areas, Detroit and Denver.

A survey carried out in Kitchener-Waterloo, ON, a highly suburbanized urban area belonging to a 414,284-resident metropolitan region, has revealed that close to half the population would consider living in a neighbourhood close to a downtown.

This interest in central area living was, however, conditional upon the downtown being revitalized into a safe, pedestrian-friendly environment where respondents could find activities compatible with their tastes, and on the availability in central neighbourhoods of their preferred types of housing.

Many of these individuals were attracted to central neighbourhoods by their mature character and the possibility of reducing dependence on the automobile. The results of the Kitchener-Waterloo study are consistent with those of recent studies documenting a housing renaissance in numerous central areas.

3

Sales and Marketing Strategies in Hotel Business

MARKETING AS PROCESS

The hotel business has changed enormously over the last 30 years, embracing special niche forms of lodging, new ways of segmenting markets brand proliferation and consolidation, new tools for acquiring customers distribution innovations and globalization. These changes in markets and in ways hotels relate to and capitalize on them have put new demands on marketing. Marketing, as addressed herein is not the sales and marketing department; I mean marketing in its broadest sense of how hotels respond to and seize on market opportunities. Definition? Marketing is a process of creating and sustaining productive relationships with desirable customers. Its goal? To produce such relationships more effectively than competitors do. Let's examine the definition and its implications.

Marketing is:

- *A process*: A process, a series of functions and actions for approaching and dealing with opportunities. *Marketing,* as used herein, is not a job but a way of proceeding to create and operate a hotel focused on customers and competitors, a way that incorporates all members of the hotel staff and its support.
- *Of creating*: The essence of marketing is creation: imagination, insight, willingness to change and evolve, and, yes, discard.
- *And sustaining*: Loyalty over time and repeat customers are the key to productivity and optimal contribution margins.
- *Productive relationships*: A relationship must be two-sided, with benefits for both partners in the relationship. In the case of customers, the benefits are wants and needs consistently fulfilled and full value received; in the case of staff, professional satisfaction and operating profits sufficient to fund improvements provide attractive compensation, and provide returns on investors' or owners' capital.

- *With desirable customers*: Not all customers are equally desirable; we want those who are willing to pay, growing in numbers, making multiple purchases, and whose needs we are able to fully satisfy. And the goal?
- To produce such relationships. *Production* implies inputs, outputs, and the measurement of productivity. Marketing productivity has been lagging for the last decade; the rising costs of acquiring customers must be reined in.
- More effectively than competitors do. Marketing success is judged in relative terms, using competitors and similar hotels as benchmarks. As a creative process, especially in a field like hospitality wherein innovations are unprotected and easily copied, the benchmarks and goals are always moving targets. Besting the competition is the constant challenge.

It will be clear that successful marketing of a hotel requires the orchestration of a wide variety of talents and skills, of which sales and marketing personnel are only a part. Chain hotels approach the process one way; independents must do so another. But in either case, market success depends on an effective integration of marketing and operations at the property level under the direction and leadership of a marketdriven general manager.

THE MARKETING PROCESS

Professor Malcolm McDonald of Cranfield University School of Management, a world authority on marketing planning, has produced numerous publications on the marketing planning process over the last 10 years. His best selling book, *Marketing Plans - How to prepare them: How to use them,* now in the Fourth Edition, describes *The Ten Steps of the Strategic Marketing Planning Process* as follows:

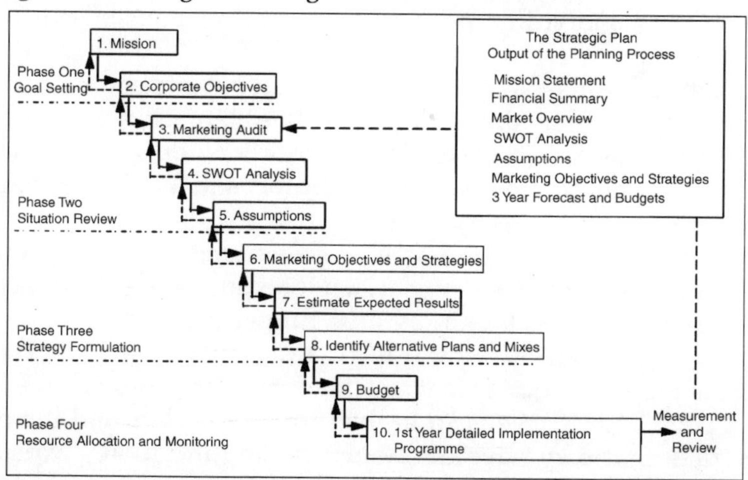

Fig. The Ten Steps of the Strategic Marketing Planning Process

In order to assist companies with the implementation of an effective Strategic Marketing Planning Process many of the techniques were implemented in software programmes. Several prototypes were developed at the Cranfield School of Management, which were widely tested in a variety of commercial environments over a number of years, in order to produce a complete and robust specification of the requirement.

HOTEL PRICING STRUCTURE

CURRENT PRICING CRITERIA

"Our pricing is market-driven, not costbased," says Scott Farrell, corporate director of distribution with Fairmont Hotels and Resorts, a Toronto-based chain of luxury properties. When the chain is setting its prices, it starts with comprehensive market research. Based on the data, the correct price for each marketplace is determined. If there is a major shift in a market, then the prices will adjust for that. However, if there is a major shift in a demand curve, then a shift of price may have no effect.

It may actually leave more money on the table. For example, if the airlines go on strike, a significant shift in the demand curve would result. Under such conditions, decreasing the rate by $50, for example, would only result in a $50 loss. If there is an opportunity to go after a new targeted market with a specific offer, enabling the chain to capture a greater market share, then lowering the rate serves its purpose. Generally, however, lowering rates across the board is not the preferred pricing strategy.

PRICING: WHO IS IN CHARGE

While independently owned properties make their own pricing decisions, in case of a chain it is usually corporate headquarters (HQ) that sets pricing guidelines. Often, individual properties are still responsible for the actual pricing.

Because they are held accountable, they must balance corporate guidelines with their autonomy to set their prices. Caroline Shin, member of the revenue management team at Starwood Hotels and Resorts Worldwide, which operates a number of upscale brands, such as Sheraton and W Hotels, stresses the cooperative nature of this relationship.

Successful pricing strategies arise from an ongoing interaction of both sides. Corporate HQ provides sophisticated tools and in-depth market analysis that would be beyond reach of individual properties.

Property managers, on the other hand, offer their experience and knowledge of regional specifics that may have gone unnoticed by the corporate team."The people who have been in the property understand the dynamics of that market, and they have developed pricing intuition," explains Shin. Some experts view intuition as a valuable part of the pricing mechanism, and even managers who are technically savvy check the numbers against their gut feeling.

PRICING: SCIENCE, ART, AND INTUITION

Pricing distribution and revenue management techniques are a mix of science and art. Recent research shows that two-thirds of managers making strategic decisions under pressure and time constraints use a combination of analysis and intuition.

The advent of modern technology, such as yield management software packages, has further strengthened this link. "Even the most sophisticated analytical model for forecasting, may it be for hotel pricing or for thermal dynamics of a nuclear plant, still needs variables based upon assumptions," says Shin, who used to work as a nuclear engineer.The more business- savvy hotel management becomes and the more they understand the hotel dynamics and the market, the more can be gained from training them how to define their experiencebased intuition and put it into numbers. In this respect, an interaction between the corporate revenue management team and individual hotels is paramount. "Every time I go out to a property, I learn something new. It only helps me when I build my analytical models to almost translate what they know into numbers," confirms Shin. The better hotels can do that, the better models they can develop. Nonetheless, inaccurate historical data remains a major limitation.

No model is ever going to be perfect, though.What seems to work best is to teach hotel managers how to use the model and to understand the direction of the pricing decisions they need to make. That is the scientific part.The art piece comes into play when they infuse the model with their knowledge and intuition.

Staff training is an important part of this process. "We can't just have Ph.D.s sitting in one room coming with all these models and we just roll it out. At the same time, we can't just have people with intuitions run around and set prices," says Shin.

Revenue management teams must make sure that hotels understand how to employ the models in their daily pricing decisions. When science is applied, the revenue team can go to their experts, ask probing questions, and get solid results. Even though intuition is a part of this process, it is based only on a hypothesis that could have been triggered by a discussion with a customer, knowledge of what is happening in the marketplace, or historic trends. That is why pure intuition is not sufficient. "Managers must have reliable data to support their hunches," cautions Scott Farrell.

CUSTOMER NEEDS

Customer satisfaction is a crucial part of marketing, pricing, and yield management. Any pricing strategy established by the hotel management must attract customers willing to pay the specified rate.While price is a determinator of the customer profile the hotel is looking for, it is also an indicator of the quality of services and the market segment the hotel is competing in.

Therefore, yield management uses information about targeted customers' purchasing Behaviour and product sales to develop pricing strategy together with inventory control that delivers products that are better matched to customer needs, create greater demand, and, on that account, produce greater revenues. Lieberman states that yield management is the process of maximizing profits from the sale of perishable assets, such as hotel rooms, by controlling price and inventory and improving service through systemization.

An exact definition of the target market is essential. There is a definite and firm perception in the psyche of the customer, who views the price as the value forthcoming. Therefore, the eventual satisfaction of the customer is the paramount task of the pricing mechanism. This is the make-or-break factor of the entire hotel, especially if the value expected does not match the price.

ROLE OF TECHNOLOGY

While the approach to hotel pricing is still ruled by supply and demand, speed and sophistication of room-rate yield or revenue maximization is now much increased due to two technological factors: yield management software and Internet bookings.

Yield management software packages enable hotels to use a higher number of roomrate levels, or buckets, and to control inventory for rate availability in real time. Each level may consist of several room rates open under given conditions to yield a maximum profit. Traditionally, hotels used between three and five rate levels; otherwise, the adjustment became too complex for the human brain to work with. The introduction of software removed this barrier, and some hotel chains now use up to ten rate levels.This allows implementation of much narrower ranges for each bucket, thus optimizing price elasticity. This further means the software model recognizes the point at which the same number of bookings can be achieved at a higher rate.

Online monitoring of room inventory in real time facilitates the timing of the adjustment. So far, the biggest limitation is the reliability of historical data. Even in its imperfect form, the system has made a difference. However, hotel managers are fully aware that it takes years to develop brand recognition and quality but just a push of a button to damage or even destroy it, if the pricing is not set up knowledgeably. As the technology becomes more sophisticated, it will eliminate such questionable practices as overbooking, which aims at compensating for last-minute cancellations by taking in more than 100 per cent reservations. Besides the question of whether overbooking is ethical and, in some countries, even illegal, better technology would definitely improve the quality of service provided by properties that engage in this practice. Another area where technological advancement had a great impact on hotel pricing is the Internet. Its use as a booking tool has created a new level of pricing transparency and tiered competition. It also penetrated the negotiation of corporate rates. Many hotels see the effect of the Internet as both good and bad.The good side is that website bookings are growing every day.

As more customers become familiar with their favourite hotel websites, hotel companies have started investing heavily in website development and upkeep, which gives them several advantages. First, the cost of online bookings is lower than for bookings made through other distribution channels. Companies do not have to pay commission because the booking is direct, circumventing all intermediaries. Online booking also provides an opportunity to monitor inventory in real time without reliance on a distributor willing to share and regularly supply data. Last but not least, it generates loyal customers by making them eligible for bonus points, which they cannot earn if they use an Internet intermediary.

That is exactly where the flip side of the Internet lies. The intermediaries are getting more powerful and growing significantly in volume. Because most of them show all hotel rates on their website, they make the information accessible to any computer user. One way to meet the challenge of more powerful intermediaries, especially if hotels need to move inventory, is to utilize auctions where the name of the hotel is not disclosed to the customer until the transaction is finalized. Such action, however, calls for extreme caution so that it does not damage a hotel's reputation or threaten its strategic partnerships.

As intermediaries become bigger, rate transparency will increase to the point where it will drive the market, especially when computer literacy and Internet access become the norm.

Moreover, the Internet allows nonbranded hotels to compete more heavily with the branded hotels because they can now be displayed just as readily. Without significant advertising expense, they can compete on price. For some markets this does not matter, especially when the brand is powerful enough to charge the premium and get the business.

In highly competitive markets, however, the competition creates an additional strain for the individual property. Many branded hotels must now compete with other brands through the traditional distribution channels and with nonbranded hotels on the Internet, which, in principle, lowers hotel rates. A frequently adopted strategy is to invest heavily in website development and customer loyalty programmes, assuring excellent website functionality and that customers are rewarded for booking directly through the hotel website rather than through the website of a thirdparty intermediary. Both Fairmont and Starwood, for example, utilize their high-quality loyalty programmes in this way.

Internet booking also changed the way corporate accounts are negotiated. Because many companies now require that their employees make business travel arrangements via the corporate website, the placement of a hotel or a brand on this booking tool is of strategic importance. Being listed first in the accommodation part, for example, may bring in a higher volume of business and thus substantiate a lower negotiated rate.

LONG-TERM STRATEGY TOR THE INTERNET

Because hotels cannot expect that Internet distributors will go out of business, they smartly conclude that a partnership with the devil is better than a fight with him. Besides using their own websites, hotel companies are also making sure that the cost of their transactions goes down continuously so they can compete even at lower rates—while maintaining a good relationship with their carefully selected online intermediaries.

There is a large number of distributors to choose from. On one end of the spectrum is, for example, Expedia, which allows participating hotels to control their rates, meaning a hotel can change its rates any time it wants.At the other end are companies, such as Hotel Reservation Network that bind hotels contractually to a locked rate that cannot be changed. Some hotel chains do not want to partner with these distributors because they like pricing flexibility and want to make sure their rates yield as much as possible.

Adaptation to new technology has been the biggest component of change for intermediaries as well. Companies that do not have the most current technology working in real time or allowing hotels to yield rates in real time are usually not considered a suitable distribution partner for some chains. On the other hand, companies that invest in real-time technology to yield rates are ideal partners because, as the industry sees it, they work with, not against the industry by permitting hotels to raise or lower rates in real time. "They work with us," says Caroline Shin.

"They give data to us very frequently so that we understand the travel pattern bookings on their website.Then we compare it with what is happening on our website and also what we are getting outside the Internet to make sure that our market mix is set appropriately." Pricing flexibility, compatibility with the desired hotel image, and protection of its strategic partnerships, together with cost, play important roles in selecting an intermediary.

THE ROLE OF CREATIVITY IN PRICING

Creativity, either of an individual or a team, can and often does lead to innovative pricing ideas. However, its application must be specific, not just directional. It is not enough to state,"We have to do something about our occupancy level." A pricing campaign must target a number of sold rooms or generated revenue that is required in order to break even or to do better. This specific approach injects efficiency into allocating marketing money to areas where it is most effective and in periods when it is desired. If there is no task direction or overall pricing leadership, the most creative idea may book only ten roomnights instead of one hundred. It may generate more customer loyalty, but that is something the hotel may not need at the moment, although it could be an acceptable outcome in a low-season month.

Pricing leadership helps team members understand the hotel's current situation and direct money and creativity to do exactly what is needed. Creativity comes up with the idea, which serves as a vehicle, but spending marketing money the smart way is a matter of experience in innovation, which turns the idea into a successful product. Creativity also plays a large part in employee satisfaction, and it lowers turnover.

In a sluggish economy, some hotels start paying attention not only to profit as the bottom line but also to revenue. This means they monitor closely the accrued cost as well as the generated revenue, thus achieving the maximum yield. Interestingly, contemporary price leadership may take different forms.

It could mean, for example, elimination of smoking rooms throughout the property. Many U.S. motels are revamping rooms, ripping off cigarette-damaged furniture and carpets, and designating them as nonsmoking. This saves on maintenance and adds to overall packaging flexibility when the business is hurt by lackluster demand. This tactic means drapes, carpets, bedding, and other furnishings must be replaced less frequently; it also mitigates fire risk and enhances cleanliness and overall safety.

THE ROLE OF HUMAN RESOURCES IN PRICING

Some large chains recognize that pricing is a complex issue and that they need to get better at it. There is a new focus on analysing the culture of pricing and how it can be improved. This approach is reflected even in the kinds of people chains are hiring. Although the majority of staff involved in strategic pricing are in the hotel industry and have a background in revenue management, others are in the airline industry and have indepth travel revenue management experience.

Some chains have sought access to this experience by hiring from outside the hotel industry. This is to encourage diversification of thinking and new ways of thought—completely out of the box, as the traditional team members are joined by researchers doing a different kind of optimization analysis. The goal could be as radical as trying to manage risk or optimize towards the railroad industry and its scheduling.

On the surface, these tactics have nothing to do with revenue management *per se*.A lot of experience in optimizing difficult travel, however, can only be gained by bringing in people with different backgrounds in consulting or with in-depth Internet experience. In order to move pricing and revenue management to a different level of thought, a new mix of people is necessary. For this approach to work, adequate training must be in place.

In this respect, basic HR functions, such as hiring and training, have an impact on pricing. What is necessary is not only to train personnel in quantitative core skills but also in strategic thinking. For example, when a hotel does not want to take a specific piece of business, it must ask such questions as:What is the revenue? What is the rate? What am I displacing by this decision? Where do I think this will go? How does it help my RevPAR?

Hotel managers must become more analytical so they can use all the new tools now available. When reports are created, team members must be taught how to use them.A lot of training must be provided for corporate executives, general managers, and regional revenue directors as well. They all must be trained to think more strategically and to understand analysis and the reports so they can help their individual properties.

DIVERSIFICATION: THE IMPROVEMENT OF THE PRICING PROCESS

As noted, exclusive hotel industry experience may lead to ossification due to one-sided judgment and the inability to see beyond the familiar. From this perspective, experience is both an asset and a liability. It is human nature to take for granted the way things are done after being in the same environment for a while.

Therefore, hotel chains are continuously creating and refining pricing strategies to accommodate not only different market segments but also different situations a hotel may face based on occupancy levels. Corporate HQ tries to identify these different situations and associated variables. "It is almost like a bag of goods, a bag of pricing strategies that should be tested," says Caroline Shin. Hotels are given the full menu and encouraged to try a certain strategy if they are in a specific situation. Depending on the region, an individual property may use one set of strategies more than another. In a weak economy, however, the chains have to work harder and be more flexible because the market is overflowing with demand.

Adapting step by step, a hotel may apply a different strategy every week.The problem for the corporate office is to identify situations a hotel might be in and seek remedy. For example, if group bookings are low this week but competitors are full, how can the property make up the difference with transient or leisure business? The general manager may ask the corporate team, "What pricing strategies can I use in order to fill my house?" Then he or she may ask, "What else worked before for other hotels, and what may work for me based on my market specifics and market characteristics?" That way he or she can test each strategy using the provided tool and personal experience.

PRICING: SUPPORT AND PROTECT

The corporate pricing structure is also in place to support and protect members of the chain in a number of areas including pricing and partnerships.

The corporate office sets guidelines for hotels in terms of pricing structure and the market segments they deal with. Fairmont Hotels and Resorts, for example, focuses on four segments: transient leisure travel, group travel, business travel, and wholesale. The corporate structure provides guidelines about how the segments fit with each other, how they cross over, and where they reside in the overall pricing structure.

This information is necessary because every segment acts differently. Most market segments are dynamic and require frequent rate adjustments. One exception is the wholesale market, where pricing is still largely done the traditional way: A wholesaler provides a net rate, marks it up, and sells it to the general population.There may be a hidden cost, however, if the distribution chain includes an operator acting as a middleman between the wholesaler and the supplier.

When setting up the overall pricing structure, one starts with the retail rate, which is a bucket of premium or best available rates charged on the open market. They usually do not carry any restrictions, such as cancellation fees, and they are fully billable. Depending on the level of occupancy, one of these rates is available on any given day when the hotel is not fully booked. It is up to the yield management system to identify which BAR to offer. All other rate types, such as discount rates and prenegotiated rates, are determined in relation to the retail rate. For instance, a corporate rate for a high-volume client will be probably set lower than the BAR rate that is estimated to sell most during the period when the contract is in place. This way the rates are nested within each other in a manner that makes economic sense.

The corporate pricing guidelines follow two main criteria: to maximize revenue and to protect key partnerships.While the hotel sales force negotiates contracts with key partners, such as longstanding corporate accounts or wholesale volume accounts, they make sure to protect these partnerships and provide them value. At the same time, they take every opportunity to maximize revenue. One cannot survive without the other, reiterates Scott Farrell. However, it is up to the hotels themselves, with guidance and additional research, to determine in their marketplace what their pricing structure should look like.

A diversified corporate team, with a mix of people with a hotel industry background and others skilled in optimization modeling, fulfills an additional function. It acts as a risk prevention mechanism, a necessary prerequisite for managing the risk inherent in pricing. Any chain with a wide variety of hotels must make sure the properties are covered in all kinds of situations. One risk containment scenario might be that the chain, in response to a changing demand curve, acquires a type of business that the brand has not catered to traditionally.

Caroline Shin explains, "Sheraton did not take on airline crew business because we did not want crew members lingering in the lobby; it affected our brand image. But we thought maybe we could start taking that when our RevPAR index or occupancy slips to a certain point. So we are trying to change the standards of different market segments we are willing to take."

On the international scale, another risk management plan would be analysing operational cost and determining whether to close down part of the hotel if market research shows occupancy will not be high enough. When PESTEL (political, economic, sociocultural, technological, environmental, legal) analysis indicates demand will drop precipitously for an extended period instead of hoping for the best and running a full house with a full staff, the hotel may decide to shut down floors or restaurants and save cost until the market picks up again.

Selection of the appropriate strategy will depend on the market specifics and protection of the image. A property may opt to close down several floors over the weekend if it caters mostly to business clientele staying during the week. It would not, however, suspend room service, although unprofitable, if that is considered an integral part of the offered product. In a worst-case scenario, the chain may decide to sell properties in global risk areas when it determines the external circumstances make it difficult to raise occupancy on an ongoing basis.

BETTER UTILIZE YOUR DISTRIBUTION CHANNELS

The Internet creates a new level of transparency as it allows the opportunity to maximize profitability.There is now a multitude of channels to choose from. Understanding the cost of each channel in relation to the value of provided service has an impact on the quality of pricing decisions. Therefore, it is necessary to determine how much revenue bookings through an Internet intermediary generate and whether or not they justify the accrued cost.There is also a tremendous risk involved.

As discussed earlier, one of key guidelines of corporate marketing is that partners are protected. Just because there is a new Internet site it does not mean a chain can use it and advertise a lower rate, which would undermine a partnership of many years. In terms of cost, the chain must review its pricing strategy not only by market segment but also by distribution channel. "Several years ago, we would not consider the cost of distribution in our ROI.Today we do," concedes Scott Farrell.

Another challenge is to keep up with new Internet sites. The chains must reevaluate constantly and prioritize their yield so as to choose which channels to keep or drop. Fairmont Hotels and Resorts, for example, applies the 80–20 rule.

They focus on the 20 per cent of the online wholesalers that capture more than 80 per cent of the business. As Scott Farrell puts it,"Why would I play with the other 10–12 per cent? I only have so many hours in a day to manage. I may as well work with the lion's share."

QUALITY ABOVE ALL?

Criteria for selecting an online distribution partner vary by price levels as well. Budget and economy properties are driven mostly by financial considerations, while upscale and luxury hotels are more concerned with compatibility.

As for chains, they ask two basic questions:

1. How can the partnership increase our brand recognition or a brand reach, and
2. How much is it going to bring us in terms of revenue or profitability?

Their choice has to match the brand first, and then it has to drive the revenue. If the brand is equaled with quality, online providers that project a connotation of cheapness will not be considered at all.The quality image refers not only to the hotel asset itself but also to how and where this asset is sold.

Fairmont Hotels and Resorts, as a quality brand on the luxury side, cannot compete on price. The quality of their product and the offering of the experience must be considered by the customer at the price being offered.

When their hotels play with price, the corporate office watches closely. Scott Farrell explains, "If our property wanted to shift their rate by $50, I would ask why? Give me the case behind it and tell me what you are going to do to make up the additional $50 you are going to lose. If they come back to me and say they are moving their rate from $300 to $250 while driving a certain volume, I would make them go through the process of determining what incremental volume they will need to make up for the $50 in loss."

In other words, pricing decisions must be driven by ROI, not only a feeling. Feelings and experience may be involved, but properties must present a strong case based on the estimated ROI and what they plan to get out of the proposed strategy. It allows them to go into the pricing change with their eyes open. They also must consider how the competition will respond.A carelessly lowered rate may lead to a price war.

SPEED AND STRATEGY

The speed and immediacy of exposure via the Internet have reshaped how marketing campaigns are conducted. Having eliminated the delay of exposure to marketing collateral material, such as brochures or newspaper advertisements, hotels can conduct targeted discount mini-campaigns on their own websites when the yield management system indicates a drop in occupancy for specific dates. In a similar manner, brand recognition can be enhanced by a carefully orchestrated online auction. The South African hospitality group Protea was among the first in the industry using this method by offering their prospective guests the opportunity to bid on a limited number of weekend getaways in their properties that needed to boost occupancy.

By setting a minimum bidding price, the integrity of the hotel image was protected. Similar auction systems, used to encourage room-night sales during slow periods, are nowadays available in the United States and Canada via several Internet intermediaries. For chains in particular, a long-term strategy in distribution pricing is paramount. It stipulates the criteria and accepts or rejects short-term adjustments depending on what is happening in the industry, what is new in the technology, and who the new players are.

In terms of corporate hierarchy, pricing is formulated and executed on three levels:

1. Strategy,
2. Tactics and execution, and
3. Measurement.

Strategy comes first, followed by tactics meant to support that strategy and their execution. Finally, the achieved outcome is measured against the set benchmarks. If the strategy is sound, it will last longer than the other two steps. Frequently, new tactics must be implemented; these drive the execution and the measurement. This requires a development of proprietary criteria for measurement and their continuous adjustment to changing conditions.

PRICE ELASTICITY

Contrary to the traditional view that hotel rates are, in the long-term, generally inelastic, price elasticity is receiving a lot of attention nowadays thanks to yield management. Its goal is to take advantage of and to cover the entire spectrum of the customers' ability to purchase. Price elasticity allows hotels to capture customers who do not mind paying the high rate as well as those who are more priceconscious.

This can be done in a number of ways. By using different room categories, a luxury hotel can have on the same day suites available at $500 and entry-level rooms at $200. Every room rate category has a different value proposition associated with the incremental revenue. If the variance between a standard room and a deluxe room is $75, the latter should provide an adequately greater value to the customer. The result is a clear product differentiation, which can be also achieved by stay restrictions or by the use of fencing. Examples of physical differences, or fences, are room type, view, amenities, and location.

Nonphysical fences may mean different customers, transactions, or consumption characteristics. These bear many similarities with airline pricing strategies, which differentiate the product by, for example, cancellation restrictions or last-minute availability of a prenegotiated corporate rate. The result is nested pricing, allowing properties to have a very high rate available on the same day as a rate that is more attractive to the lower-end customer.

NEW AREAS OF PRICING AND YIELD MANAGEMENT

Hotel pricing strategies traditionally have been limited to setting and adjusting room rates and other ongoing activities. In order to survive in the current dynamic, competitive, and even dangerous global environment, hotels and resorts are taking on other types of business, some of which are one-time projects. Organizing shows, festivals, and conferences or undergoing renovations requires a new type of core competency. Therefore, in addition to mastering current pricing strategies, hotel practitioners must acquire project management skills, such as those that are taught and practiced by Project Management Institute. Mastering these skills will make hotel team members capable of maximizing yield from project-type functions the same way as they optimize revenue from room rates.

PRODUCT DESCRIPTION

EXMAR is a process, supported by a set of associated services, for developing Strategic Marketing Plans.

It assists companies by:

- Guiding them through a logical marketing planning process
- Prompting and defining key data requirements
- Displaying information graphically to aid understanding of the business
- Providing advice at key stages
- Allowing 'what-if ' analyses
- Automatically outputting the report resulting from the analysis.

There are a number of techniques and methodologies incorporated in EXMAR including:

- Gap Analysis
- SWOT Analysis
- Ansoff Matrix
- Boston Box
- Directional Policy Matrix
- Market Segmentation
- Perceptual Maps
- Porter Matrix
- Objective and Strategy setting.

BENEFITS OF EXMAR

The competitive differentiation derived from EXMAR has been the subject of extensive research by Cranfield School of Management and can be summarised as follows:

- Provides a planning framework which ensures consistency across divisions and each division covers all the key aspects of the planning process
- Takes the 'number crunching' out of marketing analysis
- Gives new insights into the markets particularly through the market segmentation techniques
- Gives powerful graphical display which makes large volumes of data understandable

- Enables easy 'what-if ' iterations as strategy options are explored
- Facilitates team work and multidisciplinary involvement in the marketing planning process
- Improves marketing skills within the company
- Focuses planning on the customer
- Gives a clear vision of markets and the company's position in them
- Adds value to marketing database investment.

MAKING THE HOTEL AVAILABLE

Once a person in one of your target markets is interested in buying, how does he or she reach you? Your hotel's reservations office, the central reservation system, airline global distribution systems, corporate sales offices, and your property sales office are all parts of a distribution network. Travel agents, corporate travel managers and secretaries, meeting planners, and travellers themselves reach your hotel through this network.

Travel industry distribution channels are in chaos by virtue of the shift of travel agencies from commission to fee-for-service models, the rise of the Internet as a consumer's direct booking channel, and online thirdparty intermediaries like Expedia and Travelocity.

Increasingly, the Internet will become your key distribution channel, but in the meantime, you must manage two parallel systems, the traditional central reservation and travel agency channels and the new electronic channels. Are the rooms you want to offer available in both systems, with helpful and upto-date information? Are your prices sensible in each outlet? Making the hotel available is no longer a passive stance but an active part of your marketing.

In other industries, distribution channel revolutions have brought efficiencies that benefit both consumers and suppliers. In the travel distribution revolution now underway, the consumer has benefited, but costs to hotels—the suppliers—have skyrocketed. Since 1993, full-service hotel costs of distribution more than doubled, to $1,377 per occupied room per year in 2002.

Along with these new channels and thirdparty room merchants has come pressure on prices. In the downturn of 2001–2003, this was devastating. Price comparisons are quick and easy for the consumer. Packagers and auction sites unconsciously cultivate the destructive idea that a hotel room is a commodity, as is an airline seat. But hotels are not commodities; each differs in location, features, and benefits. A hotel team must resist the idea that a room is a room is a room, must emphasize their hotel's distinctive positioning, and must resist the urge to simply match the lowest price offered.

For the foreseeable future, both the traditional and Internet-based distribution systems will coexist and have to be managed. This raises a new question:What channels do you want to encourage, and what ones discourage? Conventional wisdom, in recent years, has been to make the hotel's inventory and rates available via as many channels as possible so as to capture from anywhere in the world the last drop of demand for arrival on a given day. Given their sharply differing costs, however, and the difficulty of managing coordinated presence in these new and overlapping channels, the time may be coming for a new strategy. One possibility is to starve undesirable channels with limited information and access while being fully open and transparent to others. Another approach might be to price differentially among channels to reflect their different costs. A large Hawaiian resort group is already doing that by explaining to consumers what comparative options and costs are. Other chains advertise a guarantee that the lowest price will be found on their own website, which is a low-cost channel for them.

Reservations, revenue, and channel management constitute the fastest-changing part of hotel management today. Channel management requires a comfort with and interest in technology and systems, and a knack for problem solving, anticipating, and risk taking.

CLOSING, CONFIRMING, AND MANAGING REVENUE

How one commits space—a room, meeting space, ballroom, or even a restaurant table— and at what price—determines the revenues and financial health of the hotel and determines the customer's expectation of value.

Revenues must be managed to optimize financial returns and customer satisfaction— that is, the customer's willingness to return. No one department controls the tools of revenue management. They are shared among salespeople, catering and banqueting managers, front desk agents, reservation agents, and so on. To manage properly requires frequent and open conversation between managers, good forecasting, skillful selling by customer contact people, and an appreciation of each week's goals and targets for the hotel. Poor forecasting, inflexible inventory policies, and conflicting approaches by different departments with whom the customer deals can undo all the best advertising, selling, and promotion.

Through the same forecasting disciplines, hotel teams manage their revenues to maximize the productivity of the hotel and assure its financial health. Revenue management tools and increasingly affordable yield systems can have a major and salutory effect on the financial health of the hotel.

Another part of revenue management is incentives for reservations upselling, conversion of callers, and average rate increases, and for front desk agents upselling. In the same way, F&B staff should be viewed as salespeople and given training on suggestive selling. Inventory policies for tier price quotes by forecast levels of occupancy, for stay-through restrictions, for same-rate substitutions and upgrading to clear demand inventory categories— all these are tools through which reservation and revenue managers optimize the RevPAR performance of the hotel.

It is in the area of revenue management that chains, especially multibrand management companies, have achieved significant advantage over independent hotels and franchisees that do not participate in cluster or regional revenue management. Decisions on pricing are still the domain of the property GM, but with a centralized expert staff collecting data and forecasting, the advice and guidance available has brought yield and RevPAR premiums to the chain member properties.

Revenue management requires attention to detail and analytic and forecasting skills; tolerance for ambiguity and comfort with change; and managing, training, leading, and motivating reservations agents. This is one of the most critical and dynamic areas of hotel management, one with which every aspiring general manager or director of sales and marketing should take pains to become familiar.

PREPARING TO DELIVER AND DELIGHT

A marketer of a product can count on the factory quality-control system to deliver a consistent product for sale. When the sale is closed, the customer takes the product away and uses it. In a service business, however, the product is human Behaviour, and the customer uses the product in the hotel. Because we are humans, both customers and employees, our interactions are never the same one time to the next. The job of the marketer is to help employees understand what the customer will want, need, and expect, and to sell employees on doing their job with enthusiasm.

In a full-service hotel, the conference services department embodies this preparing idea as its primary function. Conference service managers are the essential group business brokers between sales and operations. Conference services people can create loyal and repeat meeting planners; the job requires empathy, attention to detail, willingness to work unusual hours, action orientation, internal relationship building, and persuasiveness.

Preparing the hotel to fully satisfy and regularly make customers happy is as much a marketing task as attracting customers in the first place.What makes marketing hospitality services harder than marketing a tangible product is that for every market segment there must be two marketing programmes, one directed externally to customers, the other internally to employees.

RETAINING CUSTOMERS

The key to both financial health and market leadership is retaining a higher proportion of customers than do any of your competitors. Retain more customers than others do, and over time your costs drop—because of efficiency, lower advertising and selling costs, better forecasting—and your occupancy and rates rise. Numerous studies validate the high correlation between profit leadership and customer retention.

Frequent-stay rewards are often mistaken for retention programmes. They are not. Rewards can motivate returns only as long as the customer values the points or airline miles or whatever. But they do not create loyalty.They are valuable only insofar as they give employees the opportunity to come to recognize and satisfy the guest, and insofar as they give the marketing department information on who the customer is and where he or she is coming from.

Retaining customers takes more than just doing the job well. Guests and customers must come to know they are valued. Management must build relationships—the tie that binds regardless of a new hotel opening in the market or a hot promotional offer from across the street. Relationships are built on recognition and familiarity, on trust, and on appreciation.Thus, guest and customer retention must be a planned and creative activity that involves both sides of the relationship— the customers and the employees. It takes more than just smiling and trying hard. Among the talents and skills needed are analytic skills, curiosity, direct marketing planning, and management of data retrieval and direct marketing service providers.

MEASURING SATISFACTION AND EVALUATING PERFORMANCE

If the purpose of the business is, in part, to keep customers, does a financial statement of rate, occupancy, revenue, expense, and profit give enough information? No. Also needed is a scorecard of customer satisfaction, of how likely customers are to return or tell others about your good hotel. That scorecard is the guest satisfaction survey. Accounting statements tell of the hotel's financial health; a guest satisfaction scorecard tells of its reputation's health. The scorecard also helps management spot changes in expectations.

Customers are not the same from one visit to the next. Experience with a new hotel, perhaps even in another city, may raise a customer's standards. To measure satisfaction, one needs quantitative skills for tracking, analysing, and reporting data, and the ability to manage the logistics of repetitive distribution, collection, and processing.

The information helps management figure out what the hotel needs to be and to offer next in order to remain competitive and keep customers. Note, now, the return to the first step of the marketing process.

THE CIRCULAR MARKETING PROCESS

In other words, the marketing process isn't the straight-line, step-by-step process, a continuous circle around which management must go again and again as competition improves and as the customer segments in the market change.

Only by reviewing and renewing the marketing process will a hotel get ahead and continue to be the leading hotel in its market. This model of the marketing process applies to both the whole hotel and to any revenue or profit center within it. Use it like a checklist when thinking through improving the revenue and competitiveness of any operation.

MANAGEMENT OF THE PROPERTY'S MARKETING PROCESS

As should by now be clear, the marketing process is larger than any one individual's job. Further, no hotel can afford the myriad talents and skills that must be orchestrated to create and sustain a healthy marketing process; a single hotel is simply not a large enough business to afford having all those talents on staff.

Franchise companies and managed chains have the mass to employ a large proportion of those talents at headquarters, but even they must call on outside services in design, database management, advertising, direct marketing, and so on. But the chains' ability to invest in new tools and hire diverse talents has led branded chains, both management companies and franchisers, to collect increasing numbers of hotels under their umbrellas. The trend towards centralizing marketing functions to serve several hotels in a region, often even hotels of different brands, is accelerating, especially with the advent of Internet-driven information sharing. The advantages are the ability to integrate multiple sources of information, to hire experts that a single hotel might not be able to afford, to share the cost of sophisticated systems for forecasting, revenue management and customer relationships, and to reduce the expense of marketing to individual properties.

Independents must counter such attractions with cooperative activities and aggressive local marketing. The Internet has leveled the playing field somewhat, allowing independents to be found and reviewed by consumers and travel agents in a way not possible when GDS systems were the only means of access.

PROPERTY RESPONSIBILITY FOR ITS OWN MARKETING

To optimize performance, a property can neither abdicate its marketing to a chain or franchise group nor passively rely on location and presence to bring customers to the door. Each property, whether flagged or independent, must be responsible for creating and managing a marketing process tailored to its particular marketing situation—that is, its available customers; its inherent strengths, weaknesses, and employees; and its competitors. Each marketing situation is unique, even among cookie-cutter chain properties. Each has its own location, competitor, and customer dynamics.

So, given the wide range of talents and skills that must be orchestrated to create an effective marketing process, who is to lead it? Directors of sales and marketing cannot, for the process is much larger than the marketing department. Only the general manager can lead his or her marketing process; only he or she can integrate chain supports, operating departments, human resources, the controller, and—yes, marketing and sales.

THE GM AS LEADER OF THE MARKETING PROCESS

General managers must come to see themselves as the leader of their marketing process and be comfortable in the role. This does not mean becoming expert in all tools and disciplines; it does mean seeing the whole and appreciating when to bring in what talents, when to apply what tools, and how to judge the effectiveness of the process. It means using the marketing process as an organizing concept for creating the management team and a unified viewpoint of mission and challenge.

When a hotel is led by a general manager who sees herself or himself as leader of the marketing process, when that process is thoughtfully conceived and well executed, when all employees see themselves as joint operators/ marketers, that hotel becomes customer-centered, competitive, and a leader in its markets.

Few GMs are trained to do this. Many come to appreciate that location and flag are not enough; many intuitively pick up a smattering of sales, distribution, advertising, and customer retention. But it is the rare GM who weaves these parts into a coherent whole and thinks through the challenge of creating and leading the marketing process. As marketing continues to develop more complex tools and as marketing productivity becomes a more pressing matter, owners, universities, and chains must address this issue of how to develop GM candidates who are comfortable with and capable of leading a comprehensive marketing process.

THE MARKETING PROCESS MODEL AS A PROBLEM-SOLVING TOOL

One last word: The circular model of the marketing process is presented here mainly in terms of rooms marketing. But the model can be applied to every revenue department—to food and beverage outlets, catering, the health club, the business center, and even the laundry. The model can be used for planning, for business reviews, for presentations to lenders and owners, for troubleshooting, and as a checklist when preparing proposals for new services or facilities.

Use the model, make it part of your bag of management tools, and get your team to see their role in terms of this holistic and never-ending marketing process. If you achieve that, you will have gone far to create a customer- and competitor-focused organization, one in which employees see themselves as operators/marketers rather than just "in operations" or "in marketing" or "in HR." The few hotels that achieve and nurture a well-tuned marketing process and whose employees see themselves as integral parts of it become leaders—in market share, in customer and employee loyalty, and in financial returns to owners.

HOSPITALITY SALES CHALLENGING MANAGEMENT

MIS: THE NEW CHALLENGES

Management Information System is effective when it improves the profitability of an organisation considerably. The new and improvised MIS triggers the decision makers for proactive decision process. Technology has always been associated with quick decision-making that enables businesses to minimise risks and attain quality output. The hospitality industry is now keen to use technology to its full potential to offer the best services.

The management on the other hand has always been using software that played a key role in defining the performance of a hotel. Management Information System (MIS) has been one of them and has played a potent role in this industry. With time, it has become the most dependent tool, having gone through some changes apart from being customised to a company's needs. These changes in a way enabled the hospitality sector to view MIS as a complete networked platform upon which performance of a company can be viewed and dissected easily.

The competitive culture has crept into the Indian scenario as well, where constant perfection is vital to keep the revenue graph moving upwards. Hence, the new genre of MIS is all about division of departments, being web-based and offering single platform for all information across the network.

MIS Operational Platform

MIS is undertaken to take account of the day-to-day operations and the aberrations that need to be quickly addressed. It works on client-server architecture and facilitates maintenance of necessary data as well as generation of reports and queries. This software explicitly expresses the operation in a format that is conceived easily and enables quick understanding of various levels of operations. MIS is like a report card of an organisation but, experts feel, it needs to be more refined in order to figure out where the performance diversion is taking place.

This is a crucial aspect which a few software solution providers have incorporated in its software where customers (hotels) can directly pin-point the areas where things are going wrong, thereby bringing about immediate rectification. Today, hoteliers are even extending the use of MIS for keeping a bank of guest information and feedback using this real data into bringing about changes in service styles, menus, etc. An in-depth analysis can therefore be possible with the kind of information available through customisation, feeding the right inputs and evaluating the output generated.

Vital Factors

MIS primarily focuses on the soft skills of the operations. But there has to be a synergy of information flow within the managerial, operational and the top management of a hotel. To address this issue companies try to attain exactly that feature through their MIS module. In a hotel, there are different departments and MIS is made on a platform where work is divided and managed according to the departments.

MIS will be more beneficial and effective only when it considerably improves the profitability of an organisation. This will happen only when it triggers the decision-makers to be proactive, which in turn benefits the bottom line. Also, each hotel goes about customising the software according to their needs.

However, there are a few factors that are making MIS a more potent tool. Focusing on the hotel sector we have introduced a Drill Down feature. If Drill Down is provided on MIS (displaying up to voucher level data which is composed of the MIS) the management can get down to the minute details of any abnormal behaviour and can take instantaneous corrective actions. Further, we tend to forget the expense part in the budget set for each department where the emphasis is on sales. Identifying and then reducing these expenses or core areas of concern through MIS is a big boon for the management.

Going the Web Way

MIS operations have become more complex and challenging in this sector because of chain hotels which need to be linked to each other when it comes to finding out the performance of each unit. Therefore, MIS is presently being upgraded for Web-based operations too. Here, a central system is created - central MIS - that takes into account the reports generated by each property (through MIS) at the end of the day after the completion of night audit. This is done by uploading the day's report at the central Web server.

The idea is to reach the root of any discrepancy quickly and keep the profitability of the business at the optimum. This tabulation brings the performance of all properties on a single platform - single window information system - for evaluation and appraisals. Here one can figure out reasons for lacklustre performance through links provided for report generation. This also enables a company to study past trends to predict future trends. Also, MIS going the Web way not only secures data from possible theft but also ensure quick recovery from any part of the world for reference and future planning, which gives this software a status like never before.

DRIVERS OF CHANGE

Globalisation dictates the shape of the future; it reduces artificial barriers and creates the practicalities of business thereby necessitating alliances. The protagonist of this change is primarily the traveller himself who will dictate what alliances should take place in the future. The opportunity to seize and dominate a marketplace, distribution networks, introduce new products, technologies and international management talent, with the specter of competition looming overhead will require alliances to mould their collective fortunes. Rapid growth in the marketplace without ancillary support of third party services and a free economy to spur consolidation will spearhead strategic alliances. Understanding customers will become critical to establishing competitive advantage. The modalities in place will shift in angle in the age of intense competition and retaining customers will become as important as acquiring them in the first place.

In what ways will a traveller evolve to enter the next decade? In India, firstly, he will move up the value chain, creating a segment that has been there, seen that, and doesn't want the same experience anymore. But at the same time, a whole new mass will be drawn up the same value chain, taking the place of the first time traveller, for which the market and communications, and befitting alliances has already been developed. Research will lead to the better understanding of the target consumers and their behaviour, leading to more precise identification of customer segments and sub-segments, and basing alliances on the basis of this, which will further open opportunities for data mining, between different cross segments and verticals, targeting the same demographic group. Focused strategy and communication, targeted at the right persons and alliances with the right people will precede mass media as an option.

This opens a whole new untapped market - of the luxury, wellness and the experienced traveller, who's looking to combine convenience with comfort. Raymond Bickson, MD of Indian Hotels Company, elaborates, "The globetrotting wealthy traveller today is intensely important. One must understand the intricacies and subtleties for luxury clientele. These travellers influence global issues and look for value for money but one must not mistake them for bargain hunters." This will reveal new tourism products and marketing strategies to evolve, with worldwide trends moving towards shorter breaks and short haul travel during off-season.

The Way Forward

The two-edged sword of globalisation has not only made the world accessible but also brings the threat of being obsolete along with it. To stretch marketing rupees, groupings will develop to undertake joint marketing and research efforts. Cross-sector alliances will prove to be effective marketing formats, with access to database and direct marketing tools, with verticals looking at other segments to associate with. This will increase the retail, arts, cultures and others on a bigger framework and canvas than it is today.

Global opportunities will create more openings for health and wellness tourism and medical tourism - a market that the Indian government has already realised as a growing one. Its worldwide medical tourism campaign is proof enough. And not without reason; according to market statistics, the medical tourism market in India is touching US $300 million (with an estimated 1.5 lakh foreign patients visiting India every year) and growing into a US $2 billion business by 2012. The Leela Palaces & Resorts, according to its president, Peter J Leitgeb, is the first five-star hotel group in the world to offer special packages to travellers from the UK at its Kerala property after having tied-up with Globe Health Tours.

Meanwhile, hotels will try to differentiate their products even more, and expand through the management cum franchise route by integrating marketing synergies. Standalone properties are bound to integrate under the umbrella of a known brand. Alliances to differentiate the product, both with consumer brands and retail in addition to marketing alliances worldwide, will become a compulsion for Indian brands to compete against the giant franchises and managed brands.

While evolving into the next decade, it would be the visibility of a brand and its penetration into the marketplace that will be the first step to forge an alliance. Accordingly, a hotel will select the right fit for furthering its growth through the right associations, since one-size no longer fits all. And it would be the right partnership. This, in some cases, might lead to inorganic growth but nonetheless will be a win-win situation for all.

HOTEL SALES MARKETING: ORGANIZATION AND OPERATIONS

SALES AND MARKETING

Sales and marketing are related concepts, and each is an art and a science. Sales flow from marketing. Marketing, well stated by Lewis "is communicating to and giving target market customers what they want, when they want it, where they want it, and at a price they are willing and able to pay."The primary focus of sales is on the communication aspect of marketing. It involves direct personal selling to potential customers that you and your organization have the right product, in the right place, at the right time, and at the right price—be it a hotel, a restaurant, a casino, or contract food services.

Marketing is getting and keeping a customer, a macro approach to managing a successful business. In a broad sense, marketing is the development and delivery of a successful product, that is, the development and delivery of a satisfied customer. Hotel sales comprises finding that customer and matching his or her specific needs with the right product offering, a micro or one-on-one approach to customer satisfaction. For example, a meeting planner from Texas Instruments is planning an annual sales meeting to be held in Dallas. From a macro perspective, this planner has selected the city and is searching for full-service lodging accommodations for 200 TI sales representatives for a five-day conference. From a micro perspective, he or she visits several hotel alternatives and meets with the hotel sales representatives to find the best "fit." Various aspects of the meeting being planned are discussed including dates, rates, guest room accommodations, function room requirements, food and beverage services, and so forth. It is the job of the hotel sales manager to learn the specific needs and wants of the planner and "create" the right product, place, time, and price for a successful conference. A successful conference is what the planner is really buying, not bricks and mortar.

Thus, successful selling is understanding the real needs of the buyer, communicating how your product and service can best respond to those needs, and then delivering it. In another context, McDonald's Golden Arches markets fun, simplicity, good service, and a good price.

McDonald's sells friendly service, good value for price paid, convenient locations, and those delicious golden chicken nuggets on which many of us grew up. Ronald McDonald is an ancillary product, a public relations endeavor, which augments and supports the idea or concept of kids and why they are special.

Public relations, advertising, and special promotions often support the selling effort. Advertisements for the Ritz-Carlton Hotel Company are directed to their business traveller clientele. Such advertisements incorporate both the selling and marketing aspects of this upscale hotel chain. The company is simultaneously selling hotel rooms to busy business executives and marketing a hotel that "remembers your needs," and is hallmarked by the vision implicit in their slogan "ladies and gentlemen serving ladies and gentlemen."

A travel agent, a corporate travel manager, or a secretary, however, may have handled the actual purchase of the hotel room. Thus, the Ritz-Carlton advertisements support the sale, but they do not actually make the sale happen.

SALES AND OPERATIONS

Sales is the critical link between marketing and operations.While hospitality professionals may espouse marketing, all too often it becomes ignored in the daily hustle and bustle of operations. It is the role of sales to help bridge this gap and find ways for the key customer-contact members of the hotel to keep the promise of marketing.

Selling starts by the professional sales managers prospecting, making contacts, establishing relationships with clients, uncovering their specific needs and wants. But it doesn't end there. Sales is also the host or hostess greeting restaurant patrons. Sales is the front desk clerk welcoming a guest at the local Holiday Inn or at the Waldorf-Astoria in New York City. Sales is the housekeeping staff delivering the extra set of towels requested by a guest. Sales is the sommelier in a gourmet restaurant recommending wines to complement an entrée choice. Sales is the front office cashier saying, "Thank you for staying with us. We hope you enjoyed your stay." It is amazing how a simple thank-you can express appreciation for a customer's patronage and bring them back.

All client-contact personnel of a hospitality organization perform personal selling either consciously or unconsciously. This includes staff who does not regularly have guest contact, such as the credit manager. One of the authors nearly lost a $100,000 annual account when a poorly trained credit manager called the client to collect a payment that had not yet been billed. A well-trained and motivated employee who understands how a hotel works is key to successful selling. This is accomplished through the hiring and training process, and although the many facets of human resources are beyond the scope of this stage, its importance to guest satisfaction cannot be overstated.

In this particular context, however, the hotel's human resources department can perform services on behalf of the sales department by recruiting sales associates who understand the nature of the hotel industry and its place in the broader category of the services segment of business. Services are different from products and require specialized knowledge and training to be competitive.

Because hospitality is very much a part of the services industry, it is useful to understand how services differ from products. Those characteristics that are unique to the services industry product include perishability, simultaneity, heterogeneity, and intangibility.

Perishability refers to the short shelf life of the hospitality product. If it is not sold today, the potential revenue from the sales of that product is gone. A hotel room has a 24- hour shelf life. A restaurant seat has a twohour shelf life. Manufactured goods have a much longer period of durability. If a television set is not sold today, it can be sold tomorrow or next week. The potential revenue from the sale of that product is not lost. But a Tuesday-night hotel room cannot be resold on Wednesday.Tuesday has come and gone. If the hotel guest room goes unsold Tuesday, the potential revenue lost from that vacant room cannot be recouped.

Simultaneity means that production and consumption occur at the same time. How can you produce a guest experience without the guest? Our customers, in a sense, are part of the assembly line.They need to be present for final production of the product offering.A vacant guest room produces nothing. Yes, the carpeting is installed; the bed is made, the bathroom plumbing works. But it all just exists until a guest arrives to use it. Simultaneous production and consumption is a unique challenge for successful operations in hospitality management.

The guest needs to be present, because many of the facets of the service involve performances by hotel staff. A related service characteristic in hospitality is *heterogeneity*. Heterogeneity refers to the variability of service delivery. Guest service agents have their moods. Customers have their moods. All have personalities of varying shapes and sizes. Hospitality is a very peopleoriented business. Service personnel change from shift to shift, typically on an 8-hour schedule. Though operational manuals exist in most hospitality establishments, rarely are policies and procedures followed in an exact manner. Guests' "personalities," too, can change throughout their stay, and it may have nothing to do with how they were treated by service personnel. Dealing with heterogeneity in service operations is dealing with reality.

Mistakes will happen. But more importantly, mistakes can be addressed. Often a simple apology can win back a customer regardless of who was at fault when a mistake happens. *Intangibility* is a fourth major characteristic of service businesses. Some consider it the most important component to recognize. Intangibility refers to the highly intangible nature of the service product offering. Intangibility is a feeling; it is having a sense about something that one cannot fully articulate.

The intangible nature of the service product cannot be prejudged. Consumers cannot really see, touch, smell, hear, or taste a service product prior to consumption. They can only anticipate. One can test-drive a car before an automobile purchase is made to see what it feels like to drive. But a hospitality customer cannot test-drive a hotel weekend package or a restaurant meal prior to consumption. The intangibility aspect of hospitality emphasizes that service delivery is critical to customer satisfaction.

Most customers have an idea of what to expect. But, in the end, they are really not sure of what they are buying until the hospitality experience actually takes place. Finally, after the service has been consumed, the guest has only the memory of the performance. The foregoing unique characteristics represent the foundational challenge to the hotel's sales staff: they must find a way to promise performance and experience in such a way that the hotel's operations departments can deliver on the promise. If the essence of marketing is finding and keeping a customer, then the sales promise is fundamental to that effort. Operations' most important role is the keeping of that promise to the customer— having that customer walk away with a positive and memorable experience and want to return again.

MANAGEMENT OF THE SALES PROCESS

Sales management is effectively directing the personal selling efforts of a hospitality establishment. It involves managing the sales process from both an individual and team perspective. In other words, sales management addresses the logistics of sales solicitation and the development of sales account executives to enhance their sales productivity.

Sales account executives need to manage their day-to-day activity, sales teams need to coordinate their efforts, and customers need to feel that they are working with a professional and well-managed organization.

There are several components to hospitality sales management. These include sales organization, sales account management, recruitment, training and development, goal setting, and performance appraisals. Sales organization refers to departmental and individual organizational issues and inventory management. The following part focuses on the sales organization aspect of hospitality sales management.

Sales Organization

Sales organization can be viewed from three perspectives. These include departmental organization, individual planning of sales activity, and inventory management. A sales department needs to be organized, and sales managers within that organizational setup need to coordinate their efforts. Sales managers need to plan or organize their individual activities on a daily, weekly, and monthly basis.

Allocating the sale of inventory to various customer segments needs to be managed, as well. These are important issues in hospitality sales management.

Departmental Organization

Organizing a sales department means determining who is going to do what. Sales solicitation needs to take place, administrative tasks need to be completed, and managerial decisions need to be made on a regular basis. In medium- to large-size hospitality establishments, a director of sales and/or a director of marketing coordinates these efforts. In smaller operations, it is not unusual to have one individual responsible for all of the above. For most bed and breakfast operations in the United States and Canada and the small boutique hotels in Europe, for example, the owner and/or manager of the establishment typically handle sales activities.

Sales organizational setup for a midsize urban hotel targeting business clientele. The sales managers in this example are organized by target market and by geographic territory. Sales manager 1 is responsible for corporate accounts located in the immediate downtown and surrounding area. Sales manager 2 is responsible for national corporate accounts. This refers to companies based in other areas that conduct business or have the potential to conduct business at the hotel. Both of these sales managers solicit group and transient business from their account base

Sales manager 3 targets meetings and convention business from national association accounts.This business may include executive board meetings, committee meetings, regional conferences, and annual conventions.

In this example, once group events have been booked they are turned over to the conference services department for service delivery. Both the sales managers and director of conference services report to the director of sales and marketing. The sales team meets weekly to discuss issues pertinent to achieving the department's sales objectives.

Weekly sales meetings are very much a part of a sales department's organizational structure, be it a sales force of two or twelve sales account executives. They are critical for effective communication within the department.

At these meetings, each team member highlights his or her weekly activity with regard to new prospects uncovered, tentative bookings, verbal definites, cancellations, etc. (Verbal definites are bookings where clients have verbally committed their meeting or function to the facility but a signed contract is not yet in hand.) In other words, sales managers share with each other progress reports on various accounts they are currently working on. Thus, each team member gets an upto- date informal report on the status of all current sales activity.

For example, one sales manager may be working on a tentative booking but considers it weak because of strong competition for this particular account. Call this Group A. Another sales manager may have a new prospect with similar space requirements interested in the same dates. Call this Group B. Assume, however, that the property has the capability of booking only Group A or Group B over the same dates because of space limitations.

When these types of issues surface at sales meetings discussion will occur raising the following types of questions:

- What is the likelihood that either group will eventually book its business at the property?
- What is the estimated profitability and/or contribution margin for each group?
- Is either group a regular client?
- What is the likelihood of repeat business from either group? In other words, what is the long-term profitability for each?
- Can either group consider alternative dates? What would incite them to move dates?
- Do convention history reports match their current space allocation requests?

These are just a sampling of questions that need to be raised and answered. It is a never-ending process in hospitality sales management to search for the best fit for both the buyer and seller.

The organization of sales management is the process of directing the personal selling efforts of a hospitality establishment. It involves effectively managing the sales process from both an individual and team perspective.

Sales or account managers need to manage their day-to-day activity; sales teams need to coordinate their efforts. Sales account management involves developing, maintaining, and enhancing customer relationships. Sales managers develop expertise for specific market segments, industry segments, and/or customer accounts, and common traits among successful sales account executives include self-confidence, high energy, empathy, enthusiasm, and a sense of self-worth.

This stage introduces the foundation for hospitality sales and marketing. First and foremost, sales flow from marketing. If management doesn't have a marketing mindset, then sales efforts will be all for naught.

Marketing is giving the targeted customers what they want, when they want it, where they want it, at a price they are willing and able to pay. Sales is direct communication with potential customers letting them know we have what they want. In many respects, sales is the link between marketing and operations. Operations is essentially the delivery component of marketing and the final determination of a happy customer. Marketing begins, transcends, and ends with the consumer. Sales makes sure it happens.

CONSUMER DECISION RULES AND IMPLICATIONS FOR HOTEL CHOICE

Consumers' choices are influenced by the goals they attempt to achieve. Once a person has recognized a need, such as the need for accommodation when traveling for business or pleasure, he or she engages in an information search to identify alternatives from which to choose. Understanding how consumers evaluate competing alternatives in their purchase decision processes enables marketers in the hospitality industry to design better advertising and promotional campaigns leading to a more favourable evaluation of their offerings in travellers' eyes.This is an important step in increasing the likelihood that consumers will choose their offering as opposed to that of competitors.

Given that most travellers' destinations offer several hotels, how do people choose among them? The answer to this question lies, in part, in research on consumers' attitudes and their relation to purchase intentions and subsequent purchase Behaviour. This stage describes several methods consumers may use to make choices based on the evaluation of identified alternatives.

Attitude is the tendency to respond in a consistently favourable or unfavourable manner towards a target. Important to marketers is that, if measured accurately, attitudes are predictive of Behavioural intentions and relatively stable over time.

Simply put, consumers generally form intentions to choose a hotel brand towards which they hold positive attitudes. Behavioural intentions, however, do not always translate into corresponding Behaviour. For example, although some consumers have preferences and therefore form intentions to stay at Fairfield Inn when traveling across the country, they might end up choosing other forms of accommodation from time to time.Why would they act inconsistently with their intentions?

Traveling with friends who have different attitudes and preferences, temporary price reductions of competitors, or the fact that a Fairfield Inn is not readily available in a specific area might be reasons for inconsistencies between Behavioural intentions to stay at a Fairfield Inn and actual choice Behaviour.

Despite situational factors sometimes influencing travellers' choices, attitudes are ultimately useful in predicting actual Behaviour; changing or strengthening the basis of consumer attitudes may therefore increase the likelihood of consumers engaging in desired Behaviours. In order to change attitudes and subsequent related Behaviour, marketers must understand a few basic decision rules associated with consumer attitudes. We introduce decision rules likely to be implemented by different segments of consumers under varying market conditions.

DECISION RULES

Decision rules are strategies consumers use to choose among alternatives. Several factors can influence what decision rule consumers ultimately apply in a specific situation. Typically, the more important and less frequent a purchase decision is, the more time and effort consumers are willing to expend making that decision. Choosing a resort at which to spend a twenty-fifth wedding anniversary, for example, is a decision most consumers face only once and therefore are likely to take a relatively long time to make, and they are likely to be careful and thorough in evaluating alternatives.

On the other hand, a salesperson traveling frequently in a familiar territory likely chooses a hotel using a routine process where far less time and consideration are given to alternatives. Further, brand-loyal customers might choose to stay with the same hotel chain whenever possible, thereby avoiding a situation where they are forced to choose among alternatives. In general, the stronger a consumer is motivated to search and the greater the risk associated with a choice, the greater the complexity of the decision rule he or she implements.

Another important characteristic of modeling decisions is the fact that people often do not attempt to optimize choice. If a person's goal is optimal choice, considerably more time and effort is typically required to identify and evaluate alternatives.

Therefore, consumers often choose a satisfactory alternative in order to save time and effort. The use of decision rules in these instances enables people to take shortcuts in making decisions in the face of the apparently unlimited or overwhelming amounts of information available regarding all possible alternatives. Consumers usually work with a consideration set so they do not have to work as hard cognitively when required to make a decision in a given product category. They then make a final decision from this reduced set of alternatives.

Such decision rules are referred to as *heuristics* or rules of thumb. Employing heuristics, people save time and limit complex information processing while still making reasonable or satisfactory choices based on the few brand attributes or characteristics most important to them at the time of choice. In the context of hotel choice, brand attributes are things like location, room rates, and availability of a swimming pool, restaurant, and so forth.

Although the number of consumer decision rules is almost infinite and likely varies by consumer, basic categories and a few specific examples serve as useful tools in modeling and predicting traveller decisions.

Two general categories of decision rules are:

1. Compensatory and
2. Noncompensatory.

Compensatory Decision Rules

Compensatory decision rules model consumers as deriving an overall brand evaluation such that alternatives performing poorly on one attribute can *compensate* for their respective shortcomings by positive evaluations of other attributes.

For example, a high-priced hotel might not be perceived positively on the dimension of room rates by some travellers; however, these same travellers might be willing to spend more money knowing they will receive better service or that the hotel is conveniently located—that is, in this example, service and location compensate for the perceived disadvantage of high room rates. The multi-attribute attitude model described in the next part is perhaps the most popular compensatory decision rule.

MARKETING IMPLICATIONS

Once consumer evaluations of salient attributes are determined and their beliefs regarding a hotel brand's offerings are known, managers can use this information to improve their hotel's competitive positioning in the market. The goal of any marketing strategy is to increase positive attitude towards the offering or to encourage the use of certain decision rules, thereby increasing the likelihood of being chosen by consumers.

When consumers use a compensatory decision rule, the overall attitude towards a hotel is determined by the sum of the products of evaluations multiplied by beliefs regarding salient attributes associated with the offering. Consequently, travellers' overall attitudes towards a hotel can be rendered more positive by strategies targeted at increasing the evaluation of an attribute in consumers' decision making, or by changing consumers' beliefs about a hotel's offerings.

Travellers' attribute evaluations can be influenced by stressing the attribute in advertising. This strategy of influencing attribute evaluations is effective in attitude change and also relatively easy to pursue. It is, however, not a strategy always recommended for changing consumers' attitudes when they are using a compensatory model. The potential problem associated with this approach is that attribute evaluations are constant across brands in a consideration set. Travellers evaluating importance of the availability of an indoor pool is the same for all hotel brands, E, F, G, and H. If Hotel H were successful in a marketing message in increasing the evaluation of an indoor pool with a segment of consumers, say to a rating of _3, it would increase consumers' overall attitude towards its brand. At the same time, however, consumers' overall evaluation of Hotel G would increase by the same amount, as both brands do not differ with respect to consumers' beliefs about their having a great indoor pool. In the end, the attempt to increase consumers' overall attitude towards Hotel H would also benefit some of its competitors.

Thus, sometimes a more effective strategy for improving consumers' overall attitude towards a hotel's offerings is to improve consumers' brand-specific belief ratings. For example, Hotel F could strive to improve consumer belief that it offers a pleasant indoor pool by providing a picture of the pool on its website, or by stressing the availability of the indoor pool in advertisements. While consumer brand-specific beliefs are then likely to increase, Hotel F's competitors will not benefit from its strategy, and Hotel F thereby improves its competitive position.

Assuming that Hotel E cannot do anything to increase consumers' belief that it is not located in proximity of a skiing area, a strategy it may employ to increase consumers' overall attitude towards the property is to add a salient attribute to the set of attributes consumers consider when making hotel choices. For example, Hotel E could provide free accommodation for children staying with their parents. It is likely that parents would consider this option important when choosing a hotel. As long as other competitors do not offer this service, Hotel E enjoys some advantage in the choices made by its target market. It is essential that when adding a new attribute, marketers consider the following: First, the attribute added must be important enough to the hotel's target market to be included in consumers' subsequent decision making. Second, the belief that a particular hotel possesses this attribute must be stronger than the belief that any of its competitors do.

This marketing strategy, often referred to as a *strategy of differentiation,* is likely to be successful when these conditions are met. Differentiation, however, is unlikely to be sustainable— that is, over time, competitors identify what added attributes successfully attract customers and copy them, thereby creating consumer belief regarding their own properties. Thus, the hotel that introduced the new salient attribute often can expect to lose its differential advantage over time unless it maintains a unique characteristic like a special location or a fabulous chef in the kitchen.

Increasing belief strength for a hotel's attributes is not always a successful strategy, assuming a compensatory model is being used. For example, consumers may find it relatively unimportant whether the hotel offers low room rates or not. The importance rating for low room rates is _2—that is, consumers in this particular target segment evaluate low room rates negatively, perhaps because they associate low rates with low quality or with small, underfurnished rooms. In this case, stressing that a particular hotel offers low rates, thereby increasing the strength of consumers' beliefs, may adversely affect consumers' overall evaluation of a property. If you compare Hotels F and H, you will see that the strong belief that Hotel H offers low rates negatively affects its overall evaluation. Hotel F, on the other hand, benefits from consumers not being aware of low rates. It is important to note that importance weights associated with attributes vary across market segments.

For example, while business travellers on corporate expense accounts or consumers on a once-in-a-lifetime vacation, such as a honeymoon, may attach less importance to low rates, more price-sensitive market segments usually weigh low rates more heavily in their hotel choice. It is therefore important for marketers to carefully define the targeted market segment prior to conducting their research and applying evaluation weights and beliefs to similarly disposed consumers.

In general, it is crucial to find out what attributes targeted consumers feel are most salient to their decisions and, in response, increase performance regarding these attributes and commensurately inform market segments of this stronger position. The resultant positive attitude towards the offering should then increase the likelihood of the hotel being chosen by travellers using a compensatory decision-making model.

Alternatively, as a strategic move, particularly for special niche properties, marketers may want to encourage consumers to abandon the linear compensatory model. Niche market segments may exist or may be created through marketing communications; these target markets might be better served by hotels focusing on one or more of the noncompensatory decision rules presented.

For example, a segment of highly price-sensitive customers predominantly using a lexicographic decision rule with low rates as the most important attribute may constitute the primary target market for a property. In this case, travellers can be targeted by offering low prices and/or frequentstay loyalty programmes. At the same time, services deemed unnecessary or unimportant by this customer segment can be eliminated or minimized.

The fact that some customer segments expect a minimal level of performance on several attributes when they use an elimination-by-aspect or conjunctive decision rule, however, implies that focusing performance and/ or marketing on a single attribute may be inadequate for some segments of travellers. A hotel would then benefit from creating a level of "at least acceptable" attributes in addition to providing stronger packages of the same attributes offered by competitors targeting the same market segment.

Overall, knowing how consumers make decisions should help hotel managers to design better properties, packages, and services, and help them market those offerings to their respective target segment, thereby improving competitive position.

MARKET MAPPING AND SEGMENTATION WORKSHOP

The objective of the workshop is to produce a structure for the defined market, which clearly identifies the different requirements that customers look to be satisfied. These different requirements can then be used to develop the alternative strategies that need to be implemented to better access the segments and tune the product offers to suit the customer requirements. It should be noted that most organisations do not have access to the information to produce a definitive segmentation structure that is 100% accurate. However most organisations do have sufficient internal knowledge to produce something that is 'roughly right' and a reasonable starting point. Where this is not the case, the process makes it very clear where the information holes are and the importance of that information. If research is required, the process ensures a rigorous and very targeted brief can be produced.

Market Definition

A market is defined in terms of a need that can be satisfied by the products or services customers' view as alternatives. Once this is clear, the boundaries for the segmentation project can be set.

Market Mapping

A market map defines the distribution and value chain between supplier and final user, which takes into account the various buying mechanisms found in a market, including the part played by 'influencers'.

Market maps help focus attention on key decision makers within a market, and identify key target market segments within a market segmentation project. Market channels and the key players within channels can be easily identified with the help of a graphic presentation of a market. A market map can help deliver key customer and consumer insights, and ensures full awareness of the the total market place.

Market Segmentation

Market segmentation is a concept in economics and marketing. A market segment is a sub-set of a market made up of people or organizations with one or more characteristics that cause them to demand similar product and/or services based on qualities of those products such as price or function. A true market segment meets all of the following criteria: it is distinct from other segments, it is homogeneous within the segment; it responds similarly to a market stimulus, and it can be reached by a market intervention. The term is also used when consumers with identical product and/or service needs are divided up into groups so they can be charged different amounts for the services.

The people in a given segment are supposed to be similar in terms of criteria by which they are segmented and different from other segments in terms of these criteria. These can be broadly viewed as 'positive' and 'negative' applications of the same idea, splitting up the market into smaller groups.

Examples:

- Gender
- Price
- Interests
- Location
- Religion
- Income
- Size of Household

While there may be theoretically 'ideal' market segments, in reality every organization engaged in a market will develop different ways of imagining market segments, and create Product differentiation strategies to exploit these segments. The market segmentation and corresponding product differentiation strategy can give a firm a temporary commercial advantage.

Bases for Segmenting Consumer Markets

- Geographic segmentation
- Demographic segmentation
- Psychographic segmentation
- Behavioural segmentation

Geographic Segmentation

The market is segmented just as to geographic criteria- nations, states, regions, counties, cities, neigborhoods, or zip codes. Geo-cluster approach combines demographic data with geographic data to create a more accurate profile of specific

Psychographic Segmentation

Psychographics is the science of using psychology and demographics to better understand consumers.Psychographic segmentation: consumer are divided just as to their lifestyle, personality, values. People within the same demographic group can exhibit very different psychographic profiles.

"Positive" Market Segmentation

Market segmenting is dividing the market into groups of individual markets with similar wants or needs that a company divides into distinct groups which have distinct needs, wants, Behaviour or which might want different products and services.

Broadly, markets can be divided just as to a number of general criteria, such as by industry or public versus private. Although industrial market segmentation is quite different from consumer market segmentation, both have similar objectives. All of these methods of segmentation are merely proxies for true segments, which don't always fit into convenient demographic boundaries.

Consumer-based market segmentation can be performed on a *product specific* basis, to provide a close match between specific products and individuals. However, a number of generic market segment systems also exist, *e.g.* the system provides a broad segmentation of the population of the United States based on the statistical analysis of household and geodemographic data.

The process of segmentation is distinct from positioning. The overall intent is to identify groups of similar customers and potential customers; to prioritize the groups to address; to understand their Behaviour; and to respond with appropriate marketing strategies that satisfy the different preferences of each chosen segment. Revenues are thus improved.

Improved segmentation can lead to significantly improved marketing effectiveness. Distinct segments can have different industry structures and thus have higher or lower attractiveness

Once a market segment has been identified, and targeted, the segment is then subject to positioning. Positioning involves ascertaining how a product or a company is perceived in the minds of consumers.

This part of the segmentation process consists of drawing up a perceptual map, which highlights rival goods within one's industry just as to perceived quality and price. After the perceptual map has been devised, a firm would consider the marketing communications mix best suited to the product in question.

Behavioural Segmentation

In Behavioural segmentation, consumers are divided into groups just as to their knowledge of, attitude towards, use of or response to a product.

- *Occasions*: Segmentation just as to occasions.we segment the market just as to the occasions.
- *Benefits*: Segmentations just as to benefits sought by the consumer.
- Users status: nonusers, ex-users, first time users, etc.

Using Segmentation in Customer Retention

The basic approach to retention-based segmentation is that a company tags each of its active customers with 3 values:

1. *Tag No.1*: Is this customer at high risk of canceling the company's service? One of the most common indicators of high-risk customers is a drop off in usage of the company's service. For example, in the credit card industry this could be signaled through a customer's decline in spending on his or her card.
2. *Tag No.2*: Is this customer worth retaining? This determination boils down to whether the post-retention profit generated from the customer is predicted to be greater than the cost incurred to retain the customer. Managing Customers as Investments.
3. *Tag No.3*: What retention tactics should be used to retain this

customer? For customers who are deemed "save-worthy", it's essential for the company to know which save tactics are most likely to be successful. Tactics commonly used range from providing "special" customer discounts to sending customers communications that reinforce the value proposition of the given service.

Process for Tagging Customers

The basic approach to tagging customers is to utilize historical retention data to make predictions about active customers regarding:

- Whether they are at high risk of canceling their service
- Whether they are profitable to retain
- What retention tactics are likely to be most effective

The idea is to match up active customers with customers from historic retention data who share similar attributes. Using the theory that "birds of a feather flock together", the approach is based on the assumption that active customers will have similar retention outcomes as those of their comparable predecessor.

Niche Marketing

A niche is a more narrowly defined customer group who seek a distinct set of benefits. Ýdentified by dividing a segment into subsegments,distinct and unique set of needs,requires speciallization, and is not likely to attract too many competitors.

Price Discrimination

Where a monopoly exists, the price of a product is likely to be higher than in a competitive market and the quantity sold less, generating monopoly profits for the seller. These profits can be increased further if the market can be segmented with different prices charged to different segments charging higher prices to those segments willing and able to pay more and charging less to those whose demand is price elastic.

The price discriminator might need to create rate fences that will prevent members of a higher price segment from purchasing at the prices available to members of a lower price segment. This Behaviour is rational on the part of the monopolist, but is often seen by competition authorities as an abuse of a monopoly position, whether or not the monopoly itself is sanctioned. Examples of this exist in the transport industry where business class customers who can afford to pay may be charged prices many times higher than economy class customers for essentially the same service.

Ansoff Matrix

To portray alternative corporate growth strategies, Igor Ansoff presented a matrix that focused on the firm's present and potential products and markets. By considering ways to grow via existing products and new products, and in existing markets and new markets, there are four possible product-market combinations. Ansoff's matrix is shown below:

Table. Ansoff Matrix

	Existing Products	**New Products**
Existing Markets	Market Penetration	Product Development
New Markets	Market Development	Diversification

Ansoff's matrix provides four different growth strategies:

1. Market Penetration - the firm seeks to achieve growth with existing products in their current market segments, aiming to increase its market share.
2. Market Development - the firm seeks growth by targeting its existing products to new market segments.
3. Product Development - the firms develops new products targeted to its existing market segments.
4. Diversification - the firm grows by diversifying into new businesses by developing new products for new markets.

Selecting a Product-Market Growth Strategy

The market penetration strategy is the least risky since it leverages many of the firm's existing resources and capabilities. In a growing market, simply maintaining market share will result in growth, and there may exist opportunities to increase market share if competitors reach capacity limits. However, market penetration has limits, and once the market approaches saturation another strategy must be pursued if the firm is to continue to grow.

Market development options include the pursuit of additional market segments or geographical regions. The development of new markets for the product may be a good strategy if the firm's core competencies are related more to the specific product than to its experience with a specific market segment. Because the firm is expanding into a new market, a market development strategy typically has more risk than a market penetration strategy.

A product development strategy may be appropriate if the firm's strengths are related to its specific customers rather than to the specific product itself. In this situation, it can leverage its strengths by developing a new product targeted to its existing customers. Similar to the case of new market development, new product development carries more risk than simply attempting to increase market share.

Diversification is the most risky of the four growth strategies since it requires both product and market development and may be outside the core competencies of the firm. In fact, this quadrant of the matrix has been referred to by some as the "suicide cell". However, diversification may be a reasonable choice if the high risk is compensated by the chance of a high rate of return. Other advantages of diversification include the potential to gain a foothold in an attractive industry and the reduction of overall business portfolio risk.

DECISION MAKING IN BUSINESS AND MANAGEMENT

In general, business and management systems should be set up to allow decision making at the lowest possible level.

Several decision making models for business include:

- SWOT Analysis - Evaluation by the decision making individual or organization of Strengths, Weaknesses, Opportunities and Threats with respect to desired end state or objective.
- Analytic Hierarchy Process - procedure for multi-level goal hierarchy
- Buyer decision processes - transaction before, during, and after a purchase
- Complex systems - common behavioural and structural features that can be modelled
- Corporate finance:
  - The investment decision
  - The financing decision
  - The dividend decision
  - working capital management decisions
- Cost-benefit analysis - process of weighing the total expected costs vs. the total expected benefits
- Decision trees
  - Programme Evaluation and Review Technique (PERT)
  - critical path analysis
  - critical chain analysis
- Force field analysis - analizing forces that either drive or hinder movement toward a goal
- Grid Analysis - analysis done by compairing the weighted averages of ranked criteria to options. A way of comparing both objective and subjective data.
- Kepner tregoe - A Management Consultancy firm specialising in rational Problem Solving and Decision Making processes
- Linear programming - optimization problems in which the objective function and the constraints are all linear
- Min-max criterion
- Model (economics)- theoretical construct of economic processes of variables and their relationships
- Monte Carlo method - class of computational algorithms for simulating systems
- Morphological analysis - all possible solutions to a multi-dimensional problem complex

- Optimization
  - constrained optimization
- Paired Comparison Analysis - paired choice analysis
- Pareto Analysis - selection of a limited of number of tasks that produce significant overall effect
- Scenario analysis - process of analyzing possible future events
- Six Thinking Hats - symbolic process for parallel thinking
- Strategic planning process - applying the objectives, SWOTs, strategies, programmes process
- Ubiquitous command and control is a concept for dynamic decision making based on "agreement between an individual and the world", and "agreements between individuals"

Decision-makers and Influencers

In the context of industrial goods marketing, there is much theory, and even more opinion, expressed about how the various 'decision-makers' and 'influencers' (those who can only influence, not decide, the final decision) interact. Decisions are frequently taken by groups, rather than individuals, and the official buyer often does not have authority to take the decision.

Miller & Heiman, for example, offered a more complex view of industrial buying decisions (particularly in the area of 'complex sales' of capital equipment). They see three levels of decision making:

'Economic buying influence' - the decision-maker who can authorize the necessary funds for purchase

'User buying influences' - the people in the buying company who will use the product and will specify what they want to purchase

'Technical buying influence' - the `experts' (including, typically, the buying department) who can veto the purchase on technical grounds

Webster and Wind, in a similar vein, identify six roles within the 'buying centre':

'Users' - who will actually use the product or service

'Influencers' - particularly technical personnel

'Deciders' - the actual decision-makers

'Approvers' - who formally authorize the decision

'Buyers' - the department with formal authority

'Gatekeepers' - those who have the power to stop the sellers reaching other members of the `buying centre'

Some have said that true consensus involves "meeting everyone's needs." Consensus decision-making is intended to deemphasize the role of factions or parties and promote the expression of individual voices. The method also increases the likelihood of unforeseen or creative solutions by juxtaposing dissimilar ideas. Because it seeks to minimize objection, it is popular with voluntary organizations, wherein decisions are more likely to be carried out when they are most widely approved. Consensus methods are desirable when enforcement of the decision is unfeasible, such that every participant will be required to act on the decision independently.

Consensus decision-making is also found in groups where participants have different areas of expertise but are working toward a common goal. Examples of this include high technology project design teams which must integrate the opinions of people with different areas of expertise.

Minority views must be considered to a greater degree than in circumstances where a majority can take the action and enforce the decision without any further consultation with the minority voters. It is often thought that consensus can require more time and effort to achieve. Thus some groups may reserve consensus decision methods for particularly complex, risky or important decisions. However, there are many examples of groups who employ consensus decision-making in ways that enable them to both consider minority views and make decisions in a timely and efficient manner. Consensus decision making could result in group polarization, where team members make more extreme decisions compared to their prior individual positions. This could potentially have beneficial effects on team decisions (enhance commitment and conviction), or detrimental effects (escalate towards greater risk or greater conservative behaviours). Use of computer-mediated communication could further heighten the effects of group polarization.

Rather than simply list known alternatives, debate for a short time, vote, and then accept or reject by some percentage of majority (ex. over 50%, over 2/3), a consensus decision-making process involves identifying and addressing concerns, generating new alternatives, combining elements of multiple alternatives and checking that people understand a proposal or an argument.

This empowers minorities, those with objections that are hard to state quickly, and those who are less skilled in debate. Therefore, consensus decision-making can be seen as a form of grassroots democracy.

Egalitarian groups that seek to reduce the amount of power delegated to leaders, chairpersons or agenda setters often use consensus methods. Such methods can reduce the amount of harm or loss imposed on minorities (or individuals) by a majority. Consensus methods may be appropriate when personal (or emotional) risk to members is high, trust is low, and time is available for a prolonged discussion. Consensus may be used to remedy patterns of decision-making based on habit, subservience or carelessness.

Alternatively, it can be argued that in a situation of abundant trust - in which each party assumes that any objections or reservations regarding a proposal are meaningful - consensus methods may not only be appropriate, but necessary.

Like any group decision-making, consensus decision-making can disempower those not present in the debating forum, as they cannot expect to have input on the new measures that are proposed (whereas they might have had the opportunity for input into the known alternatives prior to the debate). Accordingly, most systems of consensus decision-making place a premium on participation.

Three key issues tend to define a particular type of consensus decision-making:

1. Degree of agreement or unanimity required;
2. Timing of presentation including division of time among urgent versus important matters;
3. Follow-up to action including the monitoring that arises from dissent, and from claims of majority proponents whose preferred course of action is being taken over minority objections.

There is also the question of facilitation or process leadership, which is handled

A healthy consensus decision-making process usually encourages and outs dissent early, maximizing the chance of accommodating the views of all minorities. It also often assigns a role to the dissenter, e.g. the Vatican used to assign the role of Promotor Fidei to a specific priest who argued against beatification of a saint, to ensure the case 'against' remains well represented. After the decision, the dissenting minority may have some role to play in monitoring the decision. In the Supreme Court of the United States, both the majority opinion and minority opinion are equally well documented, as the legal grounds for agreeing with either may exist in some court in the future.

Many groups consider unanimous decisions a sign of agreement, solidarity, and unity. However, there is evidence that unanimous decisions may be a sign of coercion, fear, undue persuasive power or eloquence, inability to comprehend alternatives, or plain impatience with the process of debate. (For example, elections in which 99% or 100% of the voters support the candidate are generally discredited.) When there are concerns about these aspects of unanimity, various alternatives can be pursued. These include the following:

- Unanimity minus one (or U-1), requires all delegates but one to support the decision. The individual dissenter cannot block the decision although they may be able to prolong debate (e.g. via a filibuster). The dissenter may be the ongoing monitor of the implications of the decision, and their opinion of the outcome of the decision may be solicited at some future time. Betting markets in particular rely on the input of such lone dissenters. A lone bettor against the odds profits when his or her prediction of the outcomes proves to be better than that of the majority. This disciplines the market's odds.
- Unanimity minus two (or U-2), does not permit two individual delegates to block a decision, but tends to curtail debate with a lone dissenter more quickly. Dissenting pairs can present alternate views of what is wrong with the decision under consideration. By focusing

on a pair of dissenters, and allocating less time to lone wolves or 'consensus thugs', a U-2 system tends to form stronger bonds among those who find themselves "alone on an island" with each other. Pairs of delegates can be empowered to find the common ground that will enable them to convince a third, decision-blocking, voter to join them. If the pair are unable to convince a third party to join them within a set time, their arguments are deemed to be unconvincing, immature or self-interested. If two people dissent against some common measure, it is more likely that the discussion between them can be extended to third parties easily, since it is already verbalized and illustrated. Western European court systems recognize this by strongly encouraging criminal defendants or civil plaintiffs to get an attorney's aid, so that their case can be fully heard out long before the decision.

- Unanimity minus three, (or U-3), and other such systems recognize the ability of three or more delegates to actively block a decision. However, there is controversy over whether a small group of dissenters, (e.g., militants or terrorists), is morally different from a large minority, (e.g., an opposition party with support of double-digit percentages of the population). Accordingly U-3 and lesser degrees of unanimity are usually lumped in with statistical measures of agreement, such as: 80%, mean plus one sigma, two-thirds, or greater than half (majority) levels of agreement. Such measures do not fit within the definition of consensus given at the beginning of this article.
- The IETF working group process has a tradition of "rough consensus", where there is no specific rule for "how much is enough", but it is left to the judgment of the working group chair. This makes it harder for a small number of disruptors to block a decision, but puts a lot of responsibility on the chair, and has frequently led to angry debates about whether rough consensus has in fact been correctly identified.

The quality of alternatives considered is, all else being equal, proportional to the amount of time spent gathering and comparing and combining them. The term deliberative democracy reflects the deliberation that underlies all good consensus decision-making. Ralph Nader and others have advocated deliberative measures to extend the time for "sober second thought."

A fictional example of deliberative democracy is the Entmoot from J. R. R. Tolkien's novel The Lord of the Rings. The Ents, who are large ancient living intelligent trees, spend days discussing the issue of whether to go to war, in their verbose and many-syllabled language. This is an example of a decision for which the stakes were high, the individual risk also high, and coercive force difficult or lacking; therefore suited to consensus methods.

Timeliness of decisions is an important issue. In some cases, a wrong decision taken in time can be better than a good decision taken later.

Key responsibilities of facilitators of any decision making process, but particularly in consensus decision-making, include:

- Establishing measures to place items on the agenda, or deny them time on the agenda.
- Setting deadlines for changes to the agenda (e.g. can the agenda itself be changed during the meeting?).
- Agenda forming and presentation of issues at the right time, when there is sufficient time for their debate.
- Ensuring that less urgent issues are excluded from the debate, but dealt with at another time.

To achieve a balance between urgency and importance, it is common to reserve enough time for matters that are not urgent, but are nevertheless important, (for e.g., the decision process itself, which takes care to maintain). Consensus decision processes tend to accelerate as rising trust over the course of the meeting, combined with fatigue, increase individual tolerance and the cost of dissent. Placing difficult agenda items first tends to speed a meeting, with the risk that important, but less complex decisions will not be achieved before adjournment.

Decisions about when to split up into working groups, how to handle agendas, how to deal with changes to agendas or working groups from the floor, etc., are affected by the allocation of the group's time to urgent versus important matters. These procedural matters are held to be crucial to the survival of a consensus decision process, along with issues of safety, fairness, and closure which arise from their application in practice.

Action, Monitoring and Follow-up

Action is the point of decision; without action, the decision is just talk. Military leaders from Alexander the Great to the present have emphasized that orders simply do not get carried out unless they are personally followed up by the commander. The same applies to group decisions, perhaps even more so.

One would not expect the opposing minority to do a good job of ensuring that a measure is carried out, but they can ensure that problems resulting from it are well-documented, and that inconveniences of its implementation are contained. However, they can also take steps to ensure that the inconvenience of implementation is maximized, so as to make the point that the measure was impractical and ill-advised from the beginning. A major issue in consensus decisions is whose view of the actual outcome to trust, and who to permit time to present their view.

Consensus decisions are especially vulnerable to sabotage of all kinds, so the assignment of action roles, monitoring (from the original majority and minority opinion to some future time when the results of both sets of predictions can be debated), and other follow up (e.g. assessing support of the public for a party after it has taken and publicized a particular measure), is a key responsibility of consensus decision leaders.

QUAKER-BASED CONSENSUS

The model used by the Quakers is effective because it puts in place a simple, time-tested structure that moves a group towards consensus. The Quaker model has been well-received when employed in secular settings because it gives everyone a chance to speak while limiting potential disruptors (e.g., people who want unlimited airtime, or who have a particular axe to grind).

The following aspects of the Quaker model can be effectively applied in any consensus decision-making process:

- Multiple concerns and information are shared until the sense of the group is clear.
- Discussion involves active listening and sharing of information.
- Norms limit number of times one asks to speak to ensure that each speaker is fully heard.
- Norms limit repetition and long speeches.
- Norms include a short silence after every comment so deliberations are truly thoughtful.
- Ideas and solutions belong to the group; no names are recorded.
- Differences are resolved by discussion. The facilitator ("clerk" or "convenor" in the Quaker model) identifies areas of agreement and names disagreements to push discussion deeper.
- The facilitator articulates the sense of the discussion, asks if there are other concerns, and proposes a minute of the decision.
- The group as a whole is responsible for the decision, and the decision belongs to the group.
- The facilitator can discern if one who is not uniting with the decision is acting without concern for the group or in selfish interest.
- Dissenters' perspectives are embraced.

Key components of Quaker-based consensus are: 1) that the guidance of Spirit is available to each participant who honestly seeks the truth, 2) belief in a common humanity, and, 3) the ability to decide together. The goal is "unity, not unanimity." Ensuring that group members speak only once until others are heard encourages a diversity of thought. The facilitator is understood as serving the group rather than acting as person-in-charge. By articulating the emerging consensus, members can be clear on the decision, and, as their views have been taken into account, will be likely to support it.

Many intentional communities use consensus decision-making. In many cases, with cohousing groups, business must be transacted within time constraints. Thus efficiency is important. If the group genuinely wants to make decisions by consensus, a method is needed that is both efficient and effective. An open discussion needs to be animated by a process that moves towards a timely, and sound, decision that is supported by all. Various techniques have been developed whereby this can be achieved.

In some groups, the cards are used in two ways; one for discussion and another for decisions:

A group member who wishes to speak, holds up a card:

- A green card means "I have something to say" or "I have a question." When several group members hold up a green card, they are noted and placed in a "stack" of people waiting to speak. Each person speaks in turn, in a way that is similar to Quaker-based consensus.
- A yellow card means "I can clarify" or "I need clarification (on what was just said)."
- The red card is the process card. A red card, when raised, asks members to look at the process. For example, an individual who displays a red card might say: "Are we getting off track, here?" or "What is our objective in doing this?" or even "How about we take a break?" It gives all members an equal chance to be facilitator.

Following discussion, the facilitator articulates the proposal and calls for a show of cards:

- The green card means: "I agree."
- The yellow card means: "I can live with it." This is often referred to as "standing aside"
- The red card means: "I don't agree, but am willing to work to find a better way, taking into account what has been said by all group members." Thus holding up a red card does not block progress, it signifies that the person who displayed it will work with others on the matter in question and bring it back to a subsequent meeting. This tends to ensure that red cards are not used lightly.

In the Uniting Church of Australia, orange and blue cards are used to mean "I am warm toward this" or "I am cool toward this." The use of orange and blue allows people who are colourblind, and cannot distinguish red and green, to participate in the discussion.

If groups agree to apply methods such as these, and all group members are willing to work at it, consensus decision-making can be both effective in meeting a group's goals, and time-efficient.

A similar method has come to be used in other forums, such as W3C and other computer standards bodies. There, is it known as the Quaker poll.

In lieu of coloured cards, some consensus-based groups use a system of simple hand signals.

While the nature, meaning and popularity of such signals changes from group to group, there is a common 'vocabulary':

- *Twinkle:* Wiggling of the fingers of one or both hands, with palms facing downward. Used by non-speakers to indicate agreement with the speaker. Also often used as a replacement of a raised hand to indicate a 'yea' vote to a proposal.
- *Triangle:* Forming of a triangle with the thumbs and index fingers of both hands. Used to indicate a point of order or procedure to the facilitator.
- *Crossed arms:* Forearms crossed with hands in fists. Used to indicate a strong disagreement with the speaker or to cast a 'block' vote to a proposal.

In the Internet Engineering Task Force (IETF), decisions are assumed to be taken by "rough consensus." The IETF has studiously refrained from defining a mechanical method for verifying such consensus, apparently in the belief that any such codification will lead to attempts to "game the system." Instead, a working group (WG) chair or BoF chair is supposed to "recognize it when I see it."

One tradition in support of rough consensus is the tradition of humming rather than (countable) hand-raising; this allows a WG to quickly tell the difference between "one or two objectors" or a "sharply divided community", without making it easy to slip into "majority rule". However, hand-raising is also used, especially in larger meetings, but actual counting is frowned upon.

Much of the business of the IETF is carried out on mailing lists, where all parties can speak their view at all times; the social dynamics of mailing lists is worthy of a study in itself.

MARKETING BASICS FOR THE SMALL HOTEL BUSINESS

The essence of marketing is to understand your customers' needs and develop a plan that surrounds those needs. Let's face it anyone that has a business has a desire to grow their business. The most effective way to grow and expand your business is by focusing on organic growth.

You can increase organic growth in four different ways. They include:

- Acquiring more customers
- Persuading each customer to buy more products
- Persuading each customer to buy more expensive products or up selling each customer
- Persuading each customer to buy more profitable products

All four of these increase your revenue and profit. Let me encourage you to focus on the first which is to acquire more customers. Why? Because by acquiring more customers you increase your customer base and your revenues then come from a larger base.

How can you use marketing to acquire more customers?

- Spend time researching and create a strategic marketing plan.
- Guide your product development to reach out to customers you aren't currently attracting.
- Price your products and services competitively.
- Develop your message and materials based on solution marketing.

The Importance of a Target Market

When it comes to your customers keep in mind the importance of target marketing. The reason this is important is that only a proportion of the population is likely to purchase any products or service. By taking time pitch your sales and marketing efforts to the correct niche market you will be more productive and not waste your efforts or time.

It's important to consider your virtual segmentation by selecting particular verticals to present your offerings to. Those verticals will have the particular likelihood of purchasing your products and services. Again, this saves you from wasting valuable time and money.

Marketing Differs between Small hotels and larger hotels

If you are like the majority of small hotel business owners your marketing budget is limited. The most effective way to market a small hotel business is to create a well rounded programme that combines sales activities with your marketing tactics. Your sales activities will not only decrease your out-of-pocket marketing expense but it also adds the value of interacting with your prospective customers and clients. This interaction will provide you with research that is priceless.

Small hotel businesses typically have a limited marketing budget if any at all. Does that mean you can't run with the big dogs? Absolutely not. It just means you have to think a little more creatively.

How about launching your marketing campaign by doing one of the following:

- Call your vendors or associates and ask them to participate with you in co-op advertising.
- Take some time to send your existing customers' referrals and buying incentives.
- Have you thought about introducing yourself to the media? Free publicity has the potential to boost your business. By doing this you position yourself as an expert in your field.
- Invite people into your place of business by piggybacking onto an event. Is there a concert coming to town, are you willing to sell those tickets? It could mean free radio publicity. If that is not your cup of tea, how about a walkathon that is taking place in your area, why not be a public outreach and distribute their material?

When you do spend money on marketing, do not forget to create a way to track those marketing efforts. You can do this by coding your ads, using multiple toll-free telephone numbers, and asking prospects where they heard about you. This enables you to notice when a marketing tactic stops working. You can then quickly replace it with a better choice or method. By being diligent in your marketing and creating an easy strategy such as holding yourself accountable to contact ten customers or potential customers daily five days a week you will see your business grow at an exceptional rate. The great thing is it will not take a large marketing budget to make it happen.

PROSPECT

For people who think this is the industry for them, they really think about their personality and be sure they can thrive (and survive) in the atmosphere. It truly is different from anything else. It is critical that they work for a hotel while they are still in school, preferably in a few different hotels, and departments, so they can get a feel for it and know where they would be the happiest and most successful.

The growth in the services sector of the worldwide economy has been phenomenal in the last 25 years. In the United States, services currently account for more than 75 percent of the gross domestic product (GDP), which is a popular measure of an economy's productivity. Similarly, on an international scale, services continue to account for an ever-increasing percentage of economic activity.

Most new jobs are created in the service sector, and the growth in the hospitality and tourism industry is a major contributor. Until the mid-1980s, the emphasis within the marketing community was on products. Now services have surpassed products and have taken on a more important role in marketing.

Services, such as those offered by providers in the hospitality and tourism industry, have developed marketing strategies and practices that are unique. It has been established that the strategies, tactics, and practices that have been used successfully for product marketers do not always work successfully for those who market services. With the distinct differences between products and services in mind, the field of services marketing has evolved.

Services Defined

Unlike products, which are tangible, services are usually intangible. A service is not a physical good; rather, it is the performance of an act or a deed. This performance often requires consumers to be present during the production or delivery of the service. Service industries, including hospitality and tourism, are actually selling consumers an experience. Services have been defined to "include all economic activities whose output is not a physical product or construction, is generally consumed at the time it is produced, and provides added value in forms (such as convenience, amusement, timeliness, comfort or health) that are essentially intangible concerns of its first purchaser."1 Service employees such as front desk agents, housekeepers, hostesses, wait staff, car rental agents, flight attendants, and travel agents are responsible for creating positive experiences for customers. These frontline employees are critical to the success of service firms and play boundary-spanning roles because of their direct contact with customers. These roles are important because customers' perceptions of service firms are formed as a result of their dealings with the boundary-spanning employees. Several reasons underlie the remarkable growth in services.

The numerous reasons for this growth:

- *Changing patterns of government regulation:* The reduction in government regulation has spurred the growth of services. In recent years, there has been a very noticeable shift toward the government taking a much less active role in the regulation of business activities. The most noteworthy of these shifts have been in the airline, trucking, telecommunication, and electrical generation and distribution industries. All of these industries have seen significant changes, as the barriers to entry have been removed and regulations governing such marketing elements as price have also been relaxed or entirely removed.
- *Relaxation of professional association restrictions on marketing:* A new element of competition has been introduced into professions such as law and medicine as more of the practitioners in these areas advertise their services. Bans or restrictions on promotion have been largely removed. Within the hospitality and tourism industry, standards have also changed. We have seen an increase in advertising focusing on direct comparisons, or attacks, on competitors' products and services. This type of advertising strategy creates, or sustains, the perception of superiority in the mind of the consumer in favor of the brand being advertised.
- *Privatization of some public and nonprofit services:* The term privatization was first used in Great Britain when the government adopted the policy of returning national industries from government to private ownership. This transformation has resulted in a greater emphasis on cost containment and a clearer focus on customers' needs. Later, in Central and Eastern Europe, following the fall of communism, we witnessed a continuing transformation from planned or government-run economies to market-driven economies fueled by private companies. Many of these countries' governments have released the control of airlines and travel agencies to private firms.
- *Technological innovation:* Technology continues to alter the way firms

do business and interact with consumers. In all types of businesses, consumers take a more active role in the service delivery process. For example, airlines, in an effort to reduce labour costs and increase speed of service to customers, have aggressively promoted self-check-in, both at the ticket counter and through their Web sites prior to arrival at the airport. Customers print boarding passes, receipts, and other documents without intervention by an airline employee. Express checkout for hotel guests has been in place for many years, but hotel chains continue to experiment with ways to enhance the service, thereby reducing labour costs and/or increasing the customers' perceived value.

In other settings, touch-screen computers collect feedback from guests, in much the same manner that comment cards have been used previously. The ease with which a company can maintain and access a database has permitted the development of sophisticated reservation systems and has led to more sophisticated frequent traveler Programmes. The use of more sophisticated reservations and property management systems has allowed hospitality and tourism firms to improve the level of service provided to guests. Guest history data serve as another example of how a hospitality organization can use technology to gain a competitive advantage. If a hotel guest requests a specific type of pillow, staff can record this preference within the individual's guest history file. When this guest checks into another hotel operated by the chain, the items that were previously requested can be waiting, without the guest even having to request them.

- *Growth in service chains and franchise networks:* Much of the growth in service firms, including the hospitality industry, has been the direct result of franchising efforts by some of the major companies. Franchising represents a contractual arrangement whereby one firm (the franchisor) licenses a number of other firms (the franchisees) to use the franchisor's name and business practices. Notable lodging organizations such as Choice Hotels International and Marriott International, as well as food service firms such as McDonald's, Burger King, Taco Bell, and Wendy's, have all used franchising as a major vehicle for growth. The continued growth of the hospitality industry by means of franchising has put additional stress on independent owners and operators. In fact, each year the percentage of hospitality and tourism operations that are independently operated decreases.
- *Internationalization and globalization:* Increasing shareholder value often remains directly associated with increasing company sales and profits, and globalization is one means of achieving this. As more

and more of the prime locations are developed domestically, companies look internationally for expansion opportunities. This has been particularly true for fast-food franchisors: a significant proportion of their expansion during the last few years has occurred outside of their traditional domestic markets.

- *Pressures to improve productivity:* In many industries within the service economy, competition stays very intense. This factor, when combined with the pressure from investors for higher returns on capital, has resulted in pressure to increase productivity and reduce costs. In many cases, managers seek to reduce labour costs by running leaner operations or using technology to replace humans for some tasks An example of this was when Delta Airlines encouraged passengers to check in via the Internet, thereby reducing the number of passengers who wanted to check in at the airport. They offered an incentive of 1,000 extra frequent-flyer miles to any passenger who used this service. While increasing productivity and profits remains a highly desirable goal, it must not be done at the expense of longterm customer satisfaction. Without long-term satisfaction, future profitability may exist in jeopardy.
- *The service quality movement:* With the advent of consumerism, the public's perception is that service quality has declined. In response, successful firms are using the customer's perception of quality to set performance standards, rather than relying solely on operationally defined standards for service quality. They often conduct extensive research to determine the key elements that impact the customer's perception of service quality. When Ritz-Carlton won the Malcolm Baldrige National Quality Award, this was tangible evidence that paying careful attention to customers' service expectations can have a dramatic impact on the firm.
- *Expansion of leasing and rental businesses:* The expansion of businesses that lease equipment and personnel to firms has been a contributing factor in the growth of the service sector. More and more firms are looking to outsource some elements of their operation, and they often start with elements that are not part of the firm's core product or business. For example, most hotels that host meetings and conventions have outsourced the servicing of the audiovisual needs of groups to a company that specializes in that type of business. The company in turn leases the audiovisual equipment to groups that are holding meetings in the hotel. The company is able to provide more up-to-date and specialized equipment to groups than the hotel might if it provided the service itself. The hotel does not have to maintain an inventory of equipment, and therefore capital costs are reduced.

- *Manufacturers as service providers:* Some of the firms that traditionally manufactured and distributed tangible products have found it profitable to provide services as well. For example, most automobile manufacturers have consumer credit agencies to facilitate the leasing and purchasing of automobiles. In the hospitality industry, PepsiCo decided to enter the restaurant industry and distribute its products through acquisitions such as Taco Bell and KFC, but the company later reconsidered this strategy and sold these brands to Yum! Brands, Inc. In the computer industry, firms such as IBM and Hewlett-Packard provide services in addition to hardware and software. In most cases, the profit margins on services are higher than on products, contributing significantly to the bottom line of the firm.
- *Pressures on public and nonprofit organizations to find new income sources:* All organizations are under pressure to increase sales, which often becomes difficult within the traditional products that a firm sells. There are many reasons for this, but increasing competition and mature industries are often contributing factors. In an effort to find new sources of income, firms often seek new services that will generate new net sales, without cannibalizing sales of existing products. For example, a limousine company might expand its city tour business in addition to the other services offered.
- *Hiring and promotion of innovative managers:* In the past, managers in the service industries often spent their entire careers within a single industry, or perhaps even with the same firm. This situation no longer reintroduction to services marketing mains the same, especially at the corporate level of management. Firms often hire individuals from other industries to provide a fresh perspective and fresh ideas. The results can become dramatic. One such individual is Steven Bollenback, president and CEO of Hilton Hotels. Prior to his very positive impact on Hilton Hotels, he had engineered innovative financing at both Marriott International and Trump Hotels and Resorts.

4

Human Resource Management in the Hotel Industry

HUMAN RESOURCES

Human resources has at least two meanings depending on context. The original usage derives from political economy and economics, where it was traditionally called labour, one of three factors of production. The more common usage within corporations and businesses refers to the individuals within the firm, and to the portion of the firm's organization that deals with hiring, firing, training, and other personnel issues.

Modern analysis emphasizes that human beings are not predictable commodity "resources" with definitions totally controlled by contract, but are creative and social beings that make contributions beyond "labour" to a society and to civilization. The broad term human capital has evolved to contain the complexity of this term, and in macro-economics the term "firm-specific human capital" has evolved to represent the original meaning of term "human resources".

Advocating the central role of "human resources" or human capital in enterprises and societies has been a traditional role of socialist parties, who claim that value is primarily created by their activity, and accordingly justify a larger claim of profits or relief from these enterprises or societies. Critics say this is just a bargaining tactic which grew out of various practices of medieval European guilds into the modern trade union and collective bargaining unit. A contrary view, common to capitalist parties, is that it is the infrastructural capital and (what they call) intellectual capital owned and fused by "management" that provides most value in financial capital terms. This likewise justifies a bargaining position and a general view that "human resources" are interchangeable.

A significant sign of consensus on this latter point is the ISO 9000 series of standards which requires a "job description" of every participant in a productive enterprise. In general, heavily unionized nations such as France and Germany have adopted and encouraged such descriptions especially within trade unions. One view of this trend is that a strong social consensus on political economy and a good social welfare system facilitates labour mobility and tends to make the entire economy more productive, as labour can move from one enterprise to another with little controversy or difficulty in adapting.

An important controversy regarding labour mobility illustrates the broader philosophical issue with usage of the phrase "human resources": governments of developing nations often regard developed nations that encourage immigration or "guest workers" as appropriating human capital that is rightfully part of the developing nation and required to further its growth as a civilization. They argue that this appropriation is similar to colonial commodity fiat wherein a colonizing European power would define an arbitrary price for natural resources, extracting which diminished national natural capital.

The debate regarding "human resources" versus human capital thus in many ways echoes the debate regarding natural resources versus natural capital. Over time the United Nations have come to more generally support the developing nations' point of view, and have requested significant offsetting "foreign aid" contributions so that a developing nation losing human capital does not lose the capacity to continue to train new people in trades, professions, and the arts.

An extreme version of this view is that historical inequities such as African slavery must be compensated by current developed nations, which benefitted from stolen "human resources" as they were developing. This is an extremely controversial view, but it echoes the general theme of converting human capital to "human resources" and thus greatly diminishing its value to the host society, i.e. "Africa", as it is put to narrow imitative use as "labour" in the using society.

In the very narrow context of corporate "human resources", there is a contrasting pull to reflect and require workplace diversity that echoes the diversity of a global customer base. Foreign language and culture skills, ingenuity, humor, and careful listening, are examples of traits that such programmes typically require. It would appear that these evidence a general shift to the human capital point of view, and an acknowledgement that human beings do contribute much more to a productive enterprise than "work": they bring their character, their ethics, their creativity, their social connections, and in some cases even their pets and children, and alter the character of a workplace. The term corporate culture is used to characterize such processes.

The traditional but extremely narrow context of hiring, firing, and job description is considered a 20th century anachronism. Most corporate organizations that compete in the modern global economy have adopted a view of human capital that mirrors the modern consensus as above. Some of these, in turn, deprecate the term "human resources" as useless.

As the term refers to predictable exploitations of human capital in one context or another, it can still be said to apply to manual labour, mass agriculture, low skill "McJobs" in service industries, military and other work that has clear job descriptions, and which generally do not encourage creative or social contributions.

In general the abstractions of macro-economics treat it this way - as it characterizes no mechanisms to represent choice or ingenuity. So one interpretation is that "firm-specific human capital" as defined in macro-economics is the modern and correct definition of "human resources" - and that this is inadequate to represent the contributions of "human resources" in any modern theory of political economy.

In terms of recruitment and selection it is important to consider carrying out a thorough job analysis to determine the level of skills/technical abilities, competencies, flexibility of the employee required etc. At this point it is important to consider both the internal and external factors that can have an impact on the recruitment of employees. The external factors are those out-with the powers of the organization and include issues such as current and future trends of the labour market e.g. skills, education level, government investment into industries etc. On the other hand internal influences are easier to control, predict and monitor, for example management styles or even the organizational culture.

In order to know the business environment in which any organization operates, three major trends should be considered:

- Demographics – the characteristics of a population/workforce, for example, age, gender or social class. This type of trend may have an effect in relation to pension offerings, insurance packages etc.
- Diversity – the variation within the population/workplace. Changes in society now mean that a larger proportion of organizations are made up of female employees in comparison to thirty years ago. Also over recent years organizations have become more culturally diverse and have increased the number of working patterns (part-time, casual, seasonal positions) to cope with the changes in both society and the global market. It is important to note here that an organisation must consider the ethic and legal implications of their decisions in relation to the HRM policies they enact to protect employees. Employers have to be acutely aware of the rise in discrimination, unfair dismissal and sexual/racial harassment cases in recent years and the detrimental effects this can have on the employees and the organisation. Anti-discrimination legislation over the past 30 years has provided a foundation for an increasing interest in diversity at work which is "about creating a working culture that seeks respects and values difference."
- Skills and qualifications – as industries move from manual to a more

managerial professions so does the need for more highly skilled graduates. If the market is 'tight' i.e. not enough staff for the jobs, employers will have to compete for employees by offering financial rewards, community investment etc.also the political issues

In regards to how individuals respond to the changes in a labour market the following should be understood:

- Geographical spread – how far is the job from the individual? The distance to travel to work should be in line with the pay offered by the organization and the transportation and infrastructure of the area will also be an influencing factor in deciding who will apply for a post.
- Occupational structure – the norms and values of the different careers within an organization. Mahoney 1989 developed 3 different types of occupational structure namely craft (loyalty to the profession), organization career (promotion through the firm) and unstructured (lower/unskilled workers who work when needed).
- Generational difference –different age categories of employees have certain characteristics, for example their behaviour and their expectations of the organisation.

Recruitment methods are wide and varied, it is important that the job is described correctly and any personal specifications stated. Job recruitment methods can be through job centres, employment agencies/consultants, headhunting, and local/national newspapers. It is important that the correct media is chosen to ensure an appropriate response to the advertised post.

CONCEPT AND PROCESS OF HUMAN RESOURCE PLANNING

Human resources alignment means integrating decisions about people with decisions about the results an organization is trying to obtain. By integrating human resources management (HRM) into the agency planning process, emphasizing human resources (HR) activities that support broad agency mission goals, and building a strong relationship between HR and management, agencies are able to ensure that the management of human resources contributes to mission accomplishment and that managers are held accountable for their HRM decisions.

This is especially important in light of the Government Performance and Results Act's (GPRA) push to align all agency activities, including HRM, toward achieving defined agency strategic goals and measuring progress toward those goals.

In fiscal year 1999, the U.S. Office of Personnel Management (OPM) embarked on a special study to determine how much progress Federal agencies have made toward aligning HRM with agency strategic goals in support of HRM accountability and agency mission accomplishment. Our key findings and conclusions are summarized as follows.

Many more agencies than expected include HR representatives in the agency planning process and integrate human resources management goals, objectives, and strategies into agency strategic plans. However, most agencies are still struggling in this area. Therefore, agency executives and HR leaders need to work together to fully integrate HRM into the planning process so that it will become a fundamental, contributing factor to agency planning and success.

Although some agency HR offices have begun focusing on organizational activities that assist agency decision-making, most are still emphasizing internal HR office efficiency efforts. While internal issues are important to the success of any HR programme, HR offices also need to examine the "big picture" and find ways to impact the success of the agency as a whole.

Most agencies are in some way measuring the efficiency and/or effectiveness of the HR function. These measures, however, are generally output-oriented, focus on internal HR processes and activities, and are used to make improvements to HR-specific policies and procedures. As HR refocuses its activities to broader organizational issues, HRM measures also need to be expanded to gauge the impact HRM has on agency goals and mission. Then, the measurement data can be used to inform agency-level decisions.

The relationship between HR and management is becoming more collaborative. HR executives are beginning to earn a seat at the management table. HR offices are becoming more consultative and involved in day-to-day line management activities. Nevertheless, there is still a long way to go if HR is to become a strategic partner at all levels. To do so, HR needs to build its own internal competencies to deal with organizational issues, educate itself on agency and programme missions, and find ways to offer creative and innovative solutions to organizationwide issues.

Although many National Performance Review (now known as the National Partnership for Reinventing Government) initiatives, such as downsizing, reorganizing, streamlining, and delegating HR authorities, were meant to improve HR's ability to focus on organizational issues, they have not taken hold as quickly or thoroughly as hoped. Therefore, HR is still doing most of the process work, and its ability to focus on alignment has been limited. However, as HR's role in agency planning, activities, and decision-making advances — and it is advancing — so too will the alignment of human resources management with agency mission accomplishment.

Alignment

Strategic human resources management...strategic alignment...alignment with mission accomplishment. These are just a few of the terms being used to describe the new, evolving role of Federal human resources management (HRM). What do these terms really mean? If you were to ask agency personnelists, managers, or employees, you would probably get a wide range of answers. So, it's important to establish from the beginning what we are really talking about. Human resources management alignment means to integrate decisions about people with decisions about the results an organization is trying to obtain. Our research indicates that agencies that successfully align human resources management with agency mission accomplishment do so by integrating HRM into the agency planning process, emphasizing HR activities that support mission goals, and building strong HR/management relationships.

In addition to being a vital contributor to agency mission accomplishment, HRM alignment is the ultimate level of HRM accountability, as demonstrated in the Hierarchy of Accountability. While HRM accountability must begin with basic legal compliance, it ultimately encompasses all four levels of the pyramid, including demonstrating how HRM supports achievement of the agency strategic goals.

Why Align?

Why the sudden emphasis on aligning HRM activities with agency mission accomplishment? Basically, it comes down to demonstrating the value of human resources management to the agency. In the past, one of HR's primary roles has been to ensure compliance with laws, rules, and regulations. Although this is still, and will always be, a necessary function, many recent developments have led to a strong emphasis on results.

The National Performance Review (NPR) took on the task of reinventing government to make it work better, cost less, and get results. NPR mandated many initiatives that changed the focus of HR from just compliance toward results, including downsizing the HR function, delegating HR authorities to line managers, calling for HR to demonstrate its business value, and enhancing customer service. Through these initiatives, management of human resources would become more responsive to mission-related needs because it would take place at the line level, and the HR staff would be able to expend more of its energy on broader organizational issues.

The Government Performance and Results Act (GPRA) of 1993 has also played a large part in focusing agencies on results. The purpose of GPRA is to improve Federal programme effective- ness, accountability, service delivery, decision-making, and internal management, thereby improving confidence in the Federal Government. This is achieved by demonstrating organizational results through strategic planning and performance measures.

Although the primary focus of GPRA is on programmatic functions, agencies are also required to describe how administrative resources, such as HR, are being used to achieve strategic goals. Further, the General Accounting Office (GAO) and the Office of Management and Budget (OMB) have evaluated many of these efforts, and are calling for agencies to improve their discussions of HRM alignment in strategic and annual plans. Therefore, the human resources function is increasingly being aligned to the agency strategic plan, which requires HR to show how it is supporting mission accomplishment.

Alignment has already occurred in other key administrative functions. When Congress developed a statutory framework to introduce performance-based management into the Federal Government, it initiated financial, information technology, and procurement reforms through such mandates as the Chief Financial Officer Act and Information Technology Management Reform Act. Human resources management is the administrative missing link to this comprehensive package.

The private sector has recognized that it is not just financial and technological capital that provide companies with the competitive edge, but people, or human capital. Without attracting and retaining the right people, in the right jobs, with the right skills and training, an organization cannot succeed. Therefore, people have been recognized as companies' most important asset. As the Federal Government moves toward a performance-based management approach, we, too, need to realize the importance of our human resources. A huge percentage of agencies' budgets is spent on human resources — salaries, benefits, training, work life programmes, etc. Nowhere else do you make that substantial an investment and not measure the return.

Not only do human resources provide the competitive edge, but several recent studies have confirmed that the quality and innovation of HR practices impact business results. These studies were able to draw a correlation between increased quality of HR practices and increased business success. Among other benefits, HR alignment with mission accomplishment increases HR's ability to anticipate its customers' needs, increases the agency's ability to implement strategic business goals, and provides decision-makers with critical resource allocation information. Finally, HR alignment is a vital process to advance agency accountability. By defining, maintaining, and assessing HRM goals and measures, communicating them throughout the agency, and using the information to make management decisions, agencies are able to ensure that the management of human resources contributes to mission accomplishment and that managers are held accountable for their HRM decisions in support of mission accomplishment.

HUMAN RESOURCES MANAGEMENT STRATEGIC PLAN

The Health Care Financing Administration (HCFA) has developed a very noteworthy approach to aligning human resources management with mission accomplishment. HCFA's Human Resources Management Group (HRMG), Learning Resources Group (LRG), and Office of Equal Opportunity and Civil Rights (OEOCR) collaborated to develop a draft Human Resources Strategic Plan that goes beyond each of these individual organization's human resources responsibilities and instead addresses the entire sub-component's human resources management responsibilities. It assigns accountability for specific HRM goals to HRMG, LRG, OEOCR, senior leadership, line managers, employees, the union, and/or other non-HR stakeholders. The HRMG, LRG, and OEOCR worked very closely with the HCFA strategic planning and evaluation office to tie the plan to HCFA's strategic plan.

Specifically, the plan includes challenges that HCFA will face in the future, HRM goals that will support HCFA in meeting those challenges, potential performance indicators and strategies for each goal, the roles and responsibilities of HRMG, LRG, OEOCR, managers, employees, and other stakeholders, and finally how to implement and assess its results. help determine achievement of mission goals, they should focus more on whether or not the intended outcome of the activity was achieved.

HR Strategic Plans

Approximately half of the agencies we talked to have developed separate Human Resources strategic plans. These plans generally serve one of two purposes. Either they provide direction for those agencies that have not integrated HRM into the agency strategic plan, or they are used as implementation plans which support agencywide HRM goals, strategies, and measures.

These plans are particularly important to those agencies that do not integrate HRM into the agencywide plan because it helps them map out where they want the HR programme to go. They seem less important to many of the agencies that have thoroughly integrated HRM into the agency plan. For example, the Social Security Administration (SSA) has not developed a specific HR strategic plan because HR's goals and measures are part of the agencywide approach. Then, there are some agencies that integrate HR extensively into the agency plan, but still prefer to have a separate HR operational plan supporting the agencywide plan, as is often done by other corporate functions such as information technology and financial management.

Most of these plans focus on internal HR office programme activities, rather than on agencywide accountability for the effective use of human resources in accomplishing the mission. Therefore, ownership of the plan belongs to the HR office, not the agency. The Health Care Financing Administration (a sub-component of the Department of Health and Human Services) is an interesting exception to this, as seen in the inset. As with agency strategic plans, the measures identified in HR strategic plans are typically process- oriented and tend to address what steps have been taken to achieve a goal, rather than whether the intended outcome of the goal has been achieved. A little over half of the agencies use management input in developing these plans, generally in the form of previous customer satisfaction surveys.

Strategic planning allows agencies to put down on paper where they are, where they want to go, and how they plan to get there. But the best planning in the world does nothing for an agency if it does not act on those plans. Strategic implementation of human resources management means performing activities that support agency mission accomplishment and measuring how well those activities contribute to achieving agency strategic goals.

Strategic HRM Activities

When we talk about HRM activities, we tend to focus on what the HR office, itself, is doing even though we recognize that supervisors would bear the responsibility of HR decisions in an ideal world. After all, NPR advocated deregulation and delegation and the downsizing and out- sourcing of HR office activities so that human resources management could take place at the line level, making it more responsive to mission-related needs. Additionally, the HR staff would be able to devote more time to broader organizational issues, thereby improving its contribution to mission accomplishment.

Unfortunately, deregulation and delegation, as reported in OPM's 1997 special study, Deregulation and Delegation of Human Resources Management Authority in the Federal Government, have not taken hold as quickly or thoroughly as was hoped. HR is still doing most of the HR- related work and is the nerve centre for HRM activities. That is why the focus of this section is on the HR office and what it does to support mission accomplishment.

So what are HR's contributions toward mission accomplishment? Although most line managers we interviewed cannot describe precisely which HR activities support specific agency strategic goals, they recognize that they could not accomplish their mission without HR's help. Ironically, the areas most often mentioned by managers as HR's most valued contributions are also the areas they feel need the most improvement: recruitment and staffing, employee development, and employee relations. They would like to see HR become more involved and innovative in these areas, but they also admit that it would be extremely difficult for them to get their jobs done without the help HR already provides.

With this system, HR can immediately identify available deployment candidates for selection as soon as disasters are declared. Additionally, the system allows HR to better identify employee training and promotion needs, match employee expertise with specific disaster site victim needs, and create a selection routine that rotates available employees, thereby avoiding employee burnout.

Clearly, staffing, development, and employee relations are important HR activities that make a difference to agency goal accomplishment. However, there are other areas in which HR offices contribute to and align with mission accomplishment, such as the few described below. Agency Reorganizations: Because of all of the downsizing, streamlining, and budget cuts that have been occurring in recent years, many agencies and sub-components have had to redefine their missions and restructure the programme areas that support those missions. Human resources staffs play key roles in some of these redesign efforts. Managers at the Federal Emergency Management Agency and the Department of Labour's Occupational Safety and Health Administration were particularly complimentary of all of the work the HR staffs did to redeploy and retrain the workforce, provide guidance on organizational development issues, and redesign performance standards.

Workforce Planning: In this time of budget cuts, downsizing, and an aging Federal workforce, workforce planning becomes extremely important to increasing agencies' overall ability to achieve their missions. Although few agencies have strong workforce planning systems in place, some are beginning to take steps in this direction. The Department of the Army has an automated civilian forecasting system that uses 15-year workforce data trends to project future employment patterns, up to 7 years. This is part of a developing workforce planning initiative. SSA has developed a methodology to predict the number of actual

Tracking Strategic Progress

Engineers at NASA's Kennedy Space Centre have designed and implemented an excellent strategic management tool: the Goal Performance Evaluation System. This computer system implemented a major performance management change by linking individual employee performance goals all the way up through the Centre and Agency goals.

The system tracks the status of performance plans, and allows organizations to track results achieved against their mission. Managers can access the system to see what their units and individual employees are contributing toward the agency strategic goals. The system functions as a strategic management tool, an employee performance management system, and a Centre-wide communication tool. Kennedy and Johnson Space Centres have piloted the computer system with very positive results. retirements and is developing a workforce transition plan that will identify current and future required skill sets, determine how the workforce can obtain these skills, and set action plan milestones. Additionally, OPM is in the process of developing a workforce planning model that will assist agencies in this area.

Linking Performance Management to Mission Accomplishment: When managers and employees are interviewed, they almost always cite the performance management system as a way they are held accountable for meeting agency goals. So, does this mean performance management systems are aligned with agency strategic goals? In most agencies, the answer is "not yet" — at least not fully. Recently published research has identified over a dozen agencies and agency sub- components that have started to formulate systematic approaches to aligning performance management to strategic goals.

Most are starting by linking top management performance plans and contracts to agency goals and rating and rewarding executives based on achievement of those goals.

Many of these agencies are planning to cascade the alignment down to the employee level. OPM's 1999 publication, A Handbook for Measuring Employee Performance: Aligning Employee Performance with Organizational Goals, is a very useful tool to help agencies link employee performance to the goals of the organization and measure employee accomplishments. A couple of agencies actually mandate the linkage of employee level plans to agency goals, while others are using team-based performance management approaches that include performance targets, informal team assessments, and awards that are linked to mission goals. The National Aeronautics and Space Administration (NASA), as shown in the inset, actually has an automated system that assists in the linkage. Nevertheless, as the General Accounting Office (GAO) concluded in its study, Performance Management: Aligning Employee Performance with Agency Goals at Six Results Act Pilots, aligning performance management systems with organizational missions and goals is still a "work in progress."

HR Self-Assessment: A handful of agency and sub-component HR offices are actually assessing how well their programmes align with agency mission accomplishment as part of recently established HR self-assessment programmes. These assessment programmes focus on the compliance of HR activities with law as well as how effectively HR programmes are achieving their objectives in support of mission accomplishment. Because these assessment programmes are fairly new or are in the process of being revamped, it is too soon to tell the success they will have in measuring HR's impact on organizational mission accomplishment.

HRM Measurement

In the end, HR can only determine its value to the organization by measuring it. Earlier in this report, we saw that most agencies had at least defined HR output measures in agency strategic plans, annual performance plans, and/or HR strategic plans. This is an encouraging trend, but we need to look further at whether these measures are actually being tracked and used for decision- making. The best measures in the world are meaningless if not used. HRM measures in the strategic and annual performance plans are usually tracked by the HR office and forwarded to the planning office for distribution and sharing of the information.

A few agencies, such as NASA, SSA, and Education, report actually using the information for decision- making and tracking whether goals are being met. NASA even posts the information on its web page. However, we found that most agencies look at available data without really evaluating how the information can be used to enhance goal attainment. HR staffs find that measures from HR strategic plans tend to be more useful than those in the agency strategic or annual plans, at least at the functional level. As discussed earlier, HR strategic plan measures tend to focus on internal HR programmes, policies, and processes, and can therefore point to deficiencies in these areas.

HR officials can then use this information to make improvements to the problem areas. From an organizational perspective, however, the measures are generally not very helpful in determining achievement of HR goals because they are process rather than outcome oriented. Few agencies have implemented elaborate systems to track HRM goals and measures. Nonetheless, there are quite a few interesting approaches some agencies are using to measure their HRM performance.

Benchmarking is a systematic process of measuring an organization's products, services, and practices against those of a like organization that is a recognized leader in the studied area. Many Federal HR offices are using this practice to identify ways to improve service and align with business results. The most common benchmarking effort Federal HR offices have participated in is the National Academy of Public Administration-Hackett Group HR Benchmarking Study. There are at least 19 Government agencies involved in the benchmarking of 22 HR processes within four areas: administration, risk management, employee development, and decision support. The study also helps to gauge HR alignment through decision support categories such as resource planning, organizational planning, and strategic HR planning. Most participating agencies see the value in the information but have not devised strategies for how to use it.

The Balanced Scorecard in Action

The Veterans Benefits Administration's New York Regional Office implemented a balanced scorecard that uses outcome measures linked to organizational goals at the team, core group, and division-wide levels. The purpose is to determine how successful its operations are and where improvements are needed. This "balanced scorecard" measures five performance areas: customer satisfaction, speed, accuracy, cost-per- claim, and employee development. For each element in the balanced scorecard, teams are awarded points based on how well they are performing, and the scorecard is aligned with individual employee assessments and incentive pay.

Veterans' expectations are used to define customer performance targets, and employee measures are derived from climate surveys, team development data, and technical skills inventories. HR has played an important role in designing the balanced scorecard, including developing measures, peer assessments, and other tools, as well as helping managers understand the approach and how to manage under it.

The Balanced Scorecard is a framework many agencies are using to translate strategy into operational terms by measuring a full range of perspectives: financial, customer, internal, and learning and growth. Vice President Gore advocated the use of this type of balanced set of results to evaluate agency performance at the Global Forum on Reinventing Government, January 1999. The scorecard is generally used at the business unit level, as with the Veterans Benefits Administration. To date, most agencies are in the beginning stages of implementing balanced measurement approaches.

Activity Based Costing (ABC) is a method of cost management that determines the true cost, including overhead, for a service or product. Finding the true cost allows agencies to discover cost improvement opportunities, prepare and actualize strategic and operational plans, and improve strategic decision-making. This cost management methodology involves identifying activities, determining activity costs, determining cost drivers, collecting activity data, and calculating the service cost. ABC is being explored by a number of agencies. The Patent and Trademark Office is using ABC agencywide, and the General Services Administration is using it to determine HR costs, as described on the following page.

Measuring True Cost and How to Use It

Both the General Services Administration (GSA) and the Department of Commerce's Patent and Trademark Office (PTO) have successfully used Activity Based Costing (ABC) to determine the true cost of human resources management services. The General Services Administration began tracking HR costs due to customer complaints that services were too expensive. The problem was that no one, including HR, knew the actual cost of HR services. By using Activity Based Costing, GSA was able to compute the HR activity costs and make comparisons to other Government and private sector organizations using the Hackett Benchmarking Study data. HR demonstrated to managers that its costs were actually relatively low, and it had the data to prove it.

The Patent and Trademark Office (PTO) has engaged in agencywide Activity Based Costing. All senior managers were trained in the process, and each functional area, including HR, formed teams to identify activities, activity-based drivers, and primary products. PTO has used the information to close out fiscal year 1998 financial activities and to plan the fiscal year 2000 budget. ABC has helped determine the full cost of agency activities, the proper distribution of costs, and has even influenced service rates. An additional benefit to the system is that it has encouraged strategic thinking. Managers see how much a function, such as HR, costs and starts asking what value that function really adds to the programme. This challenges HR to show its value and return on investment.

The Malcolm Baldrige and the President's Quality Award Criteria are each based on a set of core values and concepts that integrate key business requirements into a results-oriented framework. Using the criteria as a framework for management practices and measurement can help agencies to improve performance, facilitate communication and best practice sharing, and serve as a tool for managing performance, planning, training, and assessment. HR measures are 15 per cent of the total Baldrige framework score. Several agencies, most notably the Department of Navy's Inspector General's Office, have successfully used the criteria to assess agency mission programmes.

HUMAN RESOURCES WITHIN FIRMS

Though human resources have been part of business and organizations since the first days of agriculture, the modern concept of human resources began in reaction to the efficiency focus of Taylorism in the early 1900s. By 1920, psychologists and employment experts in the United States started the human relations movement, which viewed workers in terms of their psychology and fit with companies, rather than as interchangeable parts. This movement grew throughout the middle of the 20th century, placing emphasis on how leadership, cohesion, and loyalty played important roles in organizational success. Although this view was increasingly challenged by more quantitatively rigorous and less "soft" management techniques in the 1960s and beyond, human resources had gained a permanent role within the firm.

Facing mankind's problems it is opportune to mobilize as many intellectual resources as possible in order to resolve the emerging troubles. The students have to be trained to construct pertinent knowledge together (for example using the method Learning by teaching). Students can be trained in constructing knowledge outside the classroom too.

They have to adopt following attitudes:

- Be aware that they are bearing resources
- Be aware that they have to increase their own resources in order to be more attractive inside the community
- Be aware that they can increase their own resources if they communicate
- Be aware that they can increase their own resources if they share their knowledge with other people
- Ability to identify resource from other community members and to make this resource available for all the group
- Ability to search for pertinent resources outside the group
- Ability to connect people looking for proposing resources
- Ability to organize collective thinking in networks

Employee Engagement

Employee engagement is a concept that is generally viewed in terms of employees feeling a strong emotional bond to the organization that employs them. (Robinson) This is associated with people demonstrating a willingness to recommend the organization to others and commit time and effort to help the organization succeed. (Harter) It suggests that people are motivated by intrinsic factors (e.g. personal growth, working to a common purpose, being part of a larger process) rather than simply focusing on extrinsic factors (e.g. pay/ reward). (Ryan) The concept has gained popularity as various studies have demonstrated links with productivity.

In 1999, The Gallup Organization published research that showed that engaged employees are more productive, more profitable, more customer-focused, safer, and less likely to leave their employer. The review stated that "engagement with employees within a firm has shown to motivate the employee to work beyond personal factors and work more for the success of the firm." (Harter) Watson Wyatt found that high-commitment organizations (one with loyal and dedicated employees) out-performed those with low commitment by 47% in the 2000 study and by 200% in the 2002 study. (Wyatt) In a study of professional service firms, the Hay Group found that offices with engaged employees were up to 43% more productive, based on a comparison of revenue generation.

Recent research has focused on developing a better understanding of how variables such as quality of work relationships and values of the organization interact and their link to important work outcomes. From the perspective of the employee, "outcomes" range from strong commitment to the isolation of oneself from the organization. The study done by the Gallup Management Journal has shown that only 29 percent of employees are actively engaged in their jobs. Those "engaged" employees work with passion and feel a strong connection to their company. Moreover, 54 percent of employees are not engaged meaning that they go through each workday putting time but no passion into their work. Also, Seventeen percent of employees are actively disengaged, meaning that they are busy acting out of their own personal unhappiness, which undermines what their engaged co-workers are trying to accomplish.

Access to a reliable model enables organizations to conduct validation studies to establish the relationship of employee engagement to productivity/ performance and other measures linked to effectiveness.

It is an important principle of occupational psychology (i.e. the application of psychological theories, research methods, and intervention strategies involving workplace issues) that validation studies should be anchored in reliable scales (i.e. organized and related groups of items) and not simply focus on individual elements in isolation. To understand how high levels of employee engagement affect organizational performance/productivity it is important to have an a priori model that demonstrates how the scales interact. (Konrad) There is also overlap between this concept and those relating to well-being at work and the psychological contract.

As employee productivity is clearly connected with employee engagement, creating an environment that encourages employee engagement is considered to be essential in the effective management of human capital.

Employee engagement will be influenced by:

1. Employee perceptions of job importance. This study has found that "...an employees attitude toward the job['s importance] and the company had the greatest impact on loyalty and customer service then all other employee factors combined."
2. Employee clarity of job expectations. "If expectations are not clear and basic materials and equipment not provided, negative emotions such as boredom or resentment may result, and the employee may then become focused on surviving more then thinking about how he can help the organization succeed."
3. Career advancement/improvement opportunities. "Plant supervisors and managers indicated that many plant improvements were being made outside the suggestion system, where employees initiated changes in order to reap the bonuses generated by the subsequent cost savings."
4. Regular feedback and dialogue with superiors. "Feedback is the key to giving employees a sense of where they're going, but many organizations are remarkably bad at giving it." (Hay Group) "'What I really wanted to hear was 'Thanks. You did a good job.' But all my boss did was hand me a check."
5. Quality of working relationships with peers, superiors, and subordinates. "...if employee's relationship with their managers is fractured, then no amount of perks will persuade the employees to perform at top levels. Employee engagement is a direct reflection of how employees feel about their relationship with the boss."
6. Perceptions of the ethos and values of the organization. "'Inspiration and values' is the most important of the six drivers in our Engaged Performance model. Inspirational leadership is the ultimate perk. In its absence, [it] is unlikely to engage employees."

As additional research becomes available, the significance of the various factors will become more evident.

KEY ISSUES IN HRM DISCOURSE

HRM is a phenomenon of the 1980s when, according to Streeck (1987), the key issue for management was to find ways of managing in an unprecedented degree of economic uncertainty, which derived from a need for continuous rapid adjustment to an increasingly turbulent market. Hence the imperatives that HRM issues should be integrated with business strategy, and that HRM should be able to demonstrate its contribution to business performance (from the expectancy model, see high performance practices below). Issues such as commitment, quality, flexibility and adaptability became important. And so HRM was born. HRM also stresses the importance of the devolving the ownership and delivery of HR initiatives from specialist HR managers to line managers.

Others deny that HRM represents anything different or new. Armstrong claims HRM is a 'construct largely invented by academics and popularised by consultants', yet Grant and Oswick (1998) found a majority of practitioners agreed that HRM was different from personnel management. Gennard and Kelly (1995) and Torrington et al. (2002) are among those who regard HRM as the next stage in the evolution of personnel management. Equally there has been a growth in the proportion of specialists using HR in their title. These specialists are better qualified, more involved in strategic planning, more likely to use HRM practices than their counterparts using the title 'personnel', and most likely to be found in foreign-owned firms.

One outcome has been a realignment of the personnel/line manager relationship, with more personnel work being devolved down the line. Yet in the more cost-conscious and value-added environment line managers are making more, not less, use of their specialist personnel advisers. The personnel function does contribute to corporate objectives by being delivered in many different but flexible forms. It is not necessarily the case that an organization not acting strategically will mean that the workforce is not managed in a strategic way. Hence strategic management of people is not purely within the domain of the HR department, and can be diffused throughout the organization and owned and directed by the line.

The emphasis within HRM discourse has remained largely managerialist because of the emphasis on management's cost and performance concerns, hence a management practice research agenda. The management of employment also tends to be discussed in terms of bipolar opposites in and around the metaphors of 'hard' and 'soft'. Key instances include high and low trust work practices, direct control vs. responsible autonomy, control vs. commitment and 'high road' vs. 'low road'. Here managers may exercise strategic contingency choice in terms of which approach best fits their organization. In some respects these divergences are symptomatic of some of the differences between personnel management and HRM. Within personnel management people are more likely to be recognized and treated as human beings, whereas in HRM they are treated as people in the 'soft' variant and resources in the 'hard' variant.

A further criticism of HRM is that it is not gender neutral, with Townley (1994) being an exception in making gender more visible within her analysis. Dickens (1998) argues HRM policies and practices perpetuate rather than challenge gender inequality. In terms of securing employee commitment assumptions about women being less committed than men will affect the shape of the core-periphery, and determine which jobs are full-time or part-time.

Cost-cutting 'hard' HRM has underpinned existing sex segregation. Wajcman (2000) echoes these observations, pointing out that men are most likely to be found in occupations where management is convinced of a high quality strategy, whereas women are most likely to be found in low-skill jobs where management feels competition on costs is the most viable option.

High Road' or 'low road' HRM

There are two broad approaches to HRM, both of which have been found wanting. The first, a 'high road' version, is generally agreed to comprise a list of tangible practices, with 'best practice' HRM or 'bundles' of practices having the greatest impact on performance. Two groups of practices can be identified:

Some practices may be core requirements, e.g. selection, training, communications and reward. Others are more marginal because they do not necessarily have general application, e.g. family-friendly policies, profit-related pay and share ownership.

An alternative approach stresses that HRM may be contingent, with 'best fit' HRM differing according to the stage in the business life cycle, the strategy-structure configuration and the business strategy being pursued. Schuler and Jackson (1987) identify three alternative 'best fit' strategies - innovation, quality enhancement and cost-reduction - but acknowledge that organizations may pursue two or more competitive strategies simultaneously. Hence 'best fit' may embrace both 'high road' and 'low road' approaches. Espousal of the 'best practice' approach suggests that the 'sophisticated paternalist' and 'consultative' models of industrial relations management (Purcell and Sisson, 1983) triumph over 'bleak houses' and 'black holes', in effect denying them legitimacy when they undoubtedly exist. Legge (1995b) proceeds from the basis that HRM has never been anything but 'hard'.

'Some managements have always preferred a unitarist approach and have exploited their workers - HRM may have provided a language to justify that approach but was not responsible for it'. Marchington and Grugulis (2000) point out that the rhetoric of HRM disguises the way in which it reinforces managerial control, sometimes against workers' interests or wishes.

Indeed the rhetoric of 'best practice' HRM can be turned on its head to depict 'low road' HRM as the following examples show:

- The practice of teamworking can be regarded as a means to replace over the shoulder managerial control by peer surveillance.
- Empowerment is about getting workers to take more responsibility with no commensurate increase in reward.
- Using the management chain to cascade information simply denies employees any voice in what is going on around them.

In support of the contingency approach Cappelli and Crocker-Hefter (1996) caution against 'best practice' and benchmarking, suggesting each organization should develop its own set of core competencies to reflect its own distinctiveness. Conversely others have observed that international pressures have driven countries and companies to adopt similar HRM concepts, regulations and practices.

Purcell (1999) considers that a 'best practice' prescription is a cul-de-sac, while contingency and 'best fit' HRM are a chimera. Both are predicated upon the logic of rational choice and neglect other organizational processes at work.

Importantly they fail to identify circumstances in which particular HRM practices are successful. Others share Purcell's scepticism, denying that HRM can exist in the diametrically opposite forms of 'soft' and 'hard'. Policies are always both 'hard' and 'soft', e.g. McDonald's provides all the support that employees need to perform to the required level, yet it deploys a 'no excuses' policy if they do not conform. Legge (1995b) sees the implementation of Walton's soft model of mutuality being restricted to knowledge-based industries seeking value added. Even though the majority of employees may fall within this larger than normal privileged core, there may still be a minority for whom harder conditions exist.

Keenoy's (1999) metaphor of HRM as a hologram, or virtual image, usefully encapsulates why the HRM debate has become somewhat sterile. As a hologram HRM changes its appearance as we move around its image, and appears different each time we look at it. It is akin to quality, something that is always in the process of becoming (a continuous and never-ending process).

The paradox remains why so few American (Milkman, 1998) and British workplaces take the 'high road' to employment management. While the UK historical tradition does not favour this approach, it is also likely to have been undermined by the devolution of HR activities and associated budgets, which are necessary to measure the contribution of HRM. Thus line managers' HR actions will be driven by adherence to short-term financial targets, and working to budgets will drive a short-term employment relations agenda, encouraging a deterioration towards 'low road' practices.

Ultimately people are always expendable. Labour costs may be a significant proportion of operating costs, and are always far easier to trim than other fixed costs. BA cannot cut the cost of fuel or new aircraft, so it is cheaper to sack and re-employ sizeable numbers of workers because re-employment costs are lower than exit costs. It is hardly surprising, then, that the overall conclusion from WERS was that the broad approach to employment relations management in Britain was 'one of retaining control and doing what they could to control costs'.

As the HI product is highly diverse and ever-changing, there is no reason why 'high road' HRM should be effective, and there will be circumstances in which other HRM strategies, including cost-control will be effective. Indeed support for this comes from contingency models of HRM. In new businesses the personal influence of the founder and an entrepreneurial spirit will predominate over a clearly defined organization or HRM structure. As organizations mature and become more complex quality assurances, standardization, systems, structures controlling costs and increasing efficiency begin to emerge. These are heightened where there are plans to expand a chain under franchises. Concurrently more attention is given towards systematic 'people management', including motivating managers, spreading values and developing a service culture, in order to sustain the business. In short there is a mix of 'hard' and 'soft' measures that conforms to Lashley's 'promise of control and commitment'.

A Psychological Contract

A further problem with the 'best practice' approach is that it does not take account of employees' view of HRM within the psychological contract. Renewed interest in the psychological contract and taking account of employees' expectations has become an increasingly important dimension of HRM.

The concept of the psychological contract, where employees' needs are necessarily satisfied to ensure commitment to organizational objectives that will translate into business success, has remained the keystone of Torrington's philosophy of HRM as an emergent version of personnel management. Grant (1999) identifies two approaches. The first derives from Argyris (1960) and Schein (1978) who focus on employer-employee perceptions to the exchange implied by the employment relationship within the broader context of social processes.

Alternatively perceptions are shaped in the mind of the employee. All approaches draw from expectancy theory, where the state of the psychological contract is influenced by our desired goals and outcomes, while the experience we have of these goals and outcomes determines our motivation to work and our behaviour at work.

Two types of contract can be identified:

- Transactional - characterized by short-term security with most emphasis on financial reward.
- Relational - where long-term employment security is based on a mixture of loyalty, commitment and financial reward.

The nature of the contract following recruitment appears to be linked with new recruits' career motivations and intentions to stay. In transactional contracts workers may perceive regular job change as a prerequisite to career development, a point frequently noted in respect of hospitality workers. Consequently they may expect less from their employer in terms of consultation, appraisal and job security in the knowledge that they will be moving on.

While in one sense 'soft' HRM is implied in a relational contract, and 'hard' HRM is implied in a transactional contract, Grant (1999) questions the extent to which HRM policies and practices viewed across these dichotomies have led to a change in the nature of the psychological contract. Indeed employees may experience both types of psychological contract simultaneously, as noted in the case of part-time students, but it is important to emphasize that their financial reward is relatively poor.

Employees draw on past and current employment experience in order to rationalize and create their own sense of reality in relation to work. A satisfied employee will adopt and believe the prevailing HRM rhetoric. Gibb (2001) also argues that bringing employees into the equation will help to shed light on whether HRM leads to real benefits or exploitation and injustice. Fears that employees are more likely to display a preponderance of negative work attitudes have not been borne out by the WERS findings of general employee satisfaction at work. Employees are generally appreciative and positive about HRM systems, while unhappy employees may still experience effective HRM.

HRM and Service Work

The growth in importance of service work has pointed to the need to develop new theories of alternative forms of work organization and HRM. This is particularly challenging in transitional countries in Central and Eastern Europe in the post-Communist era. Clearly, front-line service work is heterogeneous.

Some forms of service work, e.g. call-centres, have been transformed by advances in digital technology. Technology cannot necessarily substitute for the personalized nature of service work that is integral to many hospitality and tourism activities. However, intensified international competition, with its attendant concentration on marketing and operational strategy, has prompted businesses to focus greater attention on managing the service encounter. The behaviour and performance of indirect service workers are also important, as poor quality food or rooms cannot be compensated by a high standard of direct service delivery. The character of service work and the HRM practices deemed necessary to support a 'best practice'.

We have already noted that the extent to which management is able to achieve its organizational goals through people will depend on the extent to which workers' or customers' aims and aspirations are met. The need to draw the employee- customer relationship into the analysis of HRM derives from the critical role of employee in determining SQ, as Redman and Mathews note: to a very real extent the employee is the service, given the absence of any tangible artefact. They carry the responsibility of projecting the image of the organisation and it is in their hands that the ultimate satisfaction of the consumer rests.

'Delighting the customer' may be marketing objective to ensure repeat business, but it is also highly dependent upon management's ability to 'manage' employees so that they display the right attitude and behaviour, an issue discussed in the previous. The simple point is, if managers are not meeting employees' or customers' expectations, this has negative implications for organizational performance, reinforcing need to consider a three-way psychological contract.

Branded hotels in particular are inevitably very concerned about customer service and quality standards. Hoque's work indicates that larger hotels do attach a large degree of importance to strategic HRM issues, although the findings should not be extrapolated to smaller hotels where 'poor' practice may be commonplace. McGunnigle and Jameson's (2000) study of high commitment in the top 50 hotel groups challenges conclusion that the hotel industry has undergone change, including finding new ways of managing staff.

Service quality and Human Resource Management

The character of service:

- Intangibility of services - cannot be evaluated until consumed.
- Inseparability of service producer from consumer - immediacy and importance of encounter.
- Heterogeneity and variability - every service encounter is different.
- Perishability - the service disappears if not consumed.

Eight key HRM practices:

- Recruitment and selection - based on identification of personality and skills needs, and uses a range of methods.
- Retention - effective programme.
- Teamworking - semi-autonomous, cross-process and multi-functional teams.
- Training and development - quality-related including teamworking process and interpersonal skills.
- Performance appraisal - goals focus on quality goals and effective behaviour, utilizing customer-driven data.
- Reward - payment systems linked to achievement of quality goals.
- Job security - high security, including support where redundancies necessary.
- Employee involvement - fosters open, supportive and participatory employment relations climate.

Case study: HRM and performance in hotels

The relationship between HRM and performance is dependent upon:

- A hotel's business strategy;
- Hotels having a quality focus within that strategy;
- HRM being introduced as an integrated and coherent 'bundle' of packages.

While it is not claimed or shown that a quality-enhancing approach leads to high performance, this study is claimed as unique in demonstrating strong contingency effects, possibly because it is a single industry study. In short high commitment HRM is practised only when there is a 'fit' with product and service strategy.

They take Peccei and Rosenthal's (1997) lead that recruitment and selection, and training and development, including performance appraisal, are all important in developing individual commitment to customer service and culture change. A clear desire for commitment, recruitment and selection is not found to be commensurate with this aim, where there is little development for line managers or strategic integration of training. In designer restaurants:

the lack of coherency both in terms of internal consistency across policy areas and the ways in which different staff groups were managed, suggest that the relationship between approaches to HRM and business strategy is a more complicated one than that suggested by the models based on notions of fit.

Lashley (1998) argues that the amount of employee discretion required to fulfil a particular customer-service need is crucial to understanding 'best fit' between the service offer and the management of employees. His model of four ideal types of HRM relates to the amount of employee involvement and participation in shaping the service encounter, hence the kind of empowerment employees are afforded. The variations on the vertical plane reflect the fact that service work is a mix of tangibles and intangibles, with the latter being regarded as the defining feature of services. Their relationship is an influential factor in determining employment strategy and the form that HRM takes.

Although within food and beverage service vending machines are wholly tangible, fast food is high in tangibles (high technology, standard products), and the intangibles of the service encounter are standardized by use of scripts. Highly personalized service in a gentleman's club might incorporate a high element of intangibles where 'delighting the customer' and considerable discretion are exercised in the conduct of work. The extent to which work needs to be standardized or customized is the most important influence on HRM strategy.

Horizontally the parameters of 'external control' and 'internal control' are broadly in keeping with the 'hard' and 'soft' approaches to the management of employment noted earlier, including direct control vs. responsible autonomy and control vs. commitment. Lashley argues these approaches are misleading in service work because employment strategy is concerned with both control and commitment, and because they fail to recognize the importance of employee discretion as an element of job design, which is crucial to an understanding of the service delivery.

While Lashley's model is a helpful start point to understanding employee management in hospitality and tourism, in practice there are likely to be many variations that reflect the fact that professional, participative, command and control and involvement are not four discrete alternatives. Further he overlooks how employee attitudes to customer service and individual and group behaviour may affect HRM practices and organizational performance in services. As many firms continually seek to reposition themselves the market place to achieve competitive advantage, these approaches are not static.

HUMAN INTERACTION MANAGEMENT

Human Interaction Management (HIM) is the set of principles and patterns for structuring, supporting and controlling human work practices proposed by Keith Harrison-Broninski in his 2005 book "Human Interactions".

Current mainstream techniques and tools for work support, whether categorized as Workflow or as Business Process Management (BPM), deal only with "mechanistic" business processes. In such business processes, human involvement is limited to key data entry and decision points. Workflow/BPM techniques and tools deal with only the externally-observable aspects of work - tasks, that are visible from outside.

HIM extends this to include support for "human-driven" processes focused on human creativity and collaboration. To achieve this, HIM deals not only with tasks, but also with those aspects of work visible from inside - information, interaction and innovation.

In HIM, a business process requiring human knowledge, judgement and experience is divided into Roles, which are then assigned to the appropriate members of an organization via a Human Interaction Management System (HIMS). A HIMS is also used to manage the work and integrate it with organizational strategy/tactics, via separation into "levels of control".

The main focus of HIM is currently on the integration of organizational objectives with human work practices, in order to implement strategy/tactics and fulfil requirements for compliance. However, HIM has application beyond the improvement of organizational efficiency, since it provides a rich set of patterns for structuring and managing collaborative work that are also finding application in spheres such as social/political negotiation, law enforcement and healthcare.

Accounting Management (Business) is the practical application of management techniques to control and report on the financial health of the organization. This involves the analysis, planning, implementation, and control of programmes designed to provide financial data reporting for managerial decision making.

This includes the maintenance of bank accounts, developing financial statements, cash flow and financial performance analysis. Accounting management is a mandatory knowledge module of any MBA programme. Cost management is the process whereby companies use cost accounting to report or control the various costs of doing business. The term CM is widely used in business today. Unfortunately there is no uniform definition. We use

CM to describe the approaches and activities of managers in short run and long run planning and control decisions that increase value for customers and lower costs of products and services. For example, managers make decisions regarding the amount and kind of material being used, changes of plant processes, and changes in product designs. Information from accounting systems helps managers make such decisions, but the information and the accounting systems themselves are not cost management.

Cost management has a broad focus. It includes – but is not confined to – the continuous reduction of costs. The planning and control of costs is usually inextricably linked with revenue and profit planning. For instance, to enhance revenues and profits, managers often deliberately incur additional costs for advertising and product modifications. Cost management is not practiced in isolation. It's an integral part of general management strategies and their implementation. Examples include programme that enhance customer satisfaction and quality as well as programmes that promote blockbuster new product development.

UNIONS AND HUMAN RESOURCE PRACTICES

The data indicate that a union presence is associated with a greater likelihood of a human resource strategy and a mission statement. However, it is wise to be somewhat sceptical about both unless they are clearly reinforced by a set of relevant practices. This subsection therefore takes us a step further by examining the presence at the new sites of the sort of practices commonly associated with human resource management.

The list is not exhaustive and it concentrates on human resource practices rather than some of those that might be associated with the more narrowly defined industrial relations aspects of the new industrial relations. This reflected the key focus of the study and also our knowledge that most of the establishments in the sample would be non-union and therefore issues like pendulum arbitration would be irrelevant.

Perhaps the most interesting result is the lack of consistent differences between union and non-union establishments. In both sets of new establishments, the use of a majority of the innovative human resource management practices is now the norm. Nevertheless significant differences emerge on seven of the items. Two of these concern status and harmonization. Here the differences are not so much between union and non-union as between non-union and single union deals on the one hand and other forms of union recognition on the other. However, in both cases it is the non-union establishments that are most likely to report these practices; and, the differences between the non-union and single union deal establishments are significant.

Therefore, although establishments with single union deals are more like the non-union establishments, they still fall some way short on single status.

The pattern is somewhat similar for two other items, merit pay and appraisal. Non-union establishments are well ahead of all forms of unionized establishment in the use of merit pay. The differences are much less marked on appraisal where it seems that the multi-union establishments are less likely to operate it.

The three remaining items are those where establishments with a single union deal stand out as most likely to have adopted a practice. One is the use of trainability as a major selection criterion; the others are concerned with integration of strategy. Establishments with single union deals are much more likely to claim that human resource policies are integrated with business strategy and that the various human resource policies are integrated with each other. This would fit with the earlier claims to be more likely to have a human resource strategy.

Taking the set of practices as a whole, it appears that they are most likely to be reported in establishments with a single union deal, closely followed by non-union establishments. However, the other unionized establishments are often little different, indicating that a union presence is no bar to most human resource practices.

Despite this, the exceptions may be important. Unionized establishments are less likely to have progressed towards single status and less likely to be using appraisal-linked merit pay. These touch on traditional trade union territory and it would seem that in this territory they are still able to exert some influence on workplace practices.

Unions and Types Strategy

There is some evidence from the preceding analysis that unionized workplaces, and more particularly those with a single union deal, are more likely to have developed a coherent human resource strategy. However, not all establishments have a strategy and not all have introduced human resource management practices. To explore whether a union presence is compatible with the kind of high utilization human resource strategy sometimes associated with best human resource practice but also often seen as inimical to a trade union presence, we can reclassify establishments.

The basis for this classification was introduced earlier. Those establishments labelled Good have a human resource strategy, defined in the questionnaire as being formally endorsed and actively supported by the top management at the site; and also a high use of human resource practices, defined arbitrarily as more than half of those listed. The Bad are the opposite in that they have no strategy and use less than half the practices listed. The Ugly have a strategy but use less than half the practices while the Lucky have no strategy but use more than half the practices.

If strategic integration is at all important, we would expect the Good to report better outcomes than the Bad. If strategic integration around a distinctive set of human resource practices confers an advantage then we would also expect to see the Good report better outcomes than the Ugly and Lucky. By comparing across the groups we can also identify whether adoption of practices without a strategy—the approach of the Lucky—also has an impact on outcomes. In our total sample of 245 establishments, 107 (43.7 per cent) were classified as Good, 70 (28.6 per cent) as Bad, 28 (11.4 per cent) as Ugly, and 40 (16.3 per cent) as Lucky.

The key question for the debate about human resource management and the new industrial relations is whether the Good are compatible with unionism.

The results confirm that a union presence is compatible with a high utilization model of human resource management. Indeed, if we examine the distribution, a higher proportion of union than non-union establishments fall in the good category. This is due to the greater likelihood that they will have a human resource strategy. In contrast, more of the non-union establishments fall into the lucky category.

They have adopted the practices but have not developed a strategy. The multivariate analysis confirms this pattern but reveals where the differences lie. It is the establishments with a single union deal that are significantly more likely to fall within the Good category while the non-union are significantly more likely to be Lucky. No group stands out as more likely to be Bad or Ugly, although, contrary to expectation, there is a slight tendency for them to be unionized rather than not.

Summarizing the results to date, we have shown that at new establishments, those set up in the 1980s or more recently, industrial relations, manifested in a trade union presence and human resource management are able to exist side by side. However, we can go further than this. It appears that, more particularly in the case of single union deals, it is less a matter of the systems coexisting as of being integrated through a coherent strategy.

Indeed, unionized workplaces are more likely than their non-union counterparts to have a human resource strategy. There do appear to be some differences between the types of union presence. Without a single union deal, there is a slightly lower use of human resource practices and slightly less evidence of the sort of strategic pursuit of a high utilization policy categorized as the Good.

We have shown that with perhaps two exceptions, represented by single status and appraisal-related merit pay, the unions do not inhibit human resource management practice. The next key question is whether they have any impact on performance.

The Impact of Unions

If we wish to conduct a rigorous test of the impact of unions on performance and other outcomes, it is firstly necessary to see if there are links between human resource policy and practice and outcomes. If there are, then it will be necessary to hold this factor constant in order to ascertain the effect which unions have on performance *per se,* irrespective of the policies which are being used. The wider and controversial literature concerning the impact of unions on performance suggests that on balance they act as a drag. However, it is plausible to hypothesize that where a union presence is part of a planned human resource strategy in a new workplace, this is less likely to be the case.

The first step is to examine the impact of human resource policy and practice on outcomes. This is an important and interesting topic in its own light. For this purpose, we retain the integrative distinction between the Good, the Bad, the Ugly, and the Lucky. These results show that there are consistent differences between the policy types and it will therefore be necessary to hold policy effects constant when testing for union effects.

It shows the strength of the links between the use of strategically integrated human resource policies and performance. Specifically, the good establishments, those with a human resource strategy and a high uptake of human resource practices, consistently report better outcomes. At the other extreme, those with the poorer outcomes, revealed most clearly are the Bad, those without a strategy or much use of human resource practices.

The Ugly and the Lucky both report consistently poorer performance than the Good on all three types of outcome. This result will be of great encouragement to those who are attempting to implement a high utilization human resource strategy. This is the first UK. study to date which demonstrates the benefits of such a strategy so clearly.

We can now hold the human resource policy variable constant while examining the impact of unions on outcomes. The resulting multivariate analysis is shown. First, however, we can examine the descriptive results.

The results reveal few significant differences between the various categories. There are some exceptions. Establishments with a single union deal claim to have weathered the recession more successfully than multi-union establishments. Industrial disputes are predictably less likely in non-union establishments. Finally there is a trend towards higher quality of staff in single union deal establishments compared with the multi-union.

Only when the controls are imposed do the differences become clearer. The unionized establishments, taken as a whole, report poorer outcomes on almost all variables.

On a number they are significant. However, as expected, there are variations according to the type of union arrangement. The rest indicates that the poorer outcomes are most likely to be found at the multi-union establishments. In particular, they appear to have poorer human resource outcomes. In contrast, the only significant factor among the single union establishments is the greater likelihood of industrial conflict compared with the non-union establishments. Indeed, on issues associated with flexibility they appear to be at an advantage.

What these results indicate is that the presence of a union still acts as a modest but sometimes significant drag on performance. The effects are greater for multi-unionism and least for single union deals.

Despite the earlier evidence of a willingness on the part of union establishments to embrace human resource practices, it seems that the unions still exert some influence on workplace outcomes. Finally, it is worth noting that the human resource strategy types appear to exert more influence than the unions. Performance is poorer in the Bad establishments than in the multi-union establishments.

The first key question we set out to explore through the study of greenfield sites is whether human resource management and trade-unionism can coexist. The answer from this study is an unequivocal yes. Most human resource management practices are just as likely to exist at unionized establishments as at those without unions. There are some variations on this general pattern.

The first important variation is the finding that the presence of a trade union is associated with a greater use of a human resource management strategy and a mission statement, which, in addition, is more likely to refer explicitly to human resource issues. This needs to be qualified by the analysis of types of trade union presence. A strategy and mission statement is particularly likely to exist where there is a single union deal. We cannot tell from this cross-sectional data whether the union presence encourages managers to think strategically or whether those who think strategically opt for a single union deal.

Although we suspect that the causal direction varies from context to context, since the choice of whether to recognize a union is an increasingly open one, we suspect that management thinks strategically about both human resource management and the new industrial relations and decides to opt for a single union deal.

Multiple unionism, by contrast, may come into operation in those establishments where a parent company already has a central collective agreement with a number of unions. It follows that the majority of such cases are likely to be British-owned. Examination of the national ownership patterns confirms that this is indeed the case. The UK- and USA-owned establishments where any union is recognized are the least likely to report a single union deal.

The pattern across the range of human resource management practices also reveals some specific differences and helps to sharpen the distinction between the new industrial relations, reflected in single union deals, and the traditional industrial relations reflected in multi-unionism. Any type of trade union presence is associated with less use of single status and use of performance appraisal and merit pay for all staff.

Single union deals on the other hand are associated with a set of practices broadly similar to non-union establishments but with the added advantage of having a more coherent human resource strategy. These results are strongly supported by Millward's analysis of the new industrial relations based on WIRS3. He finds that establishments with single union deals are consistently more likely to have a range of innovative practices, implying once again that they think strategically about single union deals and human resource management issues together.

The second major question we have explored is whether a union presence facilitates or constrains aspects of performance. The general conclusion is that unions inhibit performance and multi-unionism inhibits it more. However, this conclusion requires some qualification since single union deals have far less impact on performance, compared with non-union establishments.

The similarity between non-union establishments and those with a single union deal brings us back to the question of whether this type of unionism is an empty shell. It does not appear to constrain management. Indeed, it is associated with what managers believe to be greater commitment to the organization among lower level staff and with greater flexibility than even non-union establishments. In contrast, multi-unionism is associated with poorer outcomes on all variables except labour turnover and absenteeism; and on five of the outcomes, the differences with non-union establishments are significant. Thus multi-unionism is associated with poorer performance. This confirms the economic research on the impact of unions.

Before reaching the general conclusion that multi-unionism is bad for performance, we should recall the data on human resource management types. The Bad establishments are more clearly associated with poor outcomes than the multi-union establishments, implying that decisions about human resource strategy are more important for outcomes than decisions about multi-unionism—assuming that managers take decisions about these issues and that in practice the two can be disentangled. In one sense, this marginalizes the union issue. On the other hand, unions may always have been marginal to performance in the great majority of organizations although industrial relations specialists, with their distinctive focus on unions, have been understandably reluctant to acknowledge this.

To summarize, the new trade-unionism, reflected most strongly in single union deals, is compatible with human resource management. There is more of a question mark against multi-unionism. This raises the question of why any company will recognize a trade union at a new establishment. A single union deal has very little impact compared with non-union establishments suggesting that they turn unions into empty shells.

Multi-unionism has a somewhat negative impact. In our sample of post-1980 establishments, approximately a third recognized one or more trade unions. However, this fell to 20 per cent in the 'pure' greenfield sites compared with 42 per cent in the refurbished sites. The great majority of managers have already decided that there is no value in recognizing a trade union. So why do others do so?

The evidence from our case studies supports the more extensive data from the CLIRS2. This indicates that unions will be recognized in those companies which have a centralized system of collective bargaining which they wish to retain. Secondly, as our comparison of greenfield and refurbished sites suggests, unions may be recognized at those workplaces which are taken over, even if shut down for a while and refurbished, and where a union was already recognized.

It is possible that in some cases there may be scope for the operation of individual values. Some managers, including perhaps personnel managers in particular, may value the presence of a trade union as a counterweight to arbitrary management treatment. Since we have found little evidence of any trade union official presence in our case studies, it appears that the personnel manager may act as promoter and recruiter for the union. However, this is likely to become less common. The evidence from this study suggests that as we learn more about the impact of the new industrial relations, in the absence of any change towards a government that more actively encourages them, the outlook for trade unions is bleak.

The practices and process of 'new industrial relations' and human resource management have become the primary agenda of industrial relations research and teaching whether prescriptive or critical; notwithstanding this primacy new industrial relations and human resource management are of no use in themselves; they are propagated as mechanisms to rejuvenate the British economy, its manufacturing sector in particular, and connect with current dynamics in capitalist production. Without an evaluation of the problematic nature of the wider dynamics of capitalist production new industrial relations and human resource management are both abstract and decontextual.

In the period since 1945 the dynamics of capitalist production have been generalized under two broad headings. The post-war period is generalized as 'Fordism', centred on the mass production of standardized commodities, institutionalized collective bargaining, and Welfare State capitalism. The contemporary period is generalized as 'Post-Fordism' premissed on the demise of mass consumer markets, the rise of niche markets, and the erosion of social democracy in the institutional base of the State. In particular, it has rejected collective bargaining and trade union recognition as 'good' industrial relations.

If we accept that Fordism and Post-Fordism generalize periods in capitalist production it is equally necessary to question the degree to which national pathways in capitalist production measure up to the generalization. We contend that national pathways predominate over generalized descriptions in the development of capitalist production. In consequence we must evaluate the relationship between capital, labour, and the State within national pathways in order to illustrate how historical formation within particular nation states weakens the viability of generalized description.

We suggest that the British State has been subject to a formative influence of libertarian *laissez faire* which emphasizes freedom and liberty from centralized and institutionalized measures enacted by the State. In the post-war period plural industrial relations and voluntary regulation epitomize this influence. Equally during the post-war period the British State was subject to the contextual influence of social democracy and plural public policy manifest in 'good' industrial relations as collective bargaining and trade union recognition.

The contemporary erosion of social democracy and 'good' industrial relations has separated the State from an active interest in capitalist accumulation; in fact the disengagement of pluralism in industrial relations has wound up the contextual influence of social democracy and returned the formative influence of libertarian *laissez faire* as contemporary contextual influence in the State, its accumulation strategy, and public policy on industrial relations.

However, the disengagement of pluralism, an accumulation strategy based on flexibility, and redefined 'good' industrial relations are all caught in the permanent yet unfolding contradiction of libertarian *laissez faire;* that is, a continuity in historical formation within a particular nation state and the predominance of this over generalized pathways in capitalist production. We contend that new industrial relations is in the British case isolated and disengaged from contemporary material dynamics other than promoting what can be termed 'extra flexibility'.

This isolation illustrates the weakness of prescriptive generalization in capitalist production because Post-Fordism and Fordism are based on a presumed role for the State, which we suggest never developed in the British State. This seeks to illustrate the isolation of new industrial relations as informed by human resource management from market and production strategies which are portrayed as the (future) basis of capitalist production in the UK.

This develops a wide-ranging polemic and is eclectic in its discussion with references to the State and its current strategy of disengagement from active involvement in capitalist accumulation. Since 1945 'good' industrial relations have been a central feature of public policy.

For much of the post-war period 'good' industrial relations was constituted in terms of plural State institutions presiding over an economy where collective bargaining and trade union recognition were functional elements within an accumulation strategy centred on Fordism. By 1979 'good' industrial relations had become 'bad' industrial relations; almost overnight the Thatcher Government rejected the pluralism in the post-war settlement between capital and labour.

More significantly the Thatcher Government came to power when the period of capitalist development generalized as Fordism was exhausted. The contemporary State has initiated a libertarian, that is individual accumulation, strategy, disengaged pluralism in industrial relations, and sought to roll back much of its previous social democratic orthodoxy in areas such as employment policy, the Welfare State, nationalized industry, and industrial relations. Good industrial relations have been reconstituted and now emphasize the managerial prerogative and less industrial action as the basis of good.

This contends that the contemporary State's method of operation, disengagement from social democracy, actively frustrates its efforts to generate a positive flexible Post-Fordism in the UK. This asserts that flexibility is a means to an end in the movement between stages of capitalist development whereas in the UK it has become an end in itself.

In consequence, in the UK, flexibility is not a bridge between Fordism and Post-Fordism but a method of making the entrails of Fordism more flexible, thereby contributing to the development of a neo-Fordist low wage, low productivity, yet flexible, economy. Hence our contention that sovereign national pathways to capitalist development predominate over generalized periodizations. In order to develop this overall argument the discussion which follows is divided into four sections.

In Section 2 formative and contextual influences on the British State are briefly introduced in order to specify the limited nature of the British State. Section 3 evaluates the process of contemporary State disengagement from the post-war social democratic orthodoxy; the strategy of Conservative governments and their attempts to reconstitute good industrial relations is located in the process of disengagement.

Section 4 evaluates new industrial relations, new market and production strategies, and suggests that institutional disengagement by the State isolates new (improved) industrial relations from new market and production strategies. In consequence typology-normative description of market and production strategies are removed from their actual constitution in the UK's national pathway.

Section 5 builds on the arguments of the previous sections to illustrate the limited nature of new industrial relations in the generation of flexibility and sustainable improvement in productivity.

CUSTOMER RELATIONSHIP

Customer relationship management (CRM) covers methods and technologies used by companies to manage their relationships with clients. Information stored on existing customers (and potential customers) is analyzed and used to this end. Automated CRM processes are often used to generate automatic personalized marketing based on the customer information stored in the system.

Customer relationship management is a corporate level strategy, focusing on creating and maintaining relationships with customers. Several commercial CRM software packages are available which vary in their approach to CRM. However, CRM is not a technology itself, but rather a holistic approach to an organisation's philosophy, placing the emphasis firmly on the customer.

CRM governs an organization's philosophy at all levels, including policies and processes, front-of-house customer service, employee training, marketing, systems and information management. CRM systems are integrated end-to-end across marketing, sales, and customer service.

A CRM system should:

- Identify factors important to clients.
- Promote a customer-oriented philosophy
- Adopt customer-based measures
- Develop end-to-end processes to serve customers
- Provide successful customer support
- Handle customer complaints
- Track all aspects of sales
- Create a holistic view of customers' sales and services information

There are three fundamental components in CRM:

- Operational - automation of basic business processes (marketing, sales, service)
- Analytical - analysis of customer data and behaviour using business intelligence
- Collaborative - communicating with clients

Operational CRM provides automated support to "front office" business processes (sales, marketing and service). Each interaction with a customer is generally added to a customer's history, and staff can retrieve information on customers from the database as necessary.

According to Gartner Group operational CRM typically involves three general areas:

- *Sales force automation (SFA):* SFA automates some of a company's critical sales and sales force management tasks, such as forecasting, sales administration, tracking customer preferences and demographics, performance management, lead management, account management, contact management and quote management.
- *Customer service and support (CSS):* CSS automates certain service requests, complaints, product returns and enquiries.
- *Enterprise marketing automation (EMA) :* EMA provides information about the business environment, including information on competitors, industry trends, and macroenvironmental variables. EMA applications are used to improve marketing efficiency.

Integrated CRM software is often known as a "front office solution", as it deals directly with customers. Many call centers use CRM software to store customer information. When a call is received, the system displays the associated customer information (determined from the number of the caller). During and following the call, the call center agent dealing with the customer can add further information. Some customer services can be fully automated, such as allowing customers to access their bank account details online or via a WAP phone.

Analytical CRM

Analytical CRM analyses data (gathered as part of operational CRM, or from other sources) in an attempt to identify means to enhance a company's relationship with its clients.

The results of an analysis can be used to design targeted marketing campaigns, for example:

- Acquisition: Cross-selling, up-selling
- Retention: Retaining existing customers (antonym: customer attrition)
- Information: Providing timely and regular information to customers

Other examples of the applications of analyses include:

- Contact optimization
- Evaluating and improving customer satisfaction
- Optimizing sales coverage
- Fraud detection
- Financial forecasts
- Price optimization
- Product development
- Programme evaluation
- Risk assessment and management
- Strategic Marketing
- Operational marketing

Data collection and analysis is viewed as a continuing and iterative process. Ideally, business decisions are refined over time, based on feedback from earlier analyses and decisions. Most analytical CRM projects use a data warehouse to manage data.

Collaborative CRM

Collaborative CRM focuses on the interaction with customers (personal interaction, letter, fax, phone, Internet, e-mail etc.)

Collaborative CRM includes:

- Providing efficient communication with customers across a variety of communications channels
- Providing online services to reduce customer service costs
- Providing access to customer information while interacting with customers

Driven by authors from the Harvard Business School (Kracklauer/Mills/Seifert), Collaborative CRM also seems to be the new paradigma to succeed the leading Efficient Consumer Response and Category Management concept in the industry/ trade relationship.

In its broadest sense, CRM covers all interaction and business with customers. A good CRM programme allows a business to acquire customers, provide customer services and retain valued customers.

Customer services can be improved by:

- Providing online access to product information and technical assistance around the clock
- Identifying what customers value and devising appropriate service strategies for each customer
- Providing mechanisms for managing and scheduling follow-up sales calls
- Tracking all contacts with a customer
- Identifying potential problems before they occur
- Providing a user-friendly mechanism for registering customer complaints
- Providing a mechanism for handling problems and complaints
- Providing a mechanism for correcting service deficiencies
- Storing customer interests in order to target customers selectively
- Providing mechanisms for managing and scheduling maintenance, repair, and on-going support
- Scalability: the system should be highly scalable, as the volume of data stored in the system grows over time
- Communication channels: CRM can interface with a variety of different channels (phone, WAP, Internet etc.)
- Workflow - a company's business processes need to be represented by the system with the ability to track the individual stages and transfer information between steps
- Assignment - the ability to assign requests, such as service requests, to a person or group.
- Database - the means of storing customer data and histories (in a data warehouse)
- Customer privacy considerations, such as data encryption and legislation.

IMPROVING CUSTOMER RELATIONSHIPS

CRM applications often track customer interests and requirements, as well as their buying habits. This information can be used to target customers selectively. Furthermore, the products a customer has purchased can be tracked throughout the product's life cycle, allowing customers to receive information concerning a product or to target customers with information on alternative products once a product begins to be phased out.

Repeat purchases rely on customer satisfaction, which in turn comes from a deeper understanding of each customer and their individual needs. CRM is an alternative to the "one size fits all" approach. In industrial markets, the technology can be used to coordinate the conflicting and changing purchase criteria of the sector.

The data gathered as part of CRM raises concerns over customer privacy and enables persuasive sales techniques. However, CRM does not necessarily involve gathering new data, but also includes making better use of customer information gathered as a result of routine customer interaction.

The privacy debate generally focuses on the customer information stored in the centralized database itself, and fears over a company's handling of this information. For example, there is virtually no way a consumer can determine if the company shares private (personally identifiable) data with third parties. Furthermore, companies may not always accurately declare to the consumer the types of information collected by CRM systems and the specific purposes for which the information is used.

CRM is also important to non-profit organizations, which sometimes use the terms "constituent relationship management", "contact relationship management" or "community relationship management" to describe their information systems for managing donors, volunteers and other supporters. salesforce.com, a popular CRM service that is on demand, offers its products for free to nonprofit organizations

Financial Management

New business leaders and managers have to develop at least basic skills in financial management. Expecting others in the organization to manage finances is clearly asking for trouble. Basic skills in financial management start in the critical areas of cash management and bookkeeping, which should be done according to certain financial controls to ensure integrity in the bookkeeping process. New leaders and managers should soon go on to learn how to generate financial statements (from bookkeeping journals) and analyze those statements to really understand the financial condition of the business. Financial analysis shows the "reality" of the situation of a business — seen as such, financial management is one of the most important practices in management. This topic will help you understand basic practices in financial management, and build the basic systems and practices needed in a healthy business.

If your small business is a corporation, you would do well to find someone experienced in financial management and encourage them to be your board treasurer (your board chair has this responsibility to find someone suitable, as well). Therefore, it's important to understand the role of the board treasurer.

New, more "organic" forms or organizations (self-organizing organizations, self-managed teams, network organizations, etc.) allow organizations to be more responsive and adaptable in today's rapidly changing world. These forms also cultivate empowerment among employees, much more than the hierarchical, rigidly structured organizations of the past. Many people assert that as the nature of organizations has changed, so must the nature of management control. Some people go so far as to claim that management shouldn't exercise any form of control whatsoever. They claim that management should exist to support employee's efforts to be fully productive members of organizations and communities — therefore, any form of control is completely counterproductive to management and employees.

Some people even react strongly against the phrase "management control". The word itself can have a negative connotation, e.g., it can sound dominating, coercive and heavy-handed. It seems that writers of management literature now prefer use of the term "coordinating" rather than "controlling".

Regardless of the negative connotation of the word "control", it must exist or there is no organization at all. In its most basic form, an organization is two or more people working together to reach a goal. Whether an organization is highly bureaucratic or changing and self-organizing, the organization must exist for some reason, some purpose, some mission (implicit or explicit) — or it isn't an organization at all. The organization must have some goal. Identifying this goal requires some form of planning, informal or formal. Reaching the goal means identifying some strategies, formal or informal. These strategies are agreed upon by members of the organization through some form of communication, formal or informal. Then members set about to act in accordance with what they agreed to do. They may change their minds, fine. But they need to recognize and acknowledge that they're changing their minds.

This form of ongoing communication to reach a goal, tracking activities toward the goal and then subsequent decisions about what to do is the essence of management coordination. It needs to exist in some manner — formal or informal. The following are rather typical methods of coordination in organizations. They are used as means to communicate direction and guide behaviours in that direction. The function of the following methods is not to "control", but rather to guide. If, from ongoing communications among management and employees, the direction changes, then fine. The following methods are changed accordingly.

Note that many of the following methods are so common that we often don't think of them as having anything to do with coordination at all. No matter what one calls the following methods — coordination or control — they're important to the success of any organization.

Administrative Controls

Organizations often use standardized documents to ensure complete and consistent information is gathered. Documents include titles and dates to detect different versions of the document. Computers have revolutionized administrative controls through use of integrated management information systems, project management software, human resource information systems, office automation software, etc. Organizations typically require a wide range of reports, e.g., financial reports, status reports, project reports, etc. to monitor what's being done, by when and how.

Delegation is an approach to get things done, in conjunction with other employees. Delegation is often viewed as a major means of influence and therefore is categorized as an activity in leading (rather than controlling/ coordinating). Delegation generally includes assigning responsibility to an employee to complete a task, granting the employee sufficient authority to gain the resources to do the task and letting the employee decide how that task will be carried out.

Typically, the person assigning the task shares accountability with the employee for ensuring the task is completed. Evaluation is carefully collecting and analyzing information in order to make decisions. There are many types of evaluations in organizations, for example, evaluation of marketing efforts, evaluation of employee performance, programme evaluations, etc. Evaluations can focus on many aspects of an organization and its processes, for example, its goals and processes, outcomes.

Financial Statements

Once the organization has establish goals and associated strategies (or ways to reach the goals), funds are set aside for the resources and labour to the accomplish goals and tasks. As the money is spent, statements are changed to reflect what was spent, how it was spent and what it obtained. Review of financial statements is one of the more common methods to monitor the progress of programmes and plans. The most common financial statements include the balance sheet, income statement and cash flow statement. Financial audits are regularly conducted to ensure that financial management practices follow generally accepted standards, as well.

Performance management focuses on the performance of the total organization, including its processes, critical subsystems (departments, programmes, projects, etc.) and employees. Most of us have some basic impression of employee performance management, including the role of performance reviews. Performance reviews provide an opportunity for supervisors and their employees to regularly communicate about goals, how well those goals should be met, how well the goals are being met and what must be done to continue to meet (or change) those goals. The employee is rewarded in some form for meeting performance standards, or embarks on a development plan with the supervisor in order to improve performance.

Policies help ensure that behaviours in the workplace conform to federal and state laws, and also to expectations of the organization. Often, policies are applied to specified situations in the form of procedures. Personnel policies and procedures help ensure that employee laws are followed (e.g., laws such as the Americans with Disabilities Act, Occupational Health and Safety Act, etc.) and minimize the likelihood of costly litigation. A procedure is a step-by-step list of activities required to conduct a certain task. Procedures ensure that routine tasks are carried out in an effective and efficient fashion.

QUALITY CONTROL AND OPERATIONS MANAGEMENT

The concept of quality control has received a great deal of attention over the past twenty years. Many people recognize phrases such as "do it right the first time, "zero defects", "Total Quality Management", etc. Very broadly, quality includes specifying a performance standard (often by benchmarking, or comparing to a well-accepted standard), monitoring and measuring results, comparing the results to the standard and then making adjusts as necessary. Recently, the concept of quality management has expanded to include organization-wide programmes, such as Total Quality Management, ISO9000, Balanced Scorecard, etc. Operations management includes the overall activities involved in developing, producing and distributing products and services.

Risk, Safety and Liabilities

For a variety of reasons (including the increasing number of lawsuits), organizations are focusing a great deal of attention to activities that minimize risk, avoid liabilities and ensure safety of employees. Several decades ago, it was rare to hear of an organization undertaking contingency planning, disaster recovery planning or critical incident analysis. Now those activities are becoming commonplace.

Evaluation Activities

Evaluation, in the context of management activities, is carefully collecting information about something in order to make necessary decisions about it. There are a large number and wide variety of evaluations that can occur in businesses, whether for-profit or nonprofit. Evaluation is closely related to performance management (whether about organizations, groups, processes or individuals), which includes identifying measures to indicate results. Evaluation often includes collecting information around these measures to conclude the extent of performance.

Advertising and Promotions

Before you learn more about advertising, you should get a basic impression of what advertising is. Advertising is a major "phase" of overall product or service development and management. Advertising is specifically part of the "outbound" marketing activities, or activities geared to communicate to the market, eg, advertising, promotions, public relations, etc. Inbound" marketing activities are geared to communicate from the market, and include, eg, market research about the market.

Although your use of the latest hot marketing and sales strategies may improve the bottom line of your business, you may get into hot "legal waters" if you do not exercise the proper restraints. This article discusses the boundaries beyond which you do not want to stray lest you run afoul of the laws governing false advertising.

Two conflicting principles are involved in advertising law. On the one hand, the First Amendment, which is part of the U.S. Constitution and grants us the right of free speech, protects all forms of communication, including advertising (referred to by lawyers as "commercial speech"). On the other hand, the U.S. Constitution gives the federal government the power to regulate interstate commerce. Most state constitutions similarly give state governments the power to regulate commerce conducted solely within that state.

In exercising its power over interstate commerce, the Congress has enacted two statutes that have the greatest effect on advertising. These are the Federal Trade Commission (FTC) Act and the Lanham Act.

Employees

Your employees of usually the people who interact the most with your customers.

Ask them about products and services that customers are asking for. Ask employees about what the customers complain about.

Comment Cards

Provide brief, half-page comment cards on which they can answer basic questions such as: Were you satisfied with our services? How could we provide the perfect services? Are there any services you'd like to see that don't exist yet?

Competition

What is your competition selling? Ask people who shop there. Many people don't notice sales or major items in stores. Start coaching those around you to notice what's going on with your competition.

Customers

One of the best ways to find out what customers want is to ask them. Talk to them when they visit your facility or you visit theirs.

Documentation and Records

Notice what customers are buying and not buying from you. If you already know what customers are buying, etc., then is this written down somewhere? It should be so that you don't forget, particularly during times of stress or when trying to train personnel to help you out.

Focus Groups

Focus groups are usually 8-10 people that you gather to get their impressions of a product or service or an idea.

Surveys by Mail

You might hate answering these things, but plenty of people don't — and will fill our surveys especially if they get something in return. Promise them a discount if they return the completed form to your facility.

Competitive Analysis

Marketing should include competitor analysis. Who are your competitors? What customer needs and preferences are you competing to meet? What are the similarities and differences between their products/services and yours? What are the strengths and weaknesses of each of their products and services? How do their prices compare to yours? How are they doing overall? How do you plan to compete? Offer better quality services? Lower prices? More support? Easier access to services? How are you uniquely suited to compete with them?

Competitive Intelligence for Business Success

Some businesses think it is best to get on with their own plans and ignore the competition. Others become obsessed with tracking the actions of competitors (often using underhand or illegal methods). Many businesses are happy simply to track the competition, copying their moves and reacting to changes.

Competitor analysis has several important roles in strategic planning:

- To help management understand their competitive advantages/ disadvantages relative to competitors
- To generate understanding of competitors' past, present (and most importantly) future strategies
- To provide an informed basis to develop strategies to achieve competitive advantage in the future
- To help forecast the returns that may be made from future investments (e.g. how will competitors respond to a new product or pricing strategy?

5

Applied Modern Accountancy in Hotel Management

INTRODUCTION

The first book on accounting was written by a Croatian merchant Benedetto Cotrugli, who is also known as Benedikt Kotruljeviæ, from the city of Dubrovnik. During his life in Italy he met many merchants and decided to write, Della Mercatvra et del Mercante Perfetto (On Trade and the Perfect Merchant) in which he elaborated on the principles of modern, double-entry book-keeping. He finished his lifework in 1458. However, his work was not published until 1573, as a result of which his contributions to the field have been overlooked by the general public.

For this reason, Luca Pacioli, also known as Friar Luca dal Borgo, is credited for the "birth" of accounting. His Summa de arithmetica, geometrica, proportioni et proportionalita (Venice 1494), a synthesis of the mathematical knowledge of his time, includes the first published description of the method of keeping accounts that Venetian merchants used at that time, known as the double-entry accounting system.

Although Pacioli codified rather than invented this system, he is widely regarded as the "Father of Accounting". The system he published included most of the accounting cycle as we know it today. He described the use of journals and ledgers, and warned that a person should not go to sleep at night until the debits equalled the credits! His ledger had accounts for assets (including receivables and inventories), liabilities, capital, income, and expenses — the account categories that are reported on an organization's balance sheet and income statement, respectively. He demonstrated year-end closing entries and proposed that a trial balance be used to prove a balanced ledger. His treatise also touches on a wide range of related topics from accounting ethics to cost accounting.

The first known book in the English language on accounting was published in London by John Gouge (or Gough) in 1543. It is described as A Profitable Treatyce called the Instrument or Boke to learn to knowe the good order of the kepyng of the famouse reconynge, called in Latin, Dare and Habere, and, in English, Debitor and Creditor.

A short book of instructions was also published in 1588 by John Mellis of Southwark, in which he says, "I am but the renuer and reviver of an ancient old copie printed here in London the 14 of August 1543: collected, published, made, and set forth by one Hugh Oldcastle, Scholemaster, who, as appeareth by his treatise, then taught Arithmetics, and this booke in Saint Ollaves parish in Marko Lane." John Mellis refers to the fact that the principle of accounts he explains (which is a simple system of double entry) is "after the forme of Venice".

A book described as The Merchants Mirrour, or directions for the perfect ordering and keeping of his accounts formed by way of Debitor and Creditor, after the (so termed) Italian manner, by Richard Dafforne, accountant, published in 1635, contains many references to early books on the science of accountancy. In a chapter in this book, headed "Opinion of Book-keeping's Antiquity," the author states, on the authority of another writer, that the form of book-keeping referred to had then been in use in Italy about two hundred years, "but that the same, or one in many parts very like this, was used in the time of Julius Caesar, and in Rome long before."

An early Dutch writer appears to have suggested that double-entry book-keeping was even in existence among the Greeks, pointing to scientific accountancy having been invented in remote times.

There were several editions of Richard Dafforne's book - the second edition in 1636, the third in 1656, and another in 1684. The book is a very complete treatise on scientific accountancy, beautifully prepared and containing elaborate explanations. The numerous editions tend to prove that the science was highly appreciated in the 17th century. From this time on, there has been a continuous supply of literature on the subject, many of the authors styling themselves accountants and teachers of the art, and thus proving that the professional accountant was then known and employed.

The requirements for entry in the profession of accounting vary from country to country. Accountants may be licensed by a variety of organisations, such as the British qualified accountancy bodies including Association of Chartered Certified Accountants (ACCA) and Institute of Chartered Accountants, and are recognized by titles such as Chartered Certified Accountant (ACCA or FCCA) and Chartered Accountant (UK, Australia, New Zealand, Canada, India, Pakistan, South Africa), Certified Public Accountant (Ireland, Japan, US, Singapore, Hong Kong, the Philippines), Certified Management Accountant (Canada, U.S.), Certified General Accountant (Canada), or Certified Practising Accountant (Australia). Some Commonwealth countries (Australia and Canada) often recognise both the certified and chartered accounting bodies. The majority of "public" accountants in New Zealand and Canada are Chartered Accountants; however, Certified General Accountants are also authorized by legislation to practise public accounting and auditing in all Canadian provinces, except Ontario and Quebec, as of 2005. There is, however, no legal requirement for an accountant to be a paid-up member of one of the many Institutes and other bodies which are effectively a form of professional trade union. Unlike the Law Society, which can legally stop a solicitor from practising, accountancy institutes do not have such authority. However, auditors are regulated.

Before the Enron and other accounting scandals, there were five large firms and were called the Big Five. Since Arthur Andersen's assurance practice split (after the firm was found guilty in the Enron scandal), with a plurality joining KPMG in the US and Deloitte & Touche outside of the US, Arthur Andersen left from the group. Previous to this there were also groupings referred to as the "Big Six" (Arthur Andersen, plus Coopers & Lybrand before its merger with Price Waterhouse) and the "Big Eight" (Ernst and Young prior to their merger were Ernst & Whinney and Arthur Young and Deloitte & Touche was formed by the merger of Deloitte, Haskins and Sells with the firm Touche Ross).

Enron turned out to be only the first of a series of accounting scandals that enveloped the accounting industry in 2002. This is likely to have far-reaching consequences for the U.S. accounting industry. Application of International Accounting Standards originating in International Accounting Standards Board headquartered in London and bearing more resemblance to UK than current US practices is often advocated by those who note the relative stability of the UK accounting system (which reformed itself after scandals in the late 1980s and early 1990s). Accounting reform of a far more comprehensive sort is advocated by those who see issues with capitalism or economics, and seek ecological or social accountability.

According to Accountancy Age's 2005 league table, fee income amongst the Top 50 accounting firms in the UK rose from £6.3bn to £7.0bn. This followed two successive years in which fee income had declined, largely a result of the sale by some of the larger firms of their consultancy arms. Fee income in most business areas - audit, tax, corporate finance and consultancy - rose in the 2005 survey, with insolvency and wealth management being the only segments where revenue fell.

PricewaterhouseCoopers remains the largest firm with fee income totalling £1,780m followed by Deloitte (£1,350m), KPMG (£1,066m) and Ernst & Young (£945m). The combined revenue of the Big Four accounted for £5.0bn, 72% of the fee income of the Top 50, down from 78-79% in the years up to the 2002 survey and the third year in succession a decline in their share has occurred (Chart 1). Ernst & Young's fee income is the smallest of the largest four firms, but still over three times that of the next largest firm, Grant Thornton. The amount of fee income tapers off amongst the mid-tier firms so that in total there were only 25 firms that each generated more than £15m of revenue in the 2005 survey.

THE ACCOUNTING CYCLE

In accountancy, an account is a label used for recording and reporting a quantity of almost anything. Most often it is a record of an amount of money owned or owed by or to a particular person or entity, or allocated to a particular purpose. It may represent amounts of money that have actually changed hands, or it may represent an estimate of the values of assets, or it may be a combination of these.

Types of Accounts

1. Asset accounts: represent the different types of economic resources owned by a business, common examples of Asset accounts are cash, cash in bank, building, inventory, prepaid rent, goodwill.
2. Liability accounts: represent the different types of economic obligations by a business, such as accounts payable, bank loan, bonds payable, accrued interest.
3. Equity accounts: represent the residual equity of a business (after deducting from Assets all the liabilities) including Retained Earnings and Appropriations.
4. Revenue accounts: represent the hotel's gross earnings and common examples include Sales, Service revenue and Interest Income.
5. Expense accounts: represent the hotel's expenditures to enable itself to operate. Common examples are electricity and water, rentals, depreciation, doubtful accounts, interest, insurance.
6. Contra-accounts: from the term contra, meaning to deduct, the value of which are opposite the 5 above mentioned types of accounts. For instance, a contra-asset account is Accumulated depreciation. This label represent deductions to a relatively permanent asset like Building.

The accounting process is a series of activities that begins with a transaction and ends with the closing of the books.

Because this process is repeated each reporting period, it is referred to as the accounting cycle and includes these major steps:

1. Identify the transaction or other recognizable event.
2. Prepare the transaction's source document such as a purchase order or invoice.
3. Analyze and classify the transaction. This step involves quantifying the transaction in monetary terms (e.g. dollars and cents), identifying the accounts that are affected and whether those accounts are to be debited or credited.
4. Record the transaction by making entries in the appropriate journal, such as the sales journal, purchase journal, cash receipt or disbursement journal, or the general journal. Such entries are made in chronological order.
5. Post general journal entries to the ledger accounts.

The above steps are performed throughout the accounting period as transactions occur or in periodic batch processes. The following steps are performed at the end of the accounting period:

6. Prepare the trial balance to make sure that debits equal credits. The trial balance is a listing of all of the ledger accounts, with debits in the left column and credits in the right column. At this point no adjusting entries have been made. The actual sum of each column is not meaningful; what is important is that the sums be equal. Note that while out-of-balance columns indicate a recording error, balanced columns do not guarantee that there are no errors. For example, not recording a transaction or recording it in the wrong account would not cause an imbalance.
7. Correct any discrepancies in the trial balance. If the columns are not in balance, look for math errors, posting errors, and recording errors. Posting errors include:
   - Posting of the wrong amount,
   - Omitting a posting,
   - Posting in the wrong column, or
   - Posting more than once.
8. Prepare adjusting entries to record accrued, deferred, and estimated amounts.
9. Post adjusting entries to the ledger accounts.
10. Prepare the adjusted trial balance. This step is similar to the preparation of the unadjusted trial balance, but this time the adjusting entries are included. Correct any errors that may be found.
11. Prepare the financial statements.
    - Income statement: prepared from the revenue, expenses, gains, and losses.
    - Balance sheet: prepared from the assets, liabilities, and equity accounts.
    - Statement of retained earnings: prepared from net income and dividend information.
    - Cash flow statement: derived from the other financial statements using either the direct or indirect method.
12. Prepare closing journal entries that close temporary accounts such as revenues, expenses, gains, and losses. These accounts are closed to a temporary income summary account, from which the balance is transferred to the retained earnings account (capital). Any dividend or withdrawal accounts also are closed to capital.
13. Post closing entries to the ledger accounts.
14. Prepare the after-closing trial balance to make sure that debits equal credits. At this point, only the permanent accounts appear since the temporary ones have been closed. Correct any errors.

15. Prepare reversing journal entries (optional). Reversing journal entries often are used when there has been an accrual or deferral that was recorded as an adjusting entry on the last day of the accounting period. By reversing the adjusting entry, one avoids double counting the amount when the transaction occurs in the next period. A reversing journal entry is recorded on the first day of the new period. Instead of preparing the financial statements before the closing journal entries, it is possible to prepare them afterwards, using a temporary income summary account to collect the balances of the temporary ledger accounts (revenues, expenses, gains, losses, etc.) when they are closed. The temporary income summary account then would be closed when preparing the financial statements.

Accounting Information System

An accounting information system (AIS) is the system of records a business keeps to maintain its accounting system. This includes the purchase, sales, and other financial processes of the business. The purpose of an AIS is to accumulate data and provide decision makers (investors, creditors, and managers) with information to make decisions. While this was previously a paper-based process, most modern businesses now use accounting software. In an Electronic Financial Accounting system the steps in accounting cycle are dependent upon the system itself. Example: some systems allow direct journal posting to the various ledgers and others do not.

Accounting Reform

Accounting reform is an expansion to accounting rules that goes beyond the realm of financial measures for both individual economic entities and national economies. It is advocated by those who consider the focus of the present standards and practices wholly inadequate to the task of measuring and reporting the activity, success, and failure of modern enterprise, including government.

The basic bookkeeping concepts underlying contemporary accounting date back about 500 years to Renaissance Italian practices. Obviously, the vast majority of articulations by modern standard setters have little in common with the accounting practices then used.

Real debate concerns concepts such as whether to report transactions, such as asset acquisitions, at their cost or to report them at their current market values. The former, traditional approach, appeals for its reliability but can quickly lose its relevance due to inflation and other factors; the latter, increasingly common approach, appeals for its relevance but may be less reliable due to its resort to appraisals or other subjective measures. This trade off is essentially impossible to overcome. The relative virtue of either approach depends on the subject matter in question.

Business

Limited reforms within professional management circles have led in the past to activity-based costing, economic value added, regret and risk measures. Not only do most businesses raise capital based on numbers derived from current standards, there are extensive lobbying efforts by the accounting industry to keep those standards roughly as they are: complex, loopholed, and unable to be applied or audited easily by laymen.

Heads of the U.S. Securities and Exchange Commission since the 1980s have consistently complained that this lobbying makes it impossible for them to apply meaningful reform, even in the wake of accounting scandals, e.g. that which felled Arthur Andersen in 2002.

National Economies

Any comprehensive scheme of accounting reform is a major professional and academic enterprise; Typically it requires examination of the role of each of the fundamental factors of production, an analysis of capital indicating how many types there are and how each supports each factor of a production process. A comprehensive scheme that would affect, for instance, the United Nations standards for national accounts, the rules of the Bank for International Settlements, or listing requirements on the major stock exchanges, would have to defend any change against critics that advocated lesser reforms - making it extraordinarily difficult to achieve simultaneous consent.

Marilyn Waring, who deeply criticized the UN account system for systematically under-valuing the social and economic contributions of women, stated also that she had to read literally an entire room full of books in order even to understand the standards applied today. It seems unlikely that most advocates of reform have the stamina to do so, nor the background required to debate each issue with economists or accountants that build their careers on the detailed extension and improvement of standards that already exist. Most critics considered reform prospects bleak.

The critique from ecological economics was even more fundamental, claiming that most means of measuring well-being indicated that the developed nations were in a state of "uneconomic growth" through the 1980s and 1990s, due mostly to failures of measurement, most or all of which could be tracked back to the practice of using the Gross National Product as a means of making money supply decisions. This is perhaps the most obvious and widely-held critique of current national accounting and economic growth reporting systems - the creators of the GNP and GDP measures themselves advise against its use as a single measure of economic growth - but politicians and press typically do so without caveat nor apology.

Robert Costanza, Paul Hawken, Amory Lovins and others who advocate a consistent global system for valuing natural capital, note that failures in this area are particularly grim: promoting extinction, loss of biodiversity, climate change and destructive weather for the sake of such "growth". John McMurtry characterized this as "the cancer stage of capitalism". What makes "economic sense" under current standards, they argue, is in fact leading to ecological catastrophe, social conflict, and economic chaos.

One barrier to accounting reform are governments themselves. They have the authority to determine what are accepted accounting principles, while using questionable accounting practices themselves. Governments, for example, pay off operating costs with longer-term debt and thus overstate budgetary surpluses or conceal operating deficits. This is not unlike the allegedly fraudulent practices of some corporations.

Accounting Software

Accounting software is computer software that records and processes accounting transactions within functional modules such as accounts payable, accounts receivable, payroll and trial balance. It functions as an accounting information system. It may be developed in-house by the hotel or organization using it, may be purchased from a third party, or may be a combination of a third-party application software package with local modifications. It varies greatly in its complexity and cost. Since the mid 1990s, the market has been undergoing considerable consolidation, with many suppliers ceasing to trade or being bought by larger groups.

Modules

Accounting software is typically composed of various modules, different sections dealing with particular areas of accounting. Among the most common are:

Core Modules:

- *Accounts receivable*—where the hotel enters money received
- *Accounts payable*—where the hotel enters its bills and pays money it owes
- *General ledger*—the hotel's "books"
- *Billing*—where the hotel produces invoices to clients/customers
- *Stock/Inventory*—where the hotel keeps control of its inventory
- *Purchase Orders*—where the hotel orders inventory
- *Sales Orders*—where the hotel records customer order for the supply of inventory Non Core Modules
- *Debt Collection*—where the hotel tracks attempts to collect overdue bills (sometimes part of accounts receivable)
- *Expense*—where employee business-related expenses are entered
- *Inquiries*—where the hotel looks up information on screen without any edits or additions
- *Payroll*—where the hotel tracks salary, wages, and related taxes
- *Reports*—where the hotel prints out data

- *Timesheet*—where professionals (such as attorneys and consultants) record time worked so that it can be billed to clients

THROUGHPUT ACCOUNTING

Throughput accounting (TA) is an alternative to cost accounting proposed by Eliyahu M. Goldratt. It is not based on Standard Costing or Activity Based Costing (ABC). Throughput Accounting is not costing and it does not allocate costs to products and services. It can be viewed as business intelligence for profit maximization. Conceptually throughput accounting seeks to increase the velocity at which products move through an organization by eliminiating bottlenecks within the organization. Cost (or Management) accounting is an organization's internal method used to measure efficiency. Since no one outside the organization uses such internal accounts for investment or other decisions, any methods that an organization finds helpful can be used. Outside parties to a business depend on accounting reports prepared by financial (public) accountants who apply Generally Accepted Accounting Practices (GAAP) issued by the Financial Accounting Standards Board (FASB) and enforced by the U.S. Securities and Exchange Commission (SEC) and other regulatory agencies. Throughput accounting improves profit performance with better management decisions by using measurements that more closely reflect the effect of decisions on three critical monetary variables (throughput, inventory, and operating expense — defined below).

When cost accounting was developed in the 1890's, Labour was the largest fraction of product cost and workers might not know how many hours they would work in a week when they reported on Monday morning. Cost accountants, therefore, concentrated on how efficiently managers used Labour since it was their most important variable resource. Now, however, workers who come to work on Monday morning almost always work 40 hours or more; their cost is fixed rather than variable. Many managers are still evaluated on their Labour efficiencies, though, and many "downsizing," "rightsizing," and other Labour reduction campaigns are based on them.

Goldratt argues that, under current conditions, Labour efficiencies lead to decisions that harm rather than help organizations. Throughput accounting, therefore, removes standard cost accounting's reliance on efficiencies in general and Labour efficiency in particular from management practice. Many cost and financial accountants agree with Goldratt's critique, but they have not agreed on a replacement of their own and there is enormous inertia in the installed base of people trained to work with existing practices.

The recent development of TA is constraints accounting, which focuses more strongly on the role of the constraint in decision making.

The Concept of Throughput Accounting

Goldratt's alternative begins with the idea that each organization has a goal and that better decisions increase its value. The goal for a profit maximizing firm is easily stated, to increase profit, now and in the future. Throughput accounting applies to not-for-profit organizations too, but they have to develop a goal that makes sense in their individual cases. Throughput Accounting also pays particular attention to the concept of bottlenecks in the manufacturing or servicing processes.

Throughput accounting uses three measures of income and expense:

1. *Throughput* (T) is the rate at which the system produces "goal units." When the goal units are money (in for-profit businesses), throughput is sales revenues less the cost of the raw materials (T = S – RM). Note that T only exists when there is a sale of the product or service. Producing materials that sit in a warehouse does not count. ("Throughput" is sometimes referred to as "Throughput Contribution" and has similarities to the concept of "Contribution" in Marginal Costing which is sales revenues less "variable" costs - "variable" being defined according to the Marginal Costing philosophy.)
2. *Investment* (I) is the money tied up in the system. This is money associated with inventory, machinery, buildings, and other assets and liabilities. In earlier TOC documentation, the "I" was interchanged between "Inventory" and "Investment." The preferred term is now only "investment." Note that TOC recommends inventory be valued strictly on totally variable cost associated with creating the inventory, not with additional cost allocations from overhead.
3. *Operating expense* (OE) is the money the system spends in generating "goal units." For physical products, OE is all expenses except the cost of the raw materials. OE includes maintenance, utilities, rent, taxes, payroll, etc.

Organizations that wish to increase their attainment of The Goal should therefore require managers to test proposed decisions against three questions. Will the proposed change:

Increase Throughput? How?

Reduce Investment (Inventory) (money that cannot be used)? How?

Reduce Operating expense? How?

The answers to these questions determine the effect of proposed changes on system wide measurements:

Net profit (NP) = Throughput – Operating Expense = T–OE

Return on investment (ROI) = Net profit/ Investment = NP/I

Productivity (P) = Throughput/ Operating expense = T/OE

Investment turns (IT) = Throughput/ Investment = T/I

These relationships between financial ratios as illustrated by Goldratt are very similar to a set of relationships defined by DuPont and General Motors financial executive Donaldson Brown about 1920. Brown did not advocate changes in management accounting methods, but instead used the ratios to evaluate traditional financial accounting data. Throughput Accounting is an important development in modern accounting that allows managers to understand the contribution of constrained resources to the overall profitability of the enterprise.

MARKETING AUDIT

The first formal step in the marketing planning process is that of conducting the marketing audit. Ideally, at the time of producing the marketing plan, this should only involve bringing together the source material which has already been collected throughout the year - as part of the normal work of the marketing department.

The emphasis at this stage is on obtaining a complete and accurate picture. In a single organization, however, it is likely that only a few aspects will be sufficiently important to have any significant impact on the marketing plan; but all may need to be reviewed to determine just which 'are' the few.

In this context some factors related to the customer, which should be included in the material collected for the audit, may be:

- Who are the customers?
- What are their key characteristics?
- What differentiates them from other members of the population?
- What are their needs and wants?
- What do they expect the 'product' to do?
- What are their special requirements and perceptions?
- What do they think of the organization and its products or services?
- What are their attitudes?

A 'traditional' - albeit product-based - format for a 'brand reference book' (or, indeed, a 'marketing facts book') was suggested by Godley more than three decades ago:

1. Financial data —Facts for this section will come from management accounting, costing and finance sections.
2. Product data —From production, research and development.
3. Sales and distribution data - Sales, packaging, distribution sections.
4. Advertising, sales promotion, merchandising data - Information from these departments.
5. Market data and miscellany - From market research, who would in most cases act as a source for this information.

His sources of data, however, assume the resources of a very large organization. In most organizations they would be obtained from a much smaller set of people (and not a few of them would be generated by the marketing manager alone). It is apparent that a marketing audit can be a complex process, but the aim is simple: 'it is only to identify those existing (external and internal) factors which will have a significant impact on the future plans of the company'.

It is clear that the basic material to be input to the marketing audit should be comprehensive. Accordingly, the best approach is to accumulate this material continuously, as and when it becomes available; since this avoids the otherwise heavy workload involved in collecting it as part of the regular, typically annual, planning process itself - when time is usually at a premium. Even so, the first task of this 'annual' process should be to check that the material held in the current 'facts book' or 'facts files' actually 'is' comprehensive and accurate, and can form a sound basis for the marketing audit itself.

The structure of the facts book will be designed to match the specific needs of the organization, but one simple format - suggested by Malcolm McDonald - may be applicable in many cases. This splits the material into three groups:

1. 'Review of the marketing environment'. A study of the organization's markets, customers, competitors and the overall economic, political, cultural and technical environment; covering developing trends, as well as the current situation.
2. 'Review of the detailed marketing activity'. A study of the company's marketing mix; in terms of the 4 Ps - product, price, promotion and place.
3. 'Review of the marketing system'. A study of the marketing organization, marketing research systems and the current marketing objectives and strategies.

The last of these is too frequently ignored. The marketing system itself needs to be regularly questioned, because the validity of the whole marketing plan is reliant upon the accuracy of the input from this system, and 'garbage in, garbage out' applies with a vengeance.

The analysis of this material will, no doubt, require significant effort. In the first instance it is a matter of selection, of sorting the wheat from the chaff. What is important, and will need to be taken into account in the marketing plan that will eventually emerge from the overall process, will be different for each product or service in each situation. One of the most important skills to be learned in marketing is that of being able to concentrate on just what is important.

It is important to say not just what happened but why. The process of marketing planning encompasses all of the marketing skills. However, a number of these may be particularly relevant at this stage:

- 'Positioning'. The starting point of the marketing plan must be the consumer. It is a matter of definition that his or her needs should drive the whole marketing process. The techniques of positioning and segmentation therefore usually offer the best starting point for what has to be achieved by the whole planning process.

- 'Portfolio planning'. In addition, the coordinated planning of the individual products and services can contribute towards the balanced portfolio.
- '80:20 rule'. To achieve the maximum impact, the marketing plan must be clear, concise and simple. It needs to concentrate on the 20 per cent of products or services, and on the 20 per cent of customers, which will account for 80 per cent of the volume and 80 per cent of the 'profit'.
- '4 Ps'. The 4 Ps can sometimes divert attention from the customer, but the framework they offer can be very useful in building the action plans.

MARKETING OBJECTIVES

It is only at this stage (of deciding the marketing objectives) that the active part of the marketing planning process begins'.

This next stage in marketing planning is indeed the key to the whole marketing process. The marketing objectives state just where the company intends to be; at some specific time in the future. James Quinn succinctly defined objectives in general as: "Goals (or objectives) state 'what' is to be achieved and 'when' results are to be accomplished, but they do not state 'how' the results are to be achieved".

They typically relate to what products (or services) will be where in what markets (and must be realistically based on customer behaviour in those markets).

They are essentially about the match between those 'products' and 'markets'. Objectives for pricing, distribution, advertising and so on are at a lower level, and should not be confused with marketing objectives. They are part of the marketing strategy needed to achieve marketing objectives.

To be most effective, objectives should be capable of measurement and therefore 'quantifiable'. This measurement may be in terms of sales volume, money value, market share, percentage penetration of distribution outlets and so on. An example of such a measurable marketing objective might be `to enter the market with product Y and capture 10 per cent of the market by value within one year'. As it is quantified it can, within limits, be unequivocally monitored; and corrective action taken as necessary.

The marketing objectives must usually be based, above all, on the organization's financial objectives; converting these financial measurements into the related marketing measurements.

It is conventionally assumed that marketing objectives will be designed to maximize volume or profit (or to optimize the utilization of resources in the non-profit sector), by creating demand or rejuvenating existing demand, say; although the various sub-objectives may indicate many different routes to achieving such optimization.

However, as Kotler suggested (in the earlier edition of his book), there may be a number of other objectives:

- Synchromarketing
- Demarketing
- Counter-marketing

1. Synchromarketing - The aim may be to 'redistribute' existing sales (which are already at optimum levels) so that they occur at times, or in places, which the supplier prefers. Thus, for example, organizations which have highly seasonal sales (which make inefficient use of resources) may want to increase non-seasonal sales. Walls achieved this by balancing its summer sales of ice-cream with pies and sausages, demand for which peaks in winter. The suppliers of central-heating oil offer special deals for those customers willing to restock their tanks in summer.
2. Demarketing' - Demand may sometimes exceed supply. In these circumstances the emphasis will be on rationing scarce supplies. Occasionally the supplier, rather than bring on-stream expensive new plant, may seek to persuade customers to buy less (or be less dissatisfied with the scarcity). Some suppliers of electrical energy (electricity generators in Europe and the USA) have heavily advertised energy conservation measures to achieve this end (otherwise, the cost of meeting the peak winter loads would be very high - and unprofitable).
3. Counter-marketing - In what is usually a public-sector activity (but is occasionally undertaken by the private sector, where some uses of a product are damaging the corporate image), there may be an objective of stopping consumption completely. The anti-tobacco and anti-drug campaigns are the most obvious examples; but McDonald's campaigns to stop its customers dropping litter, or the brewers' campaigns to stop drinking and driving, fall into this category.

Emergent Strategy

In this case, the intended strategy, decided upon traditionally or incrementally, is overtaken by events in two main ways. One, which will probably be recognised by the organisation, is that of unrealised strategy; where it proves impossible to implement the chosen strategy in practice.

Less obvious is the emergent strategy which is decided by events in the external environment; and, thus, forced upon the organisation. This may not necessarily be recognised, in its totality, by the organisation - since many of its implications may be hidden. As markets become more complex, however, such emergent strategies are becoming more common.

Many organizations see both these processes in terms of failure - they have been forced, usually by unpredictable events, to abandon their own strategy. There is, accordingly, a tendency for these unwelcome facts to be ignored until they are so obvious that they cannot be avoided. This is a major error. Such deviations must be recognised (probably through one or other form of environmental analysis coupled with networking) as soon as possible-so that the organisation can react in good time.

A much more powerful approach is, though, to be proactive; so seize upon these deviations as the basis for future developments. What needs to be recognised is that emergent strategies are the most powerful of all. They must, by definition, be dierctly derived from the needs of the market - where even successful deliberate strategies may not ideally match market needs but may achieve their targets by sheer force (especially where conviction marketing lies behind them). Emergent strategies are, thus, likely to be vigorous ones.

There are two main approaches to capitalising on such emergent strategies. The first of these, favoured in the West, is the umbrella strategy. This is a form of very positive delegation, in that the overall strategies, the umbrella, are very general in nature - and allow the lower level managers, who are closest to the external environment, the freedom to react to these changes.

A much more direct, and hence even more powerful, approach is that favoured by the Japanese corporations. They integrate emergent strategies with their own. Indeed it is arguable that, in terms of marketing, to a large extent they use emergent strategies instead of their own deliberate strategies. This is evidenced as much by an attitude of mind as by any other feature.

They deliberately go out to look for symptoms of such emergent trends which can be detected in the performance of their own products. More than that, though, they often deliberately launch a range of products rather than a single one to see which is most successful. It is almost as if they deliberately seek out the emergent strategies by offering the best environment for them to develop - the very reverse of the Western approach which seeks to avoid them! The Japanese then go on to build on these emergent strategies with a number of very effective tools - most of which are designed to overcome the major problem which accompanies emergent strategies, that they emerge on the scene much later than deliberate ones (and are likely to be visible to all the competitors at the same time) so that time is the essence. Thus, time management techniques (including parallel development along with flexible manufacturing and JIT) which have been developed by the Japanese offer them a significant competitive advantage in handling such emergent strategies.

ACCOUNTING METHODS

Cash Basis

Cash-basis accounting is a method of bookkeeping that records financial events based on cash flows and cash position. Revenue is recognized when cash is received and expense is recognized when cash is paid. In cash-basis accounting, revenues and expenses are also called cash receipts and cash payments. Cash-basis accounting does not recognize promises to pay or expectations to receive money or service in the future, such as payables, receivables, and prepaid expenses.

This is simpler for individuals and organizations that do not have significant amounts of these transactions, or when the time lag between the initiation of the transaction and the cash flow is very short. Two types of cash-basis accounting exist: *strict* and *modified*. Strict cash-basis follows the cash flow exactly. Modified cash-basis includes some elements from accrual-basis accounting such as inventory and property capitalization.

Issues with Cash Basis

Cash-basis accounting fails to meet GAAP requirements because it does not adhere to the following two GAAP principles:

- *Revenue recognition principle*—Revenue should be recognized when it is realized (e.g. a credit sale)
- *Matching principle*—Revenue should be matched to the expense if possible (e.g. sales to COGS)

Additionally, cash-basis accounting is not viable for cost accounting in manufacturing operations because expenses cannot always be correctly associated with product costs.

Example: When you pay your rent, your landlord would record an income event at the time he receives your payment. The landlord would subsequently record an expense event when he pays the rental agent their fee for your apartment. It is the accounting method used by most individuals, and by some businesses, that have limited payables or receivables or whose income and expense cash flows are closely associated with each other in time.

A simplified Income Statement and Balance Sheet for cash basis accounting might look like the following:

Vandalay Industries

Income Statement

For the year ended December 31, 2004

Revenue	$1,000
Expense	$ 800
Net income	$ 200

Vandalay Industries

Balance Sheet

For the year ended December 31, 2004

Assets	
Cash	$5,500
Total assets	$5,500
Liabilities and Stockholders' Equity	
Common stock	$5,500
Total liabilities and Equity	$5,500

Accrual Basis

Accrual-basis accounting records financial events based on events that change your net worth (the amount owed to you minus the amount you owe others). Standard practice is to record and recognize revenues in the period which they incur and to match them with related expenses in a process known as matching or expense matching. Even though cash is not received or paid in a credit transaction, they are recorded because they are consequential in the future income and cash flow of the hotel. Accrual-basis is GAAP compliant.

Example: Your landlord would record an income event on the day your rent comes due (you owe it to him). He records an expense event when the fee owed to the rental agent comes due for your apartment that month (he owes it to the agent). The details of the actual cash flows and their timing are tracked by bookkeeping.

A simplified Income Statement and Balance Sheet for accrual basis accounting will look like the following (note the existence of receivable and payable):

Vandalay Industries

Income Statement

For the year ended December 31, 2004

Revenues	$1,200
Expenses	$ 800
Net income	$ 400

Vandalay Industries

Balance Sheet

For the year ended December 31, 2004

Assets	
Cash	$5,500
Accounts receivable	$ 200

Total assets	$5,700
Liabilities and Stockholders' Equity	
Accounts payable	$ 100
Common stock	$5,600
Total liabilities and Equity	$5,700

Comparison

- Using cash-basis accounting, income and expenses are recognized only when cash is received or paid out.
- Using accrual-basis accounting, receivables and payables are recognized when a sale is agreed to, even though as yet, no cash has been received or paid out.
- Cash-basis accounting defers all credit transactions to a later date. It is more conservative for the seller in that it does not record revenue until cash receipt. In a growing hotel, this results in a lower income compared to accrual-basis accounting.

A simple example

- A small business such as a fruit stand, which buys its inventory daily for cash at a wholesale market, sells the inventory for cash, and throws away what didn't sell, can get an accurate picture of its profits or losses using cash-basis accounting.
- A remodeling business that gives customers 90 days to pay and that procures materials on account at the lumber yard, must use the accrual method to gain an accurate picture of its financial condition.
- Either business will probably get a relatively accurate picture using either method over a long period of time, except for the transactions that have already begun that are not yet closed.

Standard accrual-basis financial statements (profit statements and balance sheets) do not indicate the cash inflows and outflows of a hotel. The Statement of Cash Flows is created to indicate that information for accrual-basis accounting.

Accrual-basis accounting is more costly to maintain, because it requires the bookkeeper to record many more transactions. However, the advent of accounting software has made the difference between the reporting methods less significant.

Companies that have extended or used credit significantly should use (and in the United States may be required by the Internal Revenue Service to use) the accrual-basis method of accounting. The U.S. Securities and Exchange Commission requires that all publicly traded companies follow GAAP, thus all publicly traded companies publish their financial statements using accrual-basis method.

Three kind of external stakeholders should be considered when deciding the reporting method:

- Creditors
- Stockholders
- Taxation authorities

For the creditors and stockholders of large enterprises, cash basis accounting is financially inadequate. It does not project the future cash flow of the hotel.

For tax purposes, cash basis accounting is highly favored because it defers tax burdens until the cash is received. It is often used by small businesses and organizations that are not required to use the accrual method, both for tax reasons and for its simplicity.

ACTIVITY-BASED COST ACCOUNTING

Activity-based costing (ABC) is a method of allocating costs to products and services. It is generally used as a tool for planning and control. This is a necessary tool for doing value chain analysis.

The concepts of ABC were developed in the manufacturing sector of the U.S. during the 1970s and 80s. During this time, the Consortium for Advanced Manufacturing-International, now known simply as CAM-I, provided a formative role for studying and formalizing the principles that have become more formally known as Activity-Based Costing.

Robin Cooper and Robert Kaplan, proponent of the Balanced Scorecard, brought notice to these concepts in a number of articles published in Harvard Business Review beginning in 1988. Cooper and Kaplan described ABC as an approach to solve the problems of traditional cost management systems. These traditional costing systems are often unable to determine accurately the actual costs of production and of the costs of related services. Consequently managers were making decisions based on inaccurate data especially where there are multiple products.

Instead of using broad arbitrary percentages to allocate costs, ABC seeks to identify cause and effect relationships to objectively assign costs. Once costs of the activities have been identified, the cost of each activity is attributed to each product to the extent that the product uses the activity. In this way ABC often identifies areas of high overhead costs per unit and so directs attention to finding ways to reduce the costs or to charge more for costly products.

Activity-based costing was first clearly defined in 1987 by Robert S. Kaplan and W. Bruns as a chapter in their book Accounting and Management. They initially focused on manufacturing industry where increasing technology and productivity improvements have reduced the relative proportion of the direct costs of labour and materials, but have increased relative proportion of indirect costs. For example increased automation has reduced labour, which is a direct cost, but has increased depreciation, which is an indirect cost.

Traditionally cost accountants had arbitrarily added a broad percentage onto the direct costs to allow for the indirect costs. However as the percentages of overhead costs had risen, this technique became increasingly inaccurate because the indirect costs were not caused equally by all the products. For example one product might take more time in one expensive machine than another product, but since the amount of direct labour and materials might be the same, the additional cost for the use of the machine would not be recognised when the same broad 'on-cost' percentage is added to all products. Consequently, when multiple products share common costs, there is a danger of one product subsidising another.

Like manufacturing industries, financial institutions also have diverse products which can cause cross-product subsidies. Since personnel expenses represent the largest single component of non-interest expense in financial institutions, these costs must also be attributed more accurately to products and customers. Activity based costing, even though developed for manufacturing, can therefore be a useful tool for doing this. This extended use of ABC to financial institutions was presented in 1990 in an article appearing in the Journal of Bank Cost and Management Accounting (Volume 3, Number 2) by Richard Sapp, David Crawford and Steven Rebishcke.

Direct labour and materials are relatively easy to trace directly to products, but it is more difficult to directly allocate indirect costs to products. Where products use common resources differently, some sort of weighting is needed in the cost allocation process. The measure of the use of a shared activity by each of the products is known as the cost driver. For example, the cost of the activity of bank tellers can be ascribed to each product by measuring how long each product's transactions takes at the counter and then by measuring the number of each type of transaction.

Even in activity-based costing, some overhead costs are difficult to assign to products and customers, for example the chief executive's salary. These costs are termed 'business sustaining' and are not assigned to products and customers because there is no meaningful method. This lump of unallocated overhead costs must nevertheless be met by contributions from each of the products, but it is not as large as the overhead costs before ABC is employed.

Although some may argue that costs untraceable to activities should be "arbitrarily allocated" to products, it is important to realize that the only purpose of ABC is to provide information to management. Therefore, there is no reason to assign any cost in an arbitrary manner. Management accountants can be creative in finding other ways to represent these costs on internal reporting statements.

COST ACCOUNTING

Cost accounting is the process of tracking, recording and analyzing costs associated with the products or activities of an organization. In modern accounting, costs are measured in accordance with the Generally Accepted Accounting Principles (GAAP). GAAP reporting records historical events and assigns a monetary value to each event that has taken place. Costs are measured in units of currency by convention. Cost accounting could also be defined as a kind of management accounting that translates the Supply Chain (the series of events in the production process that, in concert, result in a product) into financial values. Managers use cost accounting to support decision making to reduce a hotel's costs and improve its profitability.

There are at least four approaches:

- Standard Cost Accounting
- Activity-based Costing
- Throughput Accounting
- Marginal Costing

Cost accounting has long been used to help managers understand the costs of running a business. Modern cost accounting originated during the industrial revolution, when the complexities of running a large scale business led to the development of systems for recording and tracking costs to help business owners and managers make decisions. In the early industrial age, most of the costs incurred by a business were what modern accountants call "variable costs" because they varied directly with the amount of production. Money was spent on Labour, raw materials, power to run a factory, etc. in direct proportion to production. Managers could simply total the variable costs for a product and use this as a rough guide for decision-making.

Some costs tend to remain the same even during busy periods, unlike variable costs which rise and fall with volume of work. Over time, the importance of these "fixed costs" has become more important to managers. Examples of fixed costs include the depreciation of plant and equipment, and the cost of departments such as maintenance, tooling, production control, purchasing, quality control, storage and handling, plant supervision and engineering. In the early twentieth century, these costs were of little importance to most businesses. However, in the twenty-first century, these costs are often more important than the variable cost of a product, and allocating them to a broad range of products can lead to bad decision making. Managers must understand fixed costs in order to make decisions about products and pricing.

For example: A hotel produced railway coaches and had only one product. To make each coach, the hotel needed to purchase $60 of raw materials and components, and pay 6 laborers $40 each. Therefore, total variable cost for each coach was $300. Knowing that making a coach required spending $300, managers knew they couldn't sell below that price without losing money on each coach. Any price above $300 became a contribution to the fixed costs of the hotel. If the fixed costs were, say, $1000 per month for rent, insurance and owner's salary, the hotel could therefore sell 5 coaches per month for a total of $3000 (priced at $600 each), or 10 coaches for a total of $4500 (priced at $450 each), and make a profit of $500 in both cases.

Standard Cost Accounting

In modern cost accounting, the concept of recording historical costs was taken further, by allocating the hotel's fixed costs over a given period of time to the items produced during that period, and recording the result as the total cost of production. This allowed the *full cost* of products that were not sold in the period they were produced to be recorded in inventory using a variety of complex accounting methods, which was consistent with the principles of Generally Accepted Accounting Principles (GAAP) as established by the Financial Accounting Standards Board for reporting results of publicly owned companies. It also enabled managers to effectively ignore the fixed costs, and look at the results of each period in relation to the "standard cost" for any given product.

For example: if the railway coach hotel normally produced 40 coaches per month, and the fixed costs were still $1000/month, then each coach could be said to incur an overhead of $25 ($1000/40). Adding this to the variable costs of $300 per coach produced a full cost of $325 per coach.

This method tended to slightly distort the resulting unit cost, but in mass-production industries that made one product line, and where the fixed costs were relatively low, the distortion was very minor.

For example: if the railway coach hotel made 100 coaches one month, then the unit cost would become $310 per coach ($300 + ($1000/100)). If the next month the hotel made 50 coaches, then the unit cost = $320 per coach ($300 + ($1000/50)), a relatively minor difference.

An important part of standard cost accounting is a variance analysis which breaks down the variation between actual cost and standard costs into various components (volume variation, material cost variation, Labour cost variation, etc.) so managers can understand *why costs were different than planned* and take appropriate action to correct the situation.

Weaknesses of Standard Cost Accounting for Management Decision Making

As time went on, standard cost accounting lost its usefulness for management decision making due to a variety of reasons:

- The practice of paying workers on a 'set-piece' basis changed in favour of paying on an hourly rate.
- Modern companies tend to have relatively low truly variable costs (primarily raw material, commissions or casual workers) and very high fixed costs (worker salaries, engineering costs, quality control, etc.).
- Equipment has become more complex and specialized and may be a very significant proportion of total costs.

- Changes in the level of full cost inventory create swings in profitability that are difficult to explain or understand. An increase in inventory can "absorb" costs of production and increase profits, while a decrease in inventory level will decrease profits.
- Organizations with a wide range of products or services have processes which are common to several finished items, making cost allocation irrelevant or misleading.

As a result of the above, using standard cost accounting to analyze management decisions can distort the unit cost figures in ways that can lead managers to make decisions that do not reduce costs or maximize profits. For this reason, managers often use the terms "direct costs" and "indirect costs" to replace the standard costing, to better reflect the way allocation of overhead is actually calculated. Indirect costs (often large) are usually allocated in proportion to either labour cost, other direct costs, or some physical resource utilization.

For example: If the railway coach hotel now paid its workforce a fixed monthly rate of $8,000 (total) and its other fixed costs had risen to $2,600/ month, the total fixed costs would then be $10,600/month. The unit cost to make 40 coaches per month would still be $325 per coach ($60 material + ($10,600/40)), but producing 100 coaches would result in a unit cost of $166 per coach ($60 + ($10, 600/100)), provided the hotel had the capacity to increase production to that level.

Managers using the standard cost for 40 coaches per month would likely reject an order for 100 coaches (to be produced in one month) if the selling price was only $300 per unit, seeing that it would result in a loss of $25 per unit. If they analyzed the fixed vs. variable cost distinction, they would see clearly that filling this order would result in a contribution to fixed costs of $240 per coach ($300 selling price less $60 materials) and would result in a net profit for the month of $13,400 (($240 x 100) - 10,600).

The Development of Throughput Accounting

As companies have become more complex and begun producing a variety of products, the use of cost accounting to make decisions to maximize profitability has come under question. Managers learned in the 1980's about the theory of constraints and began to understand that *every production process has a limiting factor* somewhere in the chain of production. As managers learned to identify the constraints, they learned to use throughput accounting to manage them and *maximize the throughput dollars* from each unit of constrained resource.

For example: The railway coach hotel was offered a contract to make 15 open-topped streetcars each month, using a design which included ornate brass foundry work, but very little of the metalwork needed to produce a covered railway coach. The buyer offered to pay $280 per streetcar. The hotel had a firm order for 40 railway coaches each month for $350 per unit. The hotel accountant determined that the cost of operating the foundry vs. the metalwork shop each month was as follows:

Overhead Cost by Department	*Total Cost*	*Hours Available per month*	*Cost per hour*
Foundry	$ 7,300.00	160	$45.63
Metalshop	$ 3,300.00	160	$20.63
Total	$10,600.00	320	$33.13

The hotel was at full capacity making 40 railway coaches each month. And since the foundry was expensive to operate, and purchasing brass as a raw material for the streetcars was expensive, the accountant determined that the hotel would lose money on any streetcars it built. He showed an analysis of the estimated product costs based on standard cost accounting and recommended that the hotel decline to build any streetcars.

Standard Cost Accounting Analysis	*Streetcars*	*Railway Coach*
Monthly Demand	15	40
Price	$280	$350
Foundry Time (hrs)	3.0	2.0
Metalwork Time (hrs)	1.5	4.0
Total Time	4.5	6.0
Foundry Cost	$136.88	$ 91.25
Metalwork Cost	$ 30.94	$ 82.50
Raw Material Cost	$120.00	$ 60.00
Total Cost	$287.81	$233.75
Profit per Unit	$ (7.81)	$116.25

However, the operations manager had just made improvements in the foundry equipment, and she knew there was idle time for the workers making coaches there. The constraint was the metalwork shop. She made an analysis of profit and loss if the hotel took the contract using throughput accounting to determine the profitability of products by maximizing "throughput" (revenue less variable cost) in the metal shop.

Throughput Cost Accounting Analysis	*Decline Contract*	*Take Contract*
Coaches Produced	40	34
Streetcars Produced	0	15
Foundry Hours	80	113
Metalshop Hours	160	159
Coach Revenue	$14,000	$11,900
Streetcar Revenue	$ 0	$ 4,200
Coach Raw Material Cost	$(2,400)	$(2,040)
Streetcar Raw Material Cost	$ 0	$(1,800)
Throughput Value	$11,600	$12,260
Overhead Expense	$(10,600)	$(10,600)
Profit	$1,000	$1,660

The president saw that the metalshop capacity was limiting the hotel's profitability. They could make only 40 railway coaches per month. But by taking the contract for the streetcars, the hotel could make nearly all the railway coaches ordered, and also meet all the demand for streetcars. The result would increase throughput in the metal shop from $6.25 to $10.38 per hour of available time, and increase profitability by 66 percent.

Activity-based Costing

Activity-based costing (ABC) is a system for assigning costs to products based on the activities they require. In this case, activities are those regular actions performed inside a hotel. "Talking with customer regarding invoice questions" is an example of an activity performed inside most companies.

Accountants assign 100% of each employee's time to the different activities performed inside a hotel (many will use surveys to have the workers themselves assign their time to the different activities). The accountant then can determine the total cost spent on each activity by summing up the percentage of each worker's salary spent on that activity. Each product or service is produced and delivered via the activities performed in the hotel. The accountant can then assign the different activities to the different products using an appropriate allocation method.

A hotel can use the resulting activity cost data to determine where to focus their operational improvement efforts. For example, a job based manufacturer may find that a high percentage of their workers are spending their time trying to figure out a hastily written customer order. Via ABC, the accountants now have a currency amount that will be associated with the activity of "Researching Customer Work Order Specifications". Senior management can now decide how much focus or money to budget for the resolutions of this process deficiency. Activity-based management includes (but is not restricted to) the use of activity-based costing to manage a business.

Marginal Costing

This method is used particularly for short-term decision-making. Its principal tenets are:

- *Revenue (per product)*—Variable Costs (per product) = Contribution (per product)
- *Total Contribution*—Total Fixed Costs = Total Profit or (Total Loss)

Thus it does not attempt to allocate fixed costs in an arbitrary manner to different products. The short-term objective is to maximise contribution per unit. If constraints exist on resources, then Managerial Accounting dictates that marginal cost analysis be employed to maximise contribution per unit of the constrained resource.

Other costing Methods

More varieties of costing methods have been proposed in order to tailor for different aspects of the business. Some of the uprising ones include inventory costing method, process costing method, average costing method, target costing method. Still, the standard methods and normal costing methods are the most established methods in the world of public accounting. For management accountants in private industry, throughput accounting is rapidly becoming the standard for use in decision making in a fast-paced business environment.

MANAGEMENT ACCOUNTING

Management accounting is concerned with the provisions and use of accounting information to managers within organizations, to provide them with the basis in making informed business decisions that would allow them to be better equipped in their management and control functions. Unlike financial accountancy information (which, for the most part, is public information), management accounting information is used within an organization (typically for decision-making) and is usually confidential and access to which is only available to a select few.

According to CIMA, The Chartered Institute of Management Accountants, Management Accounting is "the process of identification, measurement, accumulation, analysis, preparation, interpretation and communication of information used by management to plan, evaluate and control within an entity and to assure appropriate use of and accountability for its resources. Management accounting also comprises the preparation of financial reports for non management groups such as shareholders, creditors, regulatory agencies and tax authorities" (CIMA Official Terminology)

Aims

1. Formulating strategies;
2. Planning and constructing business activities;
3. Making decisions;
4. Well use of resources;
5. Supporting financial reports preparation; and
6. Safeguarding assets.

Traditional vs. Innovative Management Accounting

In the late 1980s, accounting practitioners and educators were heavily criticized on the grounds that management accounting practices (and, even more so, the curriculum taught to accounting students) had changed little over the preceding 60 years, despite radical changes in the business environment. Professional accounting institutes, perhaps fearing that management accountants would increasingly be seen as superfluous in business organizations, subsequently devoted considerable resources to the development of a more innovative skills set for management accountants. The distinction between 'traditional' and 'innovative' management accounting practices can be illustrated by reference to cost control techniques. Traditionally, management accountants' principal technique was variance analysis, which is a systematic approach to the comparison of the actual and budgeted costs of the raw materials and labour used during a production period.

While some form of variance analysis is still used by most manufacturing firms, it nowadays tends to be used in conjunction with innovative techniques such as life cycle cost analysis and activity-based costing, which are designed with specific aspects of the modern business environment in mind. Lifecycle costing recognizes that managers' ability to influence the cost of manufacturing a product is at its greatest when the product is still at the design stage of its product lifecycle (i.e., before the design has been finalised and production commenced), since small changes to the product design may lead to significant savings in the cost of manufacturing the product.

Activity-based costing (ABC) recognizes that, in modern factories, most manufacturing costs are determined by the amount of 'activities' (e.g., the number of production runs per month, and the amount of production equipment idle time) and that the key to effective cost control is therefore optimizing the efficiency of these activities. Activity-based accounting is also known as Cause and Effect accounting.

Both lifecycle costing and activity-based costing recognize that, in the typical modern factory, the avoidance of disruptive events (such as machine breakdowns and quality control failures) is of far greater importance than (for example) reducing the costs of raw materials. Activity-based costing also deemphasizes direct labour as a cost driver and concentrates instead on acitivities that drive costs, such as the provision of a service or the production of a product component.

Development of Throughput Accounting

The most significant recent direction in managerial accounting is throughput accounting, which recognizes the interdependencies of modern production processes and provide managers with a tool that will allow them to measure the contribution per unit of constrained resource for any given product, customer or supplier.

An Alternative View

A seldom expressed alternative view of management accounting is that it is neither a neutral or benign influence in organizations, rather a mechanism for management control through surveillance. This view locates management accounting specifically in the context of management control theory. In throughput accounting, the cost accounting aspect of Theory of Constraints (TOC), operating expense is the money spent turning inventory into throughput. In TOC, operating expense is limited to costs that vary strictly with the quantity produced, like raw materials and purchased components. Everything else is a fixed cost, including labour unless there is a regular and significant chance that workers will not work a full-time week when they report on its first day.

FINANCIAL ACCOUNTANCY

Financial accountancy (or financial accounting) is the branch of accountancy concerned with the preparation of financial statements for decision makers, such as stockholders, suppliers, banks, government agencies, owners, and other stakeholders. The fundamental need for financial accounting is to reduce principal-agent problem by measuring and monitoring agents' performance and reporting the results to interested users. Financial Accountancy is used to prepare accounting information for people outside the organisation or not involved in the day to day running of the company. Managerial accounting provides accounting information to help managers make decisions to manage the business. Financial Accountancy is governed by both local and international accounting standards.

Basic Accounting Concepts

The accounting equation (Assets = Liabilities + Owners' Equity) and financial statements are the main topics of financial accounting. The trial balance which is usually prepared using the Double-entry accounting system forms the basis for preparing the financial statements. All the figures in the trial balance are rearranged to prepare a profit and loss statement and balance sheet. There are certain accounting standards that determine the format for these accounts (SSAP, FRS, IFS). The financial statements will display the income and expenditure for the company and a summary of the assets, liabilities, and shareholders or owners' equity of the company on the date the accounts were prepared to.

Meaning of the Accounting Equation

The value of a company can be understood simply as the useful assets that ownership of a company entitles one to claim. This value is known as Owners' Equity. Some assets of a company, however, cannot be claimed as equity by the owners of a company because other people have legal claim to them - for example if the company has borrowed money from the bank. The value of a resource claimable by a non-owner is called a liability. All of the Assets of a company can be claimed by someone, whether owner or not, so the sum of a company's equity and its liabilities must equal the value of its Assets. Thus the accounting equation describes what portion of a company's assets can by claimed by the owners.

Various account types are classified as 'credit' or 'debit' depending on the role they play in the accounting equation.

Assets = Liabilities + Equity *or* Assets - Liabilities - Equity = 0

Another way of stating it is:

Equity = Assets - Liabilities

which can be interpreted as: "Equity is what is left if all assets have been sold and all liabilities have been paid".

Managerial Finance

Managerial Finance is that branch of finance that provides tools for a company's financial managers. It encompasses corporate finance and management accounting also known as cost accounting. Financial analysts provide analysis in the corporate finance field. And, cost analysts provide analysis in the cost accounting field. Therefore, the financial-cost analyst provides analysis in the managerial finance arena. These analysts require skills of both the internal corporate financial analyst and cost analyst.

Corporate Finance

Corporate finance is a specific area of finance dealing with the financial decisions corporations make and the tools as well as analysis used to make these decisions. The primary goal of Corporate finance is to enhance corporate value, without taking excessive financial risks. The discipline may be divided among long-term and short-term decisions and techniques. Capital investment decisions comprise the long-term choices about which projects receive investment, whether to finance that investment with equity or debt, and when or whether to pay dividends to shareholders. Short-term corporate finance decisions are called working capital management and deal with the balance of current assets and current liabilities; the focus here is on managing cash, inventories, and short-term borrowing and lending (e.g., the credit terms extended to customers).

The time frames, and the goal of the discipline, are inter-related: value is enhanced when return on capital, a function of working capital management, exceeds cost of capital, a function of previous capital investment decisions. Corporate finance is closely related to managerial finance, which is slightly broader in scope, describing the financial techniques available to all forms of business enterprise, corporate or not.

Capital Investment Decisions

Longer term Corporate finance decisions - generally relating to fixed assets and capital structure - are referred to as *Capital investment decisions*. The decision here will be based on several inter-related criteria. In general, management must "maximize the value of the firm" by investing in projects which are NPV positive, when valued using an appropriate discount rate; these projects must also be financed appropriately. If no such opportunities exist, maximizing shareholder value dictates that management return excess cash to shareholders. Capital investment decisions thus comprise an investment decision, a financing decision, and a dividend decision.

The Investment Decision

Management must allocate limited resources between competing opportunities ("projects") in a process known as capital budgeting. Making this capital allocation decision requires estimating the value of each opportunity or project: a function of the size, timing and predictability of future cash flows.

Project Valuation

In general, each project's value will be estimated using a discounted cash flow (DCF) valuation, and the opportunity with the highest value, as measured by the resultant net present value (NPV) will be selected. This requires estimating the size and timing of all of the incremental cash flows resulting from the project. These future cash flows are then discounted to determine their present value. These present values are then summed, and this sum is the NPV.

The NPV is greatly influenced by the discount rate. Thus selecting the proper discount rate - the project "hurdle rate" - is critical to making the right decision. The hurdle rate is the minimum acceptable return on an investment - i.e. the project appropriate discount rate. The hurdle rate should reflect the riskiness of the investment, typically measured by volatility of cash flows, and must take into account the financing mix. Managers use models such as the CAPM or the APT to estimate a discount rate appropriate for a particular project, and use the weighted average cost of capital (*WACC*) to reflect the financing mix selected. (A common error in choosing a discount rate for a project is to apply a WACC that applies to the entire firm. Such an approach may not be appropriate where the risk of a particular project differs markedly from that of the firm's existing portfolio of assets.) In conjunction with NPV, there are several other measures used as (secondary) selection criteria in corporate finance. These are visible from the DCF and include payback, IRR, Modified IRR, equivalent annuity, capital efficiency, and ROI.

Valuing Flexibility

In many cases, for example R&D projects, a project may open (or close) paths of action to the company, but this reality will not typically be captured in a strict NPV approach. Management will therefore (sometimes) employ tools which place an explicit value on these options. So, whereas in a DCF valuation the most likely or average or scenario specific cash flows are discounted, here the "flexibile and staged nature" of the investment is modelled, and hence "all" potential payoffs are considered. The difference between the two valuations is the "option value" inherent in the project.

The two most common tools are Decision Tree Analysis (DTA) and Real options:

- The DTA approach attempts to capture flexibility by incorporating likely events and consequent management decisions into the valuation. In the decision tree, each management decision in response to an "event" generates a "branch" or "path" which the company could follow. (For example, management will only proceed with stage 2 of the project given that stage 1 was successful; stage 3, in turn, depends on stage 2. In a DCF model, on the other hand, there is no "branching" - each scenario must be modelled separately.) The highest value path (probability weighted) is regarded as representative of project value.
- The real options approach is used when the value of a project is contingent on the value of some other asset or underlying variable. (For example, the viability of a mining project is contingent on the price of gold; if the price is too low, management will abandon the mining rights, if sufficiently high, management will develop the Ore-body. Again, a DCF valuation would capture only one of these outcomes.) Here, using financial option theory as a framework, the decision to be taken is identified as corresponding to either a call option or a put option - valuation is then via the Binomial model or, less often for this purpose, via Black Scholes; see Contingent claim valuation. The "true" value of the project is then the NPV of the "most likely" scenario plus the option value.

The Financing Decision

Achieving the goals of corporate finance requires that any corporate investment be financed appropriately. As above, since both hurdle rate and cash flows (and hence the riskiness of the firm) will be affected, the financing mix can impact the valuation. Management must therefore identify the "optimal mix" of financing – the capital structure that results in maximum value. The sources of financing will, generically, comprise some combination of debt and equity. Financing a project through debt results in a liability that must be serviced - and hence there are cash flow implications regardless of the project's success. Equity financing is less risky in the sense of cash flow commitments, but results in a dilution of ownership and earnings. The cost of equity is also typically higher than the cost of debt, and so equity financing may result in an increased hurdle rate which may offset any reduction in cash flow risk. Management must also attempt to match the financing mix to the asset being financed as closely as possible, in terms of both timing and cash flows.

The Dividend Decision

In general, management must decide whether to invest in additional projects, reinvest in existing operations, or return free cash as dividends to shareholders. The dividend is calculated mainly on the basis of the company's unappropriated profit and its business prospects for the coming year. If there are no NPV positive opportunities, i.e. where returns exceed the hurdle rate, then management must return excess cash to investors - these free cash flows comprise cash remaining after all business expenses have been met. (This is the general case, however there are exceptions. For example, investors in a "Growth stock", expect that the company will, almost by definition, retain earnings so as to fund growth internally. In other cases, even though an opportunity is currently NPV negative, management may consider "investment flexibility" and potential payoff and decide to retain cash flows.)

Management must also decide on the form of the distribution, generally as cash dividends or via a share buyback. There are various considerations: where shareholders pay tax on dividends, companies may elect to retain earnings, or to perform a stock buyback, in both cases increasing the value of shares outstanding; some companies will pay "dividends" from stock rather than in cash. Today it is generally accepted that dividend policy is value neutral.

6

Capital Structuring and Investment Management

RAISING CAPITAL

To understand financial markets, let us look at what they are used for, i.e. what is their purpose? Without financial markets, borrowers would have difficulty finding lenders themselves. Intermediaries such as banks help in this process. Banks take deposits from those who have money to save. They can then lend money from this pool of deposited money to those who seek to borrow. Banks popularly lend money in the form of loans and mortgages.

More complex transactions than a simple bank deposit require markets where lenders and their agents can meet borrowers and their agents, and where existing borrowing or lending commitments can be sold on to other parties. A good example of a financial market is a stock exchange. A company can raise money by selling shares to investors and its existing shares can be bought or sold. The following table illustrates where financial markets fit in the relationship between lenders and borrowers:

Lenders

Individuals do not think of themselves as lenders but they lend to other parties in many ways. Lending activities may be:

- Putting money in a savings account at a bank;
- Contributing to a pension plan;
- Paying premiums to an insurance company;
- Investing in government bonds; or
- Investing in company shares.

Companies tend to be borrowers of capital. When companies have surplus cash that is not needed for a short period of time, they may seek to make money from their cash surplus by lending it via short term markets called money markets.

There are a few companies that have very strong cash flows. These companies tend to be lenders rather than borrowers. Such companies may decide to return cash to lenders (e.g. via a share buyback.) Alternatively, they may seek to make more money on their cash by lending it (e.g. investing in bonds and stocks.)

Borrowers

Individuals borrow money via bank loans for short term needs or longer term mortgages to help finance a house purchase. Companies borrow money to aid short term or long term cash flows. They also borrow to fund modernisation or future business expansion.

Governments often find their spending requirements exceed their tax revenues. To make up this difference, they need to borrow. Governments also borrow on behalf of nationalised industries, municipalities, local authorities and other public sector bodies. In the UK, the total borrowing requirement is often referred to as the public sector borrowing requirement.

Governments borrow by issuing bonds. In the UK, the government also borrows from individuals by offering bank accounts and Premium Bonds. Government debt seems to be permanent. Indeed the debt seemingly expands rather than being paid off. One strategy used by governments to reduce the value of the debt is to influence inflation. Municipalities and local authorities may borrow in their own name as well as receiving funding from national governments. In the UK, this would cover an authority like Hampshire County Council.

Public Corporations typically include nationalised industries. These may include the postal services, railway companies and utility companies. Many borrowers have difficulty raising money locally. They need to borrow internationally with the aid of Foreign exchange markets.

Derivative Products

During the 1980s and 1990s, a major growth sector in financial markets is the trade in so called derivative products, or derivatives for short. In the financial markets, stock prices, bond prices, currency rates, interest rates and dividends go up and down, creating *risk*. Derivative products are financial products which are used to *control* risk or paradoxically *exploit* risk.

Currency markets

Seemingly, the most obvious buyers and sellers of foreign exchange are importers/exporters. While this may have been true in the distant past, whereby importers/exporters created the initial demand for currency markets, importers and exporters now represent only 1/32 of foreign exchange dealing, according to BIS.

LONG-TERM CAPITAL MANAGEMENT

Long-Term Capital Management (LTCM) was a hedge fund founded in

1994 by John Meriwether (the former vice-chairman and head of bond trading at Salomon Brothers). On its board of directors were Myron Scholes and Robert C. Merton, who shared the 1997 Nobel Memorial Prize in Economics. Initially successful, in 1998 it lost $4.6 billion in less than four months. The fund folded in early 2000.

Founding Members

In addition to Meriwether, Scholes, Chincarrini and Merton, also joining the company as principals were Eric Rosenfeld, Greg Hawkins, Larry Hilibrand, Dick Leahy, Victor Haghani and James McEntee. On 24 February 1994, LTCM began trading with $1,011,060,243 of investor capital.

Strategy

The company had developed complex mathematical models to take advantage of fixed income arbitrage deals (termed convergence trades) usually with U.S., Japanese, and European government bonds. The basic idea was that over time the value of long-dated bonds issued a short time apart would tend to become identical. However the rate at which these bonds approached this price would be different, and that more heavily traded bonds such as US Treasury bonds would approach the long term price more quickly than less heavily traded and less liquid bonds.

Thus by a series of financial transactions (essentially amounting to buying the cheaper 'off-the-run' bond and short selling the more expensive, but more liquid, 'on-the-run' bond) it would be possible to make a profit as the difference in the value of the bonds narrowed when a new bond came on the run. As LTCM's capital base grew the need for additional returns on that expanded capital led it to undertake other trading strategies.

Although these trading strategies were non-market directional, i.e. they were not dependent on overall interest rates or stock prices going up (or down), they were not convergence trades as such. By 1998 LTCM had extremely large positions in areas such as merger arbitrage and S&P 500 options (net short long-term S&P volatility). In fact some market participants believed that LTCM had been the primary supplier of S&P 500 gamma which had been in demand by US insurance companies selling equity indexed annuities products for the prior two years.

Because these differences in value were minute — especially for the convergence trades — the fund needed to take highly-leveraged positions in order to make a significant profit.

At the beginning of 1998, the firm had equity of $4.72 billion and had borrowed over $124.5 billion with assets of around $129 billion. It had off-balance sheet derivative positions amounting to $1.25 trillion, most of which were in interest rate derivatives such as interest rate swaps. The fund also invested in other derivatives such as equity options.

1998 Downturn

The downfall of the fund started in May and June 1998 when net returns fell 6.42% and 10.14% respectively, reducing LTCM's capital by $461 million. This was further aggravated by the exit of Salomon Brothers from the arbitrage business in July 1998.

The scheme finally unraveled in August and September 1998 when the Russian government defaulted on their government bonds (GKOs). Panicked investors sold Japanese and European bonds to buy U.S. treasury bonds. The profits that were supposed to occur as the value of these bonds converged became huge losses as the value of the bonds diverged. By the end of August the fund had lost $1.85 billion in capital.

The company, which was providing annual returns of almost 40% up to this point, experienced a Flight-to-Liquidity. This prompted a bail-out of $3.625 bn by the banks, organized by the Federal Reserve Bank of New York, ostensibly in order to avoid a wider collapse in the financial markets. The fear was that there would be a chain reaction as the company liquidated its securities to cover its debt, leading to a drop in prices which would force other companies to liquidate their own debt creating a vicious cycle. The total losses were found to be $4.6 billion.

The losses in the major investment categories were (ordered by magnitude):

- $1.6 bn in swaps
- $1.3 bn in equity volatility
- $430 mn in Russian and other emerging markets
- $371 mn in directional trades in developed countries
- $215 mn in yield curve arbitrage
- $203 mn in S&P 500 stocks
- $100 mn in junk bond arbitrage
- No substantial losses in merger arbitrage

Long Term Capital was audited by Pricewaterhouse LLP. The lead partner on the engagement was John Reville (Pricewaterhouse LLP - Manhattan office).

A Deeper Understanding of the Risks Taken by LTCM

The profits from LTCM's trading strategies were generally not correlated with each other and thus normally LTCM's highly leveraged portfolio benefited from diversification. However, the general flight to liquidity in the late summer of 1998 led to a marketwide repricing of all risk leading these positions to all move in the same direction.

As the correlation of LTCM's positions increased, the diversified aspect of LTCM's portfolio vanished and large losses to its equity value occurred. Thus the primary lesson of 1998 and the collapse of LTCM for Value at Risk (VaR) users is not a liquidity one, but more fundamentally that the underlying Covariance matrix used in VaR analysis is not static but changes over time.

In the end, LTCM's basic idea was correct, in that the values of government bonds did eventually converge, but only after the firm was wiped out. Nonetheless, the incident confirms an insight often (though perhaps apocryphally) attributed to the economist John Maynard Keynes, who is said to have warned investors that although markets do tend toward rational positions in the long run, "the market can stay irrational longer than you can stay solvent."

Many of LTCM's strategies had payouts similar to those from selling an out-of-the-money option; a likely small gain balanced against a small chance of a large loss. Their basic idea was "correct" in that these large losses would not, if the positions were held to maturity, have come to pass. However, the events of 1998 increased the perceived probability of large losses, to the point where LTCM's portfolio had negative value.

Incentive Structures: Alternatives to Direct Pay for Performance

Much of the discussion here has been in terms of individual pay-for-performance contracts; but many large firms use internal labour markets as a solution to some of the problems outlined. Here, there is "pay-for-performance" in looser sense over a longer time period. There is little variation in pay within grades, and pay increases come with changes in job or job title. The incentive effects of this structure are dealt with in what is known as "tournament theory", for multi-stage tournaments in hierarchies where it is explained why CEOs are paid many times more than other workers in the firm). Workers are motivated to supply effort by the wage increase they would earn if they win a promotion. Some of the extended tournament models predict that relatively weaker agents, be they competing in a sports tournaments or in the broiler chicken industry, would take risky actions instead of increasing their effort supply as a cheap way to improve the prospects of winning. These actions are inefficient as they increase risk taking without increasing the average effort supplied.

A major problem with tournaments is that individuals' are rewarded based on how well they do relative to others, co-workers might become reluctant to help out others and might even sabotage others' effort instead of increasing one's own effort. This is supported empirically by Drago and Garvey. Why then are tournaments so popular?

Firstly, because – especially given compression rating problems – it is difficult to determine absolutely differences in worker performance. Tournaments merely require rank order evaluation.

Secondly, it reduces the danger of rent-seeking, because bonuses paid to favourite workers are tied to increased responsibilities in new jobs, and supervisors will suffer if they do not promote the most qualified person.

Thirdly, where prize structures are (relatively) fixed, it reduces the possibility of the firm reneging on paying wages. As Carmichael notes, a prize structure represents a degree of commitment, both to absolute and to relative wage levels. Lastly when the measurement of workers' productivity is difficult, e.g. say monitoring is costly, or when the tasks the workers have to perform for the job is varied in nature, making it hard to measure effort and/or performance, then running tournaments in a firm would encourage the workers to supply effort whereas workers would have shirked if there are no promotions.

Deferred Compensation

Tournaments represent one way of implementing the general principle of "deferred compensation", which is essentially an agreement between worker and firm to commit to each other. Under schemes of deferred compensation, workers are overpaid when old, at the cost of being underpaid when young. Salop and Salop argue that this derives from the need to attract workers more likely to stay at the firm for longer periods, since turnover is costly. Alternatively, delays in evaluating the performance of workers may lead to compensation being weighted to later periods, when better and poorer workers have to a greater extent been distinguished. (Workers may even prefer to have wages increasing over time, perhaps as a method of forced saving, or as an indicator of personal development. eg Loewenstein and Sicherman 1991, Frank and Hutchens 1993.)

For example Akerlof and Katz 1989: if older workers receive efficiency wages, younger workers may be prepared to work for less in order to receive those later. Overall, the evidence suggests the use of deferred compensation (eg Freeman and Medoff 1984, and Spilerman 1986 – seniority provisions are often included in pay, promotion and retention decisions, irrespective of productivity.)

The reason that employees are often paid according to hours of work rather than by direct measurement of results is that it is often more efficient to use indirect systems of controlling the quantity and quality of effort, due to a variety of informational and other issues (eg turnover costs, which determine the optimal minimum length of relationship between firm and employee). This means that methods such as deferred compensation and structures such as tournaments are often more suitable to create the incentives for employees to contribute what they can to output over longer periods (years rather than hours). These represent "pay-for-performance" systems in a looser, more extended sense, as workers who consistently work harder and better are more likely to be promoted (and usually paid more), compared to the narrow definition of "pay-for-performance", such as piece rates.

This discussion has been conducted almost entirely for self-interested rational individuals. In practice, however, the incentive mechanisms which successful firms use take account of the socio-cultural context they are embedded in, in order not to destroy the social capital they might more constructively mobilise towards building an organic, social organization, with the attendant benefits from such things as "worker loyalty and pride can be critical to a firm's success..."

BASEL II

Basel II, also called The New Accord (correct full name is the International Convergence of Capital Measurement and Capital Standards - A Revised Framework) is the second Basel Accord and represents recommendations by bank supervisors and central bankers from the 13 countries making up the Basel Committee on Banking Supervision (BCBS) to revise the international standards for measuring the adequacy of a bank's capital. It was created to promote greater consistency in the way banks and banking regulators approach risk management across national borders. The Bank for International Settlements (often confused with the BCBS) supplies the secretariat for the BCBS and is not itself the BCBS.

History

An earlier accord, Basel I, adopted in 1988, is now widely viewed as outmoded as it is risk insensitive and can easily be circumvented by regulatory arbitrage. The Basel II deliberations began in January 2001, driven largely by concern about the arbitrage issues that develop when regulatory capital requirements diverge from accurate economic capital calculations.

With the first draft (called Consultative Paper 1) published in June 1999, further consultative papers followed together with a large quantity of other releases, Quantitative Impact Studies Nos. 2, 3 and 4, and papers. A final version was issued in June 2004, with a minor revision released in November 2005. In June 2006 a Comprehensive version was published including all Basel regulations up to this date. Implementation of the Accord is expected by 2008 in many of the over 100 countries currently using the Basel I accord.

The final version aims at:

1. Ensuring that capital allocation is more risk sensitive;
2. Separating operational risk from credit risk, and quantifying both;
3. Attempting to align economic and regulatory capital more closely to reduce the scope for regulatory arbitrage.

While the final accord has largely addressed the regulatory arbitrage issue, there are still areas where regulatory capital requirements will diverge from the economic.

Basel II has largely left unchanged the question of how to actually define bank capital, which diverges from accounting equity in important respects. The Basel I definition, as modified up to the present, remains in place.

The Accord In Operation

Basel II uses a "three pillars" concept - (1) minimum capital requirements,

(2) supervisory review and (3) market discipline - to promote greater stability in the financial system. The Basel I accord only dealt with parts of each of these pillars. For example: of the key pillar one risk, credit risk, was dealt with in a simple manner and market risk was an afterthought. Operational risk was not dealt with at all.

The First Pillar

The first pillar provides improved risk sensitivity in the way that capital requirements are calculated for three major components of risk that a bank faces: credit risk, operational risk and market risk. In turn, each of these components can be calculated in two or three ways of varying sophistication. Other risks are not considered fully quantifiable at this stage.

Technical terms in the more sophisticated measures of market risk include VaR (Value at Risk), EL (Loss function) whose components are PD (Probability of Default), LGD (Loss Given Default), and EAD (Exposure At Default). Calculation of these components requires advanced data collection and sophisticated risk management techniques.

The Second Pillar

The second pillar deals with the regulatory response to the first pillar, giving regulators much improved 'tools' over those available to them under Basel I. It also provides a framework for dealing with all the other risks a bank may face, such as name risk, liquidity risk and legal risk, which the accord combines under the title of residual risk.

The Third Pillar

The third pillar greatly increases the disclosures that the bank must make. This is designed to allow the market to have a better picture of the overall risk position of the bank and to allow the counterparties of the bank to price and deal appropriately.

Criticisms

There are many criticisms that are made of Basel II. These include that the more sophisticated risk measures unfairly advantage the larger banks that are able to implement them and, from the same perspective, that the developing countries generally also do not have these banks and that Basel II will disadvantage the economically marginalized by restricting their access to credit or by making it more expensive.

The first of these is a valid point, but it is difficult to see how this can be overcome. More risk sensitive risk measures were required for the larger, more sophisticated banks and, while the less sophisticated measures are simpler to calculate, due to their lower risk sensitivity they need to be more conservative. The second criticism has elements of truth; the better credit risks will be advantaged as banks move towards true pricing for risk. Experience with these systems in the United States and the United Kingdom, however, shows that the improved risk sensitivity means that banks are more willing to lend to higher risk borrowers, just with higher prices. Borrowers previously 'locked out' of the banking system have a chance to establish a good credit history.

A more serious criticism is that the operation of Basel II will lead to a more pronounced business cycle. This criticism arises because the credit models used for pillar 1 compliance typically use a one year time horizon. This would mean that, during a downturn in the business cycle, banks would need to reduce lending as their models forecast increased losses, increasing the magnitude of the downturn. Regulators should be aware of this risk and can be expected to include it in their assessment of the bank models used.

On September 30, 2005, the four US Federal banking agencies (the Office of the Comptroller of the Currency, the Board of Governors of the Federal Reserve System, the Federal Deposit Insurance Corporation, and the Office of Thrift Supervision) announced their revised plans for the U.S. implementation of the Basel II accord. This delays implementation of the accord for US banks by 12 months.

On November 15, 2005, the committee released a revised version of the Accord, incorporating changes to the calculations for market risk and the treatment of double default effects. These changes had been flagged well in advance, as part of a paper released in July 2005.

On July 4, 2006, the committee released a comprehensive version of the Accord, incorporating the June 2004 Basel II Framework, the elements of the 1988 Accord that were not revised during the Basel II process, the 1996 Amendment to the Capital Accord to Incorporate Market Risks, and the November 2005 paper on Basel II: International Convergence of Capital Measurement and Capital Standards: A Revised Framework. No new elements have been introduced in this compilation. This version is now the current version.

Basel II and the Regulators

One of the most difficult aspects of implementing an international agreement is the need to accommodate differing cultures, varying structural models, and the complexities of public policy and existing regulation. Banks' senior management will determine corporate strategy, as well as the country in which to base a particular type of business, based in part on how Basel II is ultimately interpreted by various countries' legislatures and regulators.

To assist banks operating with multiple reporting requirements for different regulators according to geographic location, there are several software applications available. These include capital calculation engines and extend to automated reporting solutions which include the reports required under COREP/FINREP.

Implementation Progress

Regulators in most jurisdictions around the world plan to implement the new Accord, but with widely varying timelines and use of the varying methodologies being restricted. The United States of America's various regulators are yet (October 2006) to agree on a final approach - see Basel IA for a discussion. In response to a questionaire released by the Financial Stability Institute (FSI), 95 national regulators indicated they were to implement Basel II, in some form or another, by 2015.

The future

Work is apparently already underway on Basel III, at least in a preliminary sense. The goals of this project are to refine the definition of bank capital, quantify further classes of risk and to further improve the sensitivity of the risk measures.

CAPITAL EXPENDITURE

Capital expenditures ("CAPEX") are expenditures used by a company to acquire or upgrade physical assets such as equipment, property, industrial buildings. In accounting, a capital expenditure is added to an asset account (*i.e.* capitalized), thus increasing the asset's basis (i.e. the cost or value of an asset as adjusted for tax purposes).

Funds used by a company to acquire or upgrade physical assets such as property, industrial buildings or equipment. This type of outlay is made by companies to maintain or increase the scope of their operation.

These expenditures can include everything from repairing a roof to building a brand new factory. Investopedia Says: The amount of capital expenditures a company is likely to have depends on the industry it occupies. Some of the most capital intensive industries include oil, telecom and utilities.

In terms of accounting, an expense is considered to be a capital expenditure when the asset is a newly purchased capital asset or an investment that improves the useful life of an existing capital asset. If an expense is a capital expenditure, it needs to be capitalized; this requires the company to spread the cost of the expenditure over the useful life of the asset. If, however, the expense is one that maintains the asset at its current condition, the cost is deducted fully in the year of the expense.

An ongoing question of the accounting of any company is whether certain expenses should be capitalized or expensed. Costs that are expensed in a particular month simply appear on the financial statement as a cost that was incurred that month. Costs that are capitalized, however, are amortized over multiple years. Most ordinary business expenses are clearly either expensable or capitalizable, but some expenses could be treated either way, according to the preference of the company.

COST OF CAPITAL MANAGEMENT

The cost of capital for a firm is a weighted sum of the cost of equity and the cost of debt. Firms finance their operations by three mechanisms: issuing stock (equity), issuing debt (borrowing from a bank is equivalent for this purpose) (those two are external financing), and reinvesting prior earnings (internal financing). Capital (money) used to fund a business should earn returns for the capital owner who risked their saved money. For an investment to be worthwhile the estimated return on capital must be greater than the cost of capital. Otherwise stated, the risk-adjusted return on capital (incorporating not just the projected returns, but the probabilities of those projections) must be higher than the cost of capital.

The cost of debt is relatively simple to calculate, as it is composed of the interest paid (interest rate), including the cost of risk (the risk of default on the debt). In practice, the interest paid by the company will include the risk-free rate plus a risk component, which itself incorporates a probable rate of default (and amount of recovery given default). For companies with similar risk or credit ratings, the interest rate is largely exogenous.

Cost of equity is more challenging to calculate as equity does not pay a set return to its investors. Similarly to the cost of debt, the cost of equity is broadly defined as the risk-weighted projected return required by investors, where the return is largely unknown. The cost of equity is therefore inferred by comparing the investment to other investments with similar risk profiles to determine the "market" cost of equity. The cost of equity is also known as the discount rate, the rate at which projected earnings will be discounted to give a present value.

Cost of Debt

The cost of debt is computed by taking the rate on a non-defaulting bond whose duration matches the term structure of the corporate debt, then adding a default premium.

This default premium will rise as the amount of debt increases (since the risk rises as the amount of debt rises). Since in most cases debt expenses is a deductible expense, the cost of debt is computed as an after tax cost to make it comparable with the cost of equity (earnings are after-tax as well). Thus, for profitable firms, debt is discounted by the tax rate. This is used for large corporations only.

Cost of Equity

The cost of equity is calculated as the "expected" return on equity during a past or future period (usually a year or annualized) based on interest rate levels and historical average equity market return. It can be calculated for an individual company's equity, or for a whole portfolio of companies. For a diversified portfolio, the equity risk is close to the average market risk.

Expected Return

The expected return can be calculated as the "dividend capitalization model" which is (dividend per share/ price per share) + growth rate of dividends. Which is the dividend yield + growth rate of dividends.

COST OF CAPITAL

The total capital for a firm is the value of its equity (for a firm without outstanding warrants and options, this is the same as the company's market capitalization) plus the cost of its debt (the cost of debt should be continually updated as the cost of debt changes as a result of interest rate changes). Notice that the "equity" in the debt to equity ratio is the market value of all equity, not the shareholders' equity on the balance sheet.

Formula

The cost of capital is then given as:

$K_c = (1\text{-}ä)K_e + äK_d$

Where:

K_c

The weighted cost of capital for the firm

δ

The debt to capital ratio, *D/ (D + E)*

K_e

The cost of equity

K_d

The after tax cost of debt

D

The market value of the firm's debt, including bank loans and leases

E

The market value of all equity (including warrants, options, and the equity portion of convertible securities)

In writing:

WACC = (1 - debt to capital ratio) * cost of equity + debt to capital ratio * cost of debt

Capital Structure

Because of tax advantages on debt issuance, it will be cheaper to issue debt rather than new equity (this is only true for profitable firms, tax breaks are available only to profitable firms). At some point, however, the cost of issuing new debt will be greater than the cost of issuing new equity. This is because adding debt increases the default risk - and thus the interest rate that the company must pay in order to borrow money. By utilizing too much debt in its capital structure, this increased default risk can also drive up the costs for other sources (such as retained earnings and preferred stock) as well.

Management must identify the "optimal mix" of financing – the capital structure where the cost of capital is minimized so that the firms value can be maximized.

Capital Cost

Capital costs are costs incurred on the purchase of land, buildings, construction and equipment to be used in the production of goods or the rendering of services. In other words, the total cost needed to bring a project to a commercially operable status. However, capital costs are not limited to the initial construction of a factory or other business. For example, the purchase of a new machine that will increase production and last for years is a capital cost. Capital costs do not include labour costs except for the labour used for construction. Unlike operating costs, capital costs are one-time expenses, although payment may be spread out over many years. Capital costs are fixed and are therefore independent of the level of output.

A fossil fuel power plant's capital costs include the purchase of the land the plant is built on, the equipment needed to run the plant, and the cost of the plant's construction. They do not include the cost of the natural gas, fuel oil or coal used to fire the plant or any taxes on the electricity that is produced. They also do not include the labour used to run the plant or the labour and supplies needed for maintenance.

WORKING CAPITAL CYCLE

Cash flows in a cycle into, around and out of a business. It is the business's life blood and every manager's primary task is to help keep it flowing and to use the cashflow to generate profits. If a business is operating profitably, then it should, in theory, generate cash surpluses. If it doesn't generate surpluses, the business will eventually run out of cash and expire. The faster a business expands, the more cash it will need for working capital and investment. The cheapest and best sources of cash exist as working capital right within business. Good management of working capital will generate cash will help improve profits and reduce risks. Bear in mind that the cost of providing credit to customers and holding stocks can represent a substantial proportion of a firm's total profits.

There are two elements in the business cycle that absorb cash - Inventory (stocks and work-in-progress) and Receivables (debtors owing you money). The main sources of cash are Payables (your creditors) and Equity and Loans. Each component of working capital (namely inventory, receivables and payables) has two dimensions time and money. When it comes to managing working capital - time is money. If you can get money to move faster around the cycle (e.g. collect monies due from debtors more quickly) or reduce the amount of money tied up (e.g. reduce inventory levels relative to sales), the business will generate more cash or it will need to borrow less money to fund working capital. As a consequence, you could reduce the cost of bank interest or you'll have additional *free* money available to support additional sales growth or investment. Similarly, if you can negotiate improved terms with suppliers e.g. get longer credit or an increased credit limit, you effectively create *free* finance to help fund future sales.

- Collect receivables (debtors) faster
- You release cash from the cycle
- Collect receivables (debtors) slower
- Your receivables soak up cash
- Get better credit (in terms of duration or amount) from suppliers
- You increase your cash resources
- Shift inventory (stocks) faster
- You free up cash
- Move inventory (stocks) slower
- You consume more cash

It can be tempting to pay cash, if available, for fixed assets e.g. computers, plant, vehicles etc. If you do pay cash, remember that this is now longer available for working capital. Therefore, if cash is tight, consider other ways of financing capital investment - loans, equity, leasing etc. Similarly, if you pay dividends or increase drawings, these are cash outflows and, like water flowing down a plug hole, they remove liquidity from the business. More businesses fail for lack of cash than for want of profit.

Sources of Additional Working Capital

Sources of additional working capital include the following:

- Existing cash reserves
- Profits (when you secure it as cash !)
- Payables (credit from suppliers)
- New equity or loans from shareholders
- Bank overdrafts or lines of credit
- Long-term loans

If you have insufficient working capital and try to increase sales, you can easily over-stretch the financial resources of the business. This is called overtrading.

Early warning signs include:

- Pressure on existing cash
- Exceptional cash generating activities e.g. offering high discounts for early cash payment
- Bank overdraft exceeds authorized limit
- Seeking greater overdrafts or lines of credit
- Part-paying suppliers or other creditors
- Paying bills in cash to secure additional supplies
- Management pre-occupation with *surviving* rather than managing

- Frequent short-term emergency requests to the bank (to help pay wages, pending receipt of a cheque).

HANDLING RECEIVABLES (DEBTORS)

Cashflow can be significantly enhanced if the amounts owing to a business are collected faster. Every business needs to know who owes them money how much is owed how long it is owing for what it is owed.

Late Payments Erode Profits and can Lead to Bad Debts

Slow payment has a crippling effect on business, in particular on small businesses who can least afford it. If you don't manage debtors, they will begin to manage your business as you will gradually lose control due to reduced cashflow and, of course, you could experience an increased incidence of bad debt.

The following measures will help manage your debtors:

1. Have the right mental attitude to the control of credit and make sure that it gets the priority it deserves.
2. Establish clear credit practices as a matter of company policy.
3. Make sure that these practices are clearly understood by staff, suppliers and customers.
4. Be professional when accepting new accounts, and especially larger ones.
5. Check out each customer thoroughly before you offer credit. Use credit agencies, bank references, industry sources etc.
6. Establish credit limits for each customer... and stick to them.
7. Continuously review these limits when you suspect tough times are coming or if operating in a volatile sector.
8. Keep very close to your larger customers.
9. Invoice promptly and clearly.
10. Consider charging penalties on overdue accounts.
11. Consider accepting credit/debit cards as a payment option.
12. Monitor your debtor balances and ageing schedules, and don't let any debts get too large or too old.

Recognize that the longer someone owes you, the greater the chance you will never get paid. If the average age of your debtors is getting longer, or is already very long, you may need to look for the following possible defects:

- Weak credit judgement
- Poor collection procedures
- Lax enforcement of credit terms
- Slow issue of invoices or statements
- Errors in invoices or statements
- Customer dissatisfaction.

Debtors due over 90 days (unless within agreed credit terms) should generally demand immediate attention. Look for the warning signs of a future bad debt.

For example:

— Longer credit terms taken with approval, particularly for smaller orders
— Use of post-dated checks by debtors who normally settle within agreed terms
— Evidence of customers switching to additional suppliers for the same goods
— New customers who are reluctant to give credit references
— Receiving part payments from debtors.

Profits only Come from Paid Sales

The act of collecting money is one which most people dislike for many reasons and therefore put on the long finger because they convince themselves there is something more urgent or important that demand their attention now. There is nothing more important than getting paid for your product or service. A customer who does not pay is not a customer.

Here are a few ideas that may help you in collecting money from debtors:

- Develop appropriate procedures for handling late payments.
- Track and pursue late payers.
- Get external help if your own efforts fail.
- Don't feel guilty asking for money.... its yours and you are entitled to it.
- Make that call now. And keep asking until you get some satisfaction.
- In difficult circumstances, take what you can now and agree terms for the remainder. It lessens the problem.
- When asking for your money, be hard on the issue - but soft on the person. Don't give the debtor any excuses for not paying.
- Make it your objective is to get the money - not to score points or get even.

MANAGING PAYABLES (CREDITORS)

Creditors are a vital part of effective cash management and should be managed carefully to enhance the cash position. Purchasing initiates cash outflows and an over-zealous purchasing function can create liquidity problems.

Consider the following:

- Who authorizes purchasing in your company - is it tightly managed or spread among a number of (junior) people?
- Are purchase quantities geared to demand forecasts?
- Do you use order quantities which take account of stock-holding and purchasing costs?
- Do you know the cost to the company of carrying stock ?
- Do you have alternative sources of supply ? If not, get quotes from

major suppliers and shop around for the best discounts, credit terms, and reduce dependence on a single supplier.

- How many of your suppliers have a returns policy ?
- Are you in a position to pass on cost increases quickly through price increases to your customers ?
- If a supplier of goods or services lets you down can you charge back the cost of the delay ?
- Can you arrange (with confidence !) to have delivery of supplies staggered or on a just-in-time basis ?

There is an old adage in business that if you can buy well then you can sell well. Management of your creditors and suppliers is just as important as the management of your debtors. It is important to look after your creditors - slow payment by you may create ill-feeling and can signal that your company is inefficient (or in trouble!).

Remember, a good supplier is someone who will work with you to enhance the future viability and profitability of your company.

FINANCIAL MARKET

In economics a financial market is a mechanism which allows people to trade money for securities or commodities such as gold or other precious metals. In general, any commodity market might be considered to be a financial market, if the usual purpose of traders is not the immediate consumption of the commodity, but rather as a means of delaying or accelerating consumption over time.

Financial markets are affected by forces of supply and demand, and allocate resources over time through a price mechanism such as the interest rate. Typically financial markets use a market making or a bid and ask process.

Both general markets, where many commodities are traded and specialised markets (where only one commodity is traded) exist. Markets work by placing many interested sellers in one "place", thus making them easier to find for prospective buyers. An economy which relies primarily on interactions between buyers and sellers to allocate resources is known as a market economy in contrast either to a command economy or to a non-market economy that is based, such as a gift economy.

In Finance, Financial markets facilitate:

- The raising of capital (in the capital markets);
- The transfer of risk (in the derivatives markets); and
- International trade (in the currency markets).

They are used to match those who *want* capital to those who *have* it. Typically a borrower issues a receipt to the lender promising to pay back the capital. These receipts are *securities* which may be freely bought or sold. In return for lending money to the borrower, the lender will expect some compensation in the form of interest or dividends.

The term Financial markets can be a cause of much confusion. Financial markets could mean:

1. Organisations that facilitate the trade in financial products. i.e. Stock exchanges facilitate the trade in stocks, bonds and warrants.
2. The coming together of buyers and sellers to trade financial products. i.e. stocks and shares are traded between buyers and sellers in a number of ways including: the use of stock exchanges; directly between buyers and sellers etc.

In academia, students of finance will use both meanings but students of economics will only use the second meaning. Financial markets can be domestic or they can be international.

Types of financial markets

The financial markets can be divided into different subtypes:

- Capital markets which consist of:
  - Stock markets, which provide financing through the issuance of shares or common stock, and enable the subsequent trading thereof.
  - Bond markets, which provide financing through the issuance of Bonds, and enable the subsequent trading thereof.
- Commodity markets, which facilitate the trading of commodities.
- Money markets, which provide short term debt financing and investment.
- Derivatives markets, which provide instruments for the management of financial risk.
  - Futures markets, which provide standardised forward contracts for trading products at some future date.
- Insurance markets, which facilitate the redistribution of various risks.
- Foreign exchange markets, which facilitate the trading of foreign exchange.

The capital markets consist of primary markets and secondary markets. Newly formed (issued) securities are bought or sold in primary markets. Secondary markets allow investors to sell securities that they hold or buy existing securities.

INVESTMENT

Investment or investing is a term with several closely-related meanings in business management, finance and economics, related to saving or deferring consumption.

An asset is usually purchased, or equivalently a deposit is made in a bank, in hopes of getting a future return or interest from it. Literally, the word means the "action of putting something in to somewhere else" (perhaps originally related to a person's garment or 'vestment').

Types of investment

The major difference in the use of the term investment between the economics field and the finance field is that economists refer to a real investment (such as a machine or a house), while financial economists refer to a financial asset, such as money that is put into a bank or the market, which may then be used to buy a real asset.

Business Management

The investment decision (also known as capital budgeting) is one of the fundamental decisions of business management: managers determine the assets that the business enterprise obtains; these assets may be physical (e.g. buildings or machinery), intangible (e.g. patents, software, goodwill), or financial. Whatever the type of asset, the manager must assess whether the net present value of the investment to the enterprise is positive; the net present value is calculated using the enterprise's marginal cost of capital.

Economics

In Economics, investment means the purchase (and thus the production) and/or stock of capital goods and/or technology - goods which are not consumed but instead used in future production. Examples include building a railroad, or a factory, clearing land, or putting oneself through college. In measures of national income and output, investment is also a component of GDP given in the formula GDP = C + I + G + NX. The investment function in that aspect is divided into non-residential investment (such as factories, machinery etc) and residential investment (new houses).

Investment is often modeled as a function of income and interest rates, given by the relation I = (Y, i). An increase in income will encourage higher investment, whereas a higher interest rate may discourage investment as it becomes costlier to borrow money. Even if a firm chooses to use its own funds in an investment, the interest rate represents an opportunity cost of investing those funds rather than loaning them out for interest.

Finance

In finance, investment means buying securities or other monetary or paper (financial) assets in the money markets or capital markets, or in fairly liquid real assets, such as gold as an investment, real estate, or collectibles. Valuation is the method for assessing whether a potential investment is worth its price.

Types of financial investments include shares or other equity investment, and bonds (including bonds denominated in foreign currencies). These investments assets are then expected to provide income or positive future cash flows, but may increase or decrease in value giving the investor capital gains or losses. Trades in contingent claims or *derivative securities* do not necessarily have future positive expected cash flows - so are not considered to be assets, or strictly speaking, securities or investments. Nevertheless, since their cash flows are closely related to (or derived from) those of specific securities, they are often studied as or treated as investments.

Investments are often made indirectly through intermediaries, such as banks, mutual funds, pension funds, insurance companies, collective investment schemes, or even investment clubs. Though their legal and procedural details differ, an intermediary generally makes an investment using money from many individuals, each of whom receives a claim on the intermediary.

Personal finance

Within personal finance, money used to purchase shares, put in a collective investment scheme or used to buy any asset where there is an element of capital risk is deemed an investment. Saving within personal finance refers to money put aside, normally on a regular basis. This distinction is important as investment risk can cause a capital loss when an investment is realised, unlike saving(s) where the more limited risk is cash devaluing due to inflation.

In many instances the term saving and investment are used interchangeably which confuses this distinction. For example many deposit accounts are labeled as investment accounts by banks for marketing purposes. To help establish whether an asset is saving(s) or an investment you should consider where your money is invested. If the answer is cash then it is savings, if it is a type of asset which can fluctuate in value then it is investment.

The term Capital Investment has two usages in business. Firstly, Capital Investment refers to money used by a business to purchase fixed assets, such as land, machinery, or buildings. Secondly, Capital Investment refers to money invested in a business with the understanding that the money will be used to purchase fixed assets, rather than used to cover the business' day-to-day operating expenses.

INVESTMENT MANAGEMENT

Investment management, the professional management of various securities (shares, bonds etc) and other assets (e.g. real estate), to meet specified investment goals for the benefit of the investors. Investors may be institutions (insurance companies, pension funds, corporations etc.) or private investors (both directly via investment contracts and more commonly via collective investment schemes eg. mutual funds).

The term asset management is often used to refer to the investment management of collective investments, whilst the more generic fund management may refer to all forms of institutional investment as well as investment management for private investors. Investment managers who specialize in advisory or discretionary management on behalf of (normally wealthy) private investors may often refer to their services as wealth management or portfolio management often within the context of so-called "private banking".

The provision of 'investment management services' includes elements of financial analysis, asset selection, stock selection, plan implementation and ongoing monitoring of investments. Investment management is a large and important global industry in its own right responsible for caretaking of trillions of dollars, euros, pounds and yen. Coming under the remit of financial services many of the worlds largest companies are at least in part investment managers and employ millions of staff and create billions in revenue.

Fund manager (or investment advisor in the U.S.) refers to both a firm that provides investment management services and an individual(s) who directs 'fund management' decisions.

Industry Scope

The business of investment management has several facets, including the employment of professional fund managers, research (of individual assets and asset classes), dealing, settlement, marketing, internal auditing, and the preparation of reports for clients. The largest financial fund managers are firms that exhibit all the complexity their size demands. Apart from the people who bring in the money (marketers) and the people who direct investment (the fund managers), there are compliance staff (to ensure accord with legislative and regulatory constraints), internal auditors of various kinds (to examine internal systems and controls), financial controllers (to account for the institutions' own money and costs), computer experts, and "back office" employees (to track and record transactions and fund valuations for up to thousands of clients per institution).

Key Problems of Such Businesses

Key problems include:

- Revenue is directly linked to market valuations, so a major fall in asset prices causes a precipitous decline in revenues relative to costs;
- Above-average fund performance is difficult to sustain, and clients may not be patient during times of poor performance;
- Successful fund managers are expensive and may be headhunted by competitors;
- Above-average fund performance appears to be dependent on the unique skills of the fund manager; however, clients are loath to stake their investments on the ability of one or two men or women- they would rather see firm-wide success, attributable to a single philosophy and internal discipline;
- Evidence suggests that size of an investment firm correlates inversely with fund performance, i.e., the smaller the firm the better the chance of good performance.

- Analysts who can offer generate above-average returns often become sufficiently wealthy that they eschew corporate employment in favour of managing their personal portfolios.

The most successful investment firms in the world have probably been those that have been separated physically and psychologically from banks and insurance companies. That is, the best performance and also the most dynamic business strategies (in this field) have generally come from independent investment management firms.

Representing the Owners of Shares

Institutions often control huge shareholdings. In most cases they are acting as agents (intermediaries between owners of the shares and the companies owned) rather than principals (direct owners). The owners of shares theoretically have great power to alter the companies they own...via the voting rights the shares carry and the consequent ability to pressure managements, and if necessary out-vote them at annual and other meetings.

In practice, the ultimate owners of shares often do not exercise the power they collectively hold (because the owners are many, each with small holdings); financial institutions (as agents) sometimes do. There is a general belief that shareholders - in this case, the institutions acting as agents - could and should exercise more active influence over the companies in which they hold shares (e.g., to hold managers to account, to ensure Boards effective functioning). Such action would add a pressure group to those (the regulators and the Board) overseeing management.

Some institutions have been more vocal and active in pursuing such matters; for instance, some firms believe that there are investment advantages to accumulating substantial minority shareholdings (i.e, 10% or more) and putting pressure on management to implement significant changes in the business. In some cases, institutions with minority holdings work together to force management change. Perhaps more frequent is the sustained pressure that large institutions bring to bear on management teams through persuasive discourse and PR. On the other hand, some of the largest investment managers - such as Barclays Global Investors and Vanguard - advocate simply owning every company, reducing the incentive to influence management teams.

The national context in which shareholder representation considerations are set is variable and important. The USA is a litigious society and shareholders use the law as a lever to pressure management teams. In Japan it is traditional for shareholders to be low in the 'pecking order,' which often allows management and labour to ignore the rights of the ultimate owners. Whereas US firms generally cater to shareholders, Japanese businesses generally exhibit a *stakeholder* mentality, in which they seek consensus amongst all interested parties (against a background of strong unions and labour legislation).

Size of the Global Fund Management Industry

Assets of the global fund management industry increased for the second year running in 2004 to reach a record $45.9 trillion. This was up 6% on the previous year and 40% on 2002. Growth during the past two years has been due to an increase in capital inflows and strong performance of equity markets. Part of the increase in dollar terms was also a result of a 15% fall in the value of the dollar (USD index) during 2003 and a further 4% fall in its value in 2004. As shown in Chart 8, between 1999 and 2002 the value of assets under management fell as a result of declines in equity markets.

Pension assets accounted for $15.3 trillion of funds in 2004, with a further $16.2 trillion invested in mutual funds and $14.5 trillion in insurance funds. Merrill Lynch also estimates the value of private wealth at $30.8 trillion of which about a third was incorporated in other forms of conventional investment management. The US was by far the largest source of funds under management in 2004 with 43% of the world total. It was followed by Japan with 14% and the UK with 7%. The Asia-Pacific region has shown the strongest growth in recent years. Countries such as China and India offer huge potential and many companies are showing an increased focus in this region.

Philosophy, Process and People

The 3-P's (Philosophy, Process and People) are often used to describe the reasons why the manager is able to produce above average results:

- Philosophy refers to the over-arching beliefs of the investment organisation. For example, does the manager buy growth or value shares (and why), does he believe in market timing (and on what evidence), does he rely on external research or does he employ a team of researchers. It is helpful if any and all of such fundamental beliefs are supported by proof-statements.
- Process refers to the way in which the overall philosophy is implemented. For example, which universe of assets is explored before particular assets are chosen as suitable investments; how does the manager decide what to buy and when; how does the manager decide what to sell and when; who takes the decisions and are they taken by committee; what controls are in place to ensure that a rogue fund (one very different from others and from what is intended) cannot arise;
- People refers to the staff, especially the fund managers. The question is who are they, how are they selected, how old are they, who reports to whom, how deep is the team (and do all the members understand the philosophy and process they are supposed to be using), and most important of all how long has the team been working together. This last question is vital because whatever performance record was presented at the outset of the relationship with the client may or

may not relate to (have been produced by) a team that is still in place. If the team has changed greatly (high staff turnover), then arguably the performance record is completely unrelated to the existing team (of fund managers).

Investment Managers and Portfolio Structures

At the heart of the investment management industry are the managers who invest and divest client investments. A certified company investment advisor should conduct an assessment of each client's individual needs and risk profile. The advisor then recommends appropriate investments.

Asset Allocation

The different asset classes are stocks, bonds, real-estate, derivatives, and commodities. The exercise of allocating funds among these assets (and among individual securities within each asset class) is for what investment management firms are paid. Asset classes exhibit different market dynamics, and different interaction effects; thus, the allocation of monies among asset classes will have a significant effect on the performance of the fund. Some research suggests that allocation among asset classes has more predictive power than the choice of individual holdings in determining portfolio return. Arguably, the skill of a successful investment manager resides in constructing the asset allocation, and separately the individual holdings, so as to outperform certain benchmarks (e.g., the peer group of competing funds, bond and stock indices).

Long-term Returns

It is important to look at the evidence on the long-term returns to different assets, and to holding period returns (the returns that accrue on average over different lengths of investment). For example, over very long holding periods (eg. 10+ years) in most countries, equities have generated higher returns than bonds, and bonds have generated higher returns than cash. According to financial theory, this is because equities are riskier (more volatile) than bonds which are themselves more risky than cash.

Diversification

Against the background of the asset allocation, fund managers consider the degree of diversification that makes sense for a given client (given its risk preferences) and construct a list of planned holdings accordingly. The list will indicate what percentage of the fund should be invested in each particular stock or bond. The theory of portfolio diversification was originated by Markowitz and effective diversification requires management of the correlation between the asset returns and the liability returns, issues internal to the portfolio (individual holdings volatility), and cross-correlations between the returns.

Investment Styles

There are a range of different styles of fund management that the institution can implement. For example, growth, value, market neutral, small capitalisation, indexed, etc. Each of these approaches has its distinctive features, adherents and, in any particular financial environment, distinctive risk characteristics. For example, there is evidence that growth styles (buying rapidly growing earnings) are especially effective when the companies able to generate such growth are scarce; conversely, when such growth is plentiful, then there is evidence that value styles tend to outperform the indices particularly successfully.

Performance Measurement

Fund performance is the acid test of fund management, and in the institutional context accurate measurement is a necessity. For that purpose, institutions measure the performance of each fund (and usually for internal purposes components of each fund) under their management, and performance is also measured by external firms that specialise in performance measurement.

The leading performance measurement firms (e.g. Frank Russell in the USA) compile aggregate industry data e.g showing how funds in general performed against given indices and peer groups over various time periods.

In a typical case (let us say an equity fund), then the calculation would be made (as far as the client is concerned) every quarter and would show a percentage change compared with the prior quarter (e.g. +4.6% total return in US dollars). This figure would be compared with other similar funds managed within the institution (for purposes of monitoring internal controls), with performance data for peer group funds, and with relevant indices (where available) or tailor-made performance benchmarks where appropriate. The specialist performance measurement firms calculate quartile and decile data and close attention would be paid to the (percentile) ranking of any fund.

Generally speaking it is probably appropriate for an investment firm to persuade its clients to assess performance over a longer periods (e.g. 3 to 5 years) to smooth out very short term fluctuations in performance and the influence of the business cycle. This can be difficult however and, industrywide, there is a serious pre-occupation with short-term numbers and the effect on the relationship with clients (and resultant business risks for the institutions).

Absolute Versus relative Performance

In the USA and the UK, two of the world's most sophisticated fund management markets, the tradition is for institutions to manage client money relative to benchmarks. For example, an institution believes it has done well if it has generated a return of 5% when the average manager has achieved

4%. In other markets however, e.g. Switzerland, the mentality is different and clients and fund managers focus on absolute return management, i.e. returns relative to cash (e.g. Swiss franc or Yen cash) where (performance) fees are payable only if the return exceeds some absolute figure (e.g. 10% per annum).

Education or Certification

Increasingly, international business schools are incorporating the subject into their course outlines and some have formulated the title of 'Investment Management' conferred as specialist bachelors degrees. (i.e. Cass Business School, London). Due to global cross-recognition agreements with the 2 major accrediting agencies AACSB and ACBSP which accredit over 560 of the best business school programs, the Certification of MFP Master Financial Planner Professional from the American Academy of Financial Management is available to AACSB and ACBSP business school graduates with finance or financial services related concentrations.

RAISING THE EQUITY INVESTMENT FUNDS

With the bank committed to about 60 percent of the cost, the remaining 40 percent must be raised in equity commitments by investors. To pursue these, the developer prepares an offering solicitation document that meets current securities and exchange law. The nature of this document depends on the type of business entity that was formed. For limited partnerships or limited liability companies, a private placement offering circular and project description is prepared. For S or C corporations, stock offerings are prepared for sale consistent with applicable federal and state securities laws. The developer now contacts money sources that have risk capital available to invest.

These can include:

- Individual investors
- Private asset managers
- Opportunity fund managers
- Venture capital fund managers

These potential investment sources are offered the opportunity to invest in the hotel. Based on their study and evaluation of the reports, documents, and studies detailed above, they decide whether or not to offer funding to the developer. Once the loan is secured, the equity raised, and the building permit issued by the city, the land purchase option is exercised and the purchase is completed. Then the 12–16- month construction process begins. If the architect's plans work as intended, if the general contractor has no problems with subcontractors, unions, or permits, if all the furnishings, fixtures, and equipment arrive on time, if the weather cooperates, and if the employment market is such that human resources are sufficient to open a hotel, then congratulations! The hotel will open on time.

Selecting the Management Company

Often even before the construction activity commences, the owning entity selects an appropriate management company to manage the pre-opening, marketing and sales, selection and training of the opening staff, preparation of the operating budget, and day-to-day operations once the hotel is opened.

Management companies charge 3–5 percent of revenue for this service. In recent years, management companies have charged 3–4 percent of revenue and 2–3 percent of gross operating profit so they can be measured and evaluated on both sales and profitability. The franchise company may offer to provide management services to franchisees. Marriott International, Inc., for example, manages about 50 percent of all hotels that carry the Marriott flag under 20-year contracts. Independent management companies manage the remaining hotels under long-term management contracts of up to ten years' duration, often with several five-year renewal options.

This is a largely linear explanation of the complicated process that a developer goes through in order to create a hotel. It has been described in a step-by-step process, but in reality, many of the steps are carried out concurrently to save time (and money). Nevertheless, the hotel development process takes about three years from original conception to first guest. It is important to remember that during the initial stages of the process, the developer can have as much as $1 million (U.S.) or more at risk in the process before a final go/no-go decision is reached. Only after the project is approved and all financing is in place can the developer start to recover upfront costs and collect development fees. Hotel development with its component parts of hotel feasibility studies, hotel appraisal, hotel real estate finance, and hotel management are all among the career opportunities available to hotel and restaurant administration graduates.

Extended-stay Hotel Development Project

The City Development Commission in a Pacific Northwest community purchased a 1.55- acre parcel of riverfront land in the downtown area. The land was previously contaminated with industrial pollutants that made the parcel unsafe for habitation and construction. The City Development Commission used state, local, and federal grants to have the land decontaminated, created a master plan for the area, and then offered the parcel for sale and development. The City Development Commission issued a request for proposal (RFP) that outlined the asking price of $2,076,240 ($30/sq. ft.) for the land and the design requirements set down by the Commission for a building that would fit the intended look and feel of the area.

The RFP was sent to many major hotel companies and commercial real estate brokers, asking prospective buyers to submit a purchase price bid along with a statement of the buyer's development history and ability to develop a hotel of the type envisioned by the Commission. It listed a closing date by which all bids had to be submitted. An area commercial real estate broker contacted a hotel development and management company with a long history of developing and managing extended-stay hotels in the Pacific Northwest, including a property located in a similar setting to that being offered for sale.

The commercial realtor offered to represent the developer in negotiations with the City Development Commission, which would be paying the real estate commission on the sale. An agreement was reached with the commercial real estate broker to represent the buyer to the seller, and the developer went to work in preparing a proposal.

The developer conducted a feasibility study to see all of the conditions in the marketplace that would be encouraging or discouraging to this development project. Studies were conducted to estimate how many room-nights were being sold within a five-mile radius, how many extended-stay room-nights were available in the market, how many hotel rooms existed, and how many were being planned over the following five years. From this, the developer was able to estimate the number of extended-stay room-nights available needed to produce an 82 percent occupancy with an average daily room rate of $141 when the hotel achieved stabilization three years after opening. That provided the basis for a ten-year revenue estimate.

The developer proposed a nine-floor, 258- suite extended-stay hotel with an indoor pool, spa, and exercise facility, a guest laundry, offices, meeting facilities, and a three-floor parking garage with parking for 193 automobiles, all at a total cost of $38 million, or $147,286 per suite. The $38 million construction budget was broken down as follows: Land 6.0% Construction 66.0% Office Equipment 1.4% Furniture, Fixtures, Equipment 7.4% Architecture/Engineering 2.8% Permits/Fees/Environmental 2.8% Appraisal/ Legal/Tax/Insurance 1.3% Pre-Opening Expenses 1.3% Construction Loan Fee 1.1% Developer Fee 2.8% Construction Interest 2.8% Working Capital 2.1% Contingency 2.2% Total 100% The opening date for the hotel was projected at 27 months from the date of proposal acceptance.

The City Development Commission awarded the project to the developer, and work began. First, an ownership limited liability company (LLC) was formed as the ownership entity that would hold title to the hotel. The LLC, in turn, entered into a development and construction management agreement with the development company to manage the arrangements for financing and construction of the hotel. The developer, as agent for the ownership LLC, also entered into a hotel management contract with a management company to manage the pre-opening marketing, preopening hiring and training, and the day-to- day operation of the hotel once it was opened.

The arrangements called for the management company to be paid 3 percent of revenue and 2 percent of the net operating income for management services. The ownership LLC then contacted a major hotel company and applied for a franchise to allow the development and operation of an extended-stay hotel. A 20-year franchise was granted with a fee of $400 per suite or,

$102,800. This was to be followed by a 5 percent royalty and a 3 percent advertising fee once the hotel was open and operating. The developer, acting as agent for the owner, prepared a private placement memorandum document seeking investments from accredited investors.

These investors were primarily defined as people with a net worth of $1 million, or those with an income in excess of $200,000 over the previous two years and expecting an income in excess of $200,000 in the current year. (*Note:* Additional entities may also be defined as accredited investors by the Securities and Exchange Commission.) The private placement memorandum offered $100,000 units of ownership to accredited investors, guaranteeing a 9 percent priority return on the investment and a combined 50 percent ownership in the hotel.

A group of initial investors retained the other 50 percent in exchange for putting the project together. This effort was successful in raising 40 percent of the total cost of the hotel in anticipation that a lender would provide the remaining 60 percent in the form of a construction loan. In addition to the priority return, investors could expect to participate in any future capital gain realized should the hotel be sold. The development company, continuing to function as agent for the owner, then sought a commercial bank to provide three year construction financing for the project or 60 percent, of the $38 million development cost was to be borrowed; only major banks were considered as prospective lenders.

The size of the construction loan was above the lending limits of most small regional banks. After a preconstruction appraisal by a third-party appraisal firm chosen by the lender confirmed the value at $38 million upon completion of construction, and for an origination fee of $400,000, a three-year construction loan was secured.

The terms allowed the developer, as agent for the owner, to draw down the loan every 30 days after providing proof that funds had been properly disbursed in the construction process. The loan documents set an interest rate and also required that the ownership LLC seek a permanent mortgage prior to the three-year expiration date on the construction loan. The development company then negotiated with and selected a general contractor with significant hotel construction experience who acted on behalf of the developer, as agent for the owner.

The general contractor then selected design-build subcontractors and an interior designer to select colours, fabrics, furniture, fixtures, and equipment to meet the hotel franchise design requirements. Building permits were applied for, and the building design was presented to the City Development Commission for its approval, along with other groups with a stake in the appearance of the finished building in relation to the area and neighbourhood. With all of these approvals in place, construction commenced, and the hotel opened two years later. Three years after the hotel opened, the ownership

LLC had the obligation to secure permanent financing on the hotel to replace the construction loan. The September 11, 2001, terrorist attacks on the World Trade Centre and the Pentagon slowed travel throughout the United States.

As a result, the hotel did not achieve the projected occupancy or average daily rate during the three-year construction loan period. An appraisal that was primarily based on the hotel's trailing 12- month net operating income produced a value about $2 million below the original construction cost. The bank that had provided the construction loan notified the owners that they did not wish to provide permanent financing under these circumstances. The owners were forced to conduct a search for a new mortgage bank. They were able to find a mortgage, but only after buying down the loan by $2 million to bring the loan-to-value ratio back to 40 percent equity and a loan at 60 percent of the appraised.

This illustrates the risk that developers face when entering into a hotel project. However, as hotel values historically peak and decline on about a ten-year cycle, the owners look forward to the option of selling the hotel on the next peak, which will allow them to capture the original projected return through capital appreciation. Hotel development and ownership is a high-risk, high reward enterprise.

Dramatic changes have affected the hotel industry over the past 30 years. These changes have had a disproportionately high bearing on the independent hotel owner, who, in the face of increasing pressure from large, well funded chains, struggles to maintain independence and to compete on the basis of distinctive hospitality and character. Several organizations provide independent hotels and resorts with reservations and sales services. As competition has evolved and intensified, some of these organizations have modified their structure and enhanced their services to meet the changing needs of independent hotels and competitive market dynamics. Today, independent hotels may choose from among more than 20 such organizations delivering varying degrees of competitive advantage and ownership independence.

A NEW MARKET MODEL

In the new millennium, the face of the global hospitality market continues to change at a rate never before seen.

Four factors contribute to this rapidly changing environment:

- The broadening and diversification of the global consumer market. Both the demographic and psychographic characteristics of the global consumer market are growing and changing radically.
- The rapid advancement and availability of technology. This includes internal hotel operating systems, revenue management, direct-to-consumer communications and booking technology (Internet), marketing technology (customer databases), and telecommunications

and automated sales systems that enable central sales offices to become revenue producers.

- The growth and importance of global brands. Recognized brand names and brand attributes are important in reaching diverse customer segments and in creating customer loyalty.
- Consolidation of multiple brands under a single global management. The management and leveraging of multiple brands use similar technology platforms and shared sales and marketing infrastructures to consolidate and direct consumer demand. Some established ways of doing business— long-term, high-fee management contracts and franchises, a focus on traditional distribution channels, and traditional hospitality industry marketing techniques—are no longer effective in the new consumer-focused market. More and more hospitality marketing budgets are being directed toward technology enabled customer booking and communication; this shift away from traditional hospitality marketing techniques is expected to evolve over several years and involve millions of U.S. dollars in telecommunication, e-commerce, data warehousing, and one-to-one marketing investment.

The independent hotel or resort and many small branded management companies may not be able to fund this requirement. However, this shift will not affect all independent hotels and resorts simultaneously. The first wave of change will hit the global business and city hotel market. This is primarily because of brand competition and the fact that the business travel distribution network is more structured and driven by multinational corporations desiring lower and more predictable costs.

The second wave will affect the leisure market, and the changes could follow quickly. Leisure travel content, including packaging on the Internet, will increase rapidly as the presently fragmented leisure travel distribution network becomes more unified and efficient through consolidation. The emergence of e-commerce modes in the hospitality industry is not eliminating the intermediary and empowering the individual property, as once thought; instead, it is creating new, more powerful intermediaries. Some of these evolve from the hospitality industry, while others are opportunistic e-commerce companies.

Management Companies and Franchises

In the 1970s, hotel chains continued to evolve as the need for capital to invest in additional properties restricted growth opportunities. This pressure bolstered the proliferation of the management contract, whereby the chain offers the hotel owner the rights to use its brand name and established facility and service standards as well as trained operations management and reservation and marketing services—for a significant fee, usually a percentage of gross sales. The pressure to grow also fostered the development of the franchise concept and franchise system in North America.

The franchise differs from the management contract in that the owner is responsible for operations, including meeting the franchise standards. The growth of management and franchise contracts has been remarkable, and today, according to a recent study, 75 percent of the hotel rooms in North America are covered by some form of branded franchise or professional management agreement. These new business structures continued to threaten the traditional independent owner by accelerating the growth of the chains' share of the lodging market. In response, the marketing/ referral organizations formed in the 1960s began to offer a wider range of services.

While these additional offerings leveraged linkages to the global distribution systems and led to strong relationships with travel agents, the consumer was largely ignored, and the organizations did little to generate consumer brand awareness. In the United States, strong consumer branded operators are attracting increasing amounts of capital to fund their growth at the expense of unbranded operators.

Brand Development

As the consumer market became more diverse and the hospitality product more segmented, branding became increasingly important. By the late 1980s, without a recognized brand affiliation or a close relationship with the lending community, owners/developers found it difficult to obtain permanent financing on a new hotel or resort. Lenders, believing that an established brand provided greater economies of scale and established infrastructure, opted for the lower-risk alternative. In this brand-driven environment, the independent hotels' distinctive style and character became a competitive advantage, but only if they were able to meet recognized standards.

As a result, the need for independent hotels to be associated with a clearly defined, trusted brand became more critical than ever. In the late 1990s, independent hotels, particularly those in Europe, began to face the daunting costs of upgrading their technological infrastructure and facilities to accommodate changing consumer needs. Such upgrades as new property management systems, highspeed Internet access, two-line phones, inroom faxes, and leisure and health facilities became critical to maintaining competitiveness. When coupled with ever-increasing costs of consumer marketing, these costs put unprecedented strains on independent hotels' finances. As a result, these hotels became increasingly focused on leveraging greater returns from their reservation management affiliation.

RESERVATION AFFILIATIONS

The relationship of independent hotels and resorts to reservation affiliations has been long and generally successful. These relationships operated best in a market environment that was stable, somewhat homogeneous in terms of demographic market segmentation, and where travel influencers played a dominant role in transient business, group, and leisure travel. Reservation affiliations are most effective in regional hospitality markets that do not have multiple brand competition and when the goals and objectives of the reservation organization are in alignment with the goals of the independent hotel owners. A contributing element to the attractiveness of reservation affiliations has always been the networking and camaraderie opportunities for the professional management at independent hotels.

Reservation affiliations focus on traditional channels of distribution. Access to the Global Distribution Systems (GDS) is no longer a competitive advantage; the GDS is a universal pipeline. The new competitive playing field is proprietary distribution channels leveraged by consumer segmentation, e-commerce technology and partners, and innovative customer management programmes. In the new technology-driven and consumer- empowered global market, the strength and effectiveness of reservation affiliations are challenged by new market and operating imperatives. The cost to compete against chains will grow exponentially. As competition intensifies, it is probable that local and regional market share at independent hotels and resorts will be drawn off by local and regional licensees of strong global brands.

Independent hotels, therefore, need to draw more national and international business to fill occupancy gaps. This requirement runs counter to the established business model and capabilities of reservation affiliations. The average room-night contribution of reservations companies to affiliated independent hotels is less than 5 percent of available rooms.

At least four emerging factors are challenging the effectiveness of traditional reservation organizations:

1. The growing demographic and psychographic complexity of the global consumer market requires significant new expertise and resources in the area of segmentation and analysis.
2. The emergence of consumer direct-booking Internet technology requires significant new and ongoing investment.
3. The new marketplace requires innovative global brand management together with resources to establish and maintain a brand in the face of intense competition. To be competitive, a brand must attract new development and must therefore be strong enough to convince lenders to commit to permanent financing. Brand management also includes loyalty programme management and the development of regional and global partners to strengthen and extend the effectiveness of the brand.
4. The corporate objectives and governance policies of traditional reservation organizations are influenced by the need to grow and meet shareholder profit requirements. These goals for growth can

be at odds with the goals and expectations of independent hotel and resort members.

The traditional reservation affiliations must change not only their focus but also their structure if they want to succeed in this new competitive world. The traditional reservation organization must be prepared to respond to competitive challenges by expanding resources and skills necessary to increase average room-night contribution to affiliated independent hotels to 15 percent—an average growth per member hotel of at least 200 percent over present performance levels. In response to this competitive environment and the need for more cooperative and focused business relationships, a new hospitality business structure is evolving for all scales of hotels: the branded distribution company.

Characteristics of a Branded Distribution Company

The ideal branded distribution organization is a conventional equity company with ownership shared (in some cases) by the individual hotel owners, who have direct input into the corporation through an elected board of directors. This ownership structure creates a true operating partnership and a sharing of energies toward the common goal of creating value through increased brand awareness and room sales. Corporate profits must be adequate to maintain technical and managerial leadership and to support the shareholders' investment.

Unlike a reservations and representation company, a branded distribution corporation owns and builds a branded distribution network asset that, in turn. The sole focus is performance for the affiliated independent hotels and resorts. Joining such an organization is appropriate for independently owned and managed hotels and resorts that want to keep owner control but require effective and low-cost distribution, global consumer brand awareness, and group purchasing benefits without the encumbrances and costs of a traditional hotel chain franchise or management contract. Above all, it promises the independent hotel awareness of, and access to, their target consumer and rapidly emerging technology through cooperative ownership.

The Benefits of a Branded Distribution Company

This new business structure is attractive from an owner's or a developer's standpoint for a number of reasons, including:

- *Costs:* First, it requires less up-front cash; second, ongoing fees and reservation commissions are significantly lower than with either a pure franchise or management agreement. For example, a 9 or 10 percent franchise fee in many cases equals 50 percent of gross profits.
- *Contract terms:* The terms are typically shorter, easier to negotiate, and allow for substantial owner control over the operation, style, and character of the hotel. As a result, conflicts can be avoided, and

the branded distribution contract can be completed and signed in as few as 45 days.

- *Marketing:* It frees hotel management from the daunting and increasingly expensive task of acquiring profitable new customers and allows them to focus their attention and operating skills on the delivery of an exceptional hospitality experience.
- *Common objectives:* Both the owner and the branded distribution company enter into the agreement with the same primary objective: revenue.

The branded distribution company receives no revenue if it does not deliver to the hotel or resort. This shared goal strengthens and energizes the relationship between the two partners. From a branded distribution company's standpoint, this structure allows the brand to expand faster because capital is not used to subsidize additional construction or to support an older business model.

Instead, funds are used to build and maintain an uptodate global distribution network and infrastructure composed of telecommunications, e-commerce functions, reservations software, data warehousing capability, and sales and marketing. The efficiency of the operation is assured by a focus that is almost entirely on the most important part of this business relationship—the generation of brand awareness and measurable room-night revenue for each affiliated hotel or resort.

Unlike hard flags, which focus primarily on hotel operations and asset management such as the Marriott or the Westin, and reservation affiliations, which focus on professional camaraderie and traditional distribution channels such as the Best Western, the branded distribution company is primarily market focused; its full attention is on customer and travel influencer communication, relationship technology, and revenue streams.

In contrast, asset management, profitability, and operating efficiency are the major concerns of management companies, which tend to be public companies with stockholder expectations that must be met. It is often the case that strategic asset management concerns conflict with day-to-day tactical operating needs. This is evident in Marriott's recent move to separate its ownership and operating divisions, to the benefit of both. The same conflict can arise between the independent owners of a hotel property, who are focused on real estate concerns, and the management company they hire. Such misunderstandings can sour what should be a mutually supportive relationship.

The fact that management contract fees are charged and collected, even when the cash flow is negative, does not create owner confidence in the partner. A franchise relationship can cause a similar conflict and put a financial and operating burden on an owner. In contrast, participation of independent owner/operators as shareholders in a branded distribution company enables them to move beyond these concerns and focus on their operation and the consumer—the source of their revenue and the basis of their success.

A Branded Distribution Company

The owners of property within a branded distribution company must relinquish a minimal amount of control and decision making, mainly in the areas of branding and quality assurance. In certain cases, member properties may have to adopt and maintain specific quality standards. In addition, they may also be required to demonstrate their affiliation with the branded distribution company through using its logo on marketing materials as well as participating in e-commerce and inventory management initiatives. However, these drawbacks can actually enhance a hotel's operations and market positioning while allowing the hotel to maintain independent ownership and management.

Ensuring Competitive Advantage

Independent hotels face significant risk in today's marketplace. Given the advances in technology and the profitability pressures put upon chain hotels by shareholders, competition for customers is intensifying. Keeping in step with competitive chain hotels presents a significant challenge to independent owners. To address this, they currently have several options outside of the branded distribution company, including representation firms, reservations services, flagged chains, and franchise management companies. However, given the economic, societal, and technological trends that are dramatically changing the hospitality industry, several of which are analyzed in this book, many of these old economy options can offer only short-term solutions to long-term competitive pressures.

A branded distribution company has an inherent advantage going into this new competitive arena. Its sole focus is on customer acquisition and management, achieved through the development of new technologies. This competitive advantage extends to the independent hotel aligned with a branded if you ever have the chance to be involved with opening a hotel, jump at the opportunity.

Opening a hotel is one of the most rewarding jobs in the hospitality industry despite its frustrating and exhausting aspects. Walk into any hotel, anywhere, and look around. Everything you see, hear, and feel, every detail, involved many people and countless decisions.

The OPM is the third person hired, after the general manager and the director of marketing. The role of an OPM is to pull together the visions of the architect, interior designer, owner, operator, and others. When these visions are successfully melded, the hotel guest is satisfied, the owner makes money, and the architect and interior designer can add the project to their list of successful accomplishments.

The OPM oversees the following aspects of a project:

- Reviewing blueprints and specifications for the entire building
- Assisting with the creation of a model room
- Developing the pre-opening staff plan
- Developing and managing the pre-opening budget
- Developing the operational supplies and equipment budget (OS&E)
- Overseeing the purchasing, warehousing, delivery, and installation of the OS&E
- Developing the interior graphics package
- Coordinating the installation of third party vendors

7

Organizational Forms in the Global Hotels Business

INTRODCTION

One first needs to understand various organizational forms and their idiosyncrasies in the global hotel business before one can formulate hypotheses. Some of the hypotheses this chapter will propose are peculiar to the hotel business although most are applicable to other service and manufacturing sectors. Hence we first present an overview of the hotel business.

Since the focus of this chapter is the determinants of foreign strategy, we focus only on hotel properties outside the home nation of the firm. Hotel firms listed in the International Hotels Group Directory have more than half a million rooms outside their home nation. From the directory, we first identified firms that listed at least one property outside their home nation as part of their global group of hotels. The directory provides a comprehensive coverage of the business worldwide, but does not show the organizational mode (fully owned, joint venture, management contract, or franchise) for each property. This was obtained from questionnaires.

For the purpose of this chapter, therefore, a global hotel firm is defined as one that either has an equity stake in a foreign property, or operates the hotel under a management service agreement, or is a franchisor to the foreign hotel property. Thus, a company could be a global firm without any ownership of a foreign property. However, as a matter of fact, virtually every hotel company in our sample had some equity ownership in at least one foreign property, thus providing a range of organizational choices in the sample.

A questionnaire was sent to all listed firms with foreign hotel operations. The questions covered data on the hotel firm as a whole (e.g., the firm's overall size, international experience, distribution and number of hotel properties worldwide).

The questionnaire also asked what organizational mode was used for each hotel property abroad.

The questionnaire response provided a sample that covers 1,131 hotels and comprises over 60 percent of all "foreign" properties and rooms listed in the directory (355,169 out of some half million rooms). Despite reminders, a large firm response bias remains in the sample. Our data base therefore includes the organizational mode chosen for each hotel property, and other details on the global hotel company involved, as well as characteristics of the nation where the hotel property is located.

While the prevalence of management service contracts is high across all major regions where hotels are located, there appear to be variations in equity ownership and franchising by region. Equity ownership is lower, and franchising more frequent in North America. In Asia, by comparison, franchising is less common, and equity ownership modes are most common. Non-equity modes, thus, account worldwide for 65.4 percent of foreign operation properties, and arrangements involving two companies account for as much as 81.2 percent of the total number of hotels worldwide.

But this should not make us jump to the conclusion that managerial control or strategic direction are weak in the joint venture or non-equity organizational forms. In some service sectors, such as hotels, control has been de-linked from equity ownership - but control, and an overall global strategy exist.

What is the dimensions of management "control" in alliances? For both its short and long term strategy, the global firm today must deal with a multiplicity of partners and organizational forms, each having its own degrees of required control. In the international joint venture context, Schaan and Geringer and Hebert described different mechanisms whereby each firm may exercise control over the joint venture.

For alliances in general, the means of control can be classified as "participatory" control (by the act of actively participating in the management of an enterprise), control exercised by "withholding" or threatening to withhold some asset or capability desired by the other partner, and "proscriptive" control (by legal or de facto prohibitions).

We break these down further between (a) daily operational and quality control in each hotel property; (b) control over the physical assets or over the real estate and its attendant risks; (c) control over tacit expertise embedded in the routines of the firm; and (d) control over the codified assets, such as a global reservation system and the firm's internationally recognized brand name.

Equity Investments

In fully owned operations, all four control criteria (a) through (d) are under the strong control of the hotel firm. In equity joint ventures, (a), (b), and (c) are shared, although typically control of the global brand name and reservations system remains with the global hotel company to retain its leverage over the local partner. Since organizational control has many attributes, especially in international business, where culture and national differences prevail, it is difficult to develop an overall measure for control in international joint ventures. The global hotel company may retain strong control over (d) (its reservations system and global brand), but have shared control over day-to-day management, quality, and physical assets.

Tacit expertise (c) is inevitably shared with the local partner, to some extent, which may erode the global hotel company's knowledge advantage over time. Equity investment does provide stronger long-term strategic control compared with management service agreements, for the simple reason that the latter are time-bound and, on expiry of the agreement, subject to cancellation by the property owners. By comparison, an equity stake is not so easily dissolved.

MANAGEMENT SERVICE AGREEMENTS

A management service contract is a long term agreement, of up to ten years or even longer, whereby the legal owners of the property and real estate enter into a contract with the hotel firm to run and operate the hotel on a day to day basis, usually under the latter's internationally recognized name.

Quality control, daily management and senior staffing (a) principally rest with the international hotel firm and not the property owners. But the operation is run as if the property were part of the global chain. Customers cannot tell the difference. The international hotel firm, as operator, earns management fees often expressed as a percentage of gross revenues (sometimes with annual minimums and lump-sum payments).

In addition, the global hotel firm may earn extra profit margins on any supplies and material it sells to the particular property. In some cases, there may be bonuses linked, not to revenues, but to profits - as a profit-sharing formula. Finally, in several cases, the property is charged a small fee for every reservation booked through the global reservation system of the global hotel firm. Such codified strategic assets (d) remain in the control of the global firm.

Nevertheless, local partners may not always be content to merely remain as passive owners of the real estate. Since much of the middle management and staff are local personnel, they acquire tacit expertise on the job. There have been a few cases, for example, as the Oberoi Hotels Group, which initially had an agreement with Intercontinental Hotels, but learned the business well enough to launch its own international hotel chain after terminating its partnership with Intercontinental Hotels.

While it is possible that a few minority joint venture investments may provide the firm with lower control over global strategy than a management service agreement, in general we posit that a joint venture equity stake provides superior long-term strategic control, compared with contractual alternatives.

In effect, for the global hotel firm, management service agreements provide strong day-to-day (if not long term) control without ownershi. Moreover, such contracts can amount to surer returns without real estate investment risk. Even ordinary commercial or economic risk is greatly reduced since the hotel operator's take is often a percentage of revenues (akin to a royalty), and not expressed as a percentage of profits, as would be the case in an equity joint venture.

It is axiomatic that over a business cycle, revenues are far less volatile than profits. The latest indicator of this trend is Marriott Corp., which in 1993, split itself into two firms - one a profitable hotel management firm, and the other a debt-laden real estate owning company.

In franchising, (a) daily management and quality control and (b) control over physical assets reside with the franchisee, and not with the global hotel firm. In this case, the international hotel firm does not run the hotel's management, but trains and guides it under a contractual relationship, sharing only some tacit expertise (c). But it would be a mistake to assume that the franchisor exercises no control.

Typically, hotel standards are sought to be zealously enforced. Codified assets (d), such as brands and reservation systems reside with the global hotel company. The franchisor earns fees linked to revenues and profits, additional margins on material supplied to the franchise, booking fees for clients booked via the global reservations network, and training fees for personnel trained.

For the international hotel firm, even without ownership or management involvement, we hypothesize that a network of franchisees enable it to capture at least some economies of global scale in logistics, supplies, architectural design, reservations, training, and brand recognition. Certainly, not all firms replicate hotel architectural designs "cookie cutter" style in every nation; nor do all franchisees purchase from the global hotel firm's central procurement channel. But we hypothesize that enough do so to provide significant economies in a worldwide operation.

The question addressed by this chapter is:

"For a firm intending an investment in a particular hotel property located in a particular nation, what determines whether the investment will be fully owned, or an equity joint venture, or whether it will be a non-equity arrangement involving either a management service contract, or a franchise?"

This chapter is written from the perspective of a global hotel firm willing to consider different entry modes in various nations. It does not refer to the local owners of a hotel property as franchisees, or as the local partners in a management service agreement.

In this chapter we take a syncretic approach to the modal choice question, similar to Hill, Hwang and Kim, or Contractor. The approach is not merely the minimization of transaction costs, with a focus on one transaction or market entry at a time, nor does it treat only the conditions in the host nation (which was the focus of traditional market entry literature). The firm seeks the maximization of profits based on long-term global strategy. This forces a look at the revenue side as well.

Moreover, the maximization of long term global profits is not merely a matter of maximum rent extraction from a particular market, but building the capabilities and knowledge of the company as a whole. Zajac and Olsen describe the modal choice decision as determined by the need to create long-term "value" in the global firm.

Increasingly, the use of corporate allies and partners to create a global network is being seen to be as valid a pathway to building value as an ownership-linked company. Since non-equity modes are more prevalent internationally in the hotel business, this process is well along on its way in this sector. In alliances, the firm must deal with other agents, such as franchisees, local owners of the real estate, and joint venture partners, whose predilections, incentives, and motivations may differ from the strategic objectives of the global firm.

Agency theory also provides some insights into such different objectives. A robust theory of modal choice must therefore incorporate country-specific and transaction-specific variables, as well as factors relating to the strategy of the global company and the agents with which it interacts.

Interest in the modal choice question began in the marketing and international business fields, where the question was couched as the choice between exporting and foreign direct investment (FDI). Root (1994) and Goodnow and Hansz (1985) reflect the traditional marketing focus on conditions or the environment in the host country. This country focus remains as one of the legs of our empirical analysis later in the paper. Locational or country-specific advantages were one part of Dunning's (1988) OLI theory.

However, non-equity forms such as licensing were then considered of lesser interest, and joint ventures were not explicitly considered on the spectrum of governance choices until the mid-1980s. Buckley and Casson (1976) expanded the choice to include licensing as a means of reaching customers abroad. But in their perspective, the multinational firm would usually prefer to "internalize" transactions via direct equity investment rather than license its capability.

The multinational firm's raison d'etre was its superior ability to extract rents from each nation it invested in - a rent that was supposed to be almost always far higher than potential returns via cooperative or contractual modes of entry, such as licensing or franchising. Recent work by Buckley and Casson (1996) considers cooperative modes of organization as far more likely.

TRANSACTION-COST EXPLANATIONS

The core of the transaction-cost explanations deal with asset specificity, bounded rationality, the free-rider problem, and opportunism. The principal focus is on one transaction or negotiation - one market entry - at a time. The choice of organizational mode is that which minimizes transaction costs. The other strand of Dunning's (1988) OLI theory, namely Ownership, makes a related argument - that the multinational firm will prefer to "internalize" via equity ownership when the "market" for knowledge transfers "fails."

Transaction-cost explanations will comprise a significant input in the development of this chapter's hypotheses. However, since they are sufficiently well known, it would be more useful to discuss how these arguments relate to global hotel operations when formally proposing hypotheses later in the paper. The Organizational Capability Perspective: The Global Hotel Firm as a Knowledge-based Service Company

A useful perspective on many alliances is that they involve the transfer of knowledge between partners over some duration of time, rather than as a transaction. Winter (1987) focused on the creation of knowledge and competence within the enterprise, and on how expertise is embedded in tacit organizational "routines." Ghoshal (1987) has a learning focus, but on cross-affiliate knowledge transfers within the multinational enterprise.

Teece distinguishes between tacit, unwritten or informal knowledge, and formally registered intellectual property which is far more easily transferable or shared with another firm. Contractor points out that intellectual properties, such as patents, trademarks or copyrights, are only of minor strategic importance - as an all-industry generalization. However, in the hotel business, registered brand names, as well as unregistered, but proprietary reservations and logistics systems, are a potent source of control.

Control over codified strategic assets (category (d)) occurs typically in all four modes. The potential threat of withdrawing permission to use the global company's brand, reservations and support systems, moderates the opportunistic behaviour of partners in each nation. In fact, this may be one factor which explains the high prevalence of equity and non-equity alliances in the hotel business.

It is nevertheless true that codified strategic assets are only the visible, formalized tip of a vast iceberg of tacit information embedded in trained personnel and technicians, and in implicit routines. Hence the cost of transferring such knowledge to another partner firm can be protracted, difficult, costly and incomplete. This also partially depends on the "absorptive capacity" of the partner firm learning the new routines.

If the local partner is in a lesser-developed nation (here we connect the transaction-cost argument with a country variable), the transfer of complex tacit knowledge is more difficult, and we hypothesize later that non-equity forms, such as franchising, will be less prevalent in developing nations, ceteris paribus. If knowledge is so extremely embedded, or tacit, as to prevent its accurate valuation by the negotiators, then in the worst case, "bounded rationality" may prevent the "transaction" or partnership itself from taking place. In the earlier literature such "market failure" left the firm with no choice but to opt for the hierarchical, full-ownership mode. Today, however, the ubiquity of cooperative modes, especially in the hotel business, suggests that such market failure is not common.

Learning across organizational boundaries in partnerships can also be unintended, lack reciprocity, or be unequal. Unequal cross-flows of knowledge can lead to perceptions of "free riding," and unintended leakage of knowledge can lead to opportunism in the form of partners terminating the relationship to become competitors. However, retaining legal or de facto control over strategic assets, such as brands or a global reservations system, can moderate such opportunism on the part of local partners. (Here again, this firm-level literature connects with the transaction-costs arguments.)

Management of knowledge flows within and across the organizational boundary is therefore key to strategic success when dealing with multiple competitors and partners. This leads to the second sub-group of firm-specific factors affecting the choice of organizational mode.

Other Industry and Firm Strategy Variables

Whether a firm will decide to "go it alone" or cooperate with partners, and if so, under what mode of association, depends not just on the intended transaction or on the characteristics of knowledge within a firm, but on the broader structure of the firm and its industry as well. These variables include size and scale, diversification, investment in R&D and training, experience, flexibility, speed, first-mover rewards, and synergies of cooperation.

Each of these variables is complex and is not amenable to easy generalizations as to its effects on the modal choice. For example, Gomes-Casseres indicates that the quest for global economies of scale will discourage cooperative organizational modalities. Yet, in some sectors, economies of global scale may be captured equally well by quasi-integration across national borders.

To capture global economies some firms may grow larger by mergers and acquisitions, or via internal growth; others may join a coalition or network to achieve the same ends, especially if rapid growth is needed for competitive reasons.

How does "knowledge intensity" affect the modal choice? In the manufacturing sector knowledge intensity has been measured by the R&D/Sales ratio. Since hotel companies do not do R&D per se, the ratio of the amount they invest in the training of their personnel, over sales, can provide an alternate measure of knowledge intensity.

Gatignon and Anderson (1988) proposed that when the proprietary content of products or processes is high the choice will tend towards the full ownership end of the spectrum. For hotels, one can operationalize knowledge intensity by ratios such as "investment in training over sales."

AGENCY THEORY AND NON-EQUITY ORGANIZATIONAL MODES

Shane applies agency theory concepts to show that non-equity modes of entry can be efficient substitutes for equity investment. Consider the choice between a fully owned foreign hotel operation, where the global company has to hire its own staff, and a franchise. The so-called "adverse selection" and "moral hazard" problems in agency theory focus on the difficulty of assessing the abilities of foreign employees, and monitoring them for performance.

This is more difficult the greater the cultural distance between the firm and the host nation. Equity owners only have residual profit claims on the remnant of the net cash flow from a foreign operation after costs, including those of employees, are met. By contrast, not only does a local franchisee have the better local knowledge to select and monitor employees, but also promises to the franchisor the "first cut" of cash flow collections.

This is because, in franchising, lump-sum fees are paid in advance, and royalties must be paid out of sales revenue collections (regardless of profits). More specific theoretical arguments will be developed later with the hypotheses.

The Dependent Variable (M): Modal Choice for Each Property

The questionnaire responses listed, for each hotel in a foreign nation, its organizational mode, whether the hotel is a Franchise = 1; Under the company's management in a service contract = 2; Partially Owned (Joint Venture) = 3; and Fully Owned = 4. The dependent variable M is therefore a polytomous measure generally depicting rising levels of equity ownership and overall control. Overlapping categories (e.g., a hotel property under management service agreement and partial equity investment) were dropped, as Discriminant Analysis requires non-overlapping categories. This affected only 6.5 percent of cases.

Two techniques with different objectives and different methodology were used: Discriminant Analysis as a test of the robustness of the group classification based on independent variables, followed by Ordinal logistic regression using a generalized LOGIT model. Discriminant Analysis tests the validity and robustness of the modal choice categories, but is not concerned about their rank ordering. Regression is concerned about by the ordering of categories within the multinomial measure M. The hypotheses developed below relate principally to the regression analysis.

Independent Variables

A complete picture of the organizational choice question needs a syncretic approach combining transaction-cost and agency theory reasoning, as well as country-specific and firm-specific variables, as Contractor (1990) pointed out. This was echoed by Kim and Hwang (1992), and Erramilli and Rao (1993) who used all four types of factors in their empirical studies. Even earlier, while operating under the panoply of transaction-cost explanations, Gatignon and Anderson (1988) had used country indicators, such as country risk, as well as firm strategy variables, such as advertising/sales and R&D/sales ratios, and number of employees, as a proxy for firm size.

The first group relates to the country in which the hotel property is located. We will ask how country-specific variables affect the modal choice. The second groups' independent variables describe the size, international experience, and extent of foreign business of the hotel firm. The third groups' independent variables describes responses from hotel executives on the perceived importance of strategy and control variables.

In diverse international operations, the organizational form is sure to be affected by local conditions. Few companies today follow uniform policies across countries. Assume that a global hotel company is willing to consider in each country either an equity investment (fully or partially owned), or a management service agreement, or a franchise. It assesses each situation, and makes the appropriate choice of organizational mode.

Country Political and Economic Risk: Data for this independent variable were obtained from Frost and Sullivan's, International Country Risk Guide, for each nation where the sample hotel properties are located.

Development of this hypothesis rests on four arguments. The first relates to the size of resource commitments in risky nations. Kim and Hwang (1992), Agarwal and Ramaswami (1992), and Madhok (1994) propose that, ceteris paribus, higher country risk will favour entry modes with lower resource commitments or ownership. Gatignon and Anderson (1988) and Goodnow and Hansz (1985) also suggest that equity investment modes are less likely when country risk is high.

We should recall that in this business, capital investment in real estate is normally high - occasionally approaching $100 million for large resort properties. The second argument deals with "environmental uncertainty" in terms of political and currency volatility. When volatility is high, franchising is preferred over corporate ownership. Agency theory concurs and suggests that franchising can be an efficient organizational mode in risky markets, where the franchisee is responsible for employee selection and monitoring.

Control over the brand name is maintained by the global firm, tempering or eliminating franchisee opportunism. Kim and Hwang (1992) use the term "demand uncertainty" and postulate that when uncertainty is high, equity ownership will tend to be low. This is corroborated by Erramilli and Rao (1993). Third, in the international hotel business, management service contracts enable the firm to exercise a high degree of control over the foreign operation without ownership risk. Franchising involves an even lesser commitment. Finally, the inclusion of royalty-type payments in alliance agreements, where the earnings of the global hotel firm are linked to sales, and not profit of the hotel property, reduce their risk significantly in volatile environments, because royalties are linked to sales and not profits. Sales are far more stable over the business cycle compared with profits. In Buckley and Casson's (1996) words, "...as volatility increases so internalization becomes less attractive."

In risky nations then, hotel firms would be more likely to avoid the risks of equity investment and opt for management service contracts or franchising. Hence, our hypothesis:

H1: M (rising levels of equity and control) will be negatively associated with country political and economic risk.

(However, please note that because Frost & Sullivan's "Composite Risk Index" is on an inverted scale of Highest Risk = 0 to Lowest Risk = 100 our hypothesis expects a positive sign for variable CRI).

Cultural Distance: Several studies suggest that "Cultural Distance" between the home base of the firm and the intended foreign market is a powerful determinant of modal choice. There appears to be a consensus in the literature on this topic, namely, that a greater cultural distance between the firm and the foreign nation it is operating in will lead to less equity ownership, and a greater incidence of cooperative modes, ceteris paribus. Gomes-Casseres (1989) explains this in terms of needing more help from local joint venture partners in less familiar environments. Fladmoe-Lindquist and Jacque (1995) posit that "...cultural distance tends to create costly information requirements which encourage U.S. service firms to use lower-cost governance structures."

At the same time, the risk of cultural misunderstandings is higher, especially in a service industry, and one with a high local labour content. Shane's (1996) adaptation of agency theory makes a congruent hypothesis, namely that local partners ease the "adverse selection problem" in selecting and overseeing staff in culturally distant markets.

The global firm needs local partners' help all the more when the culture is unfamiliar. We should distinguish here between cultural distance risk versus political and economic country risk discussed earlier. The two are not necessarily correlated. All in all, ceteris paribus, the higher cost and risk of operating at a greater cultural distance makes the firm less inclined to make large equity investments, especially fully owned ones. Hence, the hypothesis that:

H2: High equity ownership modes will be negatively associated with increased cultural distance (CUL) between the global hotel firm and the nation where the hotel is located.

Level of Economic Development: How might a country's level of economic development affect the modal choice of prospective investors or entrants? In their study of the hotel industry over a decade ago Dunning and McQueen (1981) proposed the hypotheses that the incidence of equity ownership in the hotels business should be positively correlated with economic development. But they did not test this. Moreover, a priori reasoning tends to give greater weight to the opposite hypothesis, that higher income nations will have a relatively larger share of non-equity modes, such as franchising and management service agreements. Why?

First, the lower "absorptive capacity" of franchisees in lesser-developed nations and the consequently higher costs of adaptation and knowledge transfer would tend to support the idea that franchising would be more prevalent the more developed the nation is. Second, while the global hotel company will try to retain legal control over its brand and other intellectual property, enforcement is weaker in developing nations. Many companies which consider intellectual property protection as central to strategy, have concluded that majority or full equity ownership of developing country operations is consequently necessary.

Thirdly, emerging markets are also characterized by weaker competition, faster growth, and higher returns and profits. Recall that contractual modes, such as franchising or management service agreements, constrain the return of the global hotel company to a royalty-type return (a percentage of sales). This is a less volatile cash flow, but one that is inferior to returns on equity in absolute magnitude. In high profit potential areas, returns on equity investments far outstrip royalties.

Moreover, the contractual organization modes are subject to cancellation on expiry of the agreement, whereas a fully owned equity investment is of indefinite duration, in theory at least. For this reason, we propose:

H3: M (rising levels of equity and control) is negatively associated with the level of economic development (GDPCAP) in the country where the hotel is located.

Foreign Business Investment Penetration In The Local Economy: In an earlier study, Dunning and McQueen (1981) proposed that, other things being equal, in nations characterized by a higher penetration of FDI, the firm will choose higher control and equity-based modes.

They stated this as a hypothesis to be tested. Possible explanations involve a "follow the client" abroad hypothesis, based on the assumption that global hotel chains draw an appreciable fraction of their clientele from international business travellers. Hence, in countries whose economies are more open to international investment and trade, there should be a greater incidence of international business travellers who are particularly concerned about quality standards. To be sure, one can question some of these assumptions.

There are no data available per hotel, or per firm, on the fraction of clients who are international businesspersons, so one cannot gauge the extent of their influence. Nor can we assess whether their preferences for quality are different from other classes of customers. However, since Dunning and McQueen's work is the only other empirical study on global hotels, we thought it worthwhile to test this hypothesis. The penetration of FDI into a host nation is operationalized by the ratio of FDI over GDP.

H4: M (rising levels of equity and control) is positively associated with a country's ratio of FDI over GDP.

To summarize, three characteristics of the host nation (where the hotel property is located) are said to influence the mode of organization: Country Risk, Cultural Distance, and Foreign Business Penetration. We now turn to firm-specific factors.

Firm-specific factors have been divided into two groups. So-called Structural or Objective factors include Firm Size, International Experience, and Degree of Internationalization. The questionnaire also asked executives in the global hotel firm to give subjective Responses to Strategy and Control Questions. The latter are based on a 5-point Likert Scale (5 = Very Important.....1 = Not Important), covering the perceived strategic importance of Global Scale, Intangible Assets such as a Global Reservation System and Brand, Investment in Training and Ability to Exercise Control over Management and Quality.

How does size of the firm relate to the propensity to choose non-equity and contractual organizational modes? The majority of studies indicate that larger firms are likely to prefer high levels of equity ownership. Smaller firms, which lacked the resources or expertise to venture into foreign markets, would prefer shared control modes. This remains the accepted view, and will accordingly be stated as the hypothesis.

Nevertheless, it should be pointed out, that other studies suggest the opposite, namely, that these assumptions may not apply to several service sectors, especially the hotel business, where the advantages of size may equally well be derived by a global network of partnerships and alliances. Gatignon and Anderson (1988) state that "higher control entry modes are less likely for large foreign operations."

They base this argument on the notion that the size of global operations in many industries will force even large firms - or particularly the firms that wish to be large - to accept partners to share in the large total investment and large coverage of a global network. In this strategy, the path to becoming a large global player requires the firm to accept a lot of partners and have lower-control, non-equity relationships (in our case such as franchising). Agency theory suggests that the problems of human resource selection and management may grow even faster than the firm's growth in size, especially in international operations.

We propose to test these contrary views by formally proposing the first viewpoint:

H5: We expect a positive relationship between firm size and M (rising levels of equity ownership and control). International Experience and Degree of Globalization: More internationally experienced firms have less need for local help in the nation in which they operate and will have a lower tendency to use partners. In longitudinal studies of Scandinavian companies, as well as in Chang's (1995) study of Japanese firms, the company builds its organizational capabilities through sequential experience in overseas markets, initially taking non-equity positions, such as exporting or licensing, and later increasing its equity investment levels.

We may call this the traditional view. (It is worth noting, in passing, that there is a contrary, non-traditional view on the international experience variable namely that with greater international learning, the firm is better able to harness international partners and better assess and utilize the full spectrum modal choices. There is no empirical evidence as to which perspective applies to the hotel business. For testing purposes, the traditional view is stated in the hypotheses.)

We use two independent variables. The first, IEX is the number of years since the firm set up its first foreign operation. This time-based measure, while commonly used as a surrogate for international experience, has some caveats associated with it. For instance, mere length of time in one cultural setting may not prepare a firm for expansion into another country and culture.

For another thing, some firms may have expanded internationally faster than others; a time-based measure may therefore be somewhat biased in a cross-sectional study. For these reasons, a second independent variable, GLOP (number of properties outside the home nation of the firm divided by the global total including the home nation of the firm) was introduced as an alternative measure for the extent of globalization of the firm.

For global optimization purposes, a global company had rather not be hampered by the local preferences of local partners. Hence, a firm with a larger fraction of business globally should prefer majority or full equity ownership. IEX and GLOP are different measures. One is a measure of time since the company's first foreign excursion. The other records the proportion of foreign to total business which the firm has actually achieved.

H6: Rising levels of equity and control (M) and the number of years since the first foreign operation (IEX) will be positively associated.

H7: M and GLOP (ratio of foreign over global total number of properties) will be positively associated.

We now turn from objective data on the hotel firms to subjective responses, on a 5-point Likert scale (5 = Very Important.....1 = Not Important), from responding executives, to questions about the perceived importance of the following strategy variables. Perceived Strategic Importance of Global Scale: One view in the literature is that in order to capture the economies of global scale, a firm is required to have high control and high ownership modes of operation, unhampered by the possibly contrary sub-optimizing concerns of local partners. The executives of such companies would indicate the need for equity ownership-based control in order for the firm to capture the economies of global scale. On the other hand, we also have a diametrically opposite view expressed in the literature: To become global, a firm may be forced to accept many local partners in various markets.

If what we mean by scale economies in the hotel business relates to logistics, supply, common architectural designs etc., which can be shared with a network of franchisees and local partners at relatively low knowledge-transfer cost, then such economies can indeed be gained without ownership, or even managerial presence. Thus Galbraith and Kay's (1986) "economies of information" as the key ingredient of multinational strategy may be achievable without high equity investment or control. We thus have two diametrically opposite hypotheses in the literature, and propose to formally test the first strategy view, that:

H8: The perceived importance of scale in global hotel operations (PSCA) will be positively associated with M (rising levels of control and equity ownership).

Perceived Strategic Importance of Control Over Management and Quality: Our discussion indicated that management control is a complex and multidimensional concept. We identified Daily Management and Quality Control as one dimension of overall administrative control.

The control by the global hotel firm, in a day to day sense, rises as we go from franchising to fully owned operations. Hence we would expect, in general, that for executive respondents in the global hotel company, who indicate a greater importance for daily management and quality control (on the 5-point Likert scale), the hotel property in question would be more likely to be under a higher equity and ownership mode, ceteris paribus.

This is not tautological. Recall that executive responses indicate the firm's general strategic preferences; but in the "portfolio" of each firm there are likely to be some properties which are fully owned, some under management service contract, some franchised.

The objective here is to test the extent to which the expressed strategy preferences of executives correlates with the actual disposition of each property's management mode, and the strength of this association, statistically speaking as opposed to the influence of the other influences on the choice of organizational mode. We formally propose therefore, that:

H9: The perceived importance of operational control over management and quality (CQ) will be positively related to M (rising levels of equity and control).

Perceived Strategic Importance of Size in Global Hotel Operations: We have already discussed the SIZE variable earlier, based on an objective measure (Worldwide $ Revenue). Here, in the variable PFS, we asked managers to subjectively rate the importance of size as a strategy variable in global hotel operations (on a 5-point Likert Scale). Our reasoning for this variable is the same as for the objective SIZE, namely that executives placing greater importance on a larger size of global operations will influence, for a particular hotel, a higher level of equity investment and greater overall administrative control (i.e., a higher value for M), with better appropriability of rents, ceteris paribus.

Hence:

H10: PFS will be positively associated with M (rising levels of equity and control).

(We included both the objective measure ($ Worldwide Sales) and the subjective measure (executive responses on the perceived importance of size) conscious that the two may turn out to be collinear. If so, one would be dropped. More on this issue in the section on Empirical Tests and Methodology.) Perceived Strategic Importance of Global Reservations System and Brand: These are the two principal codified strategic assets, over which proprietary control is usually maintained by the global hotel firm, regardless of the organizational mode.

A global reservation system increases global revenues. In particular, codified assets, such as brands and reservations systems, increase the ability of a firm to have alliances for three reasons. First, codification reduces the "bounded rationality" problem of partners in each nation, who seek to assess the value they will receive from a partnership with the global hotel firm.

Second, by maintaining control (de jure and de facto) over the brand and reservation system, the global firm greatly reduces the opportunism of franchisees or partners in management service agreements, who may be tempted to strike out on their own, on expiry of the agreement. Third, while creation of brand equity and a global reservations system involves large sunk costs, the incremental costs of adding another franchisee, or non-equity partner, is low.

Thus, such strategic assets increase the likelihood of alliances in general, and franchising, in particular.

Hence, we propose:

H11: PRES (Perceived Strategic Importance of Global Reservations System and Brand) will be negatively associated with M (rising levels of equity investment and control).

Perceived Strategic Importance of Investment In Training: Gatignon and Anderson (1988) indicated that when the proprietary content of products or processes is high (operationalized by the R&D/Sales ratio), the choice will tend towards the full ownership end of the spectrum, since rents from this competitive advantage can be best exploited by full or high ownership modes.

The service sector equivalent to "R&D investment" is "investment in training" which upgrades the knowledge and organizational capabilities of the global hotel firm's management and employees. All hotels, especially the large ones, employ complex logistics, dynamic pricing, marketing and inventory control systems for everything from towels to room occupancy rates.

Such management skills and their dissemination throughout the company's organization comprises the basis for competitive advantage.

This enables the firm to appropriate higher rents which would lead to a preference for equity, and particularly, full ownership modes. At the same time, the greater the intensity of tacit knowledge in the firm (here we are not referring to codified strategic assets, but tacit organizational routines) the higher the costs of transferring such knowledge to partners, thereby lowering the likelihood of alliance. This hypothesis was verified by Kim and Hwang. Similarly, we propose that:

H12: M will be positively associated with investment in training (PINV).

Two statistical techniques will be used. Discriminant analysis merely tests the validity and robustness of the classification of the dependent variable M into four groups, and reduces the explanatory variables to a smaller number of factors. Ordinal logistic regression (using a Generalized LOGIT model) enables us to test the above twelve hypotheses, and identify independent variables which most strongly influence the choice of organizational mode.

Problems in Using Objective Firm Data, such as Dollar Sales in Research Involving Alliances: As we suspected, the objective SIZE variable (measuring Dollar sales revenues of the global hotel firm) turned out to be collinear with other variables, including PFS.

But SIZE also has other methodological problems, which often hamper its use in alliance research: (i) The sales of minority joint ventures may not be consolidated into the accounts of some of our sample companies, since accounting conventions used in the reported financial data vary across nations; (ii) franchise and management service agreement revenues may not appear under the consolidated sales figure of some companies; (iii) even if they were added to global revenues, this would greatly understate the global total sales of the entire alliance network, because franchise and management service agreement earnings are typically expressed only as a percentage of sales of the hotel property in question.

Hence for both multicollinearity reasons, as well as measurement reasons, SIZE was dropped from the subsequent analysis. Missing Data: The number of usable observations had to be reduced from the 1,131 hotels, to 720, for two reasons. 74 hotel properties were dropped because discriminant analysis cannot accept overlapping categories (typically, a hotel having both part equity investment and a management service agreement). This is a minor loss of only 6.5 percent of the data.

However, another 337 cases had to be dropped because of missing data in various independent variables, but particularly in the cultural distance CUL variable. This variable is constructed from Hofstede's (1980) data on cultural attributes, covering less than 50 nations. No other similar data exist; nor has any scholar subsequently replicated Hofstede's work, or added to his number of countries.

A researcher is thus faced with a dilemma: Either drop the cultural distance variable, considered by many scholars, such as Kogut and Singh (1988) to be a crucial determinant of modal choice, and have a larger data set, or keep the cultural distance variable and work with a reduced data set. In this study we chose the latter option, given the importance suggested for the cultural distance variable. The testing is therefore performed on a data set with n = 720 hotels, which is more than ample for statistical purposes.

TYPES OF HOTELS

Boutique Hotels

Boutique hotel is a term originating in North America to describe intimate, usually luxurious or quirky hotel environments. Boutique hotels differentiate themselves from larger chain/branded hotels and motels by providing personalized level accommodation and services/ facilities.

Sometimes known as "design hotels" or "lifestyle hotels," boutique hotels began in the 1980s in major cities like New York, London, and San Francisco. Very often it is the Morgans Hotel in Murray Hill of New York, that is awarded with the title of first boutique hotel in the world. It was opened by Ian Schrager in 1984 according to a design by Andrée Putman.

Typically boutique hotels are furnished in a themed, stylish and/or aspirational manner. Although usually considerably smaller than a mainstream hotel (often ranging from 3 to 100 guest rooms), boutique hotels can often have hundreds of rooms in major cities. Guest rooms and suites are fitted with telephony and Wi-Fi Internet, air-conditioning, honesty bars and often cable/pay TV. Guest services are attended to by 24 hour hotel staff. Many boutique hotels have on-site dining facilities, and the majority offer bars and lounges which may also be open to the general public.

Despite this definition, the popularity of the boutique term and concept has lead to some confusion about the term. Boutique hotels have typically been unique properties operated by individials or companies with a small collection. However, their successes have prompted established multi-national hotel companies to establish their own brands. The most notable is Starwood Hotels and Resorts' W Hotels.

Currently, there is one publication dedicated to the boutique hotel, boutique DESIGN magazine, which is published quarterly. Boutique hotel resources are more commonly available online. One such site dedicated to boutique hotels is Tablet Hotels. There are also a number of sytlized design and coffee table books highlighting various properties throughout the world.

Apartment Hotel

An Apartment Hotel is a type of accommodation, described as "a serviced apartment complex that uses a hotel style booking system". It is similar to renting an apartment, but with no fixed contracts and occupants can 'check-out' whenever they wish.

Apartment hotels are flexible types of accommodation; instead of the rigid format of a hotel room an apartment hotel complex usually offers a complete fully fitted apartment. These complexes are usually custom built, and similar to a hotel complex contain a varied amount of apartments. The length of stay in these apartment hotels are very varied with anywhere from a few days to months or even years. Prices tend to be cheaper than hotels. The people that stay in apartment hotels use them as a home from home therefore they are usually fitted with everything the average home would require.

Apartment hotels were first created in holiday destinations as accommodation for families that needed to 'live' in an apartment rather than 'stay' as they would in a hotel. The apartments would provide a 'holiday home' but generally be serviced. Later on these apartments evolved to be complete homes, allowing occupants to do everything they would at home, such as cleaning, washing and cooking.

Essentially the apartment hotel combines the flexibility of apartment living with the service of a hotel. Many of the apartments take advantage of prime locations with panoramic views of cities seen through wall to ceiling windows. Suites usually include high quality finishes, broadband connection & interactive TV, servicing and integrated kitchen and bathroom. High quality leather sofas in the living area and king size beds bring the hotel experience to a whole new level. Those are the luxuries, they also come with the basics: satellite or cable TV, washer, dryer, dishwasher, cooker, oven, fridge, freezer, sink, shower, bath, wardrobes, all the furnishings to be expected in a luxury home.

Bed and Breakfast

A Bed and Breakfast often referred to as a B&B is a type of boarding house typically operating out of a large single family residence.

Guests are accommodated at night in private bedrooms and breakfast is served in the morning - either in the bedroom or, more commonly, in a dining room or the host's kitchen. Bathrooms can be private or shared (with other guests or with the family in smaller establishments) or en-suite (where the ablutions are directly accessed from the guest's bedroom).

B&Bs may be operated either as a primary occupation or as a secondary source of income. Staff often consists of the house's owners and members of their family who live there. Guests are usually expected to pay for their stay upon arrival and leave before noon (or earlier) on the day of departure. A big advantage of this type of hosted accommodation is the local knowledge of the host.

When guests stay more than one night, in some smaller B&Bs they will be expected to be away from the B&B during the main part of the day. This arrangement, however, may not be inconvenient since many popular B&Bs are located in beach and mountain areas, such as Hawaii, New England, and Colorado where daytime recreation and tourism activities are popular. One advantage of staying at a B&B is readier access to popular locations "off the beaten path" which may not be convenient to the city center.

Because most B&Bs are small, rarely with room for more than about 2-12 guests, it is advisable for anyone wanting to stay at a bed and breakfast to make reservations well in advance of their travel date. Consultation with a qualified travel agent knowledgeable in this type of accommodation may be helpful; However, many B&Bs belong to associations and have a web presence. Be aware that prices and tariffs described in various books and travel guides are often obsolete by the time they are published.

The B&B arrangement is actually a very old one; before the 20th century, it was quite normal for country travellers to spend the night at a private house rather than an inn, and the custom persists in many parts of the world. However, prior to the 19th century, this was strictly an informal arrangement constrained by acquaintance and social rank; a doctor might stay with a doctor or pharmacist, while a nobleman would only stay with the local gentry. The abbreviation of 'B&B' on roadside signs first became popular in the British Isles.

In the British Isles, breakfast is usually cooked on demand for the guest and usually features bacon, eggs, sausages, tomatoes, mushrooms, baked beans, etc but increasingly, because of either a desire of owners to economise or guests to minimise their calorie intake, a 'continental breakfast' is becoming more common.

In the British Isles where hotel prices are often outrageous, B&B's are a budget option and this tradition continues in many parts of the world.

However, many B&Bs in North America and New Zealand often consciously seek to recall earlier days; they are frequently established in attractive older houses that have been renovated and filled with antique furniture. In some cases in North America an existing inn will relabel itself as a "B&B" to improve business and move itself `up-market'.

In Ireland, most B&Bs serve a traditional Irish breakfast as a point of pride. In Cuba, which opened up to tourism in the 1990s after the financial support of the Soviet Union ended, a form of B&B called casa particular ("private home") became the main form of accommodation outside the tourist resorts.

The term "bed and breakfast" is also used to refer to a meal plan where breakfast is the only meal provided, commonly in package holidays, in a major hotel that may provide other meals to only some customers.

As they are often run by amateurs, with little lodge management experience, strict laws should govern the operation of B&Bs. However, regulations vary in each jurisdiction both in content and extent and in enforcement.

The most common regulations B&Bs must follow pertain to safety. They are required to have fire resistance, a sufficient fire escape plan in place, and smoke detectors in each guest room.

Capsule Hotel

A capsule hotel, is a hotel system of extremely dense occupancy. Guest space is reduced in size to a modular plastic or fibreglass block roughly 2 m by 1 m by 1.25 m, providing room to sleep and little more, although facilities usually include a television and other electronic entertainment. These capsules are then grouped and stacked, two units high. Luggage is usually stored in a locker away from the capsule. Privacy is maintained by a curtain at the open end of the capsule but noise pollution can be high. Washing facilities are communal and there are often restaurants, or at least vending machines, and other entertainment facilities.

This style of hotel accommodation was developed in Japan and has not gained acceptance outside of the country. The Japanese capsule hotels vary widely in size, some having only fifty or so capsules and others over 700. They are often male-only. There are also capsule hotels with separate male and female sleeping quarters. Clothes and shoes are sometimes exchanged for a yukata and slippers on entry. A towel may also be provided. The benefit of these hotels is convenience and price, usually around ¥2000-4000 a night 21-29, $25–34, £15–20). Such hotels are not necessarily regarded as only an option for those with lower incomes—a typical customer would be the business salaryman after a night of drinking who has missed the last train home. Some capsule hotels offer low daytime discounts for those needing an afternoon nap.

The first capsule hotel was the Capsule Inn Osaka, designed by Kisho Kurokawa and located in the Umeda district of Osaka. It opened on February 1, 1979 and the initial room rate was ¥1,600.

These rooms can be seen in the movie The Fast and the Furious: Tokyo Drift. They were also used as a basis for sets in the film The Fifth Element. They also appear in the cyberpunk novel Neuromancer under the name of "coffin hotel."

Casa Particular

Casa particular is a phrase meaning private accommodation or private homestays in Cuba, very similar to bed and breakfast although it can also take the form of vacation rental. When the meaning is clear the term is often shortened to simply casa.

A casa particular is basically a private family establishment that provides paid lodging, usually on a short-term basis. In general under this term you can find full apartment and houses, rooms inside people homes, mini-apartments or rooms with separate entrance (studio or efficiency type rooms).

It is also considered a type of boarding house typically operated out of a single family residence where guests can be accommodated at night in private bedrooms (which may or may not be equipped with private baths) and where breakfast, sometimes continental and sometimes the full English variety, is served in the morning.

The business may be operated either as a primary occupation or as a secondary source of income, and the staff often consists of the house's owner(s) and members of their family who live there.

Because they are usually small, rarely with room for more than about 5-6 guests, it is advisable for anyone wanting to stay at a particular casa particular during high season to make advance reservations. However, outside the season there is no need because there are often many such casas, causing competition and opening opportunities to strike a deal. Prices can then drop to 15 euro or even less for longer stays. During high season they can rise to over 30 euro. Many belong to associations, have a web presence, and are described in various books and travel guides.

Casas particulares can be recognised by a small sign on the door, with two blue triangles ('roofs') against a white background, which the owners obtain after paying a fixed per-room annual tax.

In some Cuban cities and tourist resorts, like Varadero, Playa Santa Lucia and Guardalavaca, local authorities determined that casas particulares would represent a threat to the hotel industry, and passed some legislation placing regulations and limits on the industry forbidding the operation of these establishments.

"Casa particular" literally means "private house" but it started to be used to mean "private accommodation" in 1997, when the Cuban government finally allowed Cubans to rent out rooms in their houses or apartments to tourists, providing Cuban families with new sources of income. As any other type of accommodation in Cuba such as hotels, camping and motels were owned by the government, the term "casa particular" stated that this kind of paid lodging was privately operated.

Services and Facilities

All rooms are clean, safe and upgraded to tourist standards. It ranges from basic accommodation of a room with a bed, a closet, a small table to full furnished independent apartments upgraded to western standards. Other features found may be a telephone, an alarm clock, and a TV. Food and drink may be supplied by a mini-bar (which often includes a small refrigerator) containing snacks and drinks (to be paid for on departure).

It is possible to have breakfast/dinner in the casa for price. Often breakfasts/dinners sold will decide if case owner will break even or not. So if it becomes clear that one plans to generally eat out, the price may go up because this is an important source of income.

Casas particulares have several advantages over other types of lodgings:

- The guest can quickly develop genuine Cuban relationships and become deeply involved in the culture of the country. Before he/she knows it, the guest will be part of the family. In a big resort one may only meet hotel workers and other tourists.
- The guest will enjoy the free and easy atmosphere, feel completely at home in the casa particular and will be able to invite friends over. The current regulations for state-run hotels don't allow to have Cuban guests invited to hotel rooms.
- It is almost always cheaper to stay in a private room than in a hotel.
- "Guests" are not usually allowed into the hotels. Usually one can take one local "guest" into his rented casa-particular.
- By renting a casa particular, the guest will be directly contributing to a person or family's standard of living. This is often obvious through the fact that casas particulares are freshly painted.

The cost and quality of casas particulares are usually indicative of the accommodation type and type of services available. Most of the casas particulares are rented for short term to travellers. Long term accommodation is also provided by some casas, especially for foreign students. In Havana, the casas particulares are usually family apartments and a smaller number of them are houses. In other cities, private accommodation is provided mainly in family houses.

Types of Casas Particulares rentals:

- Private Room: a room is rented out most of the times with private bathroom and a key to the apartment/house is usually given to the guest.
- Private Room with independent entrance. Sometimes the house/ apartment is split in order to allow this.
- Apartment: the guest can enjoy the privacy and independency of a full furnished apartment for his/her vacations. Sometimes this apartment is part of house being split by a wall usually with a connecting door.
- Studio-type or mini-apartment: it is not an apartment with several rooms but just the bedroom, a kitchen-living-dining room and a bathroom.

Condo-hotel

A condo-hotel or a hotel-condo is a building used as both a condominium and a hotel. This type of residential building meets several needs that make it attractive. As development costs increase, the cost of hotel development can make developing new hotels difficult, especially in major cities. By selling the units as condos, the developer moves much of the development cost to the condo owners. By owning units that can be rented as hotel rooms, the owners are able to get a return on their investment allowing them the ability to own a residence in a resort or major city.

It should be noted that the U.S. Government is very strict about the type of advertising that can be done vis a vis Condo Hotel projects. Some condo projects have advertised themselves as "Real Estate Investments" - since the value of these condos as a real estate investment is not entirely clear - the U.S. Government currently disallows use of this reference when advertising condo hotels.

Condo hotels have been criticized in California for allowing developers to skirt laws designed to protect public access to beaches. Because such a facility has hotel rooms, it can be classified as a public accommodation, even though the majority of the units are privately held, and the facility does little to accommodate the public.

Destination Hotel

A destination hotel is a place of lodging whose inherent location and amenities attract visitors regardless of the route needed to arrive or the areawide features of interest. The destination hotel concept has existed at least since the 19th century and occupies a significant market share of all lodging in the world as of 2006.

From the late 1980s to the present the extent of amenities and conference facilities has greatly expanded for many destination hotels. Destination hotels are also called destination lodgings and destination resorts. Considerable academic and business analysis has been conducted in the field of destination hotels. In the Arnold Encyclopedia of Real Estate a destination hotel is characterized as a place of lodging not chosen for convenience and not chosen for people in transit to other areas.

The following typically are characteristics of a destination hotel:

- Amenities which are quite complete and self-contained
- Upscale nature of the lodging operation
- Distinctive characteristics of the building, gardens or adjacent natural feature
- Activity set which makes leaving the property unnecessary

Since the 1800s, the traditional concept of a destination hotel has been based upon a venue which is typically remote and has a natural feature as its attraction. For example, the Kviknes Hotel in Norway is a difficult to reach remote location which provides visitors access to the scenic fjord at Balestrand. Historically there were certain built-in amenities such as gourmet cuisine, music recitals and shoreline trails; however, the amenities of modern (post 1980) destination hotels dwarf the scale of these earlier models.

Many of the Las Vegas and Carribbean resort hotels have complete shopping malls, conference centers and large entertainment halls on site; thus, the contemporary version of a destination often features large on-site capital investment in activities, although the access to a local natural feature is still retained by many newer destination hotels.

Luxury Resorts

A luxury resort, sometimes referred to as an exclusive resort, is a very expensive vacation facility which is fully staffed and has been rated with five stars. Luxury resorts often boast many visitor activities and attractions such as golf, watersports, spa and beauty facilities, skiing, natural ecology and tranquility. Because of the extent of amenities offered, a luxury resort is also considered a destination resort.

A luxury resort is an elite luxury property which exhibits an exceptionally high degree of customer service and hospitality. A flawless execution of guest services will be the resort staff's and managements main concern. A luxury resort will commonly also feature a superb architectural interior and exterior design as well as an interesting physical location.

The interior design will normally be elegant with stylish bedroom decor, exceptional dining facilities, and manicured landscaping and meticulous grounds. Luxury resorts will often also be in based in exceptionally desirable and strategic worldwide locations, from beautiful tropical islands, to snow caked mountains, to scenic lakes and rivers, to exhilarating cities. The locations will often be famous for featured activities from skiing to golf, water spots, diving, fishing, sailing and nature walks to glamorous shopping and nightlife entertainment.

A luxury resort may vary greatly in character, style and theme from resort to resort. A luxury resort will, however, normally be characterized by a high level of luxury, sophistication and off course price. Accommodations are first class, whether they follow a classic and traditional nature or a more minimalist and modern styling. An unmatched level of comfort will be available at a luxury resort, as well as many personalized services and amenities.

Extended Stay Hotel

Extended stay hotels are a type of lodging with features unavailable at standard hotels. These features are intended to provide more home-like amenities. There are currently 27 extended stay chains in North America with at least 7 hotels, representing over 2,000 properties. There is substantial variation among extended stay hotels with respect to quality and the amenities that are available. Some of the economy chains attract clientele who use the hotels as semi-permanent lodging. Occasionally, these budget establishments can be the scene of criminal activity.

Extended-stay hotels typically have self-serve laundry facilities and offer discounts for extended stays, beginning at 5 or 7 days. They also have guestrooms (or "suites") with kitchens. The kitchens include at a minimum usually: a sink, a refrigerator (usually full size), a microwave oven, and a stovetop. Some kitchens also have dishwashers and conventional ovens. Extended stay hotels are popular with business travelers on extended assignments, families in the midst of a relocation, and anyone else in need of temporary housing. Extended stay hotels are also used by travelers who appreciate the larger space a typical suite provides.

Residence Inn is credited with popularizing the "extended stay" concept. The chain was launched in 1975 in Wichita, Kansas by Jack DeBoer, and acquired by Marriott Corporation in 1987. As of April 2005, there were over 450 Residence Inn hotels in the United States, Canada and Mexico. Some extended stay hotels are coming up in United Kingdom and Ireland as well.

One of today's most popular long term lodging brands came from the merger of Extended Stay America and Homestead Hotels. Both these chains were already well established when they combined in 2004 to become Extended Stay Hotels with over 670 owned and operated properties nationwide.

Another worldwide hotel chain, Choice Hotels International, franchisor for name brands such as Comfort Inn, Comfort Suites, Sleep Inn and Quality Inn, entered the extended stay market with their MainStay Suites brand. They proceeded to acquire the Suburban Extended Stay hotel chain in 2005, making them a sizeable extended stay system with over 150 hotels open and under development.

Flophouse

A flophouse or dosshouse is a place that offers very cheap lodging, generally by providing only minimal services. Occupants of flophouses generally share bathroom facilities and reside in very cramped quarters. The people who make use of these places are often transients, although some people will stay in flophouses for long periods of time—years or decades. Some people who live in flophouses may be just a step above homelessness. In the late 20th century, typical cost might be about US$6 per night. A typical flophouse might advertise its services with a sign such as "Hotel for Men; Transients Welcome".

Quarters in flophouses are very small, and may resemble office cubicles more than a regular room in a hotel or apartment building. A cubicle might only have wire mesh for a ceiling.

In the past, flophouses were sometimes called "workingmen's hotels" and catered to hobos and transient workers such as seasonal railroad and agriculture workers, or migrant lumberjacks who would travel west during the summer to work and then return to an eastern or midwestern city such as Chicago to stay in a flophouse during the winter. This is described in the 1930 novel The Rambling Kid by Charles Ashleigh and the 1976 book The Human Cougar by Lloyd Morain. Another theme in Morain's book is the gentrification which was then beginning and which has led cities to pressure flophouses to close. George Orwell also discussed flophouses in the UK in his book Down and Out in Paris and London. He described them as having rather poor cleanliness standards, often issuing unwashed and badly stained blankets, and sometimes renting beds in a large common room resembling barracks more than private rooms. He noted that at the time he wrote the book (1933) the term "dosshouse" was already falling out of use.

Some city districts that currently have or once had flophouses in abundance became well-known in their own right, such as the Bowery in New York, New York.

The movies The Blues Brothers (1980) and Staying Alive (1983) both feature their lead characters living in flophouses. Another slang term for flophouses was mentioned in the movie Kids. This variation of the definition is a house or apartment (usually apartment) where substance abusers stay to party and abuse drugs and/or alcohol. Such people, whether employed or unemployed, lead a hedonist self-destructive lifestyle. If they are employed, their money usually goes to drugs and/or alcohol. Other bums and partygoers can also temporarily stay for parties.

Some low-end flophouses have graffiti sprayed on the walls and lack beds, instead just have matresses on the floor. Some of the characters in the film Trainspotting lived in these conditions. Michael Dominic's documentary film Sunshine Hotel (2001) follows the lives of the denizens of one of the few remaining Bowery flophouses.

ORGANISATIONS CATEGORIES OF HOTEL BUSINESS

HOTEL MANAGER

The Hotel manager oversees all of a hotel's daily operations, from staffing to coordinating fresh-cut flowers for the lobby. Many, over time, are given long-term responsibility for negotiating contracts with vendors (such as maintenance supplies), negotiating leases with on-site shops, and physically upgrading the hotel.

Hotel managers usually relish "the ability to put your own distinctive style on the [hotel] experience." While managing a hotel and giving it your unique flair are wonderful, they come with full responsibility for failure. "The better you are at what you do, the more responsibilities you are given, the more chances you have to fail," mentioned one hotel manager. When things fall apart, "no one is a hotel manager's friend."

Hotel managers can feel great about their positions, create strong relationships with regular customers, and maintain an amicable working environment. But should the bottom line waver and financial woes occur, the first neck on the chopping block is the hotel manager's. Those in the hotel management industry say that sometimes it seems that you need "to be born on the planet Krypton" to be a good hotel manager because only Superman could juggle the administrative, aesthetic, and financial decisions which constitute daily life on the job. Over 70 percent of the respondents said that tired was an understatement about how they felt at the end of the day or night. A hotel manager's position as a liaison between the ownership and the staff can be difficult and isolating. But those who can put up with the long hours, the high degree of responsibility, and the variety of tasks emerge with a solid degree of satisfaction and a desire to continue in the profession. The average tenure of a hotel manager is 6.7 years, though this figure doesn't represent the number of managers who work for two years and those who work for decades. Many work at a variety of hotels, build up their resumes, and then find positions that allow them the freedom to operate their own establishments.

Aspiring hotel managers used to begin at the reception desk, as part of the wait staff, or as members of the cleaning staff, then work their way up the ladder.

As hotels have become more commercial properties and the duties of hotel managers have expanded, this avenue of advancement has closed off. Now hotel manager hopefuls go to hotel management school, and those who don't should garner as much practical hotel experience as possible. Each chain or specific hotel puts new employees through their own training programmes, so those applying for jobs should learn all they can about the scope and functioning of the specific hotels where they wish to work.

Part of life as a hotel manager can be similar to the life of a doctor, as managers can be called to duty at any time of the day or night. Hotel managers must handle any and all emergencies, and those who wish to remain in the profession and maintain respect must be quick-thinking and decisive. Candidates should have a good organizational and financial background, excellent communication and interpersonal skills, and strong self-discipline. They should also be extremely detail-oriented; when running a hotel, there is no such thing as an unimportant detail.

The good manager drives himself to improve and upgrade the hotel at every available opportunity.

A hotel manager is responsible for the day-to-day management of a hotel and its staff and has commercial accountability for planning, organising and directing all hotel services, including front-of-house (reception, concierge, reservation), banqueting and housekeeping. In larger hotels, managers often have a specific remit (guest services, accounting, marketing) and make up a general management team.

Financial management - preparing budgets and marketing strategies and achieving targets for the business - plays a major role. The manager must strike a balance between customer satisfaction and effective business management, ensuring financial viability, and facilitate a smooth-running customer service, whilst ensuring staff work together as a team.

Typical Work Activities

Typical work activities vary depending on the size and type of hotel, but may include:

- Planning and organising accommodation, catering and other hotel services;
- Promoting and marketing the business;
- Managing budgets and financial plans;
- Maintaining statistical and financial records;
- Achieving profit targets;
- Recruiting, training and monitoring staff;
- Planning work schedules;
- Meeting and greeting customers;
- Dealing with customer complaints and comments;
- Addressing problems and troubleshooting;
- Ensuring events and conferences run smoothly;
- Supervising maintenance, supplies and furnishings;
- Dealing with contractors and suppliers;
- Ensuring security is effective;
- Carrying out inspections of property and services;
- Ensuring compliance with licensing laws, health and safety and other statutory regulations.

The manager of a large hotel may have less contact with guests but will spend time meeting heads of department and planning and monitoring the progress of business strategies. In a smaller establishment, the manager is much more involved in the hands-on day-to-day running of the hotel, which may include carrying out reception duties or serving meals if the need arises. A significant number of hotel managers are self-employed and this can lead to a more general management experience, from greeting guests to managing finances.

How to Become a Hotel Manager

- Ask yourself if you have excellent interpersonal, communication and organizational skills. They are necessary for a successful hotel management career.
- Obtain a college degree in hotel management or restaurant management. Remember that a food services department contributes greatly to the profits of a hotel; a successful restaurant manager can see his or her career advance quickly.
- Take advantage of work-study programmes offered by many colleges so that you will gain solid experience working in hotels.
- Expect to go through a hotel's training programme once you are hired after college. During the first couple of years you will be handling only relatively mundane duties, instead of providing your input on issues such as staffing, hotel decor or conventions.

- Understand that you might be offered a position as a front office manager, a food and beverage manager, a convention services manager, or any of a number of administrative positions after your training period. If you are successful at different managerial positions, your career will benefit in the long run.
- Be aware that a promotion might require you to relocate for a few years if you work for a hotel chain that has properties throughout the country.
- You will need to quickly become proficient with computers because of their widespread use in hotel reservations, billing and overall management operations.
- Consider working for hotels in warm tourist destinations or snowy mountains, depending on your preferred lifestyle.
- Be prepared for long hours, night and weekend work, and the occasional unhappy guest.

Different managerial personnel working as hotel managers —

Catering managers plan, organise and manage the food and beverage services of organisations and businesses, both inside and outside the hospitality industry, with the aim of achieving good quality at low cost and maintaining high standards of hygiene and customer satisfaction.

There is a range of jobs in catering management, along with a number of different routes into the industry. Roles include: managing restaurants, bars and other outlets in hotels, resorts or liners; providing catering services at events; and running catering operations at hospitals, schools and other organisations.

With ongoing growth in the service industry, opportunities in this demanding but rewarding area continue to grow.

FOOD AND RESTAURANT MANAGER

Fast food restaurant managers are responsible for the provision of standardised food and customer service in outlets based in the high street, motor service areas, stations, airports or multiplexes.

Drawing on all the operational functions of a business, the work involves applying financial, marketing and operational know-how, and supervising and training staff.

Managers plan, organise, and co-ordinate all resources and activities in a store. The work involves: setting targets, planning budgets, and controlling stock; recruiting, training and inspiring restaurant teams; creating and driving marketing campaigns; and building bridges with the local community.

Ultimately, it is the manager's ideas, initiative and personality that shape the restaurant.

Tasks typically involve:

- Organising the store in terms of products, equipment and people;

- Planning and checking work schedules;
- Carrying out audits to check health safety, food safety and quality of service in the restaurant;
- Making sure the fast-track audit is completed daily to check the safety of equipment and that food is properly cooked, only in-date stock is used, and all other products are discarded;
- Carrying out work outside the restaurant, including 'mystery shopping' at other restaurants within the chain;
- Attending weekly meetings with senior managers;
- Dealing with problems, queries, complaints, staff and customers in the store;
- Monitoring and maintaining high standards of food, service and hygiene;
- Ensuring the company's required standards of customer care are met;
- Administering payrolls;
- Checking and securing cash receipts;
- Budgeting to ensure maximum profitability;
- Achieving set profit and loss targets;
- Maintaining and securing equipment and buildings and all company assets contained within the unit;
- Publicising and marketing restaurants in the locality;
- Motivating restaurant teams;
- Recruiting, selecting and training new staff and fully inducting the restaurant team in accordance with company policy;
- Developing all team members to their fullest potential using the performance management/review system and identifying individual training needs;
- Ensuring the implementation and maintenance of legislation, company standards and procedures;
- Recognising new trends and implementing action plans accordingly;
- Acting as a communication link between senior teams and the restaurant team;
- Leading by example, acting as a role model for the restaurant team.

A successful manager will strike the right balance between creating both a good service for restaurant customers and a fun work environment for members of staff.

CATERING MANAGER

Catering managers plan, organise and manage the food and beverage services of organisations and businesses, both inside and outside the hospitality industry, with the aim of achieving good quality at low cost and maintaining high standards of hygiene and customer satisfaction.

There is a range of jobs in catering management, along with a number of different routes into the industry. Roles include: managing restaurants, bars and other outlets in hotels, resorts or liners; providing catering services at events; and running catering operations at hospitals, schools and other organisations. With ongoing growth in the service industry, opportunities in this demanding but rewarding area continue to grow.

Typical Work Activities

The role varies according to the size and nature of the establishment: in a small operation, the catering manager has more of a 'hands on' role and will be involved in the day-to-day running of the operation; in contract catering, the catering manager will spend time negotiating with the client organisation, assessing its requirements and ensuring that it is satisfied with the service delivered.

Typical tasks will include:

- Recruiting and training permanent and casual staff;
- Organising, leading and motivating the catering team;
- Planning menus in consultation with chefs;
- Ensuring health and safety regulations are strictly observed;
- Budgeting and establishing financial targets;
- Monitoring the quality of the product and service provided;
- Keeping financial and administrative records;
- Managing the payroll and monitoring spending levels;
- Maintaining stock levels and ordering new supplies as required;
- Interacting with customers if involved with 'front of house' work;
- Liaising with suppliers and clients;
- Negotiating contracts with customers (in contract catering).

In more senior posts, principal tasks will involve:

- Setting and agreeing budgets;
- Monitoring quality standards;
- Overseeing the management of the facilities, for example checking events bookings and the allocation of resources and staff;
- Planning new promotions and initiatives, and contributing to business development;
- Dealing with staffing and client issues, as they arise.

BUSINESS PROCESS MANAGEMENT

The term Business Process Management (or BPM) refers to activities performed by businesses to optimize and adapt their processes.

Although it can be said that organizations have always been using BPM, a new impetus based on the advent of software tools (business process management systems or BPMS) which allow for the direct execution of the business processes without a costly and time intensive development of the required software. In addition, these tools can also monitor the execution of the business processes, providing managers of an organization with the means to analyze their performance and make changes to the original processes in real-time. Using a BPMS the modified process can then be merged into the current business process atmosphere.

Where Business Process Reengineering (popular in the 1990s) dealt with one-off changes to the organization, Business Process Management deals with the continuity and embedding of process orientation in the organization. Business Process Management has evolved as technology has caught up with management processes to the point that technology should no longer be the limiting factor in BPM.

The activities which constitute business process management can be grouped into three categories: design, execution and monitoring.

Process Design

This encompasses either the design or capture of existing processes. In addition the processes may be simulated in order to test them. The software support for these activities consists of graphical editors to document the processes and repositories to store the process models.

An emphasis on getting the design of the process right will logically lead to better results as the flow on effect of problems at the design stage logically affects a large number of parts in an integrated system.

Evolution of business processes requires a change to the process design to flow on into the live system. Integrating business process is also a current research area. Integration of software for process design to be used both for creating graphical representations of workflows and implementing and maintaining these workflows makes evolution of business processes less stressful, given that requirements are not as static as information systems.

Process Execution

The traditional way to achieve the automatic execution of processes is that an application is developed or purchased which executes the steps required. However, in practice, these applications only execute a portion of the overall process. Execution of a complete business process can also be achieved by using a patchwork of interfacing software with human intervention needed where applications are not able to automatically interface. In addition, certain process steps can only be accomplished with human intervention (for example, deciding on a major credit application). Due to the complexity that this approach engenders, changing a process is costly and an overview of the processes and their state is difficult to obtain.

As a response to these problems, the Business Process Management System (BPMS) category of software has evolved. BPMS allows the full business process (as developed in the process design activity) to be defined in a computer language which can be directly executed by the computer. The BPMS will either use services in connected applications to perform business operations (e.g. calculating a repayment plan for a loan) or will send messages to human workers requesting they perform certain tasks which necessitate a human attribute such as intuition as opposed to automated processes. As the process definition is directly executable, changes in the process can be (in comparison to the traditional approach of application development or maintenance) relatively quickly moved into operation. In order to work effectively a BPMS often requires that the underlying software is constructed according to the principles of a service-oriented architecture. Thus, it is often difficult to make a suite of existing legacy systems fit with a BPMS.

The commercial BPMS software market has focused on graphical process model development, rather than text-language based process models, as a means to reduce the complexity of model development. Visual programming using graphical metaphors has increased productivity in a number of areas of computing and is well accepted by users.

Business rules are a growing area of importance in BPMS as these rules provide governing behaviour to the BPMS, and a business rule engine can be used to drive process execution and resolution.

Process Monitoring

This monitoring encompasses the tracking of individual processes so that information on their state can be easily seen and the provision of statistics on the performance of one or more processes. An example of the tracking is being able to determine the state of a customer order (e.g. ordered arrived, awaiting delivery, invoice paid) so that problems in its operation can be identified and corrected. In addition, this information can be used to work with customers and suppliers to improve their connected processes. Examples of the statistics are the generation of measures on how quickly a customer order is processed, how many orders were processed in the last month etc.. These measures tend to fit into three categories: cycle time, defect rate and productivity.

Although such functions may be within the scope of current applications, the use of a BPMS is expected to ease the development of such reporting. Manufacturers of BPMSs will often offer process monitoring software as well as MIS and execution.

Business Process Management is an automated process to handle the complex business policy of any organisation. There are so many tools and programming languages to handle this process and customize the already existing tools, sometimes it's really a challenge to realize the complex business process of an organisation to automate.

The degree of monitoring depends on what information the business wants to evaluate and analyze and how business wants it to be monitored, in real-time or ad-hoc. Here, business activity monitoring (BAM) extend and expand the monitoring tools in BPMS. BAM will not only monitor a process but also monitor and analyze all processes in the business in real-time. BPM monitoring has been always ad-hoc/on-demand monitoring, and BAM compliments this feature with real-time monitoring, analysis and reporting.

Although the initial focus of BPM was on the automation of mechanistic business processes, this has since been extended to integrate human-driven processes in which human interaction takes place in series or parallel with the mechanistic processes. A common form is where individual steps in the business process which require human intuition or judgement to be performed are assigned to the appropriate members of an organization (as with workflow systems). More advanced forms are in supporting the complex interaction between human workers in performing a workgroup task. In the latter case an emerging class of BPM software known as the Human Interaction Management System is used to support and monitor these processes as well as to permit their ongoing redefinition at runtime.

BPMS can be used to understand organizations through expanded views that would not otherwise be available to organise and present. These views include the relationships of processes to each other which, when included in the process model, provide for advanced reporting and analysis that would not otherwise be available. BPM is regarded to be the crucial backbone of enterprise content management. Not all activities in business can be modelled into business process management modelling. As activities in business varies from the simplest of acquiring stationeries to complex procurement process which includes cross-countries which dealt with various legal laws and regulations.

Some processes in a business are best to be kept as it is for not to add complexity might be occurs when bringin business process management. Too dynamic changes of rules in a business process will not get the most of business process management benefit as time will be wasted on adapating the busines process to the tools. BPMS is more to a tools or platform which can be used to setup rules and define how business should be executed according to the rules. Thus, if both the rules and the business are too dynamics, it is pointless to implement business process management.

In practice, organizations often start with an objective where management have identified an area for improvement. A project team is tasked to perform Business Process Mapping and use of a common technique such as IDEF or BPMN to depict the processes as they exist before the intended changes. The team will progress to identify desired changes in work practices which will often be implemented by another team, using Kaizen or other approaches. And to successfully implements the business process management, the initiative must be a top down initiatives.

BUSINESS PROCESS

A business process is a set of linked activities that create value by transforming an input into a more valuable output. Both input and output can be artefacts and/or information and the transformation can be performed by human actors, machines, or both.

There are three types of business processes:

1. Management processes - the processes that govern the operation. Typical management processes include "Corporate Governance" and "Strategic Management".
2. Operational processes - these processes create the primary value stream, they are part of the core business. Typical operational processes are Purchasing, Manufacturing, Marketing, and Sales.
3. Supporting processes - these support the core processes. Examples include Accounting, Recruitment, IT-support.

A business process can be decomposed into several sub-processes, which have their own attributes, but also contribute to achieving the goal of the super-process. The analysis of business processes typically includes the mapping of processes and sub-processes down to activity level.

Activities are parts of the business process that do not include any decision making and thus are not worth decomposing (although decomposition would be possible), such as "Answer the phone", "produce an invoice".

A business process is usually the result of a business process design or business process reengineering activity. Business process modeling is used to capture, document and reengineer business processes. To visualize a business process, one of the graphical notations can be used such as Business Process Modeling Notation.

The concept of processes is not new. Laying out inter-related activities in a sequence and creating a flow of work has been part of organization design for more than 300 years. On of the first to describe a processes was Adam Smith (1776) in the famous example of an English pin factory. He described the production of a pin in the following way:

"One man draws out the wire, another straights it, a third cuts it, a fourth points it, a fifth grinds it at the top for receiving the head: to make the head requires two or three distinct operations: to put it on is a particular business, to whiten the pins is another... and the important business of making a pin is, in this manner, divided into about eighteen distinct operations, which in some manufactories are all performed by distinct hands, though in others the same man will sometime perform two or three of them."

Smith also first recognized how the organizational outcome could be increased through the use of advanced labour division. Previously, in a society where production was dominated by handcrafted goods, one man would perform all the activities required during the production process, while Smith described how work in a pin factory was divided into a set of simple tasks, which would be performed by specialized workers. The result of labour division in Smith's example resulted in productivity increasing by 24.000

percent (sic!), i.e. that the same number of workers made 240 times as many pins as they had been producing before the introduction of labour division.

It is worth to notice that Smith did not advocate labour division at any price and per se. He observed and noted that, under certain conditions, several tasks could very well be integrated into one, which a single worker would then perform. However, Smith did not provide any guidance for criteria that could be used for finding the optimum level of task division or integration and the determination of the appropriate level took place through experimental design of the production process.

This approach to integration could be considered as an implicit proposition of a process-oriented approach, but there is one aspect that constitutes a significant difference to the idea of business processes as it is perceived today. The integration in accordance with the idea of Smith would take place only within the same functional domain and comprise activities that are in direct sequence in the manufacturing process, whereas today's process concept includes cross-functionality as an important characteristic. It is also interesting to note that while Smith is generally accepted as the first to discuss labour division and specialization, only the division of labour was widely adopted, while the integration of tasks into functional, or cross-functional, processes was not considered as an alternative option to increase performance and productivity.

FURTHER SUPPORTING THEORIES AND CONCEPTS

Frederick Winslow Taylor developed the concept of scientific management. The concept contains aspects on the division of labour being relevant to the theory and practice around business processes. The business process related aspects of Taylor's scientific management concept are discussed in the article on Business Process Reengineering.

The Span of Control

The span of control is the number of sub-ordinates a supervisor manages within a structural organization. Introducing a business process concept has a considerable impact on the structural elements of the organization and thus also on the span of control. The implications are discussed in the Span of control article.

Large organizations that are not organized as markets need to be organized in smaller units - departments - which can be defined according to different principles. In the context of business processes, process and purpose departmentalization, as defind by Gulick and Urwick, are discussed in the departmentalization article.

INFORMATION MANAGEMENT CONCEPTS

Information Management and the organization design strategies being related to it, are a theoretical cornerstone of the business process concept. In the early 1990s, US corporations, and subsequently companies all over the world, started to adopt the concept of reengineering in an attempt to re-achieve the competitiveness that they had lost during the previous decade. A key characteristic of BPR is the focus on business processes.

Let us start our investigations with reviewing several business process definitions, as they are used in the reengineering literature. Davenport defines a (business) process as "a structured, measured set of activities designed to produce a specific output for a particular customer or market. It implies a strong emphasis on how work is done within an organization, in contrast to a product focus's emphasis on what. A process is thus a specific ordering of work activities across time and space, with a beginning and an end, and clearly defined inputs and outputs: a structure for action... Taking a process approach implies adopting the customer's point of view. Processes are the structure by which an organization does what is necessary to produce value for its customers."

This definition contains certain characteristics a process must possess. These characteristics are achieved by a focus on the business logic of the process (how work is done), instead of taking a product perspective (what is done). Following Davenports definition of a process we can conclude that a process must have clearly defined boundaries, input and output, that it consists of smaller parts, activities, which are ordered in time and space, that there must be a receiver of the process outcome- a customer - and that the transformation taking place within the process must add customer value.

Hammer & Champy's definition can be considered as a subset of Davenport's. They define a process as "a collection of activities that takes one or more kinds of input and creates an output that is of value to the customer." As we can note, Hammer & Champy have a more transformation oriented perception, and put less emphasis on the structural component–process boundaries and the order of activities in time and space.

Rummler & Brache use a definition that clearly encompasses a focus on the organization's external customers, when stating that "a business process is a series of steps designed to produce a product or service. Most processes are cross-functional, spanning the 'white space' between the boxes on the organization chart. Some processes result in a product or service that is received by an organization's external customer. We call these primary processes. Other processes produce products that are invisible to the external customer but essential to the effective management of the business. We call these support processes."

The above definition distinguishes two types of processes, primary and support processes, depending on whether a process is directly involved in the creation of customer value, or concerned with the organization's internal activities. In this sense, Rummler and Brache's definition follows Porter's value chain model, which also builds on a division of primary and secondary activities. According to Rummler and Brache, a typical characteristic of a successful process-based organization is the absence of secondary activities in the primary value flow that is created in the customer oriented primary processes. The characteristic of processes as spanning the white space on the organization chart indicates that processes are embedded in some form of organizational structure. Also, a process can be cross-functional, i.e. it ranges over several business functions.

Finally, let us consider the process definition of Johansson. They define a process as "a set of linked activities that take an input and transform it to create an output. Ideally, the transformation that occurs in the process should add value to the input and create an output that is more useful and effective to the recipient either upstream or downstream."

This definition also emphasizes the constitution of links between activities and the transformation that takes place within the process. Johansson et.al. also include the upstream part of the value chain as a possible recipient of the process output.

Summarizing the four definitions above, we can compile the following list of characteristics for a business process:

1. Definability: It must have clearly defined boundaries, input and output.
2. Order: It must consist of activities that are ordered according to their position in time and space.
3. Customer: There must be a recipient of the process' outcome, a customer.
4. Value-adding: The transformation taking place within the process must add value to the recipient, either upstream or downstream.
5. Embeddedness: A process can not exist in itself, it must be embedded in an organizational structure.
6. Cross-functionality: A process regularly can, but not necessarily must, span several functions.

Frequently, a process owner, i.e. a person being responsible for the performance and continuous improvement of the process, is also considered as a prerequisite.

PROCESS MODELING

The term process model (usually business process model) is used in different contexts. Process models are concepts which can belong in the area of Process Engineering.

A description of what process models are is provided by Colette Rolland: "Processes of the same nature are classified together into a process model. Thus, a process model is a description of a process at the type level. Since the process model is at the type level, a process is an instantiation of it. The same process model is used repeatedly for the development of many applications and thus, has many instantiations. One possible use of a process model is to prescribe 'how things must/should/could be done' in contrast to the process itself which is really what happens. A process model is more or less a rough anticipation of what the process will look like. What the process shall be will be determined during actual system development."

Main Aims

- Descriptive
  - Traces what actually happens during a process
  - Takes the point of view of an external observer who looks at the way a process has been performed and determines the improvements that have to be made to make it perform more effectively or efficiently
- Prescriptive
  - Defines desired processes and how they should/could/might be performed
  - Lays down rules, guidelines, and behaviour patterns which, if followed, would lead to the desired process performance. They range from strict enforcement to flexible guidance.
- Explanatory
  - Provides explanations about the rationale of processes
  - Explores and evaluates several possible courses of action based on rational arguments
  - Establishes an explicit link between processes and the requirements that they are to fulfill

"From a theoretical point of view, the Process Meta-Model explains which are the key concepts needed to describe what happens in the development process, on what, when it happens and why. From an operational point of view, the Process Meta-Model is aimed at providing guidance for method engineers and application developers."

The activity of modeling a business process usually predicates a need to change processes or identify issues to be corrected. This transformation may or may not require IT involvement, although that is common driver for the need to model a business process. Change management programmes are desired to put the processes into practice. With advances in technology from larger platform vendors, the vision of BPM models becoming fully executable (and capable of round-trip engineering) is coming closer to reality every day.

Process Modeling addresses the process aspects an Enterprise Business Architecture, leading to an all encompassing Enterprise Architecture. The relationships of a business processes in the context of the rest of the enterprise systems, data, org structure, strategies etc. create greater capabilities in analyzing and planning a change. One real world example is in corporate mergers and acquisitions; understanding the processes in both companies in detail, allowing management to identify redundancies resulting in a smoother merger.

BUSINESS PROCESS REENGINEERING MANAGEMENT

Business Process Reengineering is a management approach that examines aspects of a business and its interactions, and attempts to improve the efficiency of the underlying processes. It is a fundamental and radical approach by either modifying or eliminating non-value adding activities. The key steps involved in a BPR are: 1. Defining the purpose and goal of the BPR project; 2. Defining the scope of the project so as to include (or exclude) activities; A flowchart of the activities can assist to define the scope of the project; 3. Identifying the requirements that will meet the needs of the clients; 4. Assess the environment - the position of competitors, prospective changes in technology, legislation or socio-economic factors; 5. Redesign the business processes and activities in light of the above; 6. Implement the redesigned processes; 7. Monitor the success/ failure of the redesign.

Business process reengineering is also known as BPR, Business Process Redesign, Business Transformation, Process Change Management.

In 1990, Michael Hammer, a former professor of computer science at the Massachusetts Institute of Technology (MIT), published an article in the Harvard Business Review, in which he claimed that the major challenge for managers is to obliterate non-value adding work, rather than using technology for automating it. This statement implicitly accused managers of having focused the wrong issues, namely that technology in general, and more specifically information technology, has been used primarily for automating existing work. rather than using it as an enabler for making non-value adding obsolete.

Hammer's claim was simple: Most of the work being done does not add any value for customers, and this work should be removed, not accelerated through automation. Instead, companies should reconsider their processes in order to maximize customer value, while minimizing the consumption of resources required for delivering their product or service. A similar idea was advocated by Thomas Davenport and J. Short, at that time a member of the Ernst & Young research center, in a paper published in the Sloan Management Review the same year as Hammer published his paper.

This idea, to unbiased review a company's business processes, was rapidly adopted by a huge number of firms, which were striving for renewed competitiveness, which they had lost due to the market entrance of foreign competitors, their inability to satisfy customer needs, and their insufficient cost structure. Even well established management thinkers, such as Peter Drucker and Tom Peters, were accepting and advocating BPR as a new tool for (re-)achieving success in a dynamic world. During the following years, a fast growing number of publications, books as well as journal articles, was dedicated to BPR, and many consulting firms embarked on this trend and developed BPR methods. However, the critics were fast to claim that BPR was a way to dehumanize the work place, increase managerial control, and to justify downsizing, i.e. major reductions of the work force and a rebirth of Taylorism under a different label.

Despite this critique, reengineering was adopted at an accelerating pace and in 1993, as many as 65% of the Fortune 500 companies claimed to either have initiated reengineering efforts, or to have plans to do so. This trend was fueled by the fast adoption of BPR by the consulting industry, but also by the study Made in America, conducted by the MIT, that showed how companies in many US industries had lagged behind their foreign counterparts in terms of competitiveness, time-to-market and productivity.

While there are almost as many definitions of BPR as there are authors publishing on the topic, we can identify multiple aspects that they have in common. Let us first review a number of definitions.

Hammer and Champy define BPR as"the fundamental rethinking and radical redesign of business processes to achieve dramatic improvements in critical contemporary measures of performance, such as cost, quality, service, and speed".

Thomas Davenport, another well-known BPR theorist, uses the term process innovation, which he says "encompasses the envisioning of new work strategies, the actual process design activity, and the implementation of the change in all its complex technological, human, and organizational dimensions".

Additionally, Davenport points out the major difference between BPR and other approaches to organization development (OD), especially the continuous improvement or TQM movement, when he states:

"Today firms must seek not fractional, but multiplicative levels of improvement – 10x rather than 10%."

Finally, Johansson et. al. (1993) provide a description of BPR relative to other process-oriented views, such as Total Quality Management (TQM) and Just-in-time (JIT), and state:

Business Process Reengineering, although a close relative, seeks radical rather than merely continuous improvement. It escalates the efforts of JIT and TQM to make process orientation a strategic tool and a core competence of the organization. BPR concentrates on core business processes, and uses the specific techniques within the JIT and TQM "toolboxes" as enablers, while broadening the process vision.

In order to achieve the major improvements BPR is seeking for, the change of structural organizational variables, and other ways of managing and performing work is often considered as being insufficient. For being able to reap the achievable benefits fully, the use of information technology is conceived as a major contributing factor. While IT traditionally has been used for supporting the existing business functions, i.e. it was used for increasing organizational efficiency, it now plays a role as enabler of new organizational forms, and patterns of collaboration within and between organizations. BPR derives its existence from different disciplines, and we can identify four major areas being subjected to change in BPR - organization, technology, strategy, and people - where a process view is used as common framework for considering these dimensions. The approach can be graphically depicted by a modification of "Leavitt's diamond".

Business strategy is the primary driver of BPR initiatives and the other dimensions are governed by strategy's encompassing role. The organization dimension reflects the structural elements of the company, such as hierarchical levels, the composition of organizational units, and the distribution of work between them. Technology is concerned with the use of computer systems and other forms of communication technology in the business. In BPR, information technology is generally considered as playing a role as enabler of new forms of organizing and collaborating, rather than supporting existing business functions. The people, or human resources dimension deals with aspects such as education, training, motivation and reward systems. The concept of business processes - interrelated activities aiming at creating an value added output to a customer - is the basic underlying idea of BPR. These processes are characterized by a number of attributes: Process ownership, customer focus, value-adding, and cross-functionality.

Methodology

Although the names and steps being used differ slightly between the different methodologies, they share the same basic principles and elements.

BPR - A REBIRTH OF SCIENTIFIC MANAGEMENT

By its critics, BPR is often accused to be a re-animation of Taylor's principles of scientific management, aiming at increasing productivity to a maximum, but disregarding aspects such as work environment and employee satisfaction. It can be agreed that Taylor's theories, in conjunction with the work of the early administrative scientists have had a considerable impact on the management discipline for more than 50 years. However, it is not self-evident that BPR is a close relative to Taylorism and this proposed relation deserves a closer investigation.

In the late 19th century Frederick Winslow Taylor, a mechanical engineer, started to develop the idea of management as a scientific discipline. He applied the premise that work and its organizational environment could be considered and designed upon scientific principles, i.e. that work processes could be studied in detail using a positivist analytic approach. Upon the basis of this analysis, an optimal organizational structure and way of performing all work tasks could be identified and implemented. However, he was not the one to originally invent the concept. In 1886, a paper entitled "The Engineer as Economist", written by Henry Towne for the American Society of Mechanical Engineers, had laid the bedrock for the development of scientific management. The basic idea of scientific management was that work could be studied from an objective scientific perspective and that the analysis of the gathered information could be used for increasing productivity, especially of blue-collar work, significantly.

Taylor summarized his observations in the following four principles:

- Observation and analysis through time study to set the optimal production rate. In other words, develop a science for each man's task–a One Best Way.
- Scientifically select the best man for the job and train him in the procedures he is expected to follow.
- Cooperate with the man to ensure that the work is done as described. This means establishing a differential rate system of piece work and paying the man on an incentive basis, not according to the position.
- Divide the work between managers and workers so that managers are given the responsibility for planning and preparation of work, rather than the individual worker.

Scientific management's main characteristic is the strict separation of planning and doing, which was implemented by the use of a functional foremanship system. This means, that a worker, depending on the task his is performing, can report to different foreman, each of them being responsible for a small, specialized area.

Taylor's ideas had a major impact on manufacturing, but also administration. One of the most well-known examples is Ford Motor Co., which adopted the principles of scientific management at an early stage, and built its assembly line for the T-model based on Taylor's model of work and authority distribution, thereby giving name to Fordism.

Later on, Taylor's ideas were extended by the time and motion studies performed by Frank Gilbreth and his wife Lillian. Henry Gantt, a co-worker of Taylor, developed Taylor's idea further, but placed more emphasis on the worker. He developed a reward system that no longer took into account only the output of the work, but was based on a fixed daily wage, and a bonus for completing the task.

Taylor's work can be, and has been, criticized many times for degrading individuals to become machinelike. One of the most famous critiques of the situation that an application of scientific management could result in, is shown in Charles Chaplin's movie "Modern Times". Despite that fact, Taylor was inspired by the vision of creating a workplace that is beneficial to all members of the organization, both management and workers. When looking at Taylor's ideas retrospectively, we can conclude, that they very well fitted the organizations of the early 20th century. The kind of organization he proposed requires certain pre-conditions, which were satisfied in the technological and socio-economic environment of his time and the heritage from economic individualism and a Protestant view of work. However, despite the good intention of designing organizations where managers and workers could jointly contribute to the common achievements, Taylor missed the fact that he had been building his principles on wrong assumptions. There are some major critical points that can be brought forward against Taylor's concept.

The strict belief in man being totally rational, and the history of protestant ethic, which considered work as being a manifestation of religious grace, made him disregard the crucial issue of human behaviour and the fact that money is insufficient as the single source of motivation.

The lack of considering the organizational environment as a conceivable factor, and the overemphasis on organizational efficiency. As Thompson notes:

"Scientific management, focusing primarily on manufacturing or similar production activities, clearly employs economic efficiency as its ultimate criterion and achieves conceptual closure of the organization by assuming that goals are known, tasks are repetitive, output of the production process somehow disappears, and resources in uniform qualities are available."

If accepting Thompson's critique as valid and relevant, we can conclude that the strict hierarchical organization seems to be unfit to take on the challenges that are imposed by fierce competition and dynamic market structures. Due to the focus on improvement through repetition and resource uniformity, the applicability on organizations and processes without these characteristics, such as pharmaceutical R&D, can be questioned.

Peter Drucker noted a third problem related to scientific management, namely that there was no real concern about technology, i.e. that Taylor considered his theory as being general, and that it could be applied to any organization, independently of the technology used. Drucker stated:

"Scientific management was not concerned with technology. It took tools and technology as givens."

This point brings forward a clear argument against the application of Taylor's principles and methodologies for improving today's organizations. Considering that the rapid development in the IT field actually constitutes a driving force in itself, it appears to be unfit to employ organizational concepts that neglect the changing and enabling role of technology. On the other hand we can argue that the application of scientific management in the early 20st century, as we look at it retrospectively, must be considered as the contemporary use of a concept that would look and be applied in a different way today.

Taylor did not neglect technology, he considered it as an important contributor to organizational performance, but given the pace of development, he could not consider it as a major driver of change.

Looking at the suggested relationship between BPR and Taylor's principles we can conclude that primarily Thompson's and Drucker's criticism build a strong case against BPR being a successor of Taylorism. An organizational concept that does not take into account changing business environments and rapid technological advancements is not fit for serving as an improvement method today. Also the BPR literature offers a harsh critique of the continuous application of tayloristic principles in the modern business world, thus rejecting the separation of planning and doing and the strict functional division of labour. BPR proponents claim that taking BPR for Taylorism is a major misunderstanding of the concept, and responsible for a considerable number of reengineering project failures. On the other hand, there is also a similarity which stems from the methodological approach: Both scientific management and BPR have a focus on productivity and efficient use of resources that can be achieved through an optimum process design and its sub-sequent deployment. The following quote, referring to scientific management can equally be used to describe the intention of reengineering:

"To conduct the undertaking toward its objectives by seeking to derive optimum advantage from all available resources."

At the same time it cannot be denied, that the implementation of process-based organizations in practice often is accompanied by massive lay-offs and an emphasis on managerial control. A study by CSC Index from 1994 revealed that 73% of the companies applying BPR reduced their workforce with an average of 21%. Thomas Davenport, an early contributor to the BPR-field, provided a harsh critique against labeling substantial workforce reductions reengineering and in a paper from 1995 he stated that "reengineering didn't start out as a code word for mindless bloodshed. The other thing to remember about the start of reengineering is that the phrase 'massive layoffs' was never part of the early vocabulary."

Key Targets

Business Process Redesign/Reengineering can be defined as "the analysis and design of workflow and processes within and between organizations".

BPR has three key target categories:

- Customer Friendly: One of the main goals of introducing BPR is to get a competitive edge and that can only be gained by providing the customers more than what the others in the market are asking for. If a customer is looking for products tailored to their needs, for example: a car customized to the customer's taste, then that car-maker would most probably gain more customers over the competition due to the customization option.
- Effectiveness: How effective is the product or service that the business or manufacturing company providing the customer? If whatever product or service the business might be providing to the

customer is successful, then the customers would automatically want to buy that product or service again. For example: Japanese made cars like Honda and Toyota, even though they are more expensive compared to the domestic cars, they are very reliable cars causing the customers to continue going back to those brands for generations.

- Efficiency: How efficient is the company that is manufacturing the product before introducing it to the market to minimise costs? This is one of the key categories that is believed to be more important than any others. If a manufacturing company can master the skill of being efficient then they can automatically be more customer friendly and effective. Efficiency is not just about being efficient at the production floor level but the management level also has to be efficient. An example of only the production floor being efficient and not the management level would be the Japanese manufacturing companies. Now they are going through turmoil to repair their problems.

BPR, if implemented properly, can give huge returns. BPR has helped giants like Procter and Gamble Corporation and General Motors Corporation succeed after financial drawbacks due to competition. It helped American Airlines somewhat get back on track from the bad debt that is currently haunting their business practice. BPR is about the proper method of implementation.

General Motors Corporation implemented a 3-year plan to consolidate their multiple desktop systems into one. It is known internally as "Consistent Office Environment". This reengineering process involved replacing the numerous brands of desktop systems, network operating systems and application development tools into a more manageable number of vendors and technology platforms. According to Donald G. Hedeen, director of desktops and deployment at GM and manager of the upgrade programme, he says that the process "lays the foundation for the implementation of a common business communication strategy across General Motors." Lotus Development Corporation and Hewlett-Packard Development Company, formerly Compaq Computer Corporation, received the single largest non-government sales ever from General Motors Corporation. GM also planned to use Novell NetWare as a security client, Microsoft Office and Hewlett-Packard printers. According the Donald G. Hedeen, this saved GM 10% to 25% on support costs, 3% to 5% on hardware, 40% to 60% on software licensing fees, and increased efficiency by overcoming incompatibility issues by using just one platform across the entire company.

Southwest Airlines offers another successful example of reengineering their company and using Information Technology the way it was meant to be implemented. In 1992, Southwest Airlines had a revenue of $1.7 billion and an after-tax profit of $91 million. American Airlines, the largest U.S. carrier, on the other hand had a revenue of $14.4 billion dollars but lost $475 million and has not made a profit since 1989. Companies like Southwest Airlines know that their formula for success is easy to copy by new start-ups like Morris, Reno, and Kiwi Airlines. In order to stay in the game of competitive advantage, they have to continuously reengineer their strategy. BPR helps them be original. Michael Dell is the founder and CEO of DELL Incorporated, which has been in business since 1983 and has been the world's fastest growing major PC Company. Michael Dell's idea of a successful business is to keep the smallest inventory possible by having a direct link with the manufacturer. When a customer places an order, the custom parts requested by the customer are automatically sent to the manufacturer for shipment. This reduces the cost for inventory tracking and massive warehouse maintenance. Dell's website is noted for bringing in nearly "$10 million each day in sales.

Michael Dell mentions: "If you have a good strategy with sound economics, the real challenge is to get people excited about what you're doing. A lot of businesses get off track because they don't communicate an excitement about being part of a winning team that can achieve big goals. If a company can't motivate its people and it doesn't have a clear compass, it will drift." Dell's stocks have been ranked as the top stock for the decade of the 1990s, when it had a return of 57,282%.

Michael Dell is now concentrating more on customer service than selling computers since the PC market price has pretty much equalized. Michael Dell notes: "The new frontier in our industry is service, which is a much greater differentiator when price has been equalized. In our industry, there's been a pretty huge gap between what customers want in service and what they can get, so they've come to expect mediocre service. We may be the best in this area, but we can still improve quite a bit—in the quality of the product, the availability of parts, service and delivery time. Michael Dell understands the concept of BPR and really recognizes where and when to reengineer his business. Ford reengineered their business and manufacturing process from just manufacturing cars to manufacturing quality cars, where the number one goal is quality. This helped Ford save millions on recalls and warranty repairs. Ford has accomplished this goal by incorporating barcodes on all their parts and scanners to scan for any missing parts in a completed car coming off of the assembly line. This helped them guarantee a safe and quality car. They have also implemented Voice-over-IP (VoIP) to reduce the cost of having meetings between the branches.

A multi-billion dollar corporation like Procter and Gamble Corporation, which carries 300 brands and growing really has a strong grasp in re-engineering. Procter and Gamble Corporation's chief technology officer, G. Gil Cloyd, explains how a company which carry multiple brands has to contend with the "classic innovator's dilemma — most innovations fail, but companies that don't innovate die. His solution, innovating innovation...". Cloyd has helped a company like Procter and Gamble grow to $5.1 billion by the fiscal year of 2004. According to Cloyd's scorecard, he was able to raise the volume by 17%, the organic volume by 10%, sales are at $51.4 billion up by 19%, with organic sales up 8%, earnings are at $6.5 billion up 25% and share earnings up 25%. Procter and Gamble also has a free cash flow of $7.3 billion or 113% of earnings, dividends up 13% annually with a total shareholder return of 24%. Cloyd states: "The challenge we face is the competitive need for a very rapid pace of innovation. In the consumer products world, we estimate that the required pace of innovation has double in the last three years. Digital technology is very important in helping us to learn faster." G. Gil Cloyd also predicts, in the near future, "as much as 90% of P&G's R&D will be done in a virtual world with the remainder being physical validation of results and options."

The biggest problem that businesses usually face with BPR is overzealous expectations. BPR is a business tool with a high price and gradual returns. BPR is quoted as having a 30% success rate due to the time and cost involved.

BPR has been used by corporations as an excuse for job cuts which has tarnished the name with employees. Specifically, in 1995, Pacific Bell called for 10,000 job cuts, followed by Apple Computer Incorporated. Both used the word reengineering to explain the job cuts. In addition, Michael Hammer and James Champy have admitted that in their book they did not take into account the human constituent of the business process. In late 1996, Dr. Hammer made a confession on the Wall Street Journal where the article read: "Dr. Hammer points out a flaw: He and the other leaders of the $4.7 billion re-engineering industry forgot about people. 'I wasn't smart enough about that,' he says. 'I was reflecting my engineering background and was insufficient appreciative of the human dimension. I've learned that's critical." Sometimes BPR implementation was based on generic best practices by a business, not specific to a particular company. One example of using a generic idea to a particular company would be the implementation of a $28,000.00 voicemail system at Winguth, Dohahue and Co., which was later scrapped because of the computer generated voice which sounded a little too cold and clients were tired of going through all the menu prompts to reach the desired person.

Six Sigma and Total Quality Management (TQM) are terms often confused with BPR, and are not its replacements. All are change initiatives, with the main difference being BPR is focused on radical, "big bang" change, and Six Sigma and TQM both focused on continuous, incremental improvement. Methods such as that used by Riggours employ the traditional principles of BPR and acknowledge the contributions made by Six Sigma without the adherence to measurement, which while appropriate for some organisations is not suitable for those at the beginning of the BPR change ladder. In order to reanalyze BPR, it is being replaced by Business Process Management (BPM). BPM is presently taking a similar road toward many failures by focusing too heavily on automation and failing to consider people in processes.

Index